T0350222

Logic and Language Models for Computer Science

Third Edition

Logic and Language Models for Computer Science

Third Edition

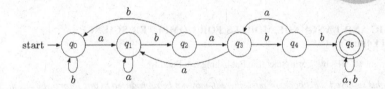

Dana Richards
Henry Hamburger

George Mason University, USA

World Scientific

NEW JERSEY · LONDON · SINGAPORE · BEIJING · SHANGHAI · HONG KONG · TAIPEI · CHENNAI · TOKYO

Published by

World Scientific Publishing Co. Pte. Ltd.
5 Toh Tuck Link, Singapore 596224
USA office: 27 Warren Street, Suite 401-402, Hackensack, NJ 07601
UK office: 57 Shelton Street, Covent Garden, London WC2H 9HE

British Library Cataloguing-in-Publication Data
A catalogue record for this book is available from the British Library.

LOGIC AND LANGUAGE MODELS FOR COMPUTER SCIENCE
Third Edition

ISBN 978-981-3229-20-4
ISBN 978-981-3230-50-7 (pbk)

Printed in Singapore

Contents

Preface

So, you are a computer science (CS) major and you are sitting down to see what this book is about. It has been assigned, the course is required, you have no choice. Still, you chose your institution, your major.

Or you are teaching a course that might use this book, maybe in discrete math, maybe including logics or formal language or both. If you want your CS students to see the applicabilility of mathematical reasoning to their own field or your math students to see the usefulness of their field outside itself, it is your students that we have in mind.

If you are a CS major, you have already noticed that this course is different from the others you have taken so far. It is not an Introduction to Computing, or to programming, problem-solving or data structures. No, this book is about something called "models" — models of language and knowledge. It is also about formal methods.

You know something about models if you have built or seen a model airplane. In Kitty Hawk, North Carolina, you can see the wind tunnel that the Wright brothers built to test the lift capabilities of various wing shapes. A model can help us simplify and think more clearly about a complex problem (powered flight) by selecting a part (the wing) and focusing on some aspect of it (its aerodynamics). The other, temporarily ignored parts and aspects must ultimately be addressed, of course, if the original problem is to be solved.

The models in this book are simplifications too, but not of material objects like airplanes. For computer scientists, the objects of study lie mainly in the world of symbols. In this book it will be computer software and especially the programming languages in which that software is written from which we draw our models and to which we apply them.

A model, then, is a collection of precisely stated interacting ideas that focus on a particular aspect or part of our subject matter. A good model can simplify a topic to its essence, stripping away the details, so that we can understand the topic better and reason precisely about it. The model keeps only those parts and processes that are of interest.

We will reason both formally and informally. Informal methods draw on analogies to your knowledge of other things in the world in general and your common sense, typically expressed in a human language like English and perhaps a diagram. Formal methods use abstract symbols — like the famous "x" of high school algebra — and clearly stated rules about how to manipulate them. A formal method based on a simple but precise model of a situation can enable us to *prove* that we have got things right, at least as reflected in the model.

If this concern with precision and proof makes you think this is a theory book, you are partly right. If you think that means it is not of practical value, we ask you to think again. It is often said that experience is the best teacher. But learning from experience means transferring ideas across situations, by seeing the essential similarities in non-identical situations. This abstracted essence, by which we learn from history or from our mistakes, is an informal model. Formalizing the model and reasoning carefully about it — that is, theory — is the scientist's and engineer's path to knowledge and action in the real world.

So what will we theorize about? We have chosen to focus on language, the crucial link between hardware and software. Programming languages permit software to be written and language processors — compilers, interpreters and assemblers — permit hardware to run that software. Sometimes a model proves to be so interesting and widely applicable that it becomes an object of study in its own right. That is the case with the logic and language models in this book.

Two key aspects of language are structure and meaning. We will study models of each. The structure of language has to do with the arrangement of symbols into permitted sequences, called "sentences" in human language and "statements" in programming languages. This topic is usually called Formal Models of Language. It underlies key aspects of compilers, the study of what computers can do efficiently and the processing of human language for translation and easy interaction between people and computers.

Symbol arrangements are of interest not only in their own right but also because they express ideas about meaning and computation. Expressing meaning can be done in various ways, including logic. Of the many logics, the simplest is propositional logic. It finds application in the tiny hardware components called "logic gates," in the conditions for branching and loops in high-level programming languages and in mathematical rules of proof that can be applied via software throughout engineering and science. Predicate logic builds on propositional logic to permit knowledge representation in database systems, artificial intelligence and in work on program correctness in software engineering.

Computer science students may notice that several phrases in the above paragraphs are the names of upper division courses in computer science. To further emphasize the practical value of the two major topics of this book, we introduce an important programming language based on each in the appendices. Prolog, a programming language whose core is based on predicate logic, supports rapid prototyping of intelligent systems. AWK is a well-known tool based on material on regular languages.

Formalisms for language and logic have ancient roots, in India for language and in Greece for logic. Each field has enjoyed renewed attention in more recent times, starting in the 19th century for logic and early in the 20th for language. These latter thrusts are more formal yet still independent of computing. The venerable histories of logic and linguistics suggest the inherent fascination that each has held for human minds. Building on that motivation, this book stresses the relationship of each to computer science. The two fields are also related to each other in various ways that emerge in this text. Watch for these important links among logic, formal language and computing.

Preface to the Second Edition

In addition to hundreds of small changes the major change has been to introduce nondeterminism in a more coherent way. After first discussing deterministic finite state automata, the nondeterministic formulations of regular languages, such as grammars, regular expressions and nondeterministic machines are grouped together. This has led to fewer and shorter proofs. It also has some unexpected benefits. For example, we no longer need to explain/allow empty-string transitions since they are now unnecessary, except briefly in one proof.

We deal with context-free languages in a more rigorous way. Unlike the first edition we no longer quote theorems without proof. We feel the proofs are more natural and shorter if we have pushdown automata that use acceptance by empty stack (instead of with accepting states). We also do not need empty-string transitions for these automata. All this requires introducing normal forms for context-free grammars; the proofs are provided but can be skipped.

Preface to the Third Edition

Again many changes have been incorporated, including simplifying some discussions of context free languages. New problems and answers have been added.

The main changes have been to chapters eight and nine. We discovered that we were working too hard, by following the lead of nearly all other texts: by having the finite automata be the first and primary focus. Now we we begin the discussion of regular languages by discussing generative models first. These models are nondeterministic and are shown to be equivalent. We show how to convert a regular grammar into a deterministic grammar. Therefore in chapter nine, where we introduce machine-based recognition models, all the proofs are straightforward. In summary, we again have reduced the number of theorems and simplified the proofs.

Chapter 1

Mathematical Preliminaries

This text is concerned with formal models that are important to the field of computer science. Because the models are formal, we will make substantial use of mathematical ideas. In many ways the topics in this book — logic, languages and automata — are a natural extension of a Discrete Mathematics course, which is generally required for Computer Science majors. This text steers clear of excessive mathematical notation, focusing instead on fundamental ideas and their application. However it is impossible to appreciate the power that comes from the rigorous methods and models in this book without a background in Discrete Mathematics. This chapter is a brief overview of the needed mathematical background and may be useful for self-evaluation, review and reference.

1.1   Sets and Sequences

A *set* is a unordered collection of distinct *elements*. The elements are typically thought of as objects such as integers, people, books, or classrooms, and are written within braces, like this: {Friday, Saturday, Sunday}. When working with sets, it can be important to specify $\mathcal{U}$, the *universe* of elements (e.g., the set of days of the week) from which the elements of particular sets are drawn. Note that the universe itself is a set: the set of all elements of a given type.

Sometimes the universe is only implicitly specified, when the reader can easily figure out what it is. The elements are said to be *in* the set and are called its *members*.

Sets can be presented in two forms. The *extensional* form enumerates the elements of the set, while the *intensional* form specifies the properties of the elements. For example:

$$S = \{11, 12, 13, 14\}$$

$$S = \{x \mid x \text{ is an integer, and } 10 < x < 15\}$$

are extensional and intensional forms of the same set. The second of these is read "those x *such that* x is an integer and ..." Note that the universe, the set of integers, is implicit in the first example and only informally specified in the second. The *empty set* is a set with no element and is denoted $\emptyset$.

Because the elements of a set are distinct, you should write sets with no repetition. For example, suppose a student database includes countries of origin and that it shows the participants in a seminar as being from China, France, China, Egypt and France. Then the set of countries represented in this class is {China, France, Egypt}. There is no concept of ordering within a set; there is no "first" element, etc. For example, the sets $\{4, 2, 3\}$ and $\{2, 3, 4\}$ are the same set.

If ordering is important then one speaks of a *sequence* of elements. In the extensional form of a sequence the elements appear in order, within parentheses, not braces. For example, the sequence $(4, 2, 3)$ is different from $(2, 3, 4)$. Further, sequences need not have distinct elements, so the sequence $(2, 3, 3, 4)$ is different from $(2, 3, 4)$. A sequence of length 2 is called an *ordered pair*. A sequence of length 3, 4 or 5 is called a *triple*, *quadruple* or *quintuple* respectively; in the general case of length n, the word is *n-tuple*. Sequences are often implemented as one-dimensional arrays or as linked lists. This leads to an intensional form for sequences, where we use subscripts, so that the extensional notation, like (x_1, x_2, x_3), can replaced with a direct definition of x_i, for each i.

The *cross-product* of S_1 and S_2, denoted $S_1 \times S_2$, is the set of ordered pairs of elements in which the first is in S_1 and the second is in S_2.

Formally,

$$S_1 \times S_2 = \{(x, y) \mid x \in S_1 \text{ and } y \in S_2\}.$$

For example, $\{a, b\} \times \{c, d, e\} = \{(a, c), (a, d), (a, e), (b, c), (b, d), (b, e)\}$. Just as the elements of $S_1 \times S_2$ are ordered pairs, the elements of $S_1 \times S_2 \times S_3$ are triples, and so on.

Set operators are discussed later, but we start with two basic ideas, the notions of membership and comparison. The notation $x \in S$ means that x is an element of the set S, while $x \notin S$ means that x is *not* in S. When $S = \{11, 12, 13, 14\}$, $12 \in S$ and $16 \notin S$. We say that S_1 is a *subset* of S_2, written $S_1 \subseteq S_2$, if each element of S_1 is also an element of S_2. For example, $\{12, 14\} \subseteq \{11, 12, 13, 14\}$. Note that $S \subseteq S$. Now consider subset T, that is *not* equal to S, because it is missing one or more elements of S. While it is correct to write $T \subseteq S$ we may choose to write $T \subset S$, which states that T is a *proper subset* of S. The empty set is a subset of any set, so we can write $\emptyset \subseteq S$, for any set S.

1.2 Relations and Functions

A *binary relation* is a set of ordered pairs. More formally, a relation R from the set S_1 to the set S_2 is a subset of the cross-product of those sets, $R \subseteq S_1 \times S_2$. For example, if E is a set of employees and P is a set of projects, we can specify a relation R between E and P that indicates which employees are assigned to which projects. In this case each element of R has to be an ordered pair (x, y) with $x \in E$ and $y \in P$. More specifically, if $E = \{e_1, e_2, e_3\}$ is the set of employees and $P = \{p_1, p_2, p_3, p_4\}$ is the set of projects, we might have $R = \{(e_1, p_2), (e_1, p_3), (e_3, p_2)\}$, indicating that employee e_1 is assigned to both p_2 and p_3, while e_3 is assigned only to p_2 and e_2 is unassigned.

It is possible to have a relation from a set to itself. In this case we say that we have a relation *on* that one set. More formally, a relation R is on the set S if $R \subseteq S \times S$. Take for example the set $S = \{\text{George VI, Elizabeth II, Prince Charles}\}$ and the relation P that relates a child to the parent. Then $P = \{(\text{Prince Charles, Elizabeth II}), (\text{Elizabeth II, George VI})\}$.

Some relations are explicitly constrained to have just one ordered pair for each possible first element; such a relation is a *function*. In the example above, if each employee had been assigned to just one project then the relation from employees to jobs would be a function. In that case we would want to use the more familiar function notation, $R(x) = y$, rather than the relation notation, $(x, y) \in R$. Since a function can be regarded as a *mapping* from one set to another, it is usually described with the notation

$$R : E \to P$$

which indicates that R is a function that maps elements of E to (unique) elements of P. E is called the *domain* of R and P is the *codomain* of R. Such function is a *one-to-one correspondence* between E and P if every element of E is mapped to an element of P and every element of P has exactly one element E mapped to it. (Such a function is also called a *bijection*, and in some texts the function is said to be "one-to-one onto.") It follows that if there is a one-to-one correspondence between E and P then those two sets have the same number of elements.

Analogous to binary relations there are also ternary (3-ary) and n-ary relations. A ternary relation is a set of triples and an n-ary one is a set of n-tuples. More formally, a relation R on the sets S_1, S_2 and S_3 is a subset of their cross-product, $R \subseteq S_1 \times S_2 \times S_3$, and similarly for n-ary relations.

The above statement that a function maps one set to another, $R : E \to P$, is more flexible than it may seem. That is because the set E (or P for that matter) may be a cross-product set. For example, consider a chart, G, of gross national product with countries and years as the rows and columns. With C as the set of countries and $\mathcal{N}$ as the set of integers (for years and dollars) we can write:

$$G : C \times \mathcal{N} \to \mathcal{N}$$

where G is a function that maps countries and years into dollars. We use the familiar binary function notation $R(x, y)$ when the domain is a cross-product. Similarly n-ary functions have a domain of n-tuples.

1.3   Operators and their Algebraic Properties

Operators are crucial to all of mathematics, starting with the first one we learn in childhood, the addition operator of ordinary arithmetic. The input to an operator are called its *operands*. Each operand of an operator must come from a specified set. For present purposes, we will say that both operands of addition are from the domain of real numbers, which includes things like -273, π, .406 and the $\sqrt{5}$. The real numbers are said to be "closed under addition," since the result of adding two of them is also a real number; that is, *closed* means staying within a domain. The codomain of the operator is the same as the domain of all its operands.

In the case of addition, the order of the operands does not affect the result. For example, 2+3 and 3+2 both are 5. More generally, $x + y = y + x$ for any x and y. Since that is the case, the operator is *commutative*. Multiplication is also commutative, but subtraction and division are not. The property of commutativity, is one of several properties of operators that will be of interest to us.

Such a property is called an *algebraic law*. A law is a strong statement. It states a property holds for all operands, not just sometimes. In other words addition is said to be commutative because it obeys the commutative law (i.e., $x + y = y + x$) for any x and y. Another algebraic law of addition is the associative law. To say that addition is *associative* — which it is — is the same as saying that $(x + y) + z = x + (y + z)$ for all x, y and z.

The *identity* element for addition is 0 (zero), since whenever it is one of the operands, the result is the other operand: $x + 0 = x$, for any x. Every real number x has an *inverse*, $-x$, such that the two of them add up to the identity: $x + (-x) = 0$.

Multiplication of reals is commutative and associative. It has an identity element, 1, and for each element x except 0 there is an inverse, $1/x$. The multiplication operator is often unwritten, as in the notation xy. Here the operator has been expressed by simply writing the operands next to each other.

A property of the interaction of addition and multiplication is *distributivity*, the fact that multiplication distributes over addition. The distributive law is written $x(y+z) = xy+xz$, for all x, y and z. (However, addition does not distribute over multiplication, since it is *not* true that $x + yz = (x + y)(x + z)$, for any x, y and z.)

An operator is really just a specific type of function[1]. For example the addition operation for two real operands can be expressed

$$Add : \mathcal{R} \times \mathcal{R} \to \mathcal{R},$$

where $\mathcal{R}$ is the set of real numbers. So $Add(5.2, 3.1)$ maps to 8.3. It is common to write such binary operators using *infix* notation, where the name of the function comes between the operands so that no parentheses are needed. However writing $Add(5.2, 3.1)$ as $5.2\,Add\,3.1$ is hard to read, so we use symbolic designations for the operators, i.e. $5.2 + 3.1$. Such a symbolic operator is still a function:

$$+ : \mathcal{R} \times \mathcal{R} \to \mathcal{R}.$$

Similarly *unary* operators, which have one operand, are written in *prefix* notation, where the operand appears before the operator; for example $-x$.

Some operators have a codomain that is {TRUE, FALSE}. Such a binary operator is known as a *relational* operator. Equality, less-than ("<") and greater-than (">") are common examples. The pairwise combinations of them are also relational operators: less-than-or-equal ("$\leq$"), greater-than-or-equal ("$\geq$"), and inequality ("$\neq$"; i.e., greater-than or less-than). An important algebraic property of all these operators except "$\neq$" is *transitivity*. For example,

---

[1] An operator is a function that is typically understood in terms of its algebraic properties.

the transitive law for the less-than operator states: if $x < y$ and $y < z$ are both true, then $x < z$ must also be true, for all x, y and z.

Operators apply not only to numbers but to other domains as well. An excellent example occurs in the next section, where set operators are introduced. We will find that not only are the two key operators, union and intersection, both commutative and associative, but also each distributes over the other. In later chapters we will see that discussions of operators and their algebraic properties are highly significant for the principal topics of this book, logic and formal languages.

1.4 Set Operators

Recall that we have already discussed two relational operators for sets: $S_1 \subseteq S_2$ and $x \in S$. As a third example consider set equality. Two sets are equal, $S_1 = S_2$, if (and only if) they contain exactly the same elements. It is important to observe that $S_1 = S_2$ exactly when $S_1 \subseteq S_2$ and $S_2 \subseteq S_1$. In fact this is taken as the *definition* of set equality. Therefore to show that $S_1 = S_2$ one needs to show that both $S_1 \subseteq S_2$ and $S_2 \subseteq S_1$.

The *cardinality* of a set S is the number of elements in S and is denoted $|S|$. For example, $|\{11, 12, 13, 14\}| = 4$. The empty set has cardinality 0, $|\emptyset| = 0$. When the cardinality is an integer the set is *finite*, otherwise it is *infinite*. Note that for finite sets, cardinality is just an operator that maps sets to integers (even though its notation is unlike other operators).

Now consider binary operators that take two sets and produce a single set as their result. The most common of these are union, intersection and subtraction (set difference). The *union* of S_1 and S_2, denoted $S_1 \cup S_2$, is the set of elements in either S_1 or S_2 or both. The *intersection* of S_1 and S_2, denoted $S_1 \cap S_2$, is the set of elements that are in S_1 as well as being in S_2. The *set difference* of S_2 from S_1, written $S_1 \setminus S_2$, is the set of elements that are in S_1 but not in S_2. The *complement* of a set S, denoted $\overline{S}$, contains exactly those elements of the current universe $\mathcal{U}$ that are *not* in S. Formally $\overline{S} = \mathcal{U} \setminus S$, which may help to stress the important point that the complement depends crucially on what the universe is understood to be. Consider a few examples, using the universe of one-digit integers, $\mathcal{U} = \{0, 1, 2, 3, 4, 5, 6, 7, 8, 9\}$.

$$\{1, 2, 3, 4\} \cup \{3, 4, 5, 6\} = \{1, 2, 3, 4, 5, 6\}$$

$$\{1, 2, 3, 4\} \cap \{3, 4, 5, 6\} = \{3, 4\}$$

$$\{1, 2, 3, 4\} \setminus \{3, 4, 5, 6\} = \{1, 2\}$$

$$\overline{\{0, 2, 4, 6, 8\}} = \{1, 3, 5, 7, 9\}.$$

The *power set* of S is the set of all subsets of S, and is typically written 2^S. For example, if $S = \{1, 2, 3\}$ then $2^S = \{\emptyset, \{1\}, \{2\}, \{3\}, \{1, 2\}, \{1, 3\}, \{2, 3\}, \{1, 2, 3\}\}$ is the power set of S. Notice that the power set in this example has exactly $8 = 2^3$ elements. This is no accident; for any set S, the cardinality of its power set, $|2^S|$, is equal to $2^{|S|}$. It is this relationship that motivates the name of the power set and the notation for it.

The power set notation allows us to express the set operators formally as a functions. Let $\mathcal{S}$ be 2^S, the set of subsets of S. So, for example, we can write

$$\cap : \mathcal{S} \times \mathcal{S} \to \mathcal{S}$$

to express, for a universe S, that $\cap$ maps two set operands into another set.

1.5   Strings and String Operators

It is commonplace in discussions of computer programming to say that "HELLO" is a "string" or a "string of 5 characters." Formally we would say it is a *sequence* of characters, of length 5, and would denote it as a 5-tuple: (H,E,L,L,O). Since such sequences are used so extensively in computer science, we adopt a more concise and natural approach.

A *string* is a finite sequence of elements. The elements are typically called *symbols* (or characters) and the set of all symbols under consideration in any example or situation is denoted Σ. The set Σ is usually called an *alphabet*, especially when each symbol is a single letter (but even in other cases). Just as the empty set is a set with no elements, it is convenient to define the *empty string* to be a string with no characters; we call it Λ. Thus if the alphabet is $\Sigma = \{a, b, c\}$ the following are examples of "strings over the alphabet Σ":

$$\Lambda, \quad ab, \quad bbc, \quad abacab$$

The principal operator for strings is concatenation. The *concatenation* of strings x and y, simply denoted xy, is a string comprised of the characters of x followed by the characters of y. For example, if $x = ab$ and $y = bca$ then $xy = abbca$. Either x or y could be the empty string; if $x = ab$ and $y = \Lambda$ then $xy = ab$. In general, concatenation is not a commutative operation, so we can *not* expect $xy = yx$. However, concatenation is an associative operation so when we extend such concatenations to three or more strings we can write the expression without parentheses: $(xy)z = x(yz) = xyz$. A *prefix* consists of consecutive characters at the beginning of a string, so ab is a prefix of $abcbb$ and x is always a prefix of xy.

The *length* of the string x, the number of characters in it, is denoted $|x|$ (the same notation used for the cardinality of a set). For example, $|ab| = 2$ and $|abacab| = 6$. The empty string has zero length, so $|\Lambda| = 0$. Recall that by definition a string is finite so $|x|$ is always an integer. Finally, note that $|xy| = |x| + |y|$.

Sets of strings are studied extensively in this text. We will use the term *language* to refer to a set of strings. For example, $L = \{ab, bbc, abacab\}$ is a language of three strings, $|L| = 3$. It is important to remember that, while a language may contain an infinite number of strings, each string in the language is finite.

We will postpone any formal discussion of strings and languages until Part II, where they receive extensive treatment.

1.6   Expressions

Arithmetic expressions are so familiar that most people are surprised
that they are hard to define. A mathematical *definition* is only useful
if it easy to describe, easy to use, and precise. To define expressions
we would need a single rule that would establish that both $a + b + c$
and $(a \times b + c) \times (d + e \times (f + c))$ are valid but $a + + b)$ is not. Actually
we want two types of definitions. First we need to know what it is
— a *syntactic* definition. Second we need to know what it means —
a *semantic* definition. We will concentrate on syntax here. (Defining
what it means to add two real numbers, for example, is beyond the
scope of this book.)

We need a *recursive definition*. The notion of recursion should be
familiar to a computer scientist because of its role in computer programming. However recursion is fundamental to all of mathematics.
A recursive definition of a set of objects is characterized by three
properties.

- A small number of straightforward cases, called "base cases."

- A rule for explaining larger objects in the set in terms of smaller
  objects.

- A statement of exclusiveness — that all objects in the set are
  covered by the definition.

In other words, an object in the set is either a base case or it is
explained in terms of smaller objects, which themselves can be explained by the same definition.

Let us make this clear with an example that runs through this section.
We start with "simple" arithmetic expressions, that have just two
operators ($+$ and $\times$) and are fully parenthesized. (We will discuss
the need for parentheses below.) For these next definitions let a
"variable" just be a letter of the roman alphabet (e.g., a or b). The
following definition regards expressions as strings over the alphabet
$\Sigma = \{a, b, \ldots, z, (,), +, \times\}$.

Definition 1.1

Let R be the set of simple arithmetic expressions.

- If ρ is a variable then $\rho \in R$,
- If $\rho_1 \in R$ and $\rho_2 \in R$ then $(\rho_1 + \rho_2) \in R$ and $(\rho_1 \times \rho_2) \in R$,
- The first two rules define every element of R.

Note the parallel to the general outline given earlier. The base cases are just variables. And more complex expressions are understood to be built from simpler expressions. For example, $(a + b)$ is in R (i.e., it is a simple arithmetic expression) because it is $(\rho_1 + \rho_2)$, with $\rho_1 = a$ and $\rho_2 = b$, and further $\rho_1 \in R$ and $\rho_2 \in R$ since a and b are variables (base cases). Similarly, $((a + b) \times c) \in R$ because it is $(\rho_1 \times \rho_2)$, with $\rho_1 = (a + b)$ and $\rho_2 = c$, and $\rho_1 \in R$ and $\rho_2 \in R$ as we just observed.

Note that a simple arithmetic expression like $((a \times b) \times (c + (d \times e)))$, is a fully parenthesized expression, since it will have a pair of parentheses for each operator. This seems excessive because we are used to using fewer parantheses, for three reasons. First we can use associativity to remove parentheses that do not matter: $(a \times b \times (c + (d \times e)))$. Second we can use precedence conventions: $((a \times b) \times (c + d \times e))$ since multiplication has "higher precedence" than addition. In formal situations we regard the parentheses as present even when not shown. Third we assume, if not told otherwise, parentheses not shown due associativity correspond to the operations being applied left to right.

We will often find it convenient to regard expressions as rooted trees. The definition above regards them as strings. Consider this analogous definition (tree terminology, if unfamiliar, is reviewed in a following section).

Definition 1.2

Let T be the set of simple arithmetic expression trees.

- If τ is a singleton tree labeled with a variable then $\tau \in T$,
- If $\tau_1 \in T$ and $\tau_2 \in T$ then the two trees, with left and right subtrees τ_1 and τ_2, and roots labeled $+$ and $\times$, respectively, are both in T.
- The first two rules define every element of T.

For example the expressions above correspond to these expression trees:

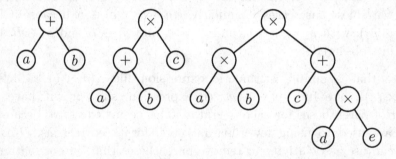

Since the two recursive definitions are essentially the same, it is natural to think of an "expression" to be a single abstraction that has two *representations*, as a string and as a tree. The fully parenthesized string version of an expression can be reconstructed from the expression tree version, simply because the recursive building processes are analogous. Similarly a fully parenthesized string version of an expression can be used to construct the expression tree version.

Expression trees have certain advantages. First they are free of the issues concerning parentheses mentioned above. Without conventions (such as precedence and left-to-right associativity) expressions represented as strings with parentheses not shown, might correspond to more than one tree. *In this text, even when we are discussing other types of expressions, we will always assume that no such ambiguity*

exists (i.e., that conventions exist so that only one tree is possible).
Second, expression trees make the *evaluation* of an expression very
clear. To evaluate an expression you must first know the (numeric)
values of the variables; given those you can assign values to the leaves
of the tree. Thereafter you can evaluate the value of each internal
node of the tree, "bottom-up", using the operators' definitions.

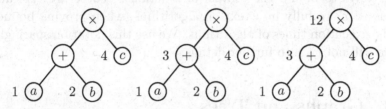

Note that our discussion of expression trees is general. For example,
the expression could be for sets using set operators and all the definitions would be analogous. In this text we encounter other types
of expressions and in all cases we will have a choice of string or tree
representations. To save space we will only give the string version of
the definitions, but we assume the tree version is also known. Therefore we can speak of an expression either way. (For example, we may
say "evaluate a set expression bottom-up.")

Recursive definitions, as used in this section, may be unfamiliar.
However they are used throughout this text and you should become
comfortable with them.

1.7 Growth Rates of Functions

A numeric function, $f(n)$, maps numbers to numbers, either integers
or reals. Sometimes we wish to discuss the growth rate of a numeric
function in rough terms. For example, for the functions $3n^2 + 12n$
and $10n^2$ it may be useful to emphasize that they are both quadratic
functions, rather than to point out their differences. The "big-O"
notation was devised to characterize the growth of functions, while
ignoring the constant coefficients and the lower order terms (such
as $12n$ above) that have negligible impact on the growth rate for
large n.

In particular, we say a numeric function "$f(n)$ is $O(g(n))$" if

$$c(n) = \frac{f(n)}{g(n)}, \quad \text{and} \quad \lim_{n \to \infty} c(n) = c$$

for some constant c. For example, $n^2 + 12n$ is $O(n^2)$. There are other ways to bound the growth of functions. These are typically discussed more fully in a text on algorithms, when proving bounds on the execution times of algorithms. We use this notation sparingly, so we will not go into further details.

1.8   Graphs and Trees

Graphs are an important mathematical concept to model relationships within a set. Formally a *graph* G is a pair of sets, $G = (V, E)$, where V is a set of elements called *vertices* and E, the set of *edges*, is a relation on V, so that $E \subseteq V \times V$. If $(x, y) \in E$ we say there is an edge from vertex x to vertex y; pictorially such an edge is drawn as an arrow from a point labeled x to another point labeled y.

As defined in the preceding paragraph, a graph is sometimes specifically called a *directed graph*, or just a *digraph*, to distinguish it from the related concept of an undirected graph. An *undirected graph* is a graph in which an edge does imply any directionality. In other words, if $(x, y) \in E$ we do *not* say that there is an edge from "x to y;" instead we simply say x and y are "adjacent." Such an undirected edge is depicted as a line (with no arrowhead). (For an undirected graph, by convention, if $(x, y) \in E$ then $(y, x) \in E$, since the (x, y) notation is not meant to imply an ordered pair.)

A directed *path* of length k from vertex x to vertex y, is a sequence of vertices

$$x = x_0, x_1, x_2, \ldots, x_k = y$$

such that $(x_{i-1}, x_i) \in E$ for each $1 \le i \le k$. An undirected path is defined analogously, but there is no implied concept of following arrowheads as one traverses such a path. A *cycle* is a path for which $x = y$. A graph is *acyclic* if it contains no cycles. An undirected graph is *connected* if there is a path from each vertex to every other vertex; a directed graph is *strongly connected* if there is a directed path from each vertex to every other vertex.

An undirected graph is a *tree* if it is connected and acyclic. A directed acyclic graph is often called a *dag*, in view of its initials. A dag is a *rooted tree* if it has a distinguished vertex, called the *root*, and a unique path from the root to every other vertex. Rooted trees, in contrast to real trees that grow in the ground, are usually drawn with the root at the top and all the edges pointing downward. When this is done consistently we omit the arrowheads in the drawings. Each edge points from a *parent* vertex to a *child* vertex. A vertex with no outward arrows (that is, no children) is called a *leaf*. Sometimes the order of the children of a parent vertex is significant, so that it is natural to speak of the "leftmost child," also called the "first child," and so on. When the children in a rooted tree have such an ordering then we have an *ordered tree*. Among the many facts known about trees, perhaps the most crucial is that the number of edges is one less than the number of vertices, $|E| = |V| - 1$. Expression trees are ordered trees. Ordered trees (with labels on their vertices) play a key role in specifying and analyzing the structure of programming languages in Part II.

Exercises

1.1 – For each of the following operators, state whether or not it is commutative, and if it is not, give an example showing this: (a) multiplication, (b) concatenation, (c) union.

1.2 – Express each of the following in formal set notation.

(a) The commutativity and associativity of union.

(b) The commutativity and associativity of intersection.

(c) The distributivity of intersection over union.

(d) The distributivity of union over intersection.

1.3 – Give an expression for the cardinality of $S_1 \times S_2$.

1.4 – What is the identity element for

   (a) the union operator?

   (b) for the intersection operator?

1.5 – For each of the following, answer the question and explain.

   (a) Is the subset relation transitive?

   (b) Is every set closed under cross-product?

1.6 – What is the cardinality of this language $\{x \mid x$ is a string over $\{a, b, c\}$ and $|x| \leq 2\}$.

1.7 – How many simple arithmetic expressions are there with 3 operators, and one repeated variable. Argue that this is the same as the number of binary trees with four leaves and with each internal node labeled in one of two ways.

1.8 – Express $f(n) = 6n^3 - n \log n + 10n$ using big-O notation.

Part I

Logic for
Computer Science

Introduction to Part I: Logic for Computer Science

Logic has many uses for computer scientists. Perhaps the best known is the role of *propositional* logic in the design and analysis of the digital circuits from which computers are built. A richer form of logic known as *predicate* logic underlies work in a much broader range of computer science topics, including artificial intelligence, databases and software engineering. There are even programming languages based on predicate logic.

But logic is not only a source of applications. It is also an aid to careful thought about precisely defined subject matter such as that of mathematics and computer science. We will see how so-called *rules of inference* can be used to establish confidence in the truth of each assertion in a sequence of assertions, culminating in proofs of important results. In fact, we will not only prove things, but also discuss proofs as problem-solving activities and stress the relationship between inference rules and everyday commonsense reasoning.

Computer science has long been concerned with the manipulation of data. Increasingly these days, it also deals with the manipulation of *knowledge*. This shift, which underlies important applications like

19

expert systems and intelligent databases, has been made possible by finding ways to write down what we know about real-world subject matter in a form that is sufficiently precise so that a computer can do useful things with it.

Because logic is a way to express knowledge, various forms of logic have played important roles in these endeavors. Here we will introduce propositional logic and predicate logic (also called predicate calculus), which are formal systems for expressing knowledge and reasoning about it to get new results. Both of these approaches to knowledge representation and reasoning ignore some aspects of knowledge. This simplification helps both the beginner and the field as a whole, by permitting clarity and rigorous proofs about how the reasoning works. There are important representation and reasoning systems (not treated here) that build on predicate logic, extending it to deal with time, uncertainty, approximation and other important aspects of knowledge.

Propositional logic is presented in Chapter 2. It then serves, in Chapter 3, as the basis of a discussion of proof techniques that are widely used in both mathematics and computer science. Building on this foundation, we move on to predicate calculus and additional proof methods that it supports, in Chapters 4 and 5, respectively. This material in turn is the basis for two very different parts of computer science. Verification, the topic of Chapter 6, is concerned with proving programs correct, as opposed to just testing them on some inputs. Finally, Chapter A shows that predicate logic can even form the basis of programming itself, by presenting the rudiments of Prolog, a logic programming language.

Chapter 2

Propositional Logic

Logic is a useful framework for models of knowledge. Logical models simplify the world in order to focus on key ideas. The focus in propositional logic is on statements that are simply *true* or *false* and on the the ways in which such statements can be combined and manipulated. Requiring statements to be true or false means that we never say something is likely or unlikely: there is never a 70% chance of rain in propositional logic. Nor do we ever say that a statement is close to the truth or far from it, and the statements themselves are never vague or approximate. These restrictions allow us to focus on essential ideas about precise reasoning and, in Chapter 3, to uncover a remarkable array of useful ways to prove important results.

2.1   Propositions

Propositional logic is about true and false statements, which we call **propositions**. Often propositions appear in the notation of arithmetic, set theory or some other formalism, but they may also be expressed as ordinary sentences in English or some other natural language. Here are a few examples:

$$5 > 3$$
FISH $\subset$ MAMMALS
It is raining.

The first of these is clearly true. The second is clearly false. The third is a bit problematic, but if we imagine that it is spoken to you as you are reading this, then it is reasonable to say that either it is true or it is false. Besides allowing ourselves this explanation about the time and place of the rain, we will also conveniently ignore borderline misty conditions. To deal with these additional factors would require a more complex system of representation. Later when we come to predicate logic, we will regard "5 > 3" as an operator with two operands. In this chapter we regard it as an indivisible statement that is true or false.

Because its focus is on true and false assertions, the formal study of propositional logic begins with the set {TRUE, FALSE}, called the set of **logical constants**. Some people refer to them as the Boolean constants in honor of George Boole, the founder of modern symbolic logic. Calling them constants contrasts them with logical variables, soon to be introduced here. Yet another term for them is the truth values, which emphasizes their similarity to numerical values in arithmetic. Just as we combine numerical values, like 2 and 3, using arithmetic operators, like plus, to get a resulting value, so here we will combine the truth values TRUE and FALSE, using logical operators, to get resulting values.

A **logical variable** (or Boolean variable) is a variable that can take on only the value TRUE or FALSE. For example, with the variable p understood to represent the idea that 5 exceeds 3, we can write $p =$ TRUE. A proposition can just be a logical constant or a logical variable or it may be a more complex expression built out of logical variables and logical constants (either or both of them) along with operators corresponding roughly to "and", "or" and "not". In particular, if we let p be the proposition that it is raining and let q be the proposition that 5 > 3, then (not surprisingly) the expression "p and q" stands for the proposition that both are true: that it is raining and 5 > 3. Similar comments apply to "p or q" and to "not p". We will also use the operator $\land$ for "and," $\lor$ for "or" and $\neg$ for "not," giving us three ways to express the propositions.

It is raining and 5 is greater than 3.	p and q	$p \wedge q$
It is raining or 5 is greater than 3.	p or q	$p \vee q$
It is not raining.	not p	$\neg p$

Although the English words "and," "or" and "not" are suggestive here, using English words can lead to ambiguity. Specifically, the word "or" is often used in English to mean "one or the other *but not both*," for example, when offering a choice between two alternatives. In logic, contrastingly, we most often use the *in*clusive interpretation: "one or the other *or both*." It is therefore actually less confusing in the long run to introduce special symbols. As shown above, we will write these expressions as $p \wedge q$, $p \vee q$, and $\neg p$, respectively. The operators $\wedge$, $\vee$ and $\neg$ are called **logical operators** (or connectives). The $\vee$ symbol is read as "or" but it is *always* understood to have the inclusive meaning (allowing the possibility of both). If we need to talk about "exclusive or", we use a different symbol (see the exercises).

The expression $p \wedge q$ is regarded as a proposition itself, as well as being an expression involving other propositions; by analogy 1+2 is a number, 3, even though it is an expression involving numbers. The following recursive definition is how we specify all such propositions.

Definition 2.1

Syntactic Structure of Propositions

- Each of the two logical constants, TRUE and FALSE, is a proposition.
- Logical variables, such as p, q, r, ..., are propositions.
- If α and β are propositions, then so are $(\alpha \wedge \beta)$, $(\alpha \vee \beta)$ and $(\neg \alpha)$.
- Nothing else is a proposition.

The reason this is called a "syntactic" definition is that it specifies how propositions appear when written out as a string of symbols. It allows us to recognize "well-formed" strings, strings that can be built up recursively from the base cases. The third line of this definition can be used repeatedly to build up complex propositions. Each of the symbols α and β can stand not only for a logical constant (TRUE or FALSE) or a logical variable, but also for any other proposition already formed in accord with this same third line of the definition. For example, with $\alpha = p$ and $\beta = (q \wedge r)$, the form $(\alpha \vee \beta)$ becomes the complex proposition, $(p \vee (q \wedge r))$. Recall our discussion of **recursive** definitions from Chapter 1.

Parentheses play an important role in the definition. Without their parentheses, the expressions $(p \vee (q \wedge r))$ and $((p \vee q) \wedge r)$ would look the same, since each would be left with just $p \vee q \wedge r$. But $(p \vee (q \wedge r))$ can have a different value than $((p \vee q) \wedge r)$, just as $(2 + 3) \times 4 \neq 2 + (3 \times 4)$. So we do need parentheses. However, the definition goes beyond what is necessary, as we discussed in the last chapter. First, it unnecessarily requires parentheses around the outside of the entire expression (if it has an operator). Second, it does not take advantage of precedence. Just as $2 + 3 \times 4$ is understood to mean that the $\times$ is to be applied before the $+$, so too is the unparenthesized expression $p \vee q \wedge r$ understood to mean that the $\wedge$ is to be applied before the $\vee$. Further $\neg$ has the highest precedence, so $\neg p \vee q$ is the same as $((\neg p) \vee q)$. Finally, recall that when an operator is associative — as $\wedge$ and $\vee$ are — we typically omit parentheses but only because we assume that such an operator associates left-to-right.

Example 2.1

The string of symbols $(\neg ((p \wedge q) \vee r))$ is proposition since it is can be built recursively. In particular, the base cases are p, q and r, from which we get $(p \wedge q)$ is a proposition, and then $((p \wedge q) \vee r)$ is seen to be a proposition, and then finally the whole string. Note that only some of these parentheses are necessary because of precedence rules. Also recall from the last chapter that recursively defined expressions can be presented as expression trees, where the parentheses are unnecessary since subtrees correspond to parenthetic subexpressions.

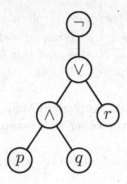

2.2 States, Operators and Semantics

We often refer to the value of a proposition as its **state**, so a proposition can be in one of two states, TRUE or FALSE. More generally, when we are dealing with a sequence of propositions, we can speak of the state of the sequence. That combined state will then be the ordered list of the states of each proposition in the sequence. For example, two propositions, p and q, can be in one of the four states listed below. Three propositions can be in one of eight states, and k propositions in one of 2^k states. A given state is sometimes called a "truth assignment."

The 4 states for p and q have these pairs of values for p, q, respectively:

1. TRUE, TRUE
2. TRUE, FALSE
3. FALSE, TRUE
4. FALSE, FALSE

The operator $\wedge$ is read "and" and is often called the **conjunction** operator. It has two operands (propositions that it operates on) and is defined by giving its value in each of the four states of those two operands. Specifically,

$p \wedge q$ = TRUE   when both p = TRUE and q = TRUE, and
$p \wedge q$ = FALSE   in the other three states.

The operator $\vee$ is read "or" and is often called the **disjunction** operator. It too is defined by giving its value in each of the four states of its two operands. Notice how this definition is inclusive in the manner mentioned above.

$p \vee q = $ FALSE   when both $p = $ FALSE and $q = $ FALSE, and
$p \vee q = $ TRUE   in the other three states.

Finally we define $\neg$, the **negation** operator:

$\neg p = $ TRUE   when $p = $ FALSE, and
$\neg p = $ FALSE   when $p = $ TRUE.

These definitions are often presented graphically as shown with the following tables, in which each cell (or box) corresponds to the combined state of the two variables p and q.

p	q T	F
T	T	F
F	F	F

$p \wedge q$

p	q T	F
T	T	T
F	T	F

$p \vee q$

p	
T	F
F	T

$\neg p$

It is of some interest to show how propositional logic can be discussed in the formal framework of sets and functions, introduced in Chapter 1. To begin, note that the logical constants constitute a 2-element set, which we will call $\mathcal{B}$, so that $\mathcal{B} = \{$TRUE, FALSE$\}$. Next, the conjunction and disjunction operators can also be regarded as *functions* of two variables. A function symbol is typically written ahead of its arguments, for example, $f(x, y)$, so by analogy you would write $\wedge (p, q)$. This is like writing $+(x, y)$ for the sum of x and y. However, it is much more common to use $\wedge$ and $\vee$ as infix operators, writing them between their arguments (or operands), as we have done except in this discussion.

We can regard the conjunction operator, $\wedge$, as a function from pairs of $\mathcal{B}$-elements to a single $\mathcal{B}$-element, that is $\wedge : \mathcal{B} \times \mathcal{B} \to \mathcal{B}$. The elements of $\mathcal{B} \times \mathcal{B}$ are the four states of (p, q) mentioned at the beginning of this section. The disjunction operator, $\vee$, involves the same sets, so $\vee : \mathcal{B} \times \mathcal{B} \to \mathcal{B}$. For the operator $\neg$, which simply has $\mathcal{B}$ as its domain, so $\neg : \mathcal{B} \to \mathcal{B}$.

Recall that Definition 2.1 provides the **syntax** or structure of the propositions. But that is just a string of symbols that has no meaning. By providing definitions of the meaning of the operator symbols in this section we have given the **semantics** or meaning of the propositions.[1]

2.3 Propositions as Functions

Consider a proposition $\alpha = \neg\,((p \wedge q) \vee r)$. We see it as a string of symbols and we understand the symbols as Boolean variables and operators and we also understand the structure — through parentheses or with an expression tree — well enough to be clear on what the arguments are for these Boolean operators. It is now just one step further to regard α itself as a Boolean function.

A proposition must be a truth-valued statement, but our α is not clearly true or false. In fact it is one or the other, but that depends on the state — truth assignment — of its variables. While α is a string of symbols, it also can be regarded as a truth-valued/Boolean function $\alpha(p, q, r)$.

Example 2.2

Again, consider the proposition $\alpha = \neg\,((p \wedge q) \vee r)$. If the variables have the truth assignment $p = \text{TRUE}$, $q = \text{FALSE}$, $r = \text{FALSE}$ we can see how to *evaluate* the proposition "bottom-up." This is shown in the diagram. First $p \wedge q = \text{FALSE}$, by the definition of $\wedge$. Next we see $(p \wedge q) \vee r$ is FALSE by appealing to the definition of $\vee$. Finally $\neg\,((p \wedge q) \vee r)$ is evaluated to TRUE.

---

[1] In formal logic this is called specifying the *model*.

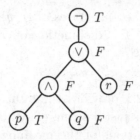

This can be captured in tabular form. Note that each node of the expression tree is the root of a subtree that corresponds to a subexpression and that we indicate what the bottom-up evaluation is for each such subexpression. For brevity, of course, we use T and F in place of TRUE and FALSE.

p	q	r	$p \wedge q$	$(p \wedge q) \vee r$	$\neg(((p \wedge q) \vee r))$
T	F	F	F	F	T

Of course the three variables could have been in any of eight possible states. Each state would lead to a different bottom-up evaluation. We can combine all eight evaluations into one table; this is called the **truth table** for α.

p	q	r	$p \wedge q$	$(p \wedge q) \vee r$	$\neg(((p \wedge q) \vee r))$
T	T	T	T	T	F
T	T	F	T	T	F
T	F	T	F	T	F
T	F	F	F	F	T
F	T	T	F	T	F
F	T	F	F	F	T
F	F	T	F	T	F
F	F	F	F	F	T

Now the final column can be taken in isolation as a complete definition of a function $\alpha(p, q, r)$. We could do the same exercise for any proposition. To illustrate consider $\beta = (\neg p \lor \neg q) \land \neg r$, which is also summarized as a function below. Notice that, when regarded as functions, α and β have the same truth table.

p	q	r	$\alpha(p,q,r)$	$\beta(p,q,r)$
T	T	T	F	F
T	T	F	F	F
T	F	T	F	F
T	F	F	T	T
F	T	T	F	F
F	T	F	T	T
F	F	T	F	F
F	F	F	T	T

Example 2.3

Consider the two propositions $\neg (p \land q)$ and $\neg p \lor \neg q$. We combine the truth tables for these two as shown below; the four states of the variables p and q are not repeated for the second proposition.

p	q	$p \land q$	$\neg (p \land q)$	$\neg p$	$\neg q$	$\neg p \lor \neg q$
T	T	T	F	F	F	F
T	F	F	T	F	T	T
F	T	F	T	T	F	T
F	F	F	T	T	T	T

Notice that the fourth and seventh columns have identical truth values, and therefore our two propositions are the same when regarded as functions.

In both of our examples we saw that in all possible states and there was no logical difference between two propositions, even though they look different syntactically.

Definition 2.2

Equivalence of Propositions

Two propositions α and β that evaluate to the same value for each and every state are **equivalent**. This is written $\alpha \equiv \beta$. This is the same as saying that when regarded as functions they are the same function; they map inputs to outputs identically. Note that $\equiv$ is *not* an operator; it is a notation used to indicate a fact.

Therefore the equivalence of the two expressions in Example 2.3 is written like this:

$$\neg (p \wedge q) \equiv \neg p \vee \neg q.$$

In general how do you show $\alpha \equiv \beta$? The truth table is a systematic and visually clear way to present an exhaustive consideration of all possible states. The table is thus a summary of a proof by **exhaustive case analysis**. The important concept of case analysis (not always exhaustive) arises again in Chapter 3, where it serves as the basis of an inference rule and is used in a proof.

Why use three bars ("$\equiv$") for equivalence instead of just the two in an ordinary equals sign ("$=$")? The difference between an equation and an equivalence is that an equivalence is always true (in all states). An equation does not make such a claim. For example, $3x^2 = 12$ is not a claim that $3x^2$ must be 12, no matter what value x has. Although an equation may hold for all values of its variables, more often the variables must have particular values (called solutions). Some equations have no solution at all, and others, like this one, may have multiple solutions (here, 2 and -2).

Example 2.4

Now consider another truth table proof, for the equivalence of the following two propositions:

$$p \wedge (q \vee r) \text{ and } (p \wedge q) \vee (p \wedge r)$$

Like in Example 2.2 there are three variables, and so eight states are needed.

p	q	r	$q \vee r$	$p \wedge (q \vee r)$	$p \wedge q$	$p \wedge r$	$(p \wedge q) \vee (p \wedge r)$
T	T	T	T	T	T	T	T
T	T	F	T	T	T	F	T
T	F	T	T	T	F	T	T
T	F	F	F	F	F	F	F
F	T	T	T	F	F	F	F
F	T	F	T	F	F	F	F
F	F	T	T	F	F	F	F
F	F	F	F	F	F	F	F

Comparing the fifth and last columns we see that they correspond exactly, each having three Ts followed by five Fs. Since the two expressions have the same truth value for each of the (eight) possible states we conclude:

$$p \wedge (q \vee r) \equiv (p \wedge q) \vee (p \wedge r).$$

There is another important kind of result, besides equivalences, that truth tables can prove. A *tautology* is a proposition that is equivalent to TRUE. (In other contexts such a proposition is said to be *valid*.) In other words, it has the value TRUE regardless of the state of its variables, so in the truth table there will be a column for that proposition that is all TRUEs. Find that column in each of the following truth tables. The first involves a single variable and proves that $p \vee \neg p$ is a tautology. A tautology involving two variables is $(p \wedge q) \vee \neg p \vee \neg q$, as is proved in the second truth table.

p	$\neg p$	$p \vee \neg p$
T	F	T
F	T	T

p	q	$\neg p$	$\neg q$	$p \wedge q$	$(p \wedge q) \vee \neg p$	$(p \wedge q) \vee \neg p \vee \neg q$
T	T	F	F	T	T	T
T	F	F	T	F	F	T
F	T	T	F	F	T	T
F	F	T	T	F	T	T

Finally, when a proposition has a truth table that has *some* TRUEs (one or more) it is said to be *satisfiable*. An expression whose column is all FALSEs is *unsatisfiable*.

2.4   Laws of Propositional Logic

This section lists some short, useful equivalences that are often called **laws of propositional logic**. You already know one of them, shown next, since it was proved in the preceding section. Below it, for comparison, is the familiar distributive law for numbers.

$$p \wedge (q \vee r) \equiv (p \wedge q) \vee (p \wedge r)$$

$$x \times (y + z) \equiv (x \times y) + (x \times z)$$

In arithmetic, multiplication distributes over addition. The logical equivalence here is similar to the arithmetic one and by analogy is also called a distributive law. It says that conjunction ($\wedge$) distributes over disjunction ($\vee$). Propositional logic, unlike arithmetic, has not just one but *two* distributive laws: each operator ($\wedge$ and $\vee$) distributes over the other. Just as we can use the distributive law of arithmetic to transform one (arithmetic) expression into another, so too we can use this propositional equivalence to transform one (propositional) expression into another. Just as in arithmetic, manipulating expressions is an important technique to generate new but equivalent expressions.

The lists in Figure 2.1 and Figure 2.2 give some of the most important equivalences which we will use for manipulating logical expressions.

Law of negation:
$$\neg\,\neg\,\alpha \equiv \alpha$$

Combining a variable with itself:

$\alpha \lor \neg\,\alpha \equiv \text{TRUE}$	Excluded middle
$\alpha \land \neg\,\alpha \equiv \text{FALSE}$	Contradiction
$\alpha \lor \alpha \equiv \alpha$	Idempotence of $\lor$
$\alpha \land \alpha \equiv \alpha$	Idempotence of $\land$

Properties of constants:
$$\alpha \lor \text{TRUE} \equiv \text{TRUE}$$
$$\alpha \lor \text{FALSE} \equiv \alpha$$
$$\alpha \land \text{TRUE} \equiv \alpha$$
$$\alpha \land \text{FALSE} \equiv \text{FALSE}$$

Figure 2.1: Equivalences with One Variable

Each equivalence can easily be established by truth tables, that is by exhaustive case analysis. Note that the laws are for general propositions like α and β rather than variables p and q. However since — like Boolean variables — propositions are truth-valued, we speak of the current state of, say, α and β and construct truth tables exactly the same way. Additional propositional equivalences will be given in the next section.

The Law of the Excluded Middle is a fundamental law. It is a essentially a restatement of the definition of a proposition: it is either true or false. The latin name "principium tertii exclusi" — the law of the excluded third — indicates that there is no third alternative. (There is a philosophical school of mathematics that prohibits this law, however almost all mathematicians use it without comment.)

Taken all together, the set of equivalences for propositional logic is richer and more symmetric than the set of analogous rules for arithmetic. An example of the richness is that there is nothing in

Commutativity:
$$\alpha \wedge \beta \equiv \beta \wedge \alpha$$
$$\alpha \vee \beta \equiv \beta \vee \alpha$$

Associativity:
$$\alpha \vee (\beta \vee \gamma) \equiv (\alpha \vee \beta) \vee \gamma$$
$$\alpha \wedge (\beta \wedge \gamma) \equiv (\alpha \wedge \beta) \wedge \gamma$$

Distributivity:
$$\alpha \vee (\beta \wedge \gamma) \equiv (\alpha \vee \beta) \wedge (\alpha \vee \gamma)$$
$$\alpha \wedge (\beta \vee \gamma) \equiv (\alpha \wedge \beta) \vee (\alpha \wedge \gamma)$$

DeMorgan's Laws:
$$\neg (\alpha \wedge \beta) \equiv \neg \alpha \vee \neg \beta$$
$$\neg (\alpha \vee \beta) \equiv \neg \alpha \wedge \neg \beta$$

Subsumption:
$$\alpha \wedge (\alpha \vee \beta) \equiv \alpha$$
$$\alpha \vee (\alpha \wedge \beta) \equiv \alpha$$

Figure 2.2: Equivalences with Multiple Variables

arithmetic like DeMorgan's laws. An example of the symmetry can be found in the two distributivity laws; many of the laws come in pairs.

The principal reason to study these laws is to allow algebraic manipulations. The goal of establishing a new equivalence like $\alpha \equiv \beta$ is not typically done by truth tables. Since the number of states grows exponentially in the number of variables truth tables are severely limited. Instead we can use the laws to algebraically manipulate a proposition into another proposition that has the same truth table. The style of algebra is so familiar and analogous to elementary algebra that little needs to be said.

Example 2.5

Consider these steps starting with left-hand side of the second subsumption law.

$$p \vee (p \wedge q) \equiv (p \vee p) \wedge (p \vee q) \equiv p \wedge (p \vee q) \equiv p$$

We have used the distributive law to get the next proposition. Next we used the idempotence of $\vee$ to get the next proposition which is the same as the left-hand side of the first subsumption law, which we know is equivalent to its right-hand side. Therefore if we were given the first subsumption law then we could *prove* the second subsumption law algebraically, without an appeal to truth tables.

Example 2.6

Let us return to the α and β of Example 2.2.

$$\alpha = \neg ((p \wedge q) \vee r) \equiv \neg (p \wedge q) \wedge \neg r \equiv (\neg p \vee \neg q) \wedge \neg r = \beta$$

The original proposition is changed with DeMorgan's law and then the subexpression $\neg (p \wedge q)$ is manipulated by the other DeMorgan's law.

While manipulating subexpressions, as in the previous example, is a common algebraic step to most of us, we should pause and consider it. What is being done is replacing a subtree of the expression tree by another subtree that is functional equivalent. Hence the entire tree that it is embedded in will have identical outcomes when it does bottom-up evaluations.

2.5 Two Important Operators

We now have a new way to prove things besides truth tables: algebraic substitution, that is, the replacement of an expression by another one that has been shown to be equivalent to it. A third approach to proving things — besides truth tables and replacing things by their equivalents — is to make use of *rules of inference*. This technique, which is the topic of Section 3.2, involves an especially important operator that we now introduce. We give it a strange name, $\triangle$, so we can talk about it without prejudging what the expression $p \triangle q$ might mean. The new operator has the following truth table:

$$
\begin{array}{c|cc}
 & \multicolumn{2}{c}{q} \\
p & \mathrm{T} & \mathrm{F} \\
\hline
\mathrm{T} & \mathrm{T} & \mathrm{F} \\
\mathrm{F} & \mathrm{T} & \mathrm{T} \\
\end{array}
$$

$$p \triangle q$$

What does this truth table tell us? First, notice that it has three T's. Therefore to assert $p \triangle q$ is a weak claim, in that it only narrows down the possible states from four to three. By contrast, asserting $p \wedge q$ is a strong claim that narrows the possible states to just one, thereby telling us what p must be (TRUE) and also what q must be (TRUE).

Suppose you were somehow assured that proposition $p \triangle q$ was TRUE. Then, consulting the truth table you would see that you were in one of the three states other than the upper right corner. That is, you could conclude the state $p = $ TRUE and $q = $ FALSE was not the current state. Now suppose you also learned that $p = $ TRUE. What can the truth of p tell you in the presence of the truth of $p \triangle q$? Well, whenever $p = $ TRUE, we are in the top half of the truth table, but whenever $p \triangle q = $ TRUE, we are not in the upper right. That leaves the upper left, where both p and q are true. So we conclude that both p and q are true.

To summarize, $p \triangle q = $ TRUE lets us use the information that $p = $ TRUE to establish that, in addition, $q = $ TRUE. In other words, it tells us that (the truth of) p leads to (the truth of) q. So we will henceforth pronounce $\triangle$ as "leads to" or "implies" and write it as $\rightarrow$. This arrow shows the direction of our reasoning. The operator it represents, is called either the **implication** or the **conditional** operator.

We also read the expression $p \to q$ as "if p then q". This English-language phrasing can be just as confusing as "or" (inclusive versus exclusive) unless we are careful to remember that as with the other operators, the definition is the truth table, not the English phrase. Even though in English "if p then q" does not seem to mean much when p is false, we have seen that it's useful to have this operator, which is defined to give TRUE in both of the states where p is FALSE. The important point is that the truth of both p and $(p \to q)$, together, ensures the truth of q, and that we can prove it with the truth table![2]

Another important operator has the truth table shown next. Once again, we use a strange name at first, this time $\diamondsuit$, to avoid any preconceptions. As you can see from the truth table, the expression $p \diamondsuit q$ is true in those (two) states for which p and q have the same truth value: either both TRUE or both FALSE.

	q	
p	T	F
T	T	F
F	F	T

$$p \diamondsuit q$$

The same kind of reasoning used for the conditional works here too. Suppose we know that $p \diamondsuit q$ is true (putting us in the either the upper left or lower right of the truth table) and we then learn that p is true (putting us in the top row). The only possible state is therefore the upper left, where both p and q are true. So from the truth of *both* p and $p \diamondsuit q$, we can conclude that $q = \text{TRUE}$ too.

So far, this reasoning is just like that for the conditional. But now notice what happens if we assume the truth of q (instead of p as before) along with the truth of $p \diamondsuit q$. The truth of q requires our state to lie in the left column. This along with the truth of $p \diamondsuit q$ (upper left or lower right) again puts us in the upper left, where $p = \text{TRUE}$. In sum, when $p \diamondsuit q = \text{TRUE}$, we can reason either from p

---

[2]This is called both *logical implication* and *material implication* and philosophers distinguish it from a *linguistic conditional*, where the $p = \text{FALSE}$ cases are treated differently.

Conditional law:
$$\alpha \to \beta \equiv \neg\, \alpha \vee \beta$$

Biconditional law:
$$\alpha \leftrightarrow \beta \equiv (\alpha \to \beta) \wedge (\beta \to \alpha)$$

Contrapositive law:
$$\alpha \to \beta \equiv \neg\, \beta \to \neg\, \alpha$$

Figure 2.3: Equivalences with the Conditional

to q or from q to p. Because each leads to the other we use a two-way arrow for this operator, writing $p \leftrightarrow q$. The $\leftrightarrow$ operator is sometimes called the **biconditional**.

We read $p \leftrightarrow q$ as "p if and only if q" or more succinctly, "p iff q". It may also help to say it less succinctly as *"p if q, and also p only if q"*. We can rephrase the *"p if q"* part as "if q, p" or "if q then p" which is the same as $q \to p$. As for the *"p only if q"* part, it indicates that when q is false, so is p; that is, $\neg\, q \to \neg\, p$. This in turn gives $p \to q$, by the contrapositive law; see the next paragraph.

There are three additional laws that involve our new operators and each is, of course, proven by truth tables. The conditional law appears in Figure 2.3; note that it quite accurately says that if you are in a state that makes $p \to q$ true then you are either in the first column (q) or the second row ($\neg\, p$). The biconditional law conditionals $p \leftrightarrow q \equiv (p \to q) \wedge (q \to p)$ certainly motivates the use of a double arrow and the phrase "if and only if." The contrapositive law is also shown.

2.6   Normal Forms

For computational purposes, it simplifies various algorithms to convert logical expressions to a normal (or standard) form. The first of the "normal" forms we will introduce here is used in artificial intelligence, the second in hardware design.[3]

---

[3]Electrical engineers use different terminology for these normal forms.

Example 2.7

Using the laws just introduced we replace the biconditional operator in $p \leftrightarrow q$ to obtain an equivalent expression only using the operators $\wedge$, $\vee$ and $\neg$.

$$
\begin{aligned}
p \leftrightarrow q &\equiv (p \to q) \wedge (q \to p) \\
&\equiv (\neg p \vee q) \wedge (\neg q \vee p)
\end{aligned}
$$

Define a **literal** to be either Boolean variable or its negation, e.g. p or $\neg q$. Define a **conjunct** as one or more literals "or"ed together, e.g. $\neg q \vee r \vee \neg p$. Next define an expression to be in **conjunctive normal form** (CNF) if it is one or more conjuncts "and"ed together. The previous example resolved to CNF.

The second normal form starts with the same definition of literal. Next we define a **disjunct** as one or more literals "and"ed together, e.g. $\neg s \wedge p \wedge \neg q$. Finally define an expression to be in **disjunctive normal form** (DNF) if it is one or more disjuncts "or"ed together; see the next example.

Example 2.8

As a further exercise, we will continue to manipulate the previous example. Continuing from above, using the distributive law twice

$$
\begin{aligned}
&\equiv (\neg p \wedge \neg q) \vee (\neg p \wedge p) \vee (q \wedge \neg q) \vee (q \wedge p) \\
&\equiv (\neg p \wedge \neg q) \vee \text{FALSE} \vee \text{FALSE} \vee (q \wedge p) \\
&\equiv (\neg p \wedge \neg q) \vee (q \wedge p)
\end{aligned}
$$

we get an equivalent expression that is in disjunctive normal form. The repeated use of the distributive law can always be used to convert an expression in CNF into DNF, and vice versa. However on large examples the exponential blow-up of the number of terms make this technique prohibitive.

As just stated, converting from CNF into DNF algebraically is problematic. There is another way. There are well-known techniques for converting a truth table for a proposition α into a CNF (or DNF) representation of α (these techniques are not covered in this text). But if converting from one form to another uses a truth table as an intermediate step then we still experience an exponential blow-up in the number of states rendering the approach untenable.

In fact there is no known efficient technique for converting between the two forms, for large inputs, and in fact this is known to be an $\mathcal{NP}$-complete problem. The last section of this book addresses what that might mean.

2.7   Logic Circuits

A primary area of computer science that makes use of propositional logic is the design of computer hardware. It is widely known that computers utilize binary values and circuitry to compute things. Unfortunately the design of hardware has a host of real-life concerns that complicate what is really a simple point. That is, nearly all circuitry is a realization of propositional formulas. In this section we merely make this point.

The binary values conceptually are TRUE and FALSE. These are often referred to as 1 and 0. In fact they are just disjoint ranges of voltages on wires. Each such value is a *bit*. But what is important is that they are understood and manipulated as if they were actually Boolean values. The entire computer age was ushered in by Claude Shannon's 1937 Master's Thesis in which he showed that circuitry could implement propositional logic. It is important to remember that what is meant by "circuitry" has changed many times but the observations made in 1937 are unchanged today; they are all *digital circuits*.

A typical computer has a clock and between each tick of the clock values race from inputs to outputs. The inputs can be from an external source or from an internal memory location. Let us confine

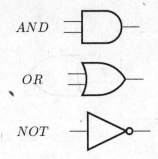

Figure 2.4: Elementary logical gates.

our attention to internal memory locations that holds one bit, called "flip-flops." The outputs can be to an external source or to an internal memory location. The basic principle is: each output value is computed to be the value of a proposition where the variables are a subset of the inputs.

We have focused on the three logical operators: AND, OR and NOT. We will continue with just those. (However we already have seen others like the conditional and biconditional operators. Hardware designers use others with names like: XOR, NAND, and NOR.) Each symbol in Figure 2.4 is a standard representation of a subcircuit that computes a Boolean operator. How those individual subcircuits are built is technology-dependent, but the symbols remain the same. The subcircuits are called "gates."

The understanding is that for, say, an OR-gate that two boolean inputs enter from the left, say p and q, and the output leaves on the right being equal to $p \lor q$. Similarly for AND-gates and NOT-gates. A proposition is implemented by cascading the inputs through a series of gates — the output of one gate being the input to the next gate — until the value of the proposition spills out on the right as the "output."

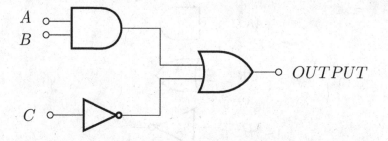

Figure 2.5: A circuit computing $(A \wedge B) \vee (\neg C)$.

Example 2.9

Consider the circuit in Figure 2.5. The output of the AND-gate is $A \wedge B$ and the output of the NOT-gate is $\neg C$. Therefore these are the inputs to the OR-gate. It follows the output of this circuit is $(A \wedge B) \vee (\neg C)$. Note that A, B, and C are just three of possibly more available inputs and this output is possibly just one of many computed from the same inputs at the same time. The values leave the inputs when the clock ticks and should arrive at the output before the next clock tick. Since there is a time delay encountered at each gate there is a technology-dependent bound on how complex a circuit can be.

Example 2.10

Consider the circuit in Figure 2.6. Like in the last example we can figure out what the output is for each gate. It follows that the output for this circuit is $(\neg (A \vee B) \wedge (B \wedge C)) \vee (\neg C)$. By DeMorgan's law and associativity this $(\neg A \wedge (\neg B \wedge B) \wedge C) \vee (\neg C)$. But this simplifies to just $\neg C$, indicating a much simpler circuit could have been used. A major concern of electrical engineering is to find simpler circuits. In reality, since portions of circuits can be used to calculate separate outputs, this is a daunting goal.

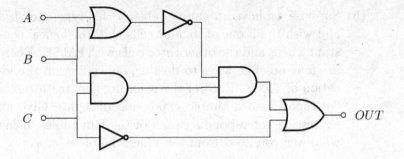

Figure 2.6: A circuit computing $(\neg (A \vee B) \wedge (B \wedge C)) \vee (\neg C)$.

This is a very brief introduction to material that require several semesters to master. Our goal is only to highlight this application area.

Exercises

2.1 – Consider the effect of parentheses.

   (a) Give a set of truth values for p, q and r for which the values of $(p \vee q) \wedge r$ and $p \vee (q \wedge r)$ are different.

   (b) What does the answer to (a) indicate about parentheses in these expressions?

   (c) Give another set of values for p, q and r that could answer (a).

2.2 – Section 2.2 introduces square 2×2 truth tables for the individual logical operators $\wedge$ and $\vee$. Each table has 4 cells.

   (a) It was noted that the binary propositional operators, $\wedge$ and $\vee$, can be regarded as functions, $f : \mathcal{B} \times \mathcal{B} \to \mathcal{B}$. Explain why there exist 16 such functions in all.

(b) Suppose we have an empty table of this type and size, and wish to fill one of its four cells with the logical constant TRUE and the other three cells with FALSE. There are four possible ways to do this, depending on the location of TRUE. Each of the resulting four truth tables corresponds to a simple expression of logic. Give an expression corresponding each of the four tables, using whatever you need from the nine symbols p, q, $\wedge$, $\vee$, $\neg$, $\leftrightarrow$, $\rightarrow$,) and (. Use as few occurrences of the operators as you can. Use parentheses only where necessary.

(c) Do the same thing as in part (b), except that this time each truth table is to have one occurrence of FALSE and three of TRUE.

2.3 – Use 2-row truth tables like the one in the text for $p \vee \neg p$ to show that each of the expressions given here is a tautology. Explain for each, in one or more complete and clear sentences, why it *should* always be true. (The latter an open-ended question just meant to engender familiarity.)

(a) $p \vee$ TRUE

(b) $\neg (p \wedge \neg p)$

(c) $p \rightarrow p$

2.4 – As in Section 2.3 show these propositions are equivalent using truth tables. For the first proof you need two identical columns in a 4-row truth table. The second requires an 8-row table.

(a) $\neg (p \vee q) \equiv \neg p \wedge \neg q$

(b) $p \vee (q \wedge r) \equiv (p \vee q) \wedge (p \vee r)$

2.5 – Use truth tables to prove the conditional, biconditional and contrapositive laws. Recall that the 2×2 truth tables introduced for $\triangle$ and $\diamond$ are actually the ones for $\rightarrow$ and $\leftrightarrow$.

(a) $p \to q \equiv \neg p \vee q$

(b) $p \leftrightarrow q \equiv (p \to q) \wedge (q \to p)$

(c) $p \to q \equiv \neg q \to \neg p$

2.6 – State a variant of DeMorgan's law for 3 terms like $\neg(q \wedge r \wedge s)$ and establish the law algebraically.

2.7 – Prove each of these equivalences algebraically, *one* step at a time. State which equivalence in Section 2.4 or 2.5 justifies each step.

(a) $((p \vee q) \wedge (\neg p \wedge \neg q)) \equiv \text{FALSE}$

(b) $p \vee q \vee r \vee s \equiv (\neg p \wedge \neg q \wedge \neg r) \to s$

2.8 – Here is a proof that the conditional operator is transitive. The proof shows that the initial expression is a tautology, since it is equivalent to TRUE; that is, it is true for any values of p, q and r. Sometimes two or more rules are used for a step. State the equivalence(s) used at each step.

$((p \to q) \wedge (q \to r)) \to (p \to r)$

$\equiv \neg((\neg p \vee q) \wedge (\neg q \vee r)) \vee (\neg p \vee r)$ i   _____

$\equiv (\neg(\neg p \vee q) \vee \neg(\neg q \vee r)) \vee (\neg p \vee r)$ ii   _____

$\equiv ((\neg \neg p \wedge \neg q) \vee (\neg \neg q \wedge \neg r)) \vee (\neg p \vee r)$ iii   _____

$\equiv (p \wedge \neg q) \vee (q \wedge \neg r) \vee \neg p \vee r$ iv   _____

$\equiv ((p \wedge \neg q) \vee \neg p) \vee ((q \wedge \neg r) \vee r)$ v   _____

$\equiv (\text{TRUE} \wedge (\neg q \vee \neg p)) \vee ((q \vee r) \wedge \text{TRUE})$ vi   _____

$\equiv \neg q \vee q \vee \neg p \vee r$ vii   _____

$\equiv \text{TRUE} \vee \neg p \vee r$ viii _____

$\equiv \text{TRUE}$ ix   _____

2.9 – Using truth tables, prove that each of the following conditional expressions is a tautology. Explain why each makes sense (where, again, this is an open-ended question).

(a) $p \to (p \vee q)$

(b) $q \to (p \to q)$

(c) $((p \to q) \land p) \to q$

(d) $((p \to q) \land \neg q) \to \neg p$

2.10 – As in Exercise 2.9, using truth tables prove that each of the following conditional expressions is a tautology. Once again, explain why each makes sense.

(a) $((p \to q) \land (q \to r)) \to (p \to r)$

(b) $((p \lor q) \land (p \to r) \land (q \to r)) \to r$

2.11 – Prove that $p \lor (\neg p \land q) \equiv (p \lor q)$ in each of the following ways:

(a) Using a truth table.

(b) Using algebraic substitution, starting with distributivity.

2.12 – For each of the conditional expressions in Exercise 2.10 use algebraic substitutions to prove they are tautologies. To do this you must show for each α that $\alpha \equiv$ TRUE. (Hints: Start by getting rid of all the conditional operators by using the conditional law. Then use DeMorgan's law repeatedly to get all the negation signs operating on the individual symbols p, q and r, getting rid of double negations wherever they crop up. You may also make use of the formula proved in Exercise 2.11.)

2.13 – Recall that converting a propositional expression from CNF (conjunctive normal form) to DNF (disjunctive normal form) is analogous to multiplying out an arithmetic expression: $(a + b) \times (c + d) = a \times c + \ldots$. Convert the following expression to DNF by algebraic methods.

$$(p \lor q) \land (r \lor s)$$

2.14 – Prove by truth tables that

$$(p \to q) \land \neg (p \leftrightarrow q) \to \neg (q \to p).$$

Explain why this tautology makes sense.

2.15 – Prove the proposition in Exercise 2.14 algebraically.

2.16 – Show algebraically that these are equivalent:

$$(p \lor q) \land r \equiv (p \land r) \lor (q \land r)$$

This shows distributivity *from the right* is valid (in this case of $\land$ over $\lor$), even though we have tacitly assumed it.

2.17 – State a law for the distributivity of $\lor$ over 3-term conjunctions like $(q \land r \land s)$ and establish the law algebraically. Hint: Recall that parentheses are suppressed for associative operators even though they are present.

2.18 – The operator "$\oplus$" expresses the idea of exclusive "or," that is, a choice between alternatives. Thus $p \oplus q$ is TRUE when exactly *one* of p, q is TRUE but it is FALSE when both or neither is TRUE.

  (a) Give the shortest possible equivalence for $p \oplus q$.

  (b) Give an expression equivalent to $p \oplus q$ containing only $\land$, $\lor$, and $\neg$ as its operators

Chapter 3

Proofs by Deduction

In this chapter we present the notion of a proof by rules of inference. The proofs are formal, since not only are they expressed in terms of symbols, but in addition each step is justified in terms of explicit rules for manipulating the symbols. The rules-of-inference approach to proving things turns out to apply much more broadly than the methods of Chapter 2. Truth tables — though essential as the foundation of other methods — have a limited role within logic. By contrast the approach introduced in this chapter, enriched with predicates (Chapter 5), applies throughout mathematics and, as we will see in Chapter 6, to computer science.

3.1   Reasons for Wanting to Prove Things

As a practical matter, it is useful to have beliefs that correctly match up with what is true in the world. Some of our beliefs are based on direct observation, some come from believing what trustworthy people tell us and still others come indirectly by reasoning. Of course, in the case of reasoning, it has to be sound reasoning if it is to yield correct results. Proofs are really just very careful reasoning in a sequence of justified steps. Rules of inference concern what kinds of steps are justifiable.

Proving things has several benefits to people in general, to technical specialists and specifically to computer scientists. A correct proof shows you that the particular thing proved is true, given that it starts from true assumptions. It also shows you why it is true, helping you to understand the subject matter more deeply. More generally, proofs give good practice in careful thinking.

Turning to computing, you know that computer programs need to be correct in general for all possible data. It is not enough for them just to work on a few arbitrary test sets of data. There are many disaster stories in the real world that turn on software error. There are several approaches to software reliability, one of which is to actually prove that a program is correct. This is discussed in Chapter 6.

The proving process itself can be automated. In fact, logic programming languages, like Prolog, actually work by proving things, as discussed in Appendix A. In other programming languages (whether logic-based or not), it is possible to write a theorem prover. Another application area for automated reasoning is expert systems. These systems apply human-like reasoning to aspects of medicine, science, engineering, law, business and education.

In common sense reasoning and in ordinary discussion, frequent informal use is made of many strategies given here, such as counter-examples and case analysis. Thus formal proofs do not differ from ordinary reasoning so much in what is an acceptable step in an argument, but rather in using symbols for precision and in proving quite subtle results by long chains of reasoning, involving many different strategies within a single proof.

3.2 Natural Deduction Proofs

A **proof** is a sequence of assertions meant to convince the reader of the truth of some particular statement. The proved statement is called a **theorem**. A theorem should always be a tautology; see Section 3.8. Usually a theorem is not obvious at the outset, but the proof is intended to inspire confidence that it is actually true. A theorem should also hold some interest, possibly because it is useful in applications or it may be of indirect use because it helps in proving other important results.

The actual presentation of the proof depends greatly on the (assumed) sophistication of the reader and the rigor of the given statement. Here we will begin with a rather formal view of proofs, rather than rough sketches of proofs, for two reasons. First, it is hard to make sense of a rough sketch of something you have never seen; in order to recognize the structure of a sketch of a formal proof we need to know the components of a formal proof. Second, formal proofs arise in several computer application areas, such as "inference engines" and "mechanical theorem provers".

Proofs succeed in convincing people by (i) starting from agreed truths and (ii) continuing by agreed methods. Some of these truths and methods may seem so simple that it is hardly worth stating them, but that's just what we want! The starting point of a proof consists of assertions chosen from among a collection of **axioms**. These simple statements are widely accepted as being clearly true. The methods for moving onward from the axioms are called **inference rules**.

In addition, we sometimes introduce an assertion tentatively, as an **assumption**, even though we do not know whether it is true or not, just to explore its consequences. A formal proof is a sequence of assertions, ending with the statement that is being proved, in which each assertion either is an axiom or an assumption or else follows by an inference rule from one or more particular assertions earlier in the sequence. It is crucial to keep track of which assertions depend on which assumptions, and to achieve the final result in such a way that it does not depend on any of the assumptions.

Proofs in real-life (in journals and books) are usually very rigorous but rarely "formal." In a rigorous proof, an axiom may be considered so common and well accepted that it is not mentioned. In arithmetic, for example, we typically do not bother to state explicitly that "4 is the successor of 3" or that "0 is the smallest element of $\mathcal{N}$" (where $\mathcal{N}$ is the set of non-negative integers). Furthermore, even when something is mentioned, a lot of "background knowledge" underlying it may be left tacit. Such facts are rigorous because they have been proven, by others in the past, to be true, i.e., a tautology. Further, our background knowledge includes inference rules about specific domains (or subject matter) that have also been proven by others. For example, continuing in the domain of non-negative integers, if $a < b$ and $b < c$, we can infer that $a < c$. This inference rule, known as the transitivity of less-than, is so common that it is often left unstated without confusing anyone.

In this chapter we avoid possible confusion about unstated background knowledge. We begin with proofs solely about propositions. The axioms and theorems will be propositions and the rules of inference will also be based on propositional logic. In later chapters we will include predicate logic for these roles. Ultimately we will apply logic-based inference to prove properties of numbers and computer programs; at that point we do assume some background knowledge.

In the last chapter we used two methods to establish that certain propositions are tautologies. First we used truth tables to establish that a given proposition is true in every state by considering every state separately; we called this proof by exhaustive case analysis. It is fairly useless for a large number of variables and, worse, it gives the reader no insight into *why* it is true; if human error created an incorrect entry in the table who would notice. Second we used laws that allowed algebraic substitutions/manipulations to transform the given proposition into some equivalent form. When the new form is the constant TRUE we have established the given proposition was a tautology. A proof that proceeds entirely in this way is sometimes called an "algebraic proof". This method can have intractable detail and also does not give much insight.

In contrast, in this chapter we use a style of proof that is often called "natural deduction." This is based on a formalization of the rigorous underpinnings of "common sense" arguments. The details of the presentation of the method differ from book to book.[1] A proof that proceeds entirely by rules of inference — without reliance

---

[1]Our presentation is based on the proof systems proposed by Gentzen, that have been very influential in the last hundred years, even if the details vary widely.

on algebraic manipulations — will sometimes be called a "natural deduction proof," or a "rules of inference proof." In Section 3.8 we formally tie together the proofs of tautologies and the deduction proofs of theorems.

In the next section we will see such inference rules, but first consider a more general setting. Suppose that in a step-by-step proof that it has been proven to the reader that α is true; also it has been proven to the reader that β is true. Further assume that before the proof was embarked upon that someone else had proven that $\phi \equiv \alpha \wedge \beta \rightarrow \gamma$ was a tautology, $\phi \equiv$ TRUE. Knowing ϕ is always true does not prevent, say, $\alpha =$ TRUE and $\beta = \gamma =$ FALSE. But *in the context of our current proof* knowing ϕ is a tautology allows us to convince the reader that γ is true. It is impossible to deny it given what is already proven. Our ϕ is a rule-of-inference. It is prior knowledge that is used to advance the proof with iron-clad logic.

3.3 Rules of Inference

A straightforward and exceedingly useful rule of inference is the one called **modus ponens** (the method of affirming). It states that if we know (the truth of) both $(\alpha \rightarrow \beta)$ and α then we can infer (the truth of) β. This inference rule follows directly from our earlier discussion of the tautology $((\alpha \rightarrow \beta) \wedge \alpha) \rightarrow \beta$. However it is not presented here as a tautology. Instead it is written this way since it is suggestive of how it will be used:

$$
\begin{array}{ll}
\text{Modus ponens:} & \alpha \rightarrow \beta \\
& \alpha \\
& \overline{} \\
& \beta
\end{array}
$$

It is suggestive since if the reader is convinced that $\alpha \rightarrow \beta$ is true and the reader is also convinced that α is true the reader must accept that β is true. It does not matter what order these first two lines appeared in proof, but we are now permitted to add the third. Notice that we indicate general propositions like α; the inference rule can be applied for any propositions, whether they are simple variables or complex examples.

Another rule of inference, called **modus tollens** (the method of denying),[2] states that if we know both $(\alpha \to \beta)$ and $\neg\, \beta$ then we can infer $\neg\, \alpha$. Notice that here we are concluding the truth of a negation, $\neg\, \alpha$. This rule can be justified if we argue that if α were true that it would lead to a contradiction. Alternatively we can justify it by proving it is a tautology. These two approaches can be used for all the inference rules in this chapter.

$$\text{Modus tollens:} \qquad \begin{array}{c} \alpha \to \beta \\ \neg\, \beta \\ \hline \neg\, \alpha \end{array}$$

Several important inference rules, including modus ponens and modus tollens, appear below in this format in Figure 3.1. First, note that each rule has a horizontal bar with an assertion below it and some number of assertions above it. The material above the bar, known as the **premises** (or antecedents) must be sufficient to justify the **conclusion** (or consequent), written below the bar. Let β be the propositional expression that appears below the bar. Above the bar we will use α for a single expression, α_1 and α_2 if there are two expressions, α_3 for a third, and so on, as needed.

$$\text{Patterns for inference rules} \qquad\qquad \begin{array}{c} \alpha_1 \end{array}$$
$$\text{with 1 or 2 premises:} \qquad \begin{array}{c} \alpha \\ \hline \beta \end{array} \qquad \begin{array}{c} \alpha_2 \\ \hline \beta \end{array}$$

Inference rules have a dual nature that we mention now and return to later. First and foremost inference rules are a given, they are not

---

[2]These names are Latin phrases. "Modus" means way or in this context a method. "Ponens" and "tollens" mean putting and taking away. Imagine that you have $p \to q$ in a container of truths. If you *put* p in, then q is in too. If you *take out* q (assert that it is false), then p comes out too.

part of the proof. *We do not need to justify them,* we simply use them. They allow the theorem prover to introduce new propositions given the acceptance of other propositions. We must remember that a proposition in a formal proof is an symbolic expression — a string or perhaps an expression tree. For example, when applying modus ponens if the expression $(\neg p) \to (q \vee r)$ has appeared in a proof (i.e. the reader has agreed it is true) and if the expression $\neg p$ has also appeared then we can confidently add the expression $(q \vee r)$. We do not need to "understand" any of these expressions. The inference rule treats these expressions as strings. A rule is carte blanche for the theorem prover, who uses it without knowing *why* it works.

The second aspect of the dual nature of inference rules seeks to explain why they were given to the theorem prover in the first place. We *could* give the theorem prover inference rules that seem arbitrary. But we don't. Why? Because the reader would lose interest. What makes the whole approach interesting is that we only choose rules that are "sound." To justify an inference rule consisting of a propositional expression α above the bar and a propositional expression β below it, we need only prove $\alpha \to \beta$ is a tautology. Similarly if $\alpha_1 \wedge \alpha_2 \to \beta$ is a tautology we justify the inference rule with α_1 and α_2 above the bar and β below. In general, there can be any number n of items above the bar, provided that we can prove the proposition $\alpha_1 \wedge \alpha_2 \wedge \ldots \wedge \alpha_n \to \beta$ is a tautology. If the corresponding proposition is a tautology we say the rule is **sound**. If the rule is sound then the reader believes that the conclusion does follow from the antecedents.

Example 3.1

Verify that the Contradiction inference rule is sound.

Consulting Figure 3.1, we see that we need to prove $\alpha \wedge \neg \alpha \to \text{FALSE}$. The truth table for this expression shows that it is a tautology.

α	$\neg \alpha$	$\alpha \wedge \neg \alpha$	FALSE	$(\alpha \wedge \neg \alpha) \to \text{FALSE}$
T	F	F	F	T
F	T	F	F	T

Example 3.2

Verify the ∨ introduction inference rule is sound.

According to Figure 3.1, it is established by proving that $\alpha \to (\alpha \vee \beta)$ is a tautology.

α	β	$\alpha \vee \beta$	$\alpha \to (\alpha \vee \beta)$
T	T	T	T
T	F	T	T
F	T	T	T
F	F	F	T

In the next section we will explain how to construct proofs using these. A curious fact will emerge. We can use some rules of inference to prove that other rules are sound. In fact we only need to be "given" two rules (several choices of two work) to prove all the rest are sound. That is only of theoretic interest. What is more important here is that we have a small but powerful set of rules, so that the reader will regard the proofs as "natural," after all the technique is called natural deduction. The list in the Figure 3.1 is arbitrary but fairly standard between textbooks.

A couple of remarks are indicated. First the Contradiction rule seems to be inconsistent with the overarching scheme of starting with true statements (axioms) and thereafter generating only true statements. That is correct. However when we introduce assumptions later, the utility of this rule will become apparent. Second the Tautology rule simply states that if there is a proposition that the reader agrees is true then it can be included. Generally this will be some previous lemma or theorem in a larger context. However in this chapter we will use this rule in a more fundamental way; the Law of Excluded Middle is a universal tautology.

Note that we *do not allow algebraic manipulation* explicitly. Certainly algebra can be put under the umbrella of "inference" inasmuch the fact that $\alpha \equiv \beta$ justifies inferring β when α is known to be true. This prohibition is a deliberate if Draconian choice. Natural

Modus ponens:	$\alpha \to \beta$	Modus tollens:	$\alpha \to \beta$
	α		$\neg \beta$
	$\overline{\hspace{2em}}$		$\overline{\hspace{2em}}$
	β		$\neg \alpha$

$\wedge$ introduction:	α	$\wedge$ elimination:	
	β		$\alpha \wedge \beta$
	$\overline{\hspace{2em}}$		$\overline{\hspace{2em}}$
	$\alpha \wedge \beta$		$\alpha \; [\text{or } \beta]$

$\vee$ introduction:	$\alpha \; [\text{or } \beta]$	$\vee$ elimination:	$\alpha \vee \beta$
	$\overline{\hspace{2em}}$	(Case analysis)	$\alpha \to \gamma$
	$\alpha \vee \beta$		$\beta \to \gamma$
			$\overline{\hspace{2em}}$
			γ

$\neg \neg$ introduction:	α	$\neg \neg$ elimination:	$\neg \neg \alpha$
	$\overline{\hspace{2em}}$		$\overline{\hspace{2em}}$
	$\neg \neg \alpha$		α

$\leftrightarrow$ introduction:	$\alpha \to \beta$	$\leftrightarrow$ elimination:	$\alpha \leftrightarrow \beta$
	$\beta \to \alpha$		$\overline{\hspace{2em}}$
	$\overline{\hspace{2em}}$		$(\alpha \to \beta) \wedge (\beta \to \alpha)$
	$\alpha \leftrightarrow \beta$		

Contradiction:	α	Tautology:	
	$\neg \alpha$	(when $\alpha \equiv \text{TRUE}$)	$\overline{\hspace{2em}}$
	$\overline{\hspace{2em}}$		α
	FALSE		

Figure 3.1: Rules of Inference

deduction is a style of proof that can be augmented by algebra, but must first be understood on its own terms.

3.4 Proof by Rules

The simplest proof is nothing more than a list of assertions each of which the reader agrees is true. The last assertion on the list being the theorem that is being proven. Each assertion can be annotated with the reason the reader has agreed to it; typically because of an inference rule.

If the reader agrees to α and from that β can be proven using rules of inference then we write:

$$\alpha \vdash \beta$$

which is called a **sequent**. It is a statement that a proof exists in which the first line is α and the last line is β. If the proof actually exists we say the sequent is **valid**. Since the reader agrees to allow α as the first line, it is axiomatic — taken as true without proof.[3]

Example 3.3

This is inspired by the subsumption law from the last chapter. Use rules of inference to show that taking p as true allows a proof of $p \wedge (q \vee p)$, that is $p \vdash p \wedge (q \vee p)$ is valid.

1.	p	given
2.	$q \vee p$	$\vee$ introduction, from line 1
3.	$p \wedge (q \vee p)$	$\wedge$ introduction, from lines 1 and 2

Notice that q can be true or false, the $\vee$ introduction rule does not care.

Example 3.4

Use rules of inference to show that taking $p \wedge q$ as true allows a proof of $p \wedge (q \vee r)$, that is $(p \wedge q) \vdash p \wedge (q \vee r)$ is valid.

1.	$p \wedge q$	given
2.	p	$\wedge$ elimination, from line 1
3.	q	$\wedge$ elimination, from line 1
4.	$q \vee r$	$\vee$ introduction, from line 3
5.	$p \wedge (q \vee r)$	$\wedge$ introduction, from lines 2 and 4

Note that we annotate each line of the proof with the inference rule that justified; the first line is the given premise.

---

[3]Sequents often have several axiomatic premises $(\alpha_1, \alpha_2, \alpha_3 \vdash \beta)$ but we will assume they are "and"ed together into one premise $(\alpha = (\alpha_1 \wedge \alpha_2 \wedge \alpha_3))$.

We cannot go much further since most interesting examples involve implications and negations. We do not have inference rules for introducing them; these are presented in the next section.

3.5 Assumptions

Assumptions play an important role in proofs; in fact, at least one of them will appear in almost every proof from this point on. An assumption is unlike an axiom in that it is only introduced tentatively. We don't claim to know that the assumption is true and it is essential to indicate that lack of commitment. To motivate how we will incorporate assumptions consider a proof of the sequent $\alpha \vdash \beta$:

1.	α	given
2.	α_1	inferred
3.	α_2	inferred
4.	...	
5.	β	inferred

Now consider the relation of the sequent $\alpha \vdash \beta$ to the proposition $\alpha \to \beta$. If the sequent is valid then the proof above exists. It was constructed with agreement with the reader that α is true. Now how would we prove the proposition to the reader. To believe it, all we have to do is prove that we are in one of three states: either α = FALSE, or both α = TRUE and β = TRUE. The reader does *not* necessarily know or even have an opinion about the truth value of α. All the reader wants to be sure of is that we are not in the state where both α = TRUE and β = FALSE! One way to do that is to show that if α = TRUE then β = TRUE (and so not FALSE). However that is exactly what a proof of the sequent $\alpha \vdash \beta$ does.

Hence there is a strong relationship between proofs of sequents and proofs of implications, even though what the reader believes is true is different. We need this important distinction to manifest itself in our formal presentation. There are two parts to the notation for an assumption. First, we put the assumed statement itself in brackets, e.g., $[\alpha]$. Second, we indent the statement *and everything else proved from it*, so that we do not confuse what is really known and what is only based on our tentative assumption. We sometimes say that the indented expressions are only true "relative to the assumption." This use of indentation is analogous to the use of stylistic indentation for readable structured programs in, say, Java or C++. The indentation makes explicit the "scope" of the assumption. The scope of an assumption is called a **subproof**.

So the proof of the above sequent justifies the indented subproof below:

1.	γ_1	some previous line
2.	$[\alpha]$	an assumption assumption
3.	α_1	inferred relative to α
4.	α_2	inferred relative to α
5.	$\cdots$	
6.	β	inferred relative to α
7.	γ_2	some line not relying on α

Seeing this the reader would have to conclude, from lines 2-6, that it is impossible for both $\alpha =$ TRUE and $\beta =$ FALSE, and therefore $\alpha \to \beta$ must be true.

While the proof of a sequent can be used as a subproof, a subproof is not restricted to this approach. The reason is that anything that came before the introduction of the assumption, like γ_1 above, is still true after adding the assumption and can be used by our rules of inference. (The proof of the sequent did not know that γ_1 is true and so never appealed to it.)

This preamble motivates the inference rule shown next which allows us to *introduce* an expression containing an instance of $\to$. Therefore, this "$\to$ introduction" inference rule is arguably the most important of all the inference rules. It states that if we assume α to be true and relative to that assumption we can prove that β would have to be true, then we can infer that $\alpha \to \beta$ must be true. Note that $\alpha \to \beta$ is *not* true relative to the assumption of α, and hence is not indented. So in our example above γ_2 could have been $\alpha \to \beta$ using this rule.

→ introduction:
$$\frac{\begin{array}{c}[\alpha]\\ \beta\end{array}}{\alpha \to \beta}$$

As an intuitive example of the idea of → introduction, suppose there is a triangle behind your back. Let p be the proposition that its angles are 30°, 60° and 90° and let q be the proposition that one of its sides is twice as long as another one. Since the triangle is behind your back, you can't see its angles so you don't know whether or not p is true and you can't see its sides so you don't know whether or not q is true. However, if you were to assume p, you would be able to prove q, so you do know that $p \to q$.

Example 3.5

Consider this proof of the sequent $p \to q \vdash (p \wedge r) \to (q \wedge r)$

1.	$p \to q$	given
2.	$[p \wedge r]$	assumption
3.	p	∧ elimination, from line 2
4.	r	∧ elimination, from line 2
5.	q	∧ modus ponens from lines 1 and 3
6.	$q \wedge r$	∧ introduction from lines 5 and 4
7.	$(p \wedge r) \to (q \wedge r)$	→ introduction, from lines 2 and 6

Note, as in all such proofs, the inferred implication was not found in the subproof, from lines 2 to 6, and so it not "exported" out of there. Instead the implication is inferred simply because that subproof exists!

Assumptions can be nested. That is, within the context of an assumption we can make an additional assumption, so that both are in force. When this happens we indent further. The indentation is a purely formal syntactic convention for the reader's benefit. By using repeated and nested indentation we make it easier to see where subproofs begin and end. It is extremely important to keep in mind that *when you leave a subproof you must abandon all assertions made there* since they are only trusted relative to an assumption that has itself been abandoned.

Example 3.6

Reconsider the previous problem in this form: $(p \to q) \to ((p \land r) \to (q \land r))$

1.	$[p \to q]$	given
2.	$[p \land r]$	assumption
3.	p	$\land$ elimination, from line 2
4.	r	$\land$ elimination, from line 2
5.	q	$\land$ modus ponens from lines 1 and 3
6.	$q \land r$	$\land$ introduction from lines 5 and 4
7.	$(p \land r) \to (q \land r)$	$\to$ introduction, from lines 2 and 6
8.	$((p \to q) \to ((p \land r) \to (q \land r)))$	$\to$ introduction, from lines 1 and 7

Another inference rule that uses an assumption is **reductio ad absurdum** ("reduction to absurdity"). It considers what we can conclude after assuming that p is true and, relative to that assumption, finding that FALSE would be a valid line later in our proof. In that context, it is absurd to allow the possibility that p could be true. Therefore the assumption that p is true must have been incorrect, so we infer that p is false; therefore, $\neg p$ is TRUE. Notice that the conclusion $\neg p$ is *not* indented, since we really do believe $\neg p$ after having found that p leads to FALSE. The rule looks like this:

$$\text{Reduction to absurdity:} \qquad \begin{array}{c} [\alpha] \\ \text{FALSE} \\ \hline \neg \alpha \end{array}$$

Notice that is the context in which we use the previously mentioned Contradiction inference rule. It indicated that when a proposition and its negation are both true that we infer "FALSE". (Some texts use the this neutral symbol $\bot$ instead of FALSE, since it is really only an indication that an assumption has led to a contradiction; it is not paradoxical since it is just evidence that an assumption should never have been used.)

Example 3.7

While the law of excluded middle, $\alpha \vee \neg \alpha$, is a tautology in the previous chapter, it is interesting to observe that it is provable using our inference rules.

1.	$[\neg (\alpha \vee \neg \alpha)]$	assumption
2.	$[\alpha]$	assumption
3.	$\alpha \vee \neg \alpha$	$\vee$ introduction, from line 2
4.	FALSE	contradiction, from lines 1 and 3
5.	$\neg \alpha$	reduction to absurdity, from lines 1 and 4
6.	$\alpha \vee \neg \alpha$	$\vee$ introduction, from line 5
7.	FALSE	contradiction, from lines 1 and 6
8.	$\neg \neg (\alpha \vee \neg \alpha)$	reduction to absurdity, from lines 1 and 7
9.	$(\alpha \vee \neg \alpha)$	double negation, from line 8

Example 3.8

Prove this proposition $((p \vee q) \wedge \neg p) \rightarrow q$, i.e., show it is a theorem.

1.	$[(p \vee q) \wedge \neg p]$	assumption
2.	$p \vee q$	$\wedge$ elimination, from line 1
3.	$\neg p$	$\wedge$ elimination, from line 1
4.	$[p]$	assumption
5.	$[\neg q]$	assumption
6.	FALSE	contradiction, from lines 3 and 4
7.	$\neg \neg q$	reduction to absurdity, lines 5 and 6
8.	q	$\neg \neg$ elimination, from line 7
9.	$p \rightarrow q$	$\rightarrow$ introduction, from lines 4 and 8
10.	$[q]$	assumption
11.	q	copied from line 10
12.	$q \rightarrow q$	$\rightarrow$ introduction, from lines 10 and 11
13.	q	case analysis, from lines 2, 9 and 12
14.	$((p \vee q) \wedge \neg p) \rightarrow q$	$\rightarrow$ introduction, from lines 1 and 13

Example 3.9

Suppose we have a contradictory assertion like $p \wedge \neg p$ and we choose
to not invoke the contradiction rule and bring the subproof to an
abrupt conclusion. It would follow that *everything* is true, surely
a bizarre and undesirable outcome. To see this consider this fragment of a larger proof, found in a subproof where the contradiction
arose.

1.	$p \wedge \neg p$	the observed contradiction
2.	p	$\wedge$ elimination, with line 1
3.	$\neg p$	$\wedge$ elimination, with line 1
4.	$[\neg q]$	assumption
5.	FALSE	contradiction, from lines 2 and 3
6.	$\neg \neg q$	reduction to absurdity, from lines 4 and 5
7.	q	$\neg \neg$ elimination, from line 6

Notice that q can be any proposition. The conclusion is that when a
contradiction happens you must halt and leave the subproof. Otherwise, the astute reader will stop reading since everything after that
is bogus.

3.6   Further Examples

We present more examples of these techniques. First we give a longer
example. Note that any algebraic law $\alpha \equiv \beta$ can be recast as $\alpha \leftrightarrow \beta \equiv$
T, since both assert that for all states α and β evaluate to the same
value. The next example applies this observation to the conditional
law, $p \rightarrow q \equiv \neg p \vee q$. It is not surprising that all of the algebraic
laws of Chapter 2 can be reinterpreted as theorems.

Example 3.10

Prove $(p \to q) \leftrightarrow (\neg p \lor q)$.

The proof structure is visible in the indentation of its several nested assumptions. Although this proof looks complex, the discussion below shows how most of it arises in a natural and straightforward manner.

$[\neg p \lor q]$	assumption
$[\neg p]$	
$[p]$	
$[\neg q]$	
FALSE	
$\neg \neg q$	
q	
$p \to q$	
$\neg p \to (p \to q)$	end of first case
$[q]$	
$[p]$	
q	
$p \to q$	
$q \to (p \to q)$	end of second case
$p \to q$	case analysis
$(\neg p \lor q) \to (p \to q)$	end of first major subproof
$[p \to q]$	assumption
$p \lor \neg p$	excluded middle (tautology)
$[p]$	
q	
$\neg p \lor q$	
$p \to (\neg p \lor q)$	end of first case
$[\neg p]$	
$\neg p \lor q$	
$\neg p \to (\neg p \lor q)$	end of second case
$\neg p \lor q$	case analysis
$(p \to q) \to (\neg p \lor q)$	end of second major subproof
$(p \to q) \leftrightarrow (\neg p \lor q)$	$\leftrightarrow$ introduction

How was this proof conceived? First look at what we have to prove; the last line. The main operator is a biconditional, $\leftrightarrow$. Any proof of a $\leftrightarrow$ must use the $\leftrightarrow$ introduction rule, and so the proof necessarily divides into two subproofs each using the $\rightarrow$ introduction rule. The first half of the proof begins by assuming the *right* side of the biconditional, $\neg p \vee q$, from which we have to prove the left side, and the second half will do the opposite. Once we make the assumption $\neg p \vee q$, it seems like a good idea to use the case analysis rule, first assuming $\neg p$ and then assuming q, and trying to prove the left side in each case. There is not much you can do with a $\vee$ except use the so-called $\vee$-elimination rule.

In the second half of the proof, it is less clear what to do. An implication like $p \rightarrow q$ is useless unless it has something else to combine with. For this part we set up a case analysis, by invoking the law of the excluded middle. Note that a *tautology* can be introduced into a proof at any time. (Also we could insert the steps in Example 3.7 rather than invoking it as a tautology.) Our decision to invoke the law of excluded middle depends on our experience with proofs, but really it is good common sense: when you cannot determine whether something is true or false, check out both possibilities.

Next we use natural deduction to justify an inference rule. Recall an inference rule $\alpha \rightarrow \beta$ is sound if it is a tautology. However if we can show $\alpha \rightarrow \beta$ is a theorem, it is provable, then the rule is justified in a more direct way. If there is a proof of a rule then we can add it to our list of allowed rules; otherwise we could always have substituted the proof of the rule in-place where we had wished to invoke it. In this way new more powerful rules can shorten proofs.

Example 3.11

We will prove modus tollens but, of course, we will not do it by using the rule modus tollens. Here, we will only use rules other than modus tollens. An exercise asks you to justify each line of this proof.

$$[(\alpha \to \beta) \land \neg \beta]$$
$$\alpha \to \beta$$
$$\neg \beta$$

$$[\alpha]$$
$$\beta$$
$$\text{FALSE}$$
$$\neg \alpha$$
$$((\alpha \to \beta) \land \neg \beta) \to \neg \alpha$$

3.7 Types of Theorems and Proof Strategies

The foregoing examples give the flavor of how formal proofs proceed. They were of the form "if α then β" and "α if and only if β". These are two very common types of theorems. We give a few hints about how to approach these kinds of theorems.

A theorem is *read* from the top down. Each line is annotated with the reason why it should follow from the lines above it. However a theorem is *written* predominantly bottom up. The last line is given as the starting point; it is the initial goal. By looking at a goal and consulting the list of inference rules the theorem prover can choose a strategy to achieve the goal. This means that new goals are set, higher up in the proof, that would justify the first goal. Sometimes we work top down, especially when we unbundle compound statements with rules like $\land$ elimination.

Example 3.12

We will begin to sketch a proof of the transitivity of the conditional operator. In symbolic form, the theorem is $((\alpha \to \beta) \land (\beta \to \gamma)) \to (\alpha \to \gamma)$. Since the main operator is a "$\to$" (the one that connects major parenthesized subexpressions), our strategy will be to use $\to$ introduction. The first thing to do is to write down the theorem itself as the *last* line of proof, preceded by the material needed to justify it, as shown in in the following sketch of a plan for the proof.

$$[(\alpha \to \beta) \wedge (\beta \to \gamma)] \qquad \text{assumption}$$
$$\vdots$$
$$\alpha \to \gamma \qquad\qquad \text{new goal to be shown}$$
$$((\alpha \to \beta) \wedge (\beta \to \gamma)) \to (\alpha \to \gamma) \qquad \to \text{introduction}$$

In the right-hand column are annotations. For $\alpha \to \gamma$, the justification is "new goal to be shown." We want to prove it, but do not yet know how we will do so. This is just a plan, not the finished proof. Next, planning to prove $\alpha \to \gamma$ is handled similarly: we again use $\to$ introduction, to plan for a (sub)proof. This leads to the following more detailed proof outline. You should try to complete it, using $\wedge$ elimination and modus ponens as needed; it is left as an exercise.

$$[(\alpha \to \beta) \wedge (\beta \to \gamma)] \qquad \text{assumption}$$
$$\vdots$$
$$[\alpha] \qquad\qquad\qquad \text{assumption}$$
$$\vdots$$
$$\gamma \qquad\qquad\qquad \text{new goal to be shown}$$
$$\alpha \to \gamma \qquad\qquad \to \text{introduction}$$
$$((\alpha \to \beta) \wedge (\beta \to \gamma)) \to (\alpha \to \gamma) \qquad \to \text{introduction}$$

The above proof, once it has been completed, establishes a theorem in the form $\alpha_1 \wedge \alpha_2 \to \beta$ and therefore justifies a new rule of inference, called the transitivity of $\to$ (below) that we can use in future proofs, as explained in the last section. Such a rule might be written:

$$\text{Transitivity of } \to : \qquad \begin{array}{c} \alpha \to \beta \\ \beta \to \gamma \\ \hline \alpha \to \gamma \end{array}$$

The issue of how to think of a proof has already been raised, especially in the discussions of the example proofs in the preceding sections. It is also important to remember that once a theorem has been proved, it can be used as part of the proof of something else. In effect, the already proved theorem is used just like an axiom or a rule of inference.

The type of theorem to be proved may suggest the style of proof. Many theorems, for example, take the form of conditional expressions. We give three strategies to obtain conditionals.

- **Direct proof:** The proof can begin by assuming that α is true and show that β would then be a consequence. In other words, use the $\rightarrow$ introduction rule. This method is used in Example 3.11 and in each of the two major subproofs in Example 3.10.

- **Indirect proof:** Alternatively, assume $\beta = \text{FALSE}$ and show that $\alpha = \text{FALSE}$ would be a consequence. This lets us conclude (by $\rightarrow$ introduction) that $\neg \beta \rightarrow \neg \alpha$, which is the contrapositive of $\alpha \rightarrow \beta$, hence equivalent to it. Making this substitution completes the proof.

- **Proof by contradiction:** Assume that $\alpha \rightarrow \beta$ — the thing we want to prove — is false, and show that this assumption leads to a contradiction, i.e. a FALSE line in our proof. Notice that the truth table definition of $\alpha \rightarrow \beta$ tells us that for it to be false we must have both $\alpha = \text{TRUE}$ and $\beta = \text{FALSE}$.

The biconditional is invariably proven by two subproofs of the above types.

Proofs are often presented informally, and this can be a good thing. Still, a sound informal proof retains the underlying structure of a formal proof and relies on inference rules even if they are not always mentioned explicitly. Proofs in the literature do not look like our formal proofs with bracketed assumptions, indented subproofs and symbolic Boolean expression of all propositions. Even so, the only "real" proofs that are compelling to the reader have the formal structure we have presented in this chapter. A sophisticated reader is typically assumed who will supply missing details and, most importantly, supply structural details that have been only implied. Unfortunately, real proofs are usually so cluttered with background knowledge (or clouded by its absence) that it can be a struggle to find the underlying formal outline of the logical proof. That's why it can be helpful to spend some time thinking about the proving process itself, as we have done here.

3.8 Soundness and Completeness

Our presentation in these two chapters has tried to emphasize the utility of propositional logic. We did this by talking about two threads at the same time, which we will now tease apart.

Initially there is the idea that a proposition is primarily defined lexically. We began by defining it as a Boolean expression which is nothing more than a string of symbols (or equivalently as a expression tree). We also said that propositions are truth-valued statements. But how do you assign such values to a string? In each chapter we gave a different answer.

First we gave a semantic interpretation to the string, by stating what the symbols mean. Formally this is called a *semantic model*. The model was in terms of constants, variables and operators. This allowed us to *evaluate* expressions given information about the variables, their state. In a more formal presentation we would use this notation (called *semantic entailment*):

$$\alpha \models \beta$$

to indicate that for every state in which α evaluates to TRUE it is also the case that β evaluates to TRUE; when that is actually the case we say "$\alpha \models \beta$ holds." (For example $q \models p \rightarrow q$ holds.) We are primarily interested in those propositions γ such that $\models \gamma$ holds. This is defined to indicate γ is a tautology, since it is always true, not just when some α is true. Note that $\alpha \models \beta$ holds if and only if $\models (\alpha \rightarrow \beta)$ holds.

Second we gave a mechanistic interpretation to the string by saying it is a theorem if by following a series of steps it can be proven. Recall that we used this notation $\alpha \vdash \beta$ to indicate that β can be proven given α; we say "$\alpha \vdash \beta$ is valid" when such a proof exists. A *theorem* α is formally defined as a proposition for which $\vdash \alpha$ is valid. Also we argued that $\alpha \vdash \beta$ is valid if and only if $\vdash \alpha \to \beta$ is valid.

The grand unifying observation for these two interpretations of propositions is:

Theorem 3.1 $-$ $\vdash \alpha$ is valid if and only if $\models \alpha$ holds, for every proposition α.

This was first proved by Kurt Gödel in 1929. This theorem is paraphrased as saying the system of propositional logic in these chapters is "sound and complete." We say the system is *sound* because $\vdash \alpha$ implies $\models \alpha$; if you can prove something it must be true. We say the system is *complete* because $\models \alpha$ implies $\vdash \alpha$; if something is true then it can be proven using natural deduction. The proof relies heavily on the fact that our rules of inference are themselves sound. Natural deduction, as a system, does not care that the rules are sound. However, by choosing only sound rules, we enabled Theorem 3.1 to be proven.

We relied on the natural deduction system of proof. It is fair game to ask whether there are yet other proof methods? Indeed there are others but they are equally powerful with respect to soundness and completeness. Another approach, which we will not discuss further, is the method of semantic tableaus, which focuses on whether an expression is satisfiable (see Section 2.3). It is used to prove that the negation of some expression of interest *must* be FALSE, that is, that it is *un*satisfiable. The method has the effect of putting an expression into disjunctive normal form (see Section 2.5). Then one looks at each of the disjuncts to see if it includes a pair of mutually contradictory literals, such as p and $\neg p$. The expression is unsatisfiable if and only if every one of the disjuncts does include such a pair.

Exercises

3.1 – Prove that the case analysis rule of inference is sound by truth tables, by giving the truth table for $((p \lor q) \land (p \to r) \land (q \to r)) \to r$.

3.2 – Annotate the proof in Example 3.11, explaining why every line is justified.

3.3 – Annotate the proof in Example 3.10 explaining why every line is justified. The annotations that are shown are merely comments tied the text.

3.4 – Complete the proof that was sketched in Example 3.12.

3.5 – Consider the formula $q \to (p \to q)$. Roughly speaking, it says that if something is true, anything implies it. This turns out to be true. Construct a *plan* for a proof in the manner of the proof-planning in Section 3.7. To begin, write down the desired final result as the last line. Then determine which " $\to$ " separates the principal parts of the expression and write those in earlier lines, using indentation and bracketing appropriately. Then proceed similarly with the other " $\to$ ". That will give you 5 lines of proof, which turns out to be all you need. Add the justifications for each line and you'll be done.

3.6 – Using rules of inference prove $(p \land (p \to q) \land (q \to r)) \to r$. Hint: The top level operator in the formula here is a conditional (the $\to$ symbol). Begin by writing everything to the left of that symbol (within the large parentheses) on the first line of the proof, in brackets and indented, as an assumption. Leave some space and put the entire formula that you are to prove as the last line, not in brackets and not indented. Try to get an indented r on the next-to-last line. Of course, the lines before it must justify putting it there.

3.7 – Use rules of inference prove the result in Exercise 2.14. Annotate the proof, by numbering each line, and for each line indicating the rule of inference that justifies it, along with the previous lines upon which it depends. No justification is needed for assumptions.

3.8 – Recall the *contrapositive* equivalence, $\alpha \rightarrow \beta \equiv \neg\beta \rightarrow \neg\alpha$. We recast this as a biconditional. Formally prove

$$(\neg\beta \rightarrow \neg\alpha) \leftrightarrow (\alpha \rightarrow \beta).$$

3.9 – Use rules of inference prove the result in Exercise 2.16. As in the previous problem, first recast the equivalence as a biconditional.

3.10 – This exercise extends the idea of case analysis to situations with *three* cases. Give a proof in the rules-of-inference format for

$$((p \vee q \vee r) \wedge (p \rightarrow s) \wedge (q \rightarrow s) \wedge (r \rightarrow s)) \rightarrow s.$$

Do not forget that even if conventions allow us to suppress parentheses when there are three or more associative operations, those parentheses are still there.

3.11 – Because of the soundness and completeness of propositional logic, every tautology is provable by natural deduction. Here are some more tautologies to try:

- $(p \rightarrow q) \rightarrow (p \rightarrow (p \wedge q))$
- $p \leftrightarrow (p \vee (p \wedge q))$
- $(p \rightarrow q) \rightarrow (p \rightarrow (p \wedge q))$
- $p \leftrightarrow p \wedge (p \vee q)$
- $((\neg p \rightarrow q) \wedge \neg q) \rightarrow p$
- $(p \rightarrow q) \leftrightarrow (\neg q \rightarrow \neg p)$

- $(p \to r) \to ((q \to r) \to ((p \lor q) \to r))$
- $(p \land q) \leftrightarrow \neg(p \to \neg q)$
- $p \to (q \to (p \land q))$
- $(p \land (q \lor p)) \leftrightarrow p$
- $(p \leftrightarrow q) \to ((q \leftrightarrow r) \to (p \leftrightarrow r))$
- $(p \to (q \to r)) \to ((p \to q) \to (p \to r))$

Chapter 4

Predicate Logic

Our study of propositions has led to some important results and has provided a relatively simple environment in which to examine three styles of proof. Unfortunately, when it comes to representing knowledge, the simplicity of propositions is a significant weakness. Recall that propositions reflect only whether a sentence is true or false, without looking at the complex conceptual structure within the sentence — at the things, properties, actions and relationships it talks about.

Predicates do look at those kinds of things, and in that way they are a big step up with respect to this issue of representing knowledge. Even with predicates, we retain the use of the logical constants, TRUE and FALSE, as the only possible values of logical expressions, so that like propositions they ignore all forms of vagueness and uncertainty. The representational power of predicate logic — sometimes called predicate *calculus* — is its greatest asset.

4.1   Predicates and Functions

In contrast to propositional logic's atomistic, true-or-false view of propositions, predicate logic breaks them apart to take a more detailed look. You may recall from Chapter 2 that our first example of a proposition was $5 > 3$. Looking now inside that proposition, we focus on the operator, ">". This operator — which is our first predicate — can be regarded as a function of two numerical arguments. To make the connection to functions clearer, we give this operator (">") a name that looks more like the name of a function and also write its name first, like this: GREATERTHAN(5,3). Thus GREATERTHAN is a function defined on pairs of numbers, each from the set of reals $\mathcal{R}$. In the terminology of Section 1.2, the domain of GREATERTHAN is thus $\mathcal{R} \times \mathcal{R}$. The codomain of this function — that is, the set to which things are mapped — is $\mathcal{B} = \{\text{TRUE}, \text{FALSE}\}$. To summarize, GREATERTHAN : $\mathcal{R} \times \mathcal{R} \to \mathcal{B}$. We are now ready to define predicates and relate them to propositions.

Definition 4.1

Predicates

A predicate is a function whose codomain is $\mathcal{B} = \{\text{TRUE}, \text{FALSE}\}$.

Thus GREATERTHAN is a predicate. It also follows from the definition that a predicate *with fixed arguments* is a member of $\mathcal{B}$ and so is a proposition. For example, GREATERTHAN(5,3) is a proposition, one whose value happens to be TRUE. Although the codomain of every predicate is $\mathcal{B}$, the *domain* is much more flexible. We used pairs of reals as the domain in this introductory example, but later examples will use predicates with domains of people, symbols and other numerical sets. Indeed the domain of a predicate can be any set whatsoever.

Predicate logic and variations of it are knowledge representation system. The language of predicate logic gives us the means to express things, but it is largely up to us what to express and how to express it. As an example of this freedom, consider a new predicate GREATERTHANTHREE, which takes one argument and yields TRUE for values greater than 3. Then the same values of x that give GREATERTHAN$(x, 3)$ = TRUE also give GREATERTHANTHREE(x) = TRUE. Despite this freedom, of course, certain sensible and conventional ways of doing things should be heeded. Thus, for example, no one has succeeded in getting a special operator symbol for the idea of GREATERTHANTHREE into widespread use, whereas the far more useful concept expressed by GREATERTHAN does have a conventional symbol ("$>$").

In reasoning about predicates it is important to understand their relationship to propositions. It is reasonable to think of a predicate as a kind of shorthand for a family of propositions, one for each element in the domain. For example, suppose that p represents the predicate we have been calling GREATERTHANTHREE. Then $p(-2)$ is a proposition whose value is FALSE and $p(7)$ is a proposition with the value TRUE. Carrying over our understanding of the $\wedge$ operator to expressions that include predicates, we have propositions like $p(-2) \wedge p(7)$. This proposition happens to be false, since $p(-2) \wedge p(7) = \text{FALSE} \wedge \text{TRUE} = \text{FALSE}$.

Example 4.1

Let q be the predicate that means its argument is less than 7. Using q along with the predicate p above, what does $r(x) = p(x) \wedge q(x)$ mean?

Here r is a predicate that is true in case both p and q are true. In other words, r is the property of being between 3 and 7. We can also write

$$r(x) = p(x) \wedge q(x) = (x > 3) \wedge (x < 7).$$

so, for instance, $r(6.8) = p(6.8) \wedge q(6.8) = \text{TRUE} \wedge \text{TRUE} = \text{TRUE}$, but $r(-16.5) = \text{FALSE}$. Although r is more complicated than p and q it is like them in that each takes only a single argument. Thus r takes one real to a logical constant, and we can write $r : \mathcal{R} \to \mathcal{B}$.

Non-numerical arguments are also of great interest. For example, let $\mathcal{P}$ be the set of persons. Then we can define MOTHER to be a predicate such that for two members, x and y, of the set $\mathcal{P}$, MOTHER(x, y) is true if and only if x is the mother of y. So MOTHER(Hillary, Chelsea) = TRUE, for example. In this case, MOTHER: $\mathcal{P} \times \mathcal{P} \to \mathcal{B}$.

It is often just assumed that there is some obvious domain or universe
of objects (reals, or persons, etc.) that can serve as possible values
for a variable. Sometimes when speaking in general terms, with no
particular universe in mind, we may just call the universe $\mathcal{U}$.

4.2   Predicates, English, and Sets

Human languages express the idea of predicates in many ways. For
example, in the preceding section we borrowed the word "mother"
from English for our logic predicate MOTHER, as in MOTHER(x, y),
meaning that x is the mother of y. Human language is not always
precise and unambiguous, and even a simple word like "mother" can
be used differently, say in a metaphor like "necessity is the mother of
invention." Still, we will assume that such examples are clear enough.
Let us look at some more examples of how predicates are expressed
in English. Of course, every other human language expresses ideas
similar to those discussed.

Nouns like "aunt," "brother" and the words for other family relations
translate readily to two- argument predicates, just like "mother."
Adjectives of nationality, like "French," can be used as one-argument
predicates, as in BELGIAN(Poirot). Notice, though, that there is
nothing about the idea or the definitions of predicate logic to stop
us from writing this idea as a two-argument predicate like CITIZEN-
SHIP(Poirot, Belgian), and indeed that may well be more convenient
from a computational viewpoint. It is up to us how to use the framework that logic provides. Names too are a matter of choice. Thus
although we meant Poirot here as fictional detective Hercule Poirot,
the constant Poirot can stand for someone (or something) else, so
long as we are consistent.

Adjectives for color can be expressed with one argument, as in
BROWN(Desk-1), but here again, as in the case of citizenship, it
is often useful to use the general idea — in this case, color — as the
predicate. Doing so again leads to two arguments: COLOR(Desk-1,
Brown). Other adjectives, like those for size, express a property that
really applies not to a single object but to the object in relation to
its class. For example, a big ant is nowhere near as big as a small

elephant. So a big ant is big with respect to ants only, and not with respect to animals or things in general. To capture this idea in predicate logic, we may wish to write BIG(Ant-3, Ant), meaning that Ant-3 is big for an ant. Taking the more general notion of size as the predicate would lead to having three arguments: SIZE(Ant-3, Ants, Big).

Example 4.2

Use the 3-argument predicate SIZE to express the fact that Jumbo the baby elephant, though small for an elephant, is a big mammal.

SIZE(Jumbo, Elephant, Small) $\wedge$ SIZE(Jumbo, Mammal, Big)

Verbs are another source of predicates. The verb "borders" corresponds to a predicate meaning that two countries border each other: BORDERS(India, Pakistan). This predicate is symmetric since its two arguments can always be interchanged without altering the value of the proposition. Another geographical example is one stating that a river runs through a country. This predicate corresponds to the meaning of a verb combined with a preposition: RUNSTHROUGH(Amazon, Brazil). Here we have a "many-many" mapping, since a river may run through more than one country and a country may have more than one river. Unlike RUNSTHROUGH, the predicate MOTHER is "one-many" since each person has exactly one (biological) mother.

Example 4.3

Let m be a function for which $m(x) = y$ means that y is the one and only mother of x. Then, with MOTHER as defined earlier, what is the meaning and truth value of MOTHER($m(x)$, x)?

This expression, which must be true for every x, says that "the mother of x is the mother of x," where the first occurrence of "mother" in this sentence is a translation of the 1-argument function m and the second comes from the 2-argument predicate MOTHER.

Each one-argument predicate has an interesting and important relationship to a particular set, namely the set of values that makes the predicate true. This set is called the **truth set** of the predicate. The truth set of p is written $\mathcal{T}(p)$. As a formal definition of $\mathcal{T}$, we write

$$\mathcal{T}(p) = \{x \mid p(x) = \text{TRUE}\}.$$

Example 4.4

Let VOWEL be a predicate that takes letters as its legal inputs. Also assume that its value is TRUE for vowels and FALSE for other letters. So VOWEL('e') = TRUE and VOWEL('g') = FALSE. The truth set of VOWEL is $\mathcal{T}(\text{VOWEL}) = \{\text{'a'}, \text{'e'}, \text{'i'}, \text{'o'}, \text{'u'}\}$. It follows that 'e' $\in \mathcal{T}(\text{VOWEL})$ but that 'g' $\notin \mathcal{T}(\text{VOWEL})$. If $\mathcal{L}$ is the set of all 26 letters, we can also write $\mathcal{T}(\text{VOWEL}) \subseteq \mathcal{L}$.

Predicates with two or more arguments also have truth sets, but the members of these sets are ordered pairs. For example, $\mathcal{T}(\text{RUNSTHROUGH})$ contains ordered pairs, like (Amazon, Brazil) and (Volga, Russia). Similarly, $(5, 3) \in \mathcal{T}(\text{GREATERTHAN})$; also note that $\mathcal{T}(\text{GREATERTHAN}) \subseteq \mathcal{R} \times \mathcal{R}$. Finally, if SEPARATES is a 3-argument predicate meaning that its first argument is a river forming part of the border between the two countries that are its other two arguments, then the ordered triple (RioGrande, Mexico, USA) is a member of $\mathcal{T}(\text{SEPARATES})$.

4.3   Quantifiers

So far we have used predicates to make assertions about only one thing at a time. **Quantifiers** give us a compact, precise, formal way to make assertions about a whole set of objects at once. The situation is somewhat analogous to loops in programming languages, which let us carry out the same operation on a whole set of entities.

(In fact, it turns out that one of the quantifiers is used to describe the consequences of a loop in proofs of program correctness; see Chapter 6.) The examples in the rest of this chapter make frequent reference to the following sets:

$\mathcal{U}$: an arbitrary set.

$\mathcal{I}$: the integers

$\mathcal{N}$: the nonnegative integers (including zero)

$\mathcal{R}$: the real numbers

$\mathcal{P}$: the set of living people

$\mathcal{Q}$: the set of all people, living or not

The **universal** quantifier means "every" or "for all" and is denoted with the symbol $\forall$. It says that every element of some set has a certain property, so to use it we need to specify the set and the property we have in mind. Properties are expressed by 1-argument predicates, so $\forall x \in \mathcal{U} : p(x)$ can be read "For all members x of the set $\mathcal{U}$, $p(x)$ is true" or more simply "Every member of $\mathcal{U}$ satisfies p." The set ($\mathcal{U}$ here) is called the **domain** or the **universe** of the quantification.

Example 4.5

Express the statement "Every integer has a square that is greater than or equal to 0" using $\forall$.

Here is one way of expressing it:

$$\forall x \in \mathcal{I} : (x^2 \geq 0).$$

This is a specific version of the more general setting:

$\forall x \in \mathcal{I} : p(x)$, where $p(x) \leftrightarrow x$ has a non-negative square

Each of the universally quantified expressions in Example 4.5 means that $0^2 \geq 0$ *and* $1^2 \geq 0$ *and* $(-1)^2 \geq 0$ and so on. Notice the use of "and" in the preceding sentence, which indicates a close relationship between conjunctions and the universal quantifier. More generally, for a universe, $\mathcal{U} = \{x_1, x_2, \ldots\}$, we might write

$$(\forall x \in \mathcal{U} : p(x)) \equiv p(x_1) \wedge p(x_2) \wedge \cdots$$

but this illustrates the power of the notation, since it conveys a large (possibly infinite) number of disjunctions without resorting to the use of "...".

The **existential quantifier** means "for some" or "there exists ... such that" and is denoted by the symbol $\exists$. It too requires us to specify a set and a property; $\exists x \in \mathcal{U} : p(x)$.

Example 4.6

Express the following statement using $\exists$: "There exists an integer between 3 and 7."

$$\exists x \in \mathcal{I} : ((x > 3) \wedge (x < 7)).$$

This existentially quantified expression means that either 0 is between 3 and 7 *or* 1 is between them *or* -1 is between them, *or* .... This use of "or" is, as usual, intended to be understood in the inclusive sense. That is, like the $\vee$ operator, $\exists$ is inclusive: it is satisfied when one or more arguments satisfy the predicate. The preceding statement is thus true because the predicate is true when $x = 4$ or 5 or 6.

A general and more formal statement of the relationship between $\exists$ and $\vee$ is

$$(\exists x \in \mathcal{U} : p(x)) \equiv p(x_1) \vee p(x_2) \vee \cdots$$

For a universe of just two elements, $\mathcal{U} = \{x_1, x_2\}$, we can rewrite the first of DeMorgan's laws from Chapter 2 as

$$\neg (p(x_1) \wedge p(x_2)) \equiv \neg p(x_1) \vee \neg p(x_2)$$

Moving to a potentially larger yet still finite universe, $\mathcal{U} = \{x_1, x_2, ..., x_n\}$, permits us to state the following generalizations of DeMorgan's laws, which are identical to the preceding equivalence when $n = 2$. They can be proved using the earlier general equivalences for the quantifiers in terms of $\land$ and $\lor$, by repeated application of the original DeMorgan's laws; see Exercise 5.6.

$$\neg\,(\forall x \in \mathcal{U} : p(x)) \equiv \exists x \in \mathcal{U} : \neg\, p(x)$$

and

$$\neg\,(\exists x \in \mathcal{U} : p(x)) \equiv \forall x \in \mathcal{U} : \neg\, p(x).$$

Now look specifically at the first equivalence. Its left side denies that every x (in the finite universe $\mathcal{U}$) satisfies p. Its right side says the same thing from a different perspective: that there is an x that fails to satisfy p. It is like the difference between saying "It is false that all dogs are brown" versus "There is (at least) one dog that is not brown". You should create a similar example with the second of the above equivalences. (We have supported the above equivalences only with informal comments. Formal proof of this generalization to arbitrary n also requires mathematical induction, introduced later in this chapter.)

Informally the DeMorgan generalizations say that negation can move through quantification while changing it from universal to existential or vice-versa. In trying to understand how negation interacts with the scope of quantifiers, it may help to think about the meanings of analogous sentences in English.

Example 4.7

Express each of the following English sentences as quantified expressions, using symbols of predicate logic, $\mathcal{P}$ for the set of people and the one-argument predicate, IsCarOwner.

It is *not* true *some*one has a car. $\neg\,\exists x \in \mathcal{P} : \text{IsCarOwner}(x)$
*Some*one does *not* have a car. $\exists x \in \mathcal{P} : \neg\,\text{IsCarOwner}(x)$
No one is without a car. $\neg\,\exists x \in \mathcal{P} : \neg\,\text{IsCarOwner}(x)$

Frequently, a form like "$x \in \mathcal{I}$" in a quantification is shortened to just "x". This is reasonable provided that the universe within which x can range is clear from the context. However, it is often clearer to give the universe explicitly. For example, it is true that

$$\exists x \in \mathcal{R} : 3 < x < 4,$$

since there are reals (like π and 3.45) that lie between 3 and 4, but replacing $\mathcal{R}$ by $\mathcal{I}$ would make this expression false. You can see that the $\mathcal{R}$ here really is more important than the x, since x could just as well be replaced throughout by y or any other variable, but $\mathcal{R}$ could not be replaced by $\mathcal{I}$. It is about $\mathcal{R}$ that we are asserting something; x is just being used to help say it. In this sense it is like a parameter of a programming function or a dummy variable in a summation or an integral! In such cases, we say that the variable is **bound** by the quantification and that it is a **bound variable**. A variable that is not bound is a **free variable**.

Example 4.8

Is the expression $\exists y \in \mathcal{N} : (y = x^2)$ about x or about y?

Note that y is bound but x is free, so, according to the above comments, the proposition says nothing about y. It does, however, say something about the free variable x: that some nonnegative integer is the square of x. Note that the expression can be encapsulated as, say, $p(x)$ since it is a property p that x may or may not have.

Empty sets can be a source of confusion. For perspective, let's look at set size in general. To discuss quantification, we have introduced sets that are infinite (e.g., the integers), large (e.g., all people), or of unspecified but finite size, $\{x_1, x_2, \ldots x_n\}$. The last-mentioned one may appear to have at least *some* members, but there is no guarantee of that, since in general it possible for n to be zero, unless that possibility is explicitly ruled out. Other set specifications too may permit a set to be either empty or not. Thus it is important to be aware of how quantification is *defined* with the empty set, which is as shown in the following formulas. Note that these hold *no matter what p is.*

$$(\forall x \in \emptyset : p(x)) \equiv \text{TRUE}$$

$$(\exists x \in \emptyset : p(x)) \equiv \text{FALSE}$$

For example, consider the set of unicorns, which is empty because the unicorn is a mythical animal that does not exist. It is FALSE that "there is a unicorn that has a horn" (even though they all did, in myth). This is reasonable in that there is no unicorn to serve in the role of horn-bearer. eneral, it is true that "every unicorn can leap tall buildings in a single bound." Let us go to a tall building and see if any unicorns fail the test. None do (none can, since none exist), so there is no fact contrary to the universal quantification.

4.4 Multiple Quantifiers

Just as one quantifier can be applied to a predicate with one variable, so two (or more) quantifiers can be applied to a predicate with two (or more) variables. We begin with examples that use only universal quantifiers and then go on to examples with both kinds of quantifiers.

Example 4.9

What do the following quantified Boolean expressions mean?

$$\forall x : \forall y : \text{MOTHER}(x, y) \leftrightarrow (\text{PARENT}(x, y) \land \text{FEMALE}(x))$$

$$\forall x : \forall y : \forall z : \text{OFFSPRING}(x, y, z) \leftrightarrow (\text{MOTHER}(y, x) \land \text{FATHER}(z, x))$$

Both of these propositions are **definitions**. The first one uses two universal quantifiers to define a mother as a female parent. The second one uses three universal quantifiers to define a predicate that expresses the three-way relationship among a person and his or her (biological) parents. What makes them definitions is that they give a method — the right-hand side of the biconditional — to determine the value of the predicate *for any* input.

Example 4.10

Write a quantified Boolean expression that expresses the property of symmetry for the predicate BORDERS, introduced earlier.

$$\forall x : \forall y : (\text{BORDERS}(x, y) \leftrightarrow \text{BORDERS}(y, x))$$

Example 4.11

Use both kinds of quantifiers in a single expression that asserts every integer has a square that is an integer. Compare this with Example 4.5, where the square is not claimed to be an integer.

$$\forall x \in \mathcal{I} : \exists y \in \mathcal{N} : y = x^2$$

In Example 4.8 we defined $p(x)$ so that the above expression is $\forall x \in \mathcal{I} : p(x)$. This illustrates the general idea that when there are multiple quantifiers it is always possible to view it as a single quantifier applied to a predicate, which is itself a quantified expression. It is because of this that some people say that quantifiers are applied left-to-right.

Although the existential quantifier claims that there is *at least* one appropriate value of y, in fact we know that there is exactly one. (Exercise 4.14 introduces a special quantifier meaning "there is exactly one," which would be useful for Example 4.11.) Whereas Example 4.11 says that numbers *have* perfect squares, Example 4.12 lets us say that if a number meets certain conditions it *is* a perfect square. In fact Example 4.12 defines the notion of a perfect square. Notice that like the definitions in Example 4.9, this one begins with a universal quantifier and contains a biconditional operator.

Example 4.12

Define the predicate ISPERFECTSQUARE, which is true of integers like 0, 1, 4, 9, 16, etc., that are perfect squares.

$$\forall x \in \mathcal{I} : \text{ISPERFECTSQUARE}(x) \leftrightarrow (\exists y \in \mathcal{I} : x = y^2).$$

The *order of quantification* is very important. In Examples 4.11 and 4.12, the existence of some y is claimed with respect to an already introduced x, and so the choice of y may depend on which value of x is under consideration, as we move through all the members of x's set. In such a case one says that y is within the **scope** of x. The scope of a quantifier extends to the end of its formula, unless otherwise indicated by parentheses. In Example 4.12, take 9 and then 49 as values of x. One of them (9) is a perfect square because of the y-value -3 or 3, and the other (49) is also a perfect square, but on the basis of a different y-value, either -7 or 7.

Reversing the order of quantification in a true expression often yields a false one, as the next example shows.

Example 4.13

Reverse the quantifier order in the expression in Examples 4.11.

The expression is false, because it states that there is a (special) number that serves as the square of every integer. (It allows that there may be additional special numbers with this property but requires at least one.)

$$\text{this is false: } \exists y \in \mathcal{N} : \forall x \in \mathcal{I} : (y = x^2)$$

Of course, there are times when we really *do* want the existential operator to come first as the next two examples show.

Example 4.14

State in a quantified expression that there is a (special) member of $\mathcal{N}$ that is less than all the others. (In fact that special member of $\mathcal{N}$ is zero.)

$$\exists y \in \mathcal{N} : \forall x \in \mathcal{N} : (y \leq x)$$

Example 4.15

A set of computers, $\mathcal{C}$, has been networked together so that the predicate DIRECT, is TRUE if its two arguments are either the same or are directly connected. Write a quantified expression that asserts there is one computer (say, the server) directly connected to all the others; there may also be other connections.

$$\exists y \in \mathcal{C} : \forall x \in \mathcal{C} : \text{DIRECT}(x, y)$$

When both quantifiers (or all of them) are of the same kind, the order of quantification does not matter. For universals, the expression $\forall x : \forall y : p(x, y)$ means that the predicate p holds for all (x, y) pairs and that is also what $\forall y : \forall x : p(x, y)$ means. As examples, look back at the definition of MOTHER at the start of this section. With existential quantifiers, the expression $\exists x : \exists y : p(x, y)$ means that the predicate p holds for at least one (x, y) pair and this is also what $\exists y : \exists x : p(x, y)$ means.

Next we give the lexical definition of expressions in predicate logic. We have already been discussing the semantics of the expressions. These expressions are called "quantified Boolean expressions" and are commonly referred to as "formulas" to distinguish them from propositions.[1]

Definition 4.2

Formulas of Predicate Logic

- If p is an n-argument predicate and each of $a_1, a_2, \ldots, a_n$ is either an object (an element of a domain $\mathcal{U}$) or a variable over a domain, then $p(a_1, a_2, \ldots, a_n)$ is a formula. By convention a predicate with $n = 0$ arguments is a simple Boolean variable.

---

[1]In a more formal setting we would refer to this system as *first-order logic* (FOL).

- If α is a formula and β is a formula then $(\neg\alpha)$, $(\alpha \vee \beta)$ and $(\alpha \wedge \beta)$ are formulas. (We naturally extend this to the other Boolean operators that have been defined in terms of these basic operators, such as $\rightarrow$)

- If α is a formula and x is a variable over a domain then $(\exists x : \alpha)$ and $(\forall x : \alpha)$ are formulas. (We also include the variants used when the domain is not implicit, such as $(\exists x \in S : \alpha)$.)

The first of the three parts of this definition establishes the **atomic formulas**. The second and third recursively build all formulas. As with propositions (Definition 2.1), we keep the definition simple by allowing an excess of parentheses. Avoiding them here would require not only specifying the precedence among the propositional operators but also a statement about what is covered by a quantification. In fact, it is understood that in the absence of parentheses *a quantifier covers everything to its right*, that is, to the end of the entire (largest) formula containing it. Another simplifying decision about the definition is that it does not bother to distinguish between free and bound variables; it allows both.

Domains, variables and quantifiers are what distinguish predicate logic from propositional logic. The elements of the domain may be numbers, people or whatever else we find useful, and the word "object" refers to any of these. Because the variables here (x, y,...), range over *objects*, they are much more flexible than the variables (p, q, ...) in the definition of propositions, which range only over *truth values*.

After defining the propositions in Chapter 2, we gave an additional definition that included their truth-values. That is harder to do here, but still possible if the universe is finite and the truth values are known (specified) for all atomic formulas without arguments. In that case, the truth value of any formula that has only bound variables can be determined in the steps listed below. A formula with no free variables has a truth value and so is a proposition.

- Eliminate quantifiers and variables, making use of the equivalences in Section 4.3 to express them in terms conjunctions and disjunctions.

- Replace each atomic formula by its truth value.

- Evaluate the result, which is a proposition, bottom up.

4.5   Logic for Data Structures

Two important data structures for computer science are the string and the graph. This section shows how to express some essential ideas of these data structures in terms of predicate logic. Both strings and graphs can be implemented as arrays, which are crucial to so many computing applications that they are found in all procedural computer languages. Arrays may have one, two or more dimensions, and may have numbers, characters or other forms of data as their elements. Strings are typically implemented as as one-dimensional arrays of characters.

The **sequence** is the abstract notion that corresponds directly to a one-dimensional array. Sequences were defined in Section 1.1.

Example 4.16

Let A be the sequence $(b, o, o, k, k, e, e, p, e, r)$. The length of A is 10, including 3 occurrences of e. The set of elements appearing in the sequence is $\{b, e, k, o, p, r\}$, which has a cardinality (size) of 6.

When the elements of a sequence are letters, characters or symbols, the sequence may be called a **string**. As Example 4.16 suggests, each word of English is a string or sequence of letters (with an occasional hyphen or apostrophe). Many programming languages implement strings as one-dimensional arrays of characters. In the study of formal language (Part II) we will regard strings as sequences of symbols.

The general notation for a finite sequence is $A = (a_1, a_2, \ldots, a_n)$. In the next few examples, A and B will each be sequences of letters, with

$A = (a_1, a_2, \ldots, a_n)$ and $B = (b_1, b_2, \ldots, b_n)$. We will use $\mathcal{I}_n$ for set of the first n positive integers, $\{1, 2, \ldots, n\}$. All quantification will be with respect to $\mathcal{I}_n$. These examples will involve formal descriptions of constraints on A and B, using quantifiers, set notation and the predicates "=", "$\neq$" and "$\prec$" as needed, where $x \prec y$ means "x precedes y alphabetically."

Example 4.17

State formally that some letter appears in the same position in the two sequences A and B specified above.

$$\exists i \in \mathcal{I}_n : a_i = b_i$$

Example 4.18

State formally that every pair of elements of A are equal to each other. Then state that every element of A is equal to its first element. Notice that these are equivalent, even though it is not clear symbolically.

$$\forall i \in \mathcal{I}_n : \forall j \in \mathcal{I}_n : a_i = a_j$$
$$\forall i \in \mathcal{I}_n : a_i = a_1$$

Note that we do not guard against the case when $i = j$, since it is not a contradictory case.

Example 4.19

Express the following quantified expression in English.

$$\forall i \in \mathcal{I}_{n-1} : a_i \prec a_{i+1}$$

This says that A is sorted in strictly alphabetical order. Notice the use of $\mathcal{I}_{n-1}$ rather than $\mathcal{I}_n$. We want to avoid comparing the last element to the one after it, since *nothing* comes after it. The situation is analogous to avoiding references beyond the bounds of an array.

Graphs were introduced in Chapter 1 are simple yet remarkably useful and whole books are devoted to graph algorithms. Here we shall confine attention to the **undirected graph** and its relationship to predicate logic. Recall that an undirected graph $G = (V, E)$ consists of a set V of vertices and a set E of edges which are (unordered) pairs of elements of V. Vertices and edges can be, respectively, computers and cables, airports and roundtrip flights, people and friendships, nations and bilateral treaties or whatever else we find it useful to apply them to. Each edge represents a *direct* connection.

To make the connection with logic, let $\text{EDGE}(x, y)$ be the predicate that x and y are connected by an edge, that is, $(x, y) \in E$. Note EDGE is a symmetric predicate.

Example 4.20

Suppose that $V = \{a, b, c, d\}$ and that there are three edges: (a, b), (b, c) and (a, d). State whether the following quantified expressions is TRUE or FALSE.

$$\forall x \in V : \exists y \in V : \text{EDGE}(x, y)$$

This is true for the given graph, since for each vertex there is a vertex connected to it, in particular $\text{EDGE}(a, b)$ $\text{EDGE}(b, c)$ $\text{EDGE}(c, b)$ $\text{EDGE}(d, a)$ are true.

Also, evaluate the following quantified expression.

$$\exists x \in V : \forall y \in V : (x = y) \vee \text{EDGE}(x, y)$$

This is false. It claims that one particular vertex is connected to all the others and this is not so.

In the previous exercise the two formulas can be regarded as two properties that a graph might possess. In fact all properties of graphs can be cast as quantified boolean expressions; these properties can be thing like the graph is connected, bipartite, regular, etc. In fact all properties of mathematical objects are formally *defined* this way.

Exercises

4.1 – Express in predicate logic the meaning of each of the following sentences of English. Use negation, whatever quantifiers you need and the one-argument predicate IsCarOwner which is true for anyone who owns at least one car. Also, state which of your answers are equivalent to each other. Leave the domain implicit.

(a) Someone has a car.

(b) It is not the case that everyone has a car.

(c) No one has a car.

(d) Everyone is without a car.

(e) It is false that everyone is without a car.

4.2 – Consider the definitions in Examples 4.9 and 4.12 of Section 4.5. Definitions often make use of the biconditional operator. Why? Definitions often make use of the universal quantifier. Why?

4.3 – Assume the predicate Different(x, y) is defined to be true iff x and y not identical. Further we assume that the predicates Parent and Female have been defined.

(a) Use Parent and Different along with quantifiers as needed (but no other predicates) to define ParentInCommon(x, y), meaning that x and y have one of the following (biological) relationships: sister, brother, half-sister or half-brother. Someone does not have a parent in common with themself.

(b) Now define Sister(x, y) to mean that x is either the sister or half-sister of y. You can use the one-argument predicate Female and ParentInCommon from (a).

(c) Define FIRSTCOUSIN(x, y) to mean that x is the first cousin of y. Note that first cousins must have a grand-parent in common, but they must be different people with different parents. (You may assume that married pairs do not share a parent.)

4.4 – With $\mathcal{U} = \{a, b, c\}$, rewrite the following equivalence from Section 4.3 without using any quantifiers. Use the $\wedge$ and $\vee$ operators. Consider the equivalences in Section 4.3.

$$\neg\,(\forall x \in \mathcal{U} : p(x)) \equiv \exists x \in \mathcal{U} : \neg\,p(x)$$

4.5 – The existential quantifier says that there is at least one of something, but sometimes we have more accurate information than that. Express the fact that there is exactly one integer between 4 and 6, by using an existential quantifier to state that there is at least one such integer and also that if there were two such integers (say x and y), they would have to be equal to each other.

4.6 – The Pythagoreans of ancient Greece studied what they called triangular numbers as well as the squares. These are 1, 3, 6, 10, ..., which are equal to 1, 1+2, 1+2+3, 1+2+3+4, and so on. Define a predicate TRIANGULAR that is true of these numbers and no others. Your definition may allow zero to be triangular.

4.7 – *Evaluate* each of the following formulas and explain your reasoning for arriving at your result. $\mathcal{N}$ is the set of non-negative integers, $\{0, 1, 2, \dots\}$. $\mathcal{I}^+$ is the set of positive integers, $\{1, 2, \dots\}$. $\mathcal{I}$ is the set of all integers, including the negatives. To evaluate an expression means to find the constant to which it is equal or equivalent. For a proposition, that means determining that it is equivalent to TRUE or to FALSE.

(a) $\forall i \in \mathcal{N} : \forall j \in \mathcal{N} : i^2 + j^2 \geq 0$

(b) $\exists i \in \mathcal{I}^+ : \exists j \in \mathcal{I}^+ : (5 < i^2 + j^2 < 10) \wedge (i \neq j)$

(c) $\forall i \in \mathcal{I} : \exists j \in \mathcal{I} : (i + 2j = 0) \vee (i + 2j = 1)$

(d) $\exists j \in \mathcal{I} : \forall i \in \mathcal{I} : ij = -i$

4.8 – Consider the undirected graph $G = (V, E)$ with vertices, V, and edges, E. (We assume G has no self-loops, so $\text{EDGE}(x, x)$ is never true.) Define $\text{EDGE}(x, y)$, as in the Section 4.5.

(a) Write a formula (a quantified Boolean expression) stating that for every pair, (x, y), of vertices in V there is a path of length 2 connecting x to y.

(b) Let $\text{PATH}(x, y)$ be the predicate for the property that there is a sequence of 0, 1, 2 or more edges connecting x and y. Using quantifiers and EDGE, give a *recursive* definition of PATH.

(c) Let $\text{PATH2}(x, y)$ be the predicate for the property that there is a sequence of 2 or more edges connecting x and y, using vertices other than x and y. Using part (b) write a definition for PATH2. (You can define another predicate.)

4.9 – Continuing Exercise 4.8, we let $V = \{a, b, c, d\}$. The formulas below give four properties of undirected graphs. Paraphrase each property and evaluate each formula when

(a) $\text{EDGE}(a, b)$, $\text{EDGE}(b, c)$ and $\text{EDGE}(b, d)$ are TRUE, but these are the only edges.

(b) $\text{EDGE}(a, b)$, $\text{EDGE}(b, c)$ and $\text{EDGE}(c, d)$ are TRUE, but these are the only edges.

(i) $\forall x \in V : \forall y \in V : (x \neq y) \rightarrow \text{EDGE}(x, y)$

(ii) $\forall x \in V : \forall y \in V : \text{PATH}(x, y)$

(iii) $\exists x \in V : \exists y \in V : \text{EDGE}(x, y) \wedge \text{PATH2}(x, y)$

4.10 – Continuing Exercise 4.8, what graph property does this convey:

$$\exists\, S \in 2^V : \forall\, (u,v) \in E : u \in S \leftrightarrow v \notin S.$$

4.11 – As in the sequence examples of Section 4.5, let A and B each be sequences of letters, with $A = (a_1, a_2, \ldots, a_n)$ and $B = (b_1, b_2, \ldots, b_n)$. Make a formal assertion for each of the following situations, using quantifiers with respect to $\mathcal{I}_n$, set notation and the relational operators "$=$", "$\neq$" and "$\prec$" (precedes alphabetically) as needed.

(a) Some letter appears twice in A.

(b) No letter appears twice in A.

(c) A and B are identical, the same sequence of characters.

(d) The set of letters appearing in A is a subset of the set of letters appearing in B.

(e) The set of letters appearing in A is the same as the set of letters appearing in B.

(f) Each letter of A is no later in the alphabet than the corresponding letter of B.

4.12 – Using the notation of Exercise 4.11 above, give a formal specification of conditions that are both necessary and sufficient to make A occur earlier in an ordinary dictionary than B. In such a case we say that A *lexicographically* precedes B. You may assume that both sequences have the same length, n, and are padded on the right by blanks, which alphabetically precede all the letters. Also note that $\mathcal{I}_1 = \{1\}$ and $\mathcal{I}_0 = \emptyset$.

4.13 – Two solutions are provided to the question posed in Example 4.18. Argue that one of them corresponds to an algorithm with a single loop and in that way is preferable to the other, which in effect specifies a less efficient algorithm with nested looping.

4.14 – The quantifier ∃! is sometimes used to assert that exactly one of something exists. That is $\exists!x \in \mathcal{I} : p(x)$ means that there is exactly one integer with property p. (Do not use this quantifier to answer other exercises!) Use this quantifier to state that

(a) A sequence A of n integers contains exactly one even integer.

(b) Every integer has exactly one square.

Chapter 5

Proving with Predicates

Predicates and quantification when combined with the earlier apparatus of propositional logic provide a much broader foundation for proving important results. We will prove results within logic itself — as we did in Chapter 3 — but now we can prove theorems in other areas of mathematics and computer science. With a view to achieving these results, the first two sections develop new inference rules and strategies for using them within the same natural deduction framework we have been using. The application of logical inference beyond logic itself then makes its first appearance in the last two sections, preparing the way for an application to computer science in the next chapter.

5.1   Inference Rules with Predicates

As we begin to prove things about subject matter expressed with predicates, it is important to remember that propositions are still part of the picture, because, as noted, a formula in predicate logic with no free variables, *is* a proposition. Therefore our propositional rules of inference will still be used as before; they still provide the structure of all our proofs. Moreover, many inference rules for propositions have analogous versions for predicates. For these reasons, proofs by rules of inference with predicates may have a reassuringly familiar look. Here is the predicate version of → introduction. We

99

use the same name as before, but it will be clear from context which rule is meant.

$\rightarrow$ Introduction:

$$[p(x)]$$
$$q(x)$$

$$\overline{\qquad\qquad\qquad}$$
$$p(x) \rightarrow q(x)$$

To realize that the preceding rule is not really new, remember that $p(x)$ is a proposition: that x satisfies the predicate p. The variable x above and below the line is the same variable. When a variable is first used it is a blank slate, though it is assumed to be from some domain; as a computer scientist would say, the variable is typed (integer, real, etc.). This is generally done formally by asserting this as an assumption; this will start a new subproof which is the scope of the variable since it is unknown outside of this. (Of course the introduction of variables is so common that this is implicit in all but the most formal proofs.) So in the above inference rule the antecedents and the conclusion are all within the scope of x. The $\exists$ Elimination rule below is an exception to this.

Of course, some inference rules with predicates go beyond just restating propositional rules. We begin the $\forall$ *Introduction* rule. This rule is based on the following insight: $\forall x \in S : p(x)$ and $(x \in S) \rightarrow p(x)$ are the same proposition. In both cases we are saying "when $x \in S$ then $p(x)$ will evaluate to true; it is silent on whether $p(x)$ is true for other values x may be allowed to take on. So the next rule, below, is just a restatement of the $\rightarrow$ Introduction inference rule for propositions.

$\forall$ Introduction:

$$[\text{new } x \in \mathcal{U}]$$
$$q(x)$$

$$\overline{\qquad\qquad\qquad}$$
$$\forall y \in \mathcal{U} : q(y)$$

Note that x is assumed to be a new variable and all we know about it is that it belongs to some set, $\mathcal{U}$. Thus x is a completely *arbitrary* element of $\mathcal{U}$. The second line says that this (weak) assumption has led to the truth of $q(x)$. Thus the predicate q must hold for every member of $\mathcal{U}$, as concluded below the line. The variable x is unknown outside the subproof; we could have used x instead of y below the line, but it would have been a new x. (The bound variables of any formula are always new variables, known only within that formula.)

The next rule is often called *instantiation*, but we call it $\forall$ *Elimination* to emphasize that it generalizes the propositional rule, $\wedge$ Elimination. In fact, with a domain of just two elements, this rule is identical to $\wedge$ elimination. It states that if the predicate p is true for all possible arguments it must be true for any particular one.

$$\forall \text{ Elimination:} \qquad \forall x \in \mathcal{U} : p(x)$$
$$\overline{\qquad p(y) \vee y \notin \mathcal{U} \qquad}$$

Note that y is not regarded as a new variable, even though might happen to be free of prior properties.

We turn now to the existential quantifier. When a variable in a proof has been proven to be simultaneously in a domain and to have property associated with predicate p then this rule is clearly sound.

$$\exists \text{ Introduction:} \qquad x \in \mathcal{U} \wedge p(x)$$
$$\overline{\qquad \exists y \in \mathcal{U} : p(y) \qquad}$$

The variable y is a bound variable within the quantified Boolean expression.

Finally, consider how to make use of the knowledge that *some* member of $\mathcal{U}$ satisfies p. In this event we proceed to name that thing "y".

$$\exists \text{ Elimination:} \qquad \exists x \in \mathcal{U} : p(x)$$
$$\overline{\qquad \text{new } y \in \mathcal{U} \wedge p(y) \qquad}$$

This y is a new variable. It is not created by an assumption. The variable y must *not* be assumed to be some particular member of $\mathcal{U}$; all we know about y is that $y \in \mathcal{U}$ and it possesses property p. Since it is new it must *not* be known at this point in the proof.

Example 5.1

These rules can be nested of course. Consider a proof of the formula $\forall x \in \mathcal{N} : \forall y \in \mathcal{N} : p(x, y)$. The framework would be:

$$[x \in \mathcal{N}]$$
$$[y \in \mathcal{N}]$$
$$\vdots$$
$$p(x, y)$$
$$\forall b \in \mathcal{N} : p(x, y)$$
$$\forall a \in \mathcal{N} : \forall b \in \mathcal{N} : p(x, y)$$

However recall that when two of the same quantifier are consecutive it does not matter what the order is. In other words $\forall x \in \mathcal{N} : \forall y \in \mathcal{N} : p(x, y)$ is the same as $\forall (x, y) \in \mathcal{N} \times \mathcal{N} : p(x, y)$. So it can be more natural to use a framework like:

$$[x \in \mathcal{N} \wedge y \in \mathcal{N}]$$
$$\vdots$$
$$p(x, y)$$
$$\forall a \in \mathcal{N} : \forall b \in \mathcal{N} : p(x, y)$$

5.2   Proof Strategies with Predicates

The foregoing rules of inference, like the ones for propositions, allow us to prove many important results. Here are a few common types of theorems and proof strategies for each.

1. Theorems of the form "$\exists x \in \mathcal{U} : p(x)$"

   Theorems like this can be proven using $\exists$ introduction simply by *exhibiting* a specific $x \in \mathcal{U}$ and showing that it is the case that $p(x)$ is true. (It is a common mistake to use this proof technique when a universal quantification is to be proved; in that case a "proof by example" is inadequate and is not a proof.) Sometimes, rather than explicitly showing such an x, we can give a technique for finding such an x (and argue the technique cannot fail); this is called an *algorithmic proof.*

2. Theorems of the form "$\forall x \in \mathcal{U} : p(x)$"

   This kind of theorem clearly requires $\forall$ introduction. As noted above, though, the theorem really says that $(x \in \mathcal{U}) \to p(x)$ is a true proposition. So the proof, using the $\to$ introduction rule, assumes $x \in \mathcal{U}$ and shows $p(x)$ is a consequence. It is crucial that when using this technique you assume x is an *arbitrary* element of $\mathcal{U}$; making any further assumption about x invalidates the proof.

3. Theorems of the form "$\neg \forall x \in \mathcal{U} : p(x)$"

   Here we are to prove that p does not hold throughout $\mathcal{U}$. By DeMorgan's law, this is equivalent to "there exists an $x \in \mathcal{U}$ such that $\neg p(x)$". Using strategy 1 above, we can prove this by exhibiting an x such that $\neg p(x)$ is true. This is a *proof by counterexample.*

4. Theorems of the form "$\forall x \in \mathcal{N} : p(x)$"

   This is an extremely common type of theorem; we want to show that p holds for all integers x such that $x \geq 0$. One technique used in to prove such theorem is *mathematical induction,* which is sufficiently novel and important that we devote an entire section to it.

5.3   Applying Logic to Mathematics

Logic has been playing a double role in many of our examples. Its rules of inference have been our principal source of reasoning techniques and it has also served as the domain of application. We have applied logic to logic. However, the power and significance of logic are clearer when its proof methods are put to use outside of logic. The most important applications of logic lie within mathematics and computer science, because, like logic itself, they are expressed in general terms and so are broadly applicable. Chapter 6 applies logic to computer science, specifically to the challenge of proving the correctness of programs. This section and the next one pave the way, by applying logic to arithmetic, or more precisely to number theory. In this domain, the claims are easy to understand but not trivial to prove, so it is a good place to start.

For any new application domain, it is necessary to develop new predicates and sometimes even new inference rules specific to that domain. Sometimes the special predicates and inference rules for a particular topic are given explicitly, but usually they are tacit or couched as definitions. Part of the difficulty of understanding and writing proofs is to recognize these components of our background knowledge. For example, below are four items of background knowledge for numbers and sets. The task of casting them into the inference rule format of Chapter 3 is left as an exercise.

- Subset rule:

  $A \subseteq B$ follows from the assertion $\forall x \in A : (x \in B)$.

- Set equality rule:

  $A = B$ follows from $A \subseteq B$ and $B \subseteq A$.

- Transitivity of $<$:

  This inference rule states that $a < c$ follows from the combination of $a < b$ and $b < c$. We saw in Chapter 3 that the conditional operator, $\rightarrow$, is also transitive. Several other operators and relations, including equality, equivalence and subset are transitive as well.

- Pigeon-hole principle:

    If $n+1$ occurrences are assigned to n categories, there
    must be one category with at least two occurrences;
    e.g., given 8 people, at least two were born on the
    same day of the week.

Some inference rules follow directly from definitions. For example,
we defined the predicate IsPERFECTSQUARE in Example 4.12, which
is true for each of the perfect squares. Therefore if in a proof we
have a line asserting that IsPERFECTSQUARE(a) is true then we can
infer that there exists an integer b such that $a = b^2$. The proof in
Example 5.2 below uses this rule, though very informally. The proof
in Example 5.3, which is more formal, defines the predicate ODD,
converts it to a rule of inference and uses that in a proof that the
product of odd numbers is odd.

Example 5.2

Prove that every perfect square is either a multiple of 3 or one greater
than a multiple of 3.

This proof is informal, but we will point out its use of some formal
rules of inference, specifically case analysis and $\vee$ introduction. The
basic idea of the proof is that when examining numbers in the context of multiples of 3, each integer falls into one of three categories,
depending on its value modulo 3. That is, for every n, one of the
following holds:

$$n = 3m, \text{ for some } m, \text{ or}$$
$$n = 3m + 1, \text{ for some } m, \text{ or}$$
$$n = 3m + 2, \text{ for some } m,.$$

The disjunctive form of this statement (its use of "or") suggests a
proof by *case analysis*, with three cases; see Exercise 3.10. To complete the proof, we show that each case leads to the result. A perfect
square is the square of an integer n, so continuing each of the cases,
the square, n^2, is one of these:

$$n^2 = (3m)^2 = 3(3m^2) \text{ or}$$
$$n^2 = (3m+1)^2 = 3(3m^2 + 2m) + 1 \text{ or}$$
$$n^2 = (3m+2)^2 = 3(3m^2 + 4m + 1) + 1.$$

In the first case the square is a multiple of 3 and in the other two cases it is one greater than a multiple of 3. Now look at the problem statement. It can be written in the form $p(n^2) \vee q(n^2)$, where p is the property of being a multiple of 3 and q is the property of being 1 more than a multiple of 3. In one of the three cases we have proved $p(n^2)$ and in the other two cases we have proved $q(n^2)$. In each case, one then uses $\vee$ *introduction*, a step so straightforward it often goes unmentioned.

Example 5.3

Prove that if the integers a and b are odd then ab is odd.

In other words, the product of two odd numbers is itself odd. This proof will be more formal than that of Example 5.2, but they are alike in using the idea of domain specific inference rules. The first step is to give a formal *definition* of "a is odd":

$$\forall x \in \mathcal{I} : \text{ODD}(x) \leftrightarrow \exists w \in \mathcal{I} : (x = 2w + 1).$$

The proof uses this definition as an inference rule in two ways, replacing its left-hand side by its right-hand side, and vice versa. Nearly all theorem statements have their logical structure hidden by the use of ordinary (English) language. Our earlier phrasing, "the product of odd numbers is itself odd" is an example of such informality. To clarify what is really being said, it is helpful, at this point, to state explicitly the logical structure of what is to be proved:

$$\forall a \in \mathcal{I} : \forall b \in \mathcal{I} : (\text{ODD}(a) \wedge \text{ODD}(b)) \rightarrow \text{ODD}(ab).$$

The main idea is that, taking x and y to be arbitrary integers, $2x+1$ and $2y+1$ are arbitrary odd numbers, and their product, can be manipulated by algebraic equivalences into $2(2xy + x + y) + 1$, which must be odd. Here is a (more nearly) formal proof.

$$[a \in \mathcal{I} \wedge b \in \mathcal{I}]$$

$[\textsc{Odd}(a) \wedge \textsc{Odd}(b)]$	
$\textsc{Odd}(a)$	
$\exists w \in \mathcal{I} : (a = 2w + 1)$	definition of $\textsc{Odd}$
$a = 2x + 1$	$\exists$ elimination, x new
$\textsc{Odd}(b)$	
$\exists w \in \mathcal{I} : (b = 2w + 1)$	definition of $\textsc{Odd}$
$b = 2y + 1$	$\exists$ elimination, y new
$ab = 2(2xy + x + y) + 1$	
$ab = 2z + 1$	
$\exists w \in \mathcal{I} : (ab = 2w + 1)$	$\exists$ introduction
$\textsc{Odd}(ab)$	definition of $\textsc{Odd}$

$$(\textsc{Odd}(a) \wedge \textsc{Odd}(b)) \rightarrow \textsc{Odd}(ab)$$

$$\forall a \in \mathcal{I} : \forall b \in \mathcal{I} : ((\textsc{Odd}(a) \wedge \textsc{Odd}(b)) \rightarrow \textsc{Odd}(ab)) \qquad \forall \text{ introduction, twice}$$

The foregoing proof begins with the assumption that we have an arbitrary a and b from the domain, which is how we typically prove any universally quantified logical expression. Our earlier definition of $\textsc{Odd}$ is used in both directions, as promised, 'forward' in the fourth and seventh lines and then 'backward' in the third-to-last line. When we "use" the definition we are compressing several inference steps; for example, $\forall$ elimination, then $\leftrightarrow$ elimination, then $\wedge$ elimination, and then modus ponens.

The rule of $\exists$ elimination is used twice in this proof, each time to let use choose a name for something we know exists. Also used here is $\exists$ introduction, which lets us say that if something is true of a particular number then it is true of some number.

Finally note that we have used the initial assumption, that a and b are integers, in two subtle ways: we used $\textsc{Odd}(a)$ which is only defined for integers and we perform algebraic manipulations, from our background knowledge, that are allowed for integer variables.

5.4 Mathematical Induction

This section introduces a technique called **mathematical induction** that is used to prove things about infinite sets. In particular it is used prove things about integer variables, variables that can take on an unbounded number of values. Computer scientists need to know things about infinite sets, they need to be proficient in reasoning about the set of integers. For example, consider a while loop and a predicate p, where each $p(i)$ (for $i = 0, 1, 2, \ldots$) asserts something that is supposed to be true after i iterations of the loop. How would we prove it? We want to show $p(i)$ is true for every $i \in \mathcal{N}$. Now $\mathcal{N}$ is an infinite set, but every member of it is a finite integer. Would it be easier to avoid any mention of infinite sets; after all everything in the real world is finite.[1] Actually it is more complicated and less useful. Suppose we did limit a loop to, say, 10,000 iterations. Proving 10,000 propositions one by one is ludicrous, and it does not inform us about more iterations. In contrast, many proofs for infinite sets are not very difficult.

In Chapter 6 we do consider proofs about the behavior of loops, but here we will use easier examples about integers, so we can focus our attention on the methods of proof. You have already seen one proof of an infinite set of propositions. This was the proof that the product of any two odd numbers is odd. The proof was done rather formally, concluding be using the rule of inference known as ∀ introduction. This sort of direct proof, is usually avoided, because our new technique is simpler.

Mathematical induction (MI) is used solely for theorems of the form $\forall n \in \mathcal{N} : p(n)$. However such theorems are extremely common, especially for computer scientists, since integers are the archetypical discrete mathematical object. Suppose we are trying to prove $p(n)$ for an arbitrary natural number n. This may be hard. The key idea of MI is that when trying to prove proposition $p(n)$ it may be much easier if we assume that the truth of $p(n-1)$ has already been established. To simplify our presentation below we will instead ask if assuming $p(n)$ makes it easier to prove $p(n + 1)$. This assumption is called the **inductive hypothesis**.

---

[1]We are not going to delve into the philosophy of science here, though we could point out that computer programs go into "infinite loops."

This assumption can be helpful, as we will see, but is it justified? To see that it is, let us be a little more precise. First, it is important to realize that a proof by MI has two parts, proof of a base case and proof of the so called inductive step. Typically, the **base case** (or basis) is $p(0)$. Typically the **inductive step** is to prove that $p(n) \to p(n+1)$. If this step is carried out with no assumptions about n except that $n \geq 0$, then it is true for any $n \geq 0$, so the base case together with all the results that come from the inductive step are:

$$p(0)$$
$$p(0) \quad \to \quad p(1)$$
$$p(1) \quad \to \quad p(2)$$
$$p(2) \quad \to \quad p(3)$$
$$\vdots$$
$$p(n) \quad \to \quad p(n+1)$$
$$\vdots$$

From the first two lines, modus ponens allows us infer $p(1)$. From $p(1)$ and the third line, modus ponens lets us infer $p(2)$. Then we can infer $p(3)$, and so on, to any $p(n)$. Thus, starting with the base case, repeated appeals to the inductive step with modus ponens justifies all these arrows, for any positive integer n.

$$p(0) \to p(1) \to p(2) \to p(3) \to \cdots \to p(n)$$

Having introduced the general idea of mathematical induction, we now move on to showing how it can be used. You will notice that nothing we have said tells you *what* to prove, how to choose p. MI is only a method of proof. Such theorems, we will see, involve loops in programs, recursive functions in programs, recursive definitions, universal quantification ($\forall$), summations (Σ) and products (Π). MI is useful even when $\mathcal{N}$ is not explicitly mentioned, it often is tacit in the statement of theorems.

Example 5.4

Show that, for any nonnegative integer n, the sum of the first n integers is $n(n+1)/2$. That is, prove the propositions $p(n)$ is true for all $n \geq 0$, where $p(n)$ is the following statement:

$$\sum_{i=1}^{n} i = \frac{n(n+1)}{2}$$

Proof: We show, by MI, that $\forall n \in \mathcal{N} : p(n)$. The base case, $p(0)$, is the proposition that the sum of no (zero) numbers is $0(0+1)/2$ or 0^2, which is clearly true. To establish $p(n)$ we proceed as follows:

$$\sum_{i=1}^{n+1} i = (n+1) + \sum_{i=1}^{n} i$$

$$= (n+1) + \frac{n(n+1)}{2} = \frac{2(n+1) + n(n+1)}{2} = \frac{(n+1)(n+2)}{2}$$

Note that we appealed to the inductive hypothesis, $p(n)$, when we went to the second line.

The above discussion and example are motivation for our formal statement. Mathematical induction can be expressed as a *rule of inference*. Above the bar are, as usual, the things that must be proved before invoking the rule. So for MI, we must prove the base case, which is the first line, as well as the inductive step, the second line. The final line is the result that is being proved by MI.

Mathematical Induction: $p(0)$
                            $\forall\, n \in \mathcal{N} : p(n) \to p(n+1)$

$\forall\, n \in \mathcal{N} : p(n)$

Notice that the second line, the inductive step, is expressed in terms of $\forall$ (universal quantification) and $\to$ (conditional). We will need to

---

[2]We use the familiar convention that if S is a set of numbers then the sum of the elements of S is 0 when $S = \emptyset$.

get results in a form that includes these symbols in order to make use of this rule of inference, so we should expect to use $\forall$ introduction and $\rightarrow$ introduction along the way. For $\forall$ introduction, recall that proving something true of all positive integers can be achieved by proving that it is true of n, where we make no assumptions about n except that it is a positive integer. For $\rightarrow$ introduction, we assume the left-hand side and, using that assumption, proceed to prove the right-hand side. Notice that in the context of MI, assuming the left-hand side is called using the inductive hypothesis. Taken together, this give the general framework for proofs by mathematical induction. The framework can be seen to guide the proof in Example 5.5.

$p(0)$	base case proved
$[n \in \mathcal{N}]$	assumption
$[p(n)]$	assumption: inductive hypothesis
$\vdots$	steps for proving inductive conclusion
$p(n+1)$	inductive conclusion proved
$p(n) \rightarrow p(n+1)$	$\rightarrow$ introduction
$\forall n \in \mathcal{N} : p(n) \rightarrow p(n+1)$	$\forall$ introduction
$\forall n \in \mathcal{N} : p(n)$	mathematical induction

Example 5.5

Give a *formal proof* of the formula in Example 5.4, that the sum of the first n integers is $n(n+1)/2$.

1.	$\sum_{i=1}^{0} i = 0 = \frac{0(0+1)}{2}$	base case
2.	$[n \in \mathcal{N}]$	assumption
3.	$[\sum_{i=1}^{n} i = \frac{n(n+1)}{2}]$	inductive hypothesis
4.	$\sum_{i=1}^{n+1} i = (n+1) + \sum_{i=1}^{n} i = \ldots = \frac{(n+1)(n+2)}{2}$	algebra rules
5.	$\sum_{i=1}^{n+1} i = \frac{(n+1)(n+2)}{2}$	inductive conclusion
6.	$\sum_{i=1}^{n} i = \frac{n(n+1)}{2} \rightarrow \sum_{i=1}^{n+1} i = \frac{(n+1)(n+2)}{2}$	$\rightarrow$ introduction
7.	$\forall n \in \mathcal{N} : \sum_{i=1}^{n} i = \frac{n(n+1)}{2} \rightarrow \sum_{i=1}^{n+1} i = \frac{(n+1)(n+2)}{2}$	$\forall$ introduction
8.	$\forall n \in \mathcal{N} : \sum_{i=1}^{n} i = \frac{n(n+1)}{2}$	mathematical induction

Although it is instructive to put one MI proof into our standard proof format, we must admit that by doing so we have made the proof of

a relatively simple result look much more complex and forbidding
than is usual. The essence of this longer proof lies in lines 1 and 4,
which made up the entirety of the earlier informal proof in Example
5.4. In effect, the implicit structure for that informal proof was the
formal MI framework above.

Variations

As stated MI is more restrictive than it is in practice, because there
are some equivalent variants presentations that are often more nat-
ural. First let us define $\mathcal{I}_i^+ = \{k \in \mathcal{I} \mid i \leq k\}$; so $\mathcal{N} = \mathcal{I}_0^+$. Also we
define $\mathcal{I}_i^j = \{k \in \mathcal{I} \mid i \leq k \leq j\}$.

Not starting at 0

Sometimes, as in Example 5.6 below, the base case does not seem
to be tied to 0. In particular, if a predicate $q(n)$ is true for all
integers $n \geq k$ but false for $n = k - 1$ the theorem to be proved is
$\forall n \in \mathcal{I}_k^+ : q(n)$. Now we can define $p(n) = q(n + k)$ and use MI
with p to prove the theorem about q. However it is more natural to
deal with q directly using this rule, and its expansion with the above
framework.

$$\text{Induction variant:} \qquad \begin{array}{l} q(k) \\ \forall\, n \in \mathcal{I}_k^+ : q(n) \to q(n+1) \\ \hline \forall\, n \in \mathcal{I}_k^+ : q(n) \end{array}$$

To make the presentation easier to read, we typically use $n \geq k$
instead of $n \in \mathcal{I}_k^+$, leaving membership in $\mathcal{I}$ implicit for the reader.

Strong induction

Recall that when we conclude that $p(0) \to \cdots \to p(n+1)$ using modus
ponens repeatedly that not only was $p(n)$ true just before we proved
$p(n) \to p(n+1)$ but all of the propositions, $p(0)$, $p(1)$, $p(2)$, ..., $p(n)$
were true, that is, $p(0) \wedge p(1) \wedge p(2) \wedge \cdots \wedge p(n)$ was true. The idea
behind "strong induction" is that instead of proving $p(n) \to p(n+1)$

we might find it easier to prove $(p(0) \land p(1) \land p(2) \land \cdots \land p(n)) \to p(n+1)$, since we will still be able to invoke modus ponens to get $p(n+1)$.

Strong induction:
$$p(0)$$
$$\forall n \in \mathcal{N} : (\forall i \in \mathcal{I}_0^n : p(i)) \to p(n+1)$$
$$\overline{\forall n \in \mathcal{N} : p(n)}$$

We can show that this version is *not* any "stronger" than normal induction by showing it is equivalent to it. The key insight is to introduce a new predicate $q(n) = \forall i \in \mathcal{I}_0^n : p(i)$. We leave it as exercise to show that $p(0) \equiv q(0)$, that $\forall n \in \mathcal{N} : (\forall i \in \mathcal{I}_0^n : p(i)) \to p(n+1) \equiv \forall n \in \mathcal{N} : q(n) \to q(n+1)$, and that $\forall n \in \mathcal{N} : p(n) \equiv \forall n \in \mathcal{N} : q(n)$.

Strong induction with a larger basis

Sometime the basis is not established by showing that the predicate p is true for a single value, like $p(0)$. The more natural argument starts by showing that the predicate is true for several values. Example 5.7 below, about Fibonacci numbers, will illustrate this.

Larger basis:
$$\forall n \in \mathcal{I}_0^l : p(n)$$
$$\forall n \in \mathcal{I}_l^+ : (\forall i \in \mathcal{I}_0^n : p(i)) \to p(n+1)$$
$$\overline{\forall n \in \mathcal{N} : p(n)}$$

So you begin by showing $p(0), p(1), \ldots, p(l)$ for some $l \geq 0$. Then you show that $p(l+1), p(l+2), \ldots$ can all be shown to follow from the previously proven predicates. Note that this is the same as before when $l = 0$. Of course, this is not stronger than normal induction and can be reduced to it. Also this can be combined with the above variant using $\mathcal{I}_k^l$ instead of $\mathcal{I}_0^l$, etc.

Implicit natural numbers

Sometime MI is used when there is no apparent natural numbers in the theorem. For example, we might encounter "For all sets the property p holds." To use induction we can implicitly (or explicitly) recast the theorem as "For all sets S, $|S| = n$, the property $p(S)$ holds, for all $n \geq 0$." In this case the proof will typically begin with something like "We will prove this by induction on the cardinality of the set."

Change of variables

Suppose that we wish to prove "$q(n)$ is true for all odd positive integers." If we let $p(n) = q(2n + 1)$ then it becomes $\forall n \in \mathcal{N} : p(n)$. And suppose we wish to prove "$q(n)$ is true for all powers of 2." If we now let $p(n) = q(2^n)$ then it becomes $\forall n \in \mathcal{N} : p(n)$.

Using $p(n - 1) \rightarrow p(n)$

Often you will encounter a proof in which the author uses $p(n - 1)$ as the inductive hypothesis, showing $p(n - 1) \rightarrow p(n)$ instead of $p(n) \rightarrow p(n+1)$. This is essentially a change of variable and corresponds to this rule:

$$\text{Induction variant:} \qquad \begin{array}{c} p(0) \\ \forall\, n \in \mathcal{I}_1^+ : p(n - 1) \rightarrow p(n) \\ \hline \forall\, n \in \mathcal{N} : p(n) \end{array}$$

The switch to $\mathcal{I}_1^+$ needs to be adhered to; ignoring it can cause errors.

There are other variations. For example, if the proof of $p(n) \rightarrow p(n + 1)$ is by *contradiction* (rather than a *direct proof*), this might be called a "proof by smallest counter-example."

5.5   Examples of Mathematical Induction

First an algebraic tip. Often predicate $p(n)$ is an equation, say $L(n) = R(n)$, such as $\sum_{i=1}^{n} i = \frac{n(n+1)}{2}$. When you can show that $L(n + 1) = L(n) + \alpha = \cdots = R(n) + \beta = R(n + 1)$ then also try to show that the expressions α and β are equal. Together with the induction hypothesis $p(n)$, that $L(n) = R(n)$, this will complete the proof. This approach guided Example 5.4.

Example 5.6

Prove that $\forall n \geq 5 : 2^n > n^2$.

1.	$2^5 = 32 > 25 = 5^2$	base case
2.	$[n \geq 5]$	assumption
3.	$n^2 > 2n + 1$	algebra
4.	$[2^n > n^2]$	inductive hypothesis
5.	$2^{n+1} = 2 \times 2^n > 2n^2 = n^2 + n^2 > n^2 + 2n + 1$	algebra rules
6.	$2^{n+1} > (n+1)^2$	inductive conclusion
7.	$2^n > n^2 \rightarrow 2^{n+1} > (n+1)^2$	$\rightarrow$ introduction
8.	$\forall n \geq 5 : 2^n > n^2 \rightarrow 2^{n+1} > (n+1)^2$	$\forall$ introduction
9.	$\forall n \geq 5 : 2^n > n^2$	mathematical induction

Note that we used $n \geq 5$ instead of $n \in I_5^+$. Let $p(n) = (2^n > n^2)$; $p(n)$ is false for $n = 4$, but it is true for all integers ≥ 5. This suggests we use the variant strategy mentioned above, which allows a starting point other than $p(0)$. We take $p(5)$ as the base case. Like every MI proof there are two nested assumptions. Notice that line 3 (which is used in line 5) follows from the first assumption only. This assumption is often ignored in informal MI proofs, but can be crucial (if we did not know that $n > 2$ then line 3 would not be accepted by the reader).

Recurrence relations are common in computer science, especially in the analysis of algorithms. They can be studied as a separate topic in a course on discrete mathematics. They can sometimes be solved with a variety of methods. Here we want to highlight how they naturally dovetail with MI. A recurrence relation defines a function of the integer n in terms of the same function for smaller arguments; also a boundary condition must be given. We will focus on the best known recurrence relation, the Fibonacci sequence. It is defined by:

$$F_0 = 0, \quad F_1 = 1, \quad F_{n+1} = F_n + F_{n-1}, \text{ for all } n \geq 1.$$

Therefore $F_2 = 1$, $F_3 = 2$, $F_4 = 3$ and so on. F_0 and F_1 constitute a "boundary condition."

Example 5.7

The Fibonacci sequence may be the most studied sequence. There are literally thousands of facts proven about it. Here is just one theorem:

$$\forall n \in \mathcal{N} : F_n \leq \left(\frac{5}{3}\right)^{n-1}.$$

Here the predicate $p(n)$ is $(F_n \leq (\frac{5}{3})^{n-1})$. This will be proved without the formal indentation, using the variant of strong induction with a basis of two propositions: $p(0)$ and $p(1)$. We observe that $F_0 = 0 \leq \frac{3}{5} = (\frac{5}{3})^{0-1}$ and $F_1 = 1 \leq 1 = (\frac{5}{3})^{1-1}$. Now we assume that $n \geq 1$. We further assume that $p(i)$ is true for all $0 \leq i \leq n$. The next steps show how recurrence relations naturally combine with an appeal to the inductive hypothesis.

$$F_{n+1} = F_n + F_{n-1} \leq \left(\frac{5}{3}\right)^{n-1} + \left(\frac{5}{3}\right)^{n-2}$$

$$= \left(\frac{3 \times 5 + 3^2}{5^2}\right) \times \left(\frac{5}{3}\right)^n < \left(\frac{5}{3}\right)^n.$$

Hence $p(n + 1)$ is true.

5.6 Limits of Logic

How many rules of inference are there? How many do we need? How many should we use? So far, we have not asked such questions but have been content to look at individual rules and evaluate them in isolation. We have been careful to only use a rule that is give will guarantee truth (is a tautology). Recall, such a rule is said to be sound. Clearly we want only sound rules. It may also appear that we are evaluating a rule positively when we make favorable comments about how reasonable it seems. For example, we observed that rules like case analysis seem to make good common sense. Reasonableness is nice, but for formal proofs, soundness is essential.

Now recall that some sound rules, like case analysis and modus ponens, were collected together into a kind of starter set or initial set of inference rules in a figure (Figure 3.1), whereas other equally sound rules, like transitivity of the conditional we saw fit to prove not by truth tables but from other inference rules (whether from the initial set or previously proved or both). How should one decide which rules to start with and which to prove using other rules? Even if there are an infinite number of sound inference rules we must start with a finite number; hopefully a very small number. However, we certainly do want to start with a big enough or diverse enough collection to be able to prove everything that is true.

Recall that in Section 3.8 we stated that propositional logic is sound and complete. This was proved by Gödel. Actually Gödel proved the same thing about the predicate logic we have introduced in these chapters.

Theorem 5.1 – $\vdash \alpha$ is valid if and only if $\models \alpha$ holds, for every α in predicate logic.

However the symbols in this theorem require many new definitions that are beyond the scope of this book. For example, $\models \alpha$ indicates that α is necessarily *true in every model*. Here a model is the filling out of the details about the truth values of the variables and what each predicate is defined to be; since the predicates are over infinite domains the number of models are not finite. ("Deciding" if $\models \alpha$ holds is impossible, in general; what this means is deferred until the final chapter.)

Things get worse, though. Before that we need to pause to introduce the formal basis of $\mathcal{N}$ the set of natural numbers. The history of logic is intertwined with developments in Set Theory and this set in particular. The most influential definition is called "Peano's axioms," which we paraphrase:

Definition 5.1

Peano's definition of $\mathcal{N}$:

- $0 \in \mathcal{N}$
- If $n \in \mathcal{N}$ then $n + 1 \in \mathcal{N}$
- If $n \in \mathcal{N}$ then $n + 1 \neq 0$
- If $n, m \in \mathcal{N}$ and $n + 1 = m + 1$ then $n = m$
- If $p(n) \to p(n + 1)$ when $n \in \mathcal{N}$ and $p(0)$ is true then $p(n)$ is true for all $n \in \mathcal{N}$

We use the notation $n + 1$ for what is formally called the "successor" of n.

You will recognize the last axiom as MI. Even though we motivated MI by a discussion involving modus ponens, etc., in fact MI was already agreed to as soon as we started using $\mathcal{N}$. In other words, we were really operating with an informal commonplace definition of the natural numbers. This is always dangerous when dealing with infinite sets. It is pedagogically difficult to begin with these axioms, though.

A *system* of logic is informally defined as a set of axioms and a finite set of rules of inference. (The axioms may be infinite in number but there is a finite description of them, they are "effectively generated".) A system is **consistent** if it is impossible to prove any expression to be both true and false. A system that makes it possible to have a proof for everything is said to be **complete**; in particular, in the system every (well-formed) expression is provably true or provably false. Everyone wants a system that is complete and consistent. Unfortunately logic is not always so clean and intuitive.

It turns out that if we look at systems of logic, our expectations can not always be met. This was first discovered by Gödel in the 1931 and it revolutionized mathematics. He considered a minimal system for proving statements about number theory (such as the statements in Section 5.3 above). He was able to show that if the system was consistent then it must be incomplete! After Gödel, people have replicated this paradoxical situation with many other systems. It is known that if a system is sufficiently complex, in a very technical sense, it cannot be both consistent and complete — there will always be a true but unprovable expression!

It is beyond the scope of this book to even sketch the rationale behind these results. The minimal system alluded to above, that Gödel used, combined Peano's axioms with other axioms that effectively defined the operations of addition and multiplication. (Curiously, addition without multiplication does not cause the same problems; that is an indication of how subtle the result is). Gödel also proved that these systems cannot prove their own consistency. There are several books in the bibliography that *do* explain, in popular language, how Gödel proved it, but many chapters are required.

Exercises

5.1 – Recast the following inference rules into the formal line-by-line notation introduced in Chapter 3.

(a) Subset rule.

(b) Set equality rule.

(c) Transitivity of the conditional operator.

(d) Pigeon-hole principle. Hint: Let f be a function from set A to set B; that is, $f : A \to B$. Remember that $|A|$ is the number of elements in A.

5.2 – Prove by mathematical induction that the sum of the first n positive odd integers is n^2, for all $n \geq 0$. State the theorem as a formula and give the complete formal proof, with indentation.

5.3 – Prove that, for all $n \geq 0$:

$$\left(\sum_{i=1}^{n} i\right)^2 = \sum_{i=1}^{n} i^3.$$

You may make use of the fact that $\sum_{i=1}^{n} i = \frac{n(n+1)}{2}$. Your mathematical induction proof can be "informal."

An informal induction proof does not use the formal syntax. And it usually does not explicitly give the last three lines, since they are the same in every proof. However an informal proof must still clearly stated what the base case is, what assumptions are being made, and how the inductive conclusion follows from the assumptions.

5.4 – Informally prove by mathematical induction that for any integer $n \geq 10$, $2^n > n^3$.

5.5 – Informally prove that $\vee$ distributes over n-component conjunctions like

$$(q_1 \wedge q_2 \wedge \ldots \wedge q_n)$$

using the algebraic law given in Chapter 2 for $n = 2$.

5.6 – As in the previous exercise, informally prove DeMorgan's law generalized from 2 components to n.

5.7 – Informally prove by mathematical induction that $F_n > (\frac{3}{2})^{n-1}$, when $n > 5$.

5.8 – Example 5.7 and the previous exercise show that the Fibonacci sequence has a growth rate that is lower bounded and upper bounded by some exponential function. Actually there is a sharper result. Informally prove by mathematical induction that $F_n = (\phi^n - (1 - \phi)^n)/\sqrt{5}$, where $\phi = (1 + \sqrt{5})/2$, for all $n \geq 0$.

5.9 – Suppose stamps are only issued in 3¢ and 7¢ denominations. So you can make postage for 13¢ (with two 3¢ stamps and one 7¢ stamp) but you cannot make postage for 11¢. Prove that you can make any postage of 12¢ or more. Prove this both with normal induction and again with the variant of strong induction.

5.10 – Prove by induction that for any undirected graph that the sum of the degrees of all the vertices is twice the number of edges.

5.11 – Argue that these statements which were stated during the discussion of strong inductions are true: $p(0) \equiv q(0)$,

$$\forall n \in \mathcal{N} : (\forall i \in \mathcal{I}_0^n : p(i)) \rightarrow p(n+1) \equiv \forall n \in \mathcal{N} : q(n) \rightarrow q(n+1),$$

and $\forall n \in \mathcal{N} : p(n) \equiv \forall n \in \mathcal{N} : q(n)$.

Chapter 6

Program Verification

Often we write computer programs that we believe to be correct. Still, it would be desirable, especially for important programs, to *know* that they are correct, by proving it. But how would you prove a program correct? This question defines the challenge of **program verification**, a subfield of software engineering. This chapter lays out a predicate logic approach to verification, incorporating special new rules of inference to express our background knowledge of computer programming. The material can thus sharpen your predicate logic skill while demonstrating their relevance.

6.1   The Idea of Verification

When a program compiles successfully, the compiler has, in effect, certified that the program is *syntactically* correct. But this means only that it consists of permitted symbols in recognized categories that have been strung together in ways that the programming language allows. As an example for English "Fast trees see" is syntactically correct in that an adjective, "fast," precedes and combines with a noun, "trees," to make a plural subject for the verb "see." However, this is a very weak notion of correctness, having nothing to do with whether the sentence means anything. Since trees have neither speed nor sight, the words do not combine in a meaningful way. The sentence is syntactically acceptable but since it has no meaning, we say that it is *semantically* unacceptable.

Semantics is the formal study of meaning. The idea is to introduce notation for the semantics of each kind of programming statement and to have these combine to give the semantics of whole programs. Here we will take the semantics of a programming statement to be its effect on the values of variables and on the properties of those values, such as being an odd integer, a positive real or less than another number. We will use new inference rules to describe these effects. These rules are language dependent, in that some of the rules for C++ have to be different from those for Perl. However, the rules introduced here are for central concepts, shared by many programming languages.

Our intent is to prove, for a given program, that it accomplishes its goal. We begin by specifying that goal — what the program is supposed to compute — in the form of a logical assertion. We also describe in logic the initial state of the program. The process of program verification then consists of repeatedly applying our new inference rules (for the statement types in our programming language) to successive statements in the program until, finally, the inference rule for the last statement allows us to infer the logical assertion which was originally given as the goal of the program. In other words we are trying to prove a theorem of the form "executing the code S when p is known to be true will result in q being true".

This process has actually been automated and used to verify the correctness of relatively small programs, but we are far from achieving that for large real-life programs. The last section of this chapter is a consideration of some of the difficulties in program verification. But now let's see what all this really looks like.

6.2   Definitions

Typically the *proof* that a program is correct is divided in to two subproofs. First, one shows the program's **partial correctness**: if the program **terminates** then it indeed computes what it should. Second, one shows that, in fact, the program terminates. This chapter treats only the first part, proofs of partial correctness, since proofs of termination can be very subtle and problematic.

In order to keep our discussion largely language independent we will constrain our attention to just a few types of statements common to most procedural languages. In particular, in addition to some elementary statements, such as assignment statements, we will use the three standard mechanisms for generating structured code out of elementary statements: sequencing of statements ("S_1 ; S_2" for S_1 followed by S_2), conditional statements ("if B then S_1 else S_2") and iteration statements ("while B do S"). (It is worth noting that these last three kinds of statements are the core of Structured Programming and that they are also the easiest to prove assertions about. This supports the notion that programmers who use Structured Programming will write code that is most readily shown correct, however informal that proof might be.)

We choose to write programming statements not in any real programming language but in "pseudocode" that captures key ideas, yet keeps us from appearing to rely on the peculiarities of any particular real language. This approach lets us promote clarity. It also lets us avoid C's and C++'s use of the equals sign for assignment statements, so that the mathematical equals signs in the proofs will be unambiguous. Users of C++ will find it easy enough to read "while B do S", for example, as "while (B) S". We use new-line breaks and indentation where possible to indicate program structure (avoiding **begin/end** bracketing, etc.). Recall, as is typical in any discussion of Structured Programming, a "statement" S can be a compound statement, which can be an arbitrarily large block of code.

We *specify* what a program is supposed to compute by giving two propositions. First we give the **initial assertion** which indicates the initial state of the computation. This will be a conjunction of propositions about the initial values of the variables used by the program. Second we give the **final assertion** which specifies the final state of the computation. This too is a conjunction of propositions, in this case about the final values of the variables and/or the output of the program. Notice that the specification says nothing about the method used to compute the desired final state; any number of programs based on different methods could all be correct.

The notation that is typically used in program verification is called the **Hoare triple:** $p \{S\} q$. This notation is equivalent to this assertion: If the proposition p is true for the initial state of the code S and, further, S terminates then q is true for the final state. Recall that S need not be a single statement; it can be any block of code, including the entire program. We call p the **precondition** and q the **postcondition**. When S is the entire program then the precondition is the initial assertion and the postcondition is the final assertion.

6.3   Inference Rules

The simplest inference rules are for the elementary statements, like the assignment statement. We will use " $\Leftarrow$ " as the assignment operator, rather than the "=" of C and C++, to emphasize that our reasoning is language-independent. With this notation, the general form of an assignment statement is v $\Leftarrow$ e, where v is a variable and e is an expression like 3 or x+1 or 2*sin(theta). The assignment statement has the following semantics (meaning): Evaluate e and assign the resulting value to v. The rule of inference for assignment statements is that the following Hoare triple is a tautology:

Assignment: $p(e) \{\text{v} \Leftarrow \text{e}\} p(v)$

The idea here is that if the value of e satisfies some predicate p before the statement is executed, then the value of v will satisfy that same predicate afterwards. Of course, this assumes that all variables other than v will retain their values, i.e., our pseudocode does not allow "side-effects."

Example 6.1

Letting p be the predicate ODD, which is true when its argument is odd, permits the following Hoare triples:

$$\text{ODD}(3)\ \{y \Leftarrow 3\}\ \text{ODD}(y)$$

$$\text{ODD}(y)\ \{x \Leftarrow y + 2\}\ \text{ODD}(x)$$

$$\text{ODD}(x)\ \{x \Leftarrow x + 1\}\ \text{EVEN}(x)$$

In the first triple, the precondition, ODD(3), is true from arithmetic and does not really need to be written. Arithmetic steps are often omitted from correctness proofs. Thus the second triple uses the fact that the sum of 2 and an odd number is odd (i.e., $y + 2$ is odd), without mentioning it. In the third triple, it is important to distinguish two different meanings of x. The value of x is odd in the precondition, before execution so $x + 1$ is even, and x inherits that property, after execution.

The rule of inference for the sequencing of statements is:

$$\textbf{Sequence:} \qquad \frac{p\ \{S_1\}\ q \\ q\ \{S_2\}\ r}{p\ \{S_1; S_2\}\ r}$$

This inference rule is applicable when we have analyzed two successive statements, S_1 and S_2, and have established that q, the *pre*condition of the second, is also the *post*condition of the first. Thus S_1 establishes what S_2 requires. In such a case, it is correct to conclude that we know the precondition and postcondition for the two-statement sequence as a whole. Note that a sequence is itself a kind of statement, a compound statement. Therefore repeated use of this rule on longer and longer compound statements allows us handle programs of any size.

Example 6.2

Suppose it is known that x must be 1 on entry to the code
$$\text{y} \Leftarrow 3; \ \text{z} \Leftarrow \text{x} + \text{y} \ .$$
Substitute appropriate parts of this code into the sequence rule for
the values of S_1, S_2, p, q and r. (You will need to use your knowledge
of elementary arithmetic and programming to get the postconditions.

$(x = 1)$	$\{\ \text{y} \Leftarrow 3\ \}$	$(x = 1) \wedge (y = 3)$
$(x = 1) \wedge (y = 3)$	$\{\ \text{z} \Leftarrow \text{x} + \text{y}\ \}$	$(z = 4)$

$(x = 1)$	$\{\ \text{y} \Leftarrow 3;\ \text{z} \Leftarrow \text{x} + \text{y}\ \}$	$(z = 4)$

Example 6.3

For the compound statement $\{\text{x} \Leftarrow \text{x} + 2;\ \text{y} \Leftarrow \text{y} + 1\}$, show that
if the equality $x = 2y$ holds on entry to the code it also holds
on exit.

$(x = 2y)$	$\{\ \text{x} \Leftarrow \text{x} + 2\ \}$	$(x = 2y + 2)$
$(x = 2(y + 1))$	$\{\ \text{y} \Leftarrow \text{y} + 1\ \}$	$(x = 2y)$

$(x = 2y)$	$\{\ \text{x} \Leftarrow \text{x} + 2;\ \text{y} \Leftarrow \text{y} + 1\ \}$	$(x = 2y)$

In the second line, note that with $e = y + 1$ the precondition for the
assignment is $x = 2e$, so the postcondition is $x = 2y$.

Example 6.3 illustrates a situation where the precondition is the same
as the postcondition. Although each of the variables x and y has un-
dergone a change in value, we are able to prove that the relationship
of equality between them is maintained by the statement sequence
as a whole. Such a relationship is called an **invariant condition** for

that chunk of code. This idea is important in the discussion of loops below.

The next rules of inference are for the conditional statements, involving if, then and possibly else.

If-Then: $(p \wedge B) \{S\} q$

$(p \wedge \neg B) \rightarrow q$

$$\overline{\quad p \, \{\text{if } B \text{ then } S\} \, q \quad}$$

If-Then-Else: $(p \wedge B) \{S_1\} q$

$(p \wedge \neg B) \{S_2\} q$

$$\overline{\quad p \, \{\text{if } B \text{ then } S_1 \text{ else } S_2\} \, q \quad}$$

Focusing only on the If-Then rule, notice that whereas the first line is a Hoare triple, the second line is an ordinary expression in propositional logic. Also notice that the proposition p appears at the start of each, conjoined with B in one case and with $\neg B$ in the other. Together, therefore, they justify the concluding Hoare triple, in the bottom line, since when p is true, q either becomes true by execution of S when B is true or was already true when B is false, as shown by modus ponens in the second line. The If-Then-Else rule has a similar explanation, left as an exercise.

Example 6.4

For the statement $\{\text{if } \text{y} < \text{x} \text{ then } \text{y} \Leftarrow \text{x}\}$ show that from a precondition of $x = 7$ we can assure a postcondition of $y \geq 7$.

In this If-Then statement the condition B is $y < x$ and statement S is the assignment, $\text{y} \Leftarrow \text{x}$. Notice that $\neg B$, which in this example, is $\neg (y < x)$, can be rewritten as $y \geq x$, since y's relation to x must be one of $\{>, =, <\}$. Also p is $x = 7$ and q is $y \geq 7$. Putting all this into the If-Then inference rule gives the tableau shown below. Our goal is the result below the bar; to prove it we must establish the two lines above the bar. Each is easy. The first line is true because x is initially 7 and is copied to y, making y equal 7, so certainly $y \geq 7$ (by $\vee$ Introduction, strictly speaking). The second line is all arithmetic: $y \geq x = 7$, so again $y \geq 7$. By the way, the 7 here could just as well have been replaced by whatever value x might have at the outset. Since x is not reassigned in the code, we actually have the more general conclusion $y \geq x$ after the If-Then statement is executed.

$$(x = 7 \wedge y < x) \qquad \{\ \text{y} \Leftarrow \text{x}\ \} \qquad\qquad\qquad (y \geq 7)$$
$$(x = 7 \wedge y \geq x) \qquad\quad \rightarrow \qquad\qquad\qquad\qquad (y \geq 7)$$

$$\overline{(x = 7) \qquad\quad \{\ \text{if y < x then y} \Leftarrow \text{x}\ \} \quad (y \geq 7)}$$

Example 6.5

Implement the absolute value function and verify the code.

The code is below the bar.

$$(\text{TRUE} \wedge x < 0) \quad \{\ \text{abs} \Leftarrow \text{-x}\ \} \qquad\qquad\qquad (abs = |x|)$$
$$(\text{TRUE} \wedge x \geq 0) \quad \{\ \text{abs} \Leftarrow \text{x}\ \} \qquad\qquad\qquad\ \ (abs = |x|)$$

$$\overline{(\text{TRUE}) \qquad\quad \{\ \text{if x<0 then abs} \Leftarrow \text{-x else abs} \Leftarrow \text{x}\ \} \quad (abs = |x|)}$$

We use the precondition $p = \text{TRUE}$ to indicate that we need no prior assumptions to draw our conclusion. (In all our examples we suppress assumptions about the data type of variables.) This, like all our examples, treats the code in a very isolated way; in fact there will be a lot of facts in the precondition, like the type of the variable x and information about all the other variables in the program, which pass unchanged into the postcondition.

6.4 Loop Invariants

The inference rule for the while iteration statement is shown below. The condition p in the rule is called the **loop invariant**. It is an invariant condition for the loop body S because when S is allowed to execute — that is, when B is true — p is both a precondition and postcondition for S.

While:
$$(p \wedge B)\,\{S\}\,p$$
$$\overline{\qquad\qquad\qquad\qquad\qquad}$$
$$p\,\{\texttt{while } B \texttt{ do } S\}\,(p \wedge \neg B)$$

The correctness of this inference rule relies on a proof by mathematical induction. To see this, imagine that we are trying to prove the following theorem: "The assertion p is true after n iterations of the While loop, for every $n \geq 0$." An induction proof has a basis, for $n = 0$, which is trivially true here since this rule can only be invoked when p is true initially. The inductive step of an induction proof would try to show that if p is true after n iterations, then it is also true after $n + 1$ iterations. That is essentially what it means for p to be an invariant condition for S. Note, that we only have shown p is an invariant condition for S as long as B remains true, but if there is an $n + 1$st iteration then B must have been true before it.

It is important to remember that if a proposition is proposed as the loop invariant it must satisfy two criteria. First it must already be true when the loop is encountered. Otherwise the inference can not be used in a valid proof. Second it must satisfy the Hoare triple above the line in the inference rule.

Notice the occurrence of $\neg B$ in the postcondition of the While rule. The inference rule does not address why B must become false. We know that $\neg B$ holds at this point since what terminates the loop is a violation of B. Since we are only doing partial correctness we can assume that the loop does halt after n iterations, for some integer n, without proof.

Example 6.6

Find a loop invariant for the following program and use it to prove that the program computes $n!$. You can assume $n \geq 1$.

```
i ⇐ 1;
f ⇐ 1;
while i < n do
    i ⇐ i+1
    f ⇐ f*i
```

How do we come up with a loop invariant? To answer this we need to think about the *purpose* of the code. Here the purpose is to compute $n!$ in the variable f. Therefore we will take as part of the invariant that $f = i!$ inside the loop. At the time of exit, we will have $i = n$, making $f = n!$. In light of these considerations we take the loop invariant p to be $(f = i!) \wedge (i \leq n)$. Note that p is true initially as it must be. To show p is a loop invariant we need to argue that:

$$(f = i!) \wedge (i \leq n) \wedge (i < n) \; \{\texttt{i} \Leftarrow \texttt{i} + 1; \; \texttt{f} \Leftarrow \texttt{f} * \texttt{i}\} \; (f = i!) \wedge (i \leq n).$$

While this can easily be seen to be true, we could break the argument down into two steps, and use the sequencing inference rule:

$$(f = i!) \wedge (i \leq n) \wedge (i < n) \; \{\texttt{i} \Leftarrow \texttt{i} + 1\} \; (f = (i-1)!) \wedge (i \leq n).$$

$$(f = (i-1)!) \wedge (i \leq n) \; \{\texttt{f} \Leftarrow \texttt{f} * \texttt{i}\} \; (f = i!) \wedge (i \leq n).$$

Once we have established p as a loop invariant, the inference rule gives:

$$(f = i!) \wedge (i \leq n) \; \{\texttt{while} \; (\texttt{i} < \texttt{n}) \; \texttt{do} \; \texttt{S}\} \; (f = i!) \wedge (i \leq n) \wedge (i \geq n).$$

so that when the loop terminates $i = n$ and so $f = n!$. The Hoare triple style of presentation highlights what is being proven. Another style also illustrates what is happening altogether, not separately. We do this by annotating the code with assertions; these assertions are the postconditions of the preceding code and the precondition for the following code. For example:

```
i ⇐ 1;
f ⇐ 1;
// (f = i!) ∧ (i ≤ n)
while i < n do
        // (f = i!) ∧ (i ≤ n) ∧ (i < n)
        i ⇐ i+1
        // (f = (i − 1)!) ∧ (i ≤ n)
        f ⇐ f*i
        // (f = i!) ∧ (i ≤ n)
// (f = i!) ∧ (i ≤ n) ∧ (i ≥ n)
```

Example 6.7

Look for the loop invariant in the following pseudocode, which is for reading characters from input until a non-blank is found.

```
read(c)
while c=' ' do
        read (c)
```

This loop does not seem to have a loop invariant. In fact the loop invariant p is just TRUE, which is trivially proven. From the inference rule we conclude

$$(\text{TRUE}) \{\texttt{while } c = \text{' '} \texttt{ do read}(c)\} (\text{TRUE}) \wedge (c \neq \text{' '})$$

so that really all we get is $c \neq$ ' '. Note that this is a good example of why these arguments are only for partial correctness. We do not claim to prove that the loop terminates, but only that if it terminates then $c \neq$ ' '.

Example 6.8

Consider the problem of searching for a key K in a binary search tree (BST) rooted at T. We assume the reader is familiar with this algorithm. Recall that the nodes of the tree hold a key value and keys are ordered by "$<$". Every node t in the tree holds $key(t)$, as well as $L(t)$ and $R(t)$ which are the roots of t's left and right subtrees. An empty tree has root nil.

To simplify our formulas we define the notation "$K \in t$" to be the proposition $\exists x \in tree(t) : K = key(x)$, where $tree(t)$ is the set of nodes in the subtree rooted at t. Let $\mathcal{T}$ be the set of BSTs over some key domain D. $\mathcal{T}$ is defined recursively:

Definition T is the root of a tree in $\mathcal{T}$ if
1) $T \neq nil \rightarrow \forall K \in D : (K < key(T) \rightarrow K \notin R(T)) \wedge (K \geq key(T) \rightarrow K \notin L(T))$
2) $L(T)$ and $R(T)$ are roots of trees in $\mathcal{T}$.

Other definitions of BSTs are used but can be shown to be equivalent to this definition. Note that $tree(t) = \{t\} \cup tree(L(t)) \cup tree(R(t))$ and $tree(nil) = \emptyset$.

Our specification has $t = nil$ if the search is unsuccessful; otherwise t will be the root of the subtree where $K = key(t)$. This is the algorithm.

```
t ⇐ T;
while t ≠ nil ∧ K ≠ key(t) do
    if K < key(t) then
        t ⇐ L(t)
    else
        t ⇐ R(t)
```

To prove the code is correct we use the loop invariant p which is $K \notin T \vee K \in t$. Note that after the initialization, $t \Leftarrow T$, p is true by the law of excluded middle. We need to establish

$$p \wedge B \{ \text{if K < key(t) then } t \Leftarrow L(t) \text{ else } t \Leftarrow R(t) \} p \quad (6.1)$$

where B is $t \neq nil \wedge K \neq key(t)$. Therefore using the If-Then-Else rule we need to show

$$p \wedge B \wedge (K < key(t)) \, \{ \, \mathtt{t} \Leftarrow \mathtt{L(t)} \, \} \, p \qquad (6.2)$$

$$p \wedge B \wedge (K \geq key(t)) \, \{ \, \mathtt{t} \Leftarrow \mathtt{R(t)} \, \} \, p \qquad (6.3)$$

First note that the left-hand side of (6.2) is

$$(K \notin T \vee K \in t) \wedge (t \neq nil \wedge K \neq key(t)) \wedge (K < key(t))$$

$$\begin{aligned} &\equiv \quad t \neq nil \wedge (K \notin T \vee K \in t) \wedge (K \neq key(t) \wedge K \notin R(t)) \\ &\equiv \quad t \neq nil \wedge ((K \notin T \wedge K \neq key(t) \wedge K \notin R(t)) \\ &\qquad \vee (K \in t \wedge K \neq key(t) \wedge K \notin R(t))) \\ &\equiv \quad t \neq nil \wedge (K \notin T \vee K \in L(t)) \end{aligned}$$

so (6.2) is

$$(t \neq nil) \wedge (K \notin T \vee K \in L(t)) \, \{ \mathtt{t} \Leftarrow \mathtt{L(t)} \, \} \, K \notin T \vee K \in t.$$

And (6.3) is handled similarly. Now given that this proves (6.1) we can infer that after the loop terminates we have, using $\neg B$:

$$(K \notin T \vee K \in t) \wedge (t = nil \vee K = key(t))$$

$$\begin{aligned} &\equiv \quad (K \notin T \wedge t = nil) \vee (K \notin T \wedge K = key(t)) \vee (K \in t \wedge t = nil) \\ &\qquad \vee (K \in t \wedge K = key(t)) \\ &\equiv \quad (K \notin T \wedge t = nil) \vee FALSE \vee FALSE \vee (K = key(t)) \\ &\equiv \quad (K \notin T \wedge t = nil) \vee K = key(t). \end{aligned}$$

This is the expected postcondition for a search of a BST. Note $t \neq nil$ if and only if the search was successful.

Example 6.9

Now consider the algorithmically related problem of searching a sorted array of distinct keys $A[1 \ldots n]$ using binary search. Note that a sorted array has a recursive structure similar to a BST: the subarrays $A[1 \ldots t-1]$ and $A[t+1 \ldots n]$ are both sorted arrays and further, for any $1 \leq t \leq n$:

$$\forall K \in D : (K < A[t] \to K \notin A[t+1 \ldots n]) \wedge (K \geq A[t] \to K \notin A[1 \ldots t-1])$$

where we let $K \in A[n_1 \ldots n_2]$ denote $\exists i \in \mathcal{N} : (n_1 \leq i \leq n_2) \wedge (K = A[i])$. In the code mid(i,j) computes the midpoint $\lfloor \frac{i+j}{2} \rfloor$.

```
i ⇐ 1;   j ⇐ n
while i ≤ j ∧ K ≠ A[mid(i,j)] do
    if K < A[mid(i,j)] then
            j ⇐ mid(i,j)-1
    else
            i ⇐ mid(i,j)+1
if i>j then t ⇐ 0 else t ⇐ mid(i,j)
```

Of course we would not usually recompute mid(i,j) but we wish to emphasize the analogous structure of these two search algorithms. To see the parallelism note that "A[mid(i,j)]" serves as the "root" of the subarray $A[i \ldots j]$, and that "i ≤ j" serves as "t ≠ nil." In fact, with these substitutions the previous proof of correctness can be reused. In particular, loop invariant

$$K \notin A[1 \ldots n] \vee K \in A[i \ldots j]$$

can be proven the same way, leading to the postcondition

$$(K \notin A[1 \ldots n] \wedge i > j) \vee K = A[\lfloor \frac{i+j}{2} \rfloor]$$

which justifies the trailing **if** statement. (An unsuccessful search leaves $t = 0$.)

Further, our observation above about the recursive nature of sorted arrays, did *not* assume t was the midpoint and works for other choices. For example if mid(i,j) was i instead then we would also prove the correctness of searching with a left-to-right scan. (It can also justify the so-called "interpolation search" and other schemes.)

Both of the previous examples, BST-Search and Binary-Search, can be found in textbooks with recursive implementations. This is not surprising as there is a fundamental relationship between any **while**-loop and recursive procedures. Before discussing this we first discuss how to handle ordinary procedures

6.5 Proofs with Procedures

We will consider how to prove the correctness of code that calls procedures (or any similar mechanism for encapsulating code). A fuller treatment, that included function calls, is beyond the scope of this short introduction. The technique is general, even though our example happens to be recursive.

Every procedure will have a precondition that states what is true when that code commences; in particular, what is known about it parameters. The postcondition states what is true when that code terminates; again what is true of it's returning parameters. (Our examples will not access global variables, or have any other kind of side-effects, which simplifies the technique.) We need to prove that the postcondition does indeed follow from the precondition and the execution of the body of the procedure.

Further, whenever this procedure is invoked we must show that the precondition does hold for the parameters at the time of the call. If so we will be able to assert the postcondition holds for the parameters immediately after returning from the procedure. The beauty of this is that we do the exact same thing when the invocation is within the procedure, that is when it is recursive.

Example 6.10

Consider a procedure for computing binomial coefficients $C(m, n) = \binom{m}{n}$, $0 \leq n \leq m$, using the standard recursive definition: $C(m, n) = 1$ if $n = 0$ or $n = m$, and $C(m, n) = C(m - 1, n) + C(m - 1, n - 1)$ otherwise. The procedure `Binom(m,n,b)` has the pre-condition $0 \leq n \leq m$ and has the post-condition $b = C(m, n)$.

The code is annotated with assertions and these are justified using the If-Then-Else rule.

```
Binom (m, n, b)
// 0 ≤ n ≤ m
if n = 0 ∨ n = m then
      b ⇐ 1
      // b = C(m, n)
else
      // 1 ≤ n ≤ m − 1
      Binom (m-1, n, b1)
      // b1 = C(m − 1, n)
      // 0 ≤ n − 1 ≤ m − 1
      Binom (m-1, n-1, b2)
      // b2 = C(m − 1, n − 1)
      b ⇐ b1 + b2
      // b = C(m, n)
   // b = C(m, n)
```

Recall the annotation style where any statement (i.e., a block of code) together with the assertions before and after it, comprise a Hoare triple which we should be able to prove. In particular, the first and last assertions are the given pre- and postconditions for the procedure.

6.6　Loop Invariants and Tail Recursion

There is a simpler type of recursion that is common. *Tail recursion* describes a recursive procedure where there is only one recursive call and it is always last, that is no further statements are executed after the call returns. In this section we illustrate how to rewrite code with While-loops as tail recursive procedures. It also true that we can readily convert tail recursion into non-recursive looping code, but we do not illustrate it. What is relevant in this section is the relationship between loop invariants and the pre- and postcondition in such examples.

Example 6.11

Consider this recursive version of the BST search algorithm. It is annotated with relevant propositions. Very little has to be said since these propositions are virtually the same as those for the iterative code. Again, the first and last assertions are the given pre- and postconditions for the procedure. This procedure must be initially invoked using the root of the tree, BSTSearch(T, K).

```
BSTSeach(t, K)
// K ∉ T ∨ K ∈ t
if t ≠ nil ∧ K ≠ key(t) then
    if K < key(t) then
        // t ≠ nil ∧ (K ∉ T ∨ K ∈ L(t))
        t ⇐ L(t)
        // K ∉ T ∨ K ∈ t
        BSTSearch(t, K)
        // (K ∉ T ∧ t = nil) ∨ K = key(t)
    else
        // t ≠ nil ∧ (K ∉ T ∨ K ∈ r(t))
        t ⇐ R(t)
        // K ∉ T ∨ K ∈ t
        BSTSearch(t, K)
        // (K ∉ T ∧ t = nil) ∨ K = key(t)
// (K ∉ T ∧ t = nil) ∨ K = key(t)
```

Note that before a recursive call is invoked the precondition is met, so the postcondition holds afterwards. The $t \Leftarrow L(t)$ and $t \Leftarrow R(t)$ statements are artifacts of the fact we are not using a function call, but instead use t as a return parameter. We leave doing the same transformation of Binary Search as an exercise.

The main observation is, for this type of conversion, the precondition is the loop invariant p, and the postcondition is $p \wedge \neg B$, which is what is true after the While-loop terminates.

It should be noted that these examples are "natural" inasmuch as the underlying data objects — BSTs and sorted arrays — are "recursive." Hence a recursive algorithm suggests itself, and since it is tail-recursive it can be interpreted as iterative code. In Computer Science most objects are hierarchical, if not recursive, leading to clean code with natural proofs of correctness.

6.7 The Debate About Formal Verification

For at least forty years the value of formal proofs of the correctness of programs has been appreciated. Much research has been done on designing languages and systems that facilitate such proofs, and on the underlying mathematical logic. There has also been much effort to teach programmers to incorporate these techniques as they build software.

Work on correctness proofs has had only limited success. No large or even moderate-sized software projects have been formally proven to be correct. Additional reasons have been put forward for not using these techniques.

- that they are too sophisticated for most programmers.

- that they lead to straightforward algorithms and code reuse, stifling creativity.

- that they assume the specifications are correct when, in fact, the major source of real-life errors is in the specifications.

- that they prove the underlying algorithm is correctly implemented but the program runs on a complicated collection of hardware and software components which may or may not be correct.

The hope is that the process can be automated, since the inference rules can be applied mechanically. However the construction of the various preconditions, postconditions, and loop invariants seems to involve the programmer to some degree.

The good news is that a knowledge of formal verification techniques helps *inform* the programmer even when only informal verification is being practiced. We already mentioned that structured programming principles derive from the desire to create code that is easily (either formally or informally) proven correct. Similarly all good programmers will document their subroutines with the preconditions and postconditions for that code (that is, what is known about the parameters and about what the subroutine returns). And, in general, a good programmer will always know and document at key points the state of the program, that is, the things that must be true about the values of important variables.

Finally, a note about partial correctness versus correctness. It usually is not difficult to argue that a program, or a section of code, will terminate. For example, binary search will halt after $\lceil \log_2(n + 1) \rceil$ iterations. However it is a deep result (from Turing Machine theory) that we will never have a single technique that will always allow us to decide if a program will terminate. (This is known as the "Halting Problem" and is discussed in Section 12.6.)

Exercises

6.1 – The sequence rule could be used more widely and still be correct if it only required the postcondition of S_1 to *imply*, not to equal, the precondition of S_2. Express this revised rule formally.

6.2 – For this code present a loop invariant and prove it. Assume $n \geq 1$.

```
i ⇐ 0;
x ⇐ 1;
while i < n do
    i ⇐ i + 1
    x ⇐ x + x
```

6.3 – For this code present a loop invariant and prove it. Assume $n \geq 0$.

```
i ⇐ 0;
s ⇐ 0;
while i < n do
    i ⇐ i + 1
    s ⇐ s + i
```

6.4 – For this code present a loop invariant and prove it. Assume $n \geq 1$ and y is a constant.

```
i ⇐ 1;
x ⇐ 1;
while i < n do
    x ⇐ x * y
    i ⇐ i + 1
```

6.5 – Since $(i + 1)^2 = i^2 + i + (i + 1)$ you can compute $(i + 1)^2$ from i^2 by adding i, incrementing i and adding i again.

(a) Use this observation to write a pseudocode for computing n^2 by repeated addition, $n \geq 1$.

(b) For this pseudocode present a loop invariant and prove it.

(c) Apply the **while** inference rule to establish that it does compute n^2.

6.6 – For this pseudocode present a loop invariant and prove it, $n \geq 0$.

```
i ⇐ 0;
s ⇐ 2;
while i < n do
    i ⇐ i + 1
    s ⇐ s * s
```

6.7 – Consider the following puzzle. You begin with a bag of M white and N black balls, say 17 white and 10 black balls. Then you repeatedly randomly draw two balls from the bag. If the two balls are of opposite color, you put the white one back. If they are the same color, you put a black ball back in the bag. (Assume you have a large enough supply of extra black balls to always be able to do this.) Note that at each iteration the number of balls in the bag decreases by 1, so eventually there will only be one ball left. Presented as pseudocode we have:

```
m ⇐ M
n ⇐ N
while (m+n > 1) do
    a ⇐ randomly selected ball
    if (a is white) then m-- else n--
    b ⇐ randomly selected ball
    if (b is white) then m-- else n--
    if (a and b same) then n++ else m++
```

The puzzle is: What is the color of that final ball? It may seem that the answer depends on how the balls are selected at each step, but that is not so. For the particular example of 17 white and 10 black balls, the final ball must be white, regardless of the sequence leading to it. This remarkable conclusion is based on the loop invariant!

State and prove the appropriate loop invariant.

6.8 – This code computes the product $Y * Z$ of two positive integer variables by repeated additions. It is actually an ancient algorithm! For this the function `odd` is the simple parity check and `floor` rounds down to the next integer. For this code present a loop invariant, which will involve the quantity `Y * Z`, and prove it. Finally invoke the **while** inference rule to get the intended final assertion.

```
x ⇐ 0;
y ⇐ Y;
z ⇐ Z;
while z > 0 do
        if odd(z) then x ⇐ x + y
        y ⇐ y + y
        z ⇐ floor(z / 2)
```

6.9 – Consider the Fibonacci sequence of integers; $F_0 = 0, F_1 = 1,$ $F_n = F_{n-1} + F_{n-2}$, for all $n > 1$.

(a) Give simple iterative pseudocode to compute F_n for $n \geq 0$. State and prove the loop invariant.

(b) Give a simple recursive procedure `Fib(n, f)` which returns with `f` equal to F_n, for $n \geq 0$. Annotate the procedure, as discussed in the text. Note that this procedure does *not* exhibit tail recursion, so it does not lead back to (a).

6.10 – Consider an array such as in Example 6.9, but assume it is unsorted.

(a) Give pseudocode to determine the maximum element, using a simple left-to-right scan. State and prove the loop invariant.

(b) Give a simple recursive procedure `Max(A, n, max)` which returns `max`, for $n \geq 1$. It will first compute the maximum of the subarray of the first $n-1$ elements and then compare it to the last element. Annotate the procedure, as discussed in the text. Note that this procedure does *not* exhibit tail recursion.

Part II

Language Models for Computer Science

Introduction to Part II: Language Models for Computer Science

Language models are related to programming languages, which are central to practical computing. The study of language models addresses concepts and issues that are relevant to all programming languages. The field thereby seeks a better understanding of language in general, as opposed to a single language. In moving to this more general level, we follow our modeling strategy focusing on a relatively small number of widely applicable concepts. The resulting language models clarify issues about compilers, the software that translates your programs into executable form. The study of language models can also help you to learn and even design new languages.

Language models have another more abstract function. We use them to define problems formally. We will turn to this aspect when we have discussed more background.

In addition to modeling language, we will also be modeling computing machinery, by introducing simple abstract machines called automata. We will see some surprisingly close relationships between automata and language models. The study of automata also leads to the Theory of Computation. A category of automata known as Turing Machines provides a simple but apparently universal way to model what it means to compute. Then, given a model of what computation is, it becomes possible to talk about incomputability. That is, one can actually prove that for some computational problems there cannot be a general solution. From a practical standpoint, this work helps us to formulate real problems in ways that are computable.

Chapter 7

Language and Models

The aim of this chapter is to motivate the study of language models and lay out fundamental conceptual themes. We set the stage by relating language models to actual programming languages. Attention is also directed to relating our field of study with other parts of computer science. This chapter introduces formal notation that is needed and will also provide a foundation for the chapters that follow. The later sections address the major recurring questions that have driven the development of the field.

7.1 Programming Languages and Computer Science

Programming languages are central to computing. They lie between software and hardware, and connect the two of them. Software (a program) is written in a high-level language that people can understand. It is translated (compiled) into a machine language that some hardware understands. More precisely, the program is translated into a structured collection of commands that a particular kind of computer has been built to be responsive to. Just as it is important to understand general principles of hardware (architecture in general, as well as the design of individual machines) and general principles of software (software engineering, as well as particular applications), so too it is important to understand not just individual languages but ideas of language in general. For this purpose, we study models of language.

Why do programming languages take the forms they do and how does a computer process the programs you write? To gain insight into questions like these, we model not only language but also mechanisms for processing it. The language-processing models that one uses are simple, formal machines called **automata** and the field of study that seeks understanding of both language structure and processing is often called "Formal Languages and Automata." This field occupies Part II of this book.

The study of language models begins with the observation that the two key aspects of language are structure and meaning. As noted in the Preface, a good model strips away the details of a topic, to simplify it, as an aid to understanding. In the case of formal models of language, which is the study of language structure, we make a gross oversimplification: we begin by throwing out language meaning! Of course, meanings have to be addressed, but not right now, that is, not while we are in the midst of looking at structure. Expressing meaning can be done in various ways, many of them related to predicate logic, a topic introduced in Part I.

Practical treatment of the questions and issues raised in the study of Formal Languages and Automata takes place in courses on Programming Languages and Compiler Design. The modeling approach used here is good preparation for these practical topics. Books on compilers typically begin with several chapters on formal languages, and compiler tools are based directly on them.

7.2   Formal Languages

Models ignore details to allow a clear focus on particular aspects of interest. The field of formal language models makes a startling choice: it focuses on the statements themselves — the sequencing of their basic symbols — while it ignores the meaning, except in the most simplistic way. There is no attempt to specify or characterize the meaning of a sentence or a programming statement. (The study of formal languages can been extended, in several ways, to incorporate the meaning, or *semantics*, of sentences; discussions of formal semantics are beyond the scope of this book.)

As just noted, the field of formal models of language focuses on sequences of symbols. These will be called strings, a term that is neutral between the statements of programming languages and the sentences of human languages, and that may also serve to remind us that meaning has been stripped away. Recall in Chapter 1 we gave several definitions concerning strings, which we repeat here to keep this chapter self-contained.

The specification of any particular language begins with an **alphabet** which is defined to be a finite set of symbols, for which we adopt the name Σ. A **string** is defined to be a finite sequence of symbols from an alphabet; we say it is a string "over the alphabet." A formal language — called just a **language** hereafter — is defined simply as a set of strings. One can also say that a language is a subset of all the possible strings that can be formed using its alphabet. A key question will be, for any particular language or class of languages that interests us, how can we specify precisely which strings are to be included?

According to these definitions, everything is built up from symbols in some alphabet Σ. What is a symbol? For composing the strings (sentences) of English, Σ might be the words of English, a huge set. For a programming language, Σ might be the keywords and variables. While this might seem natural we adopt a far simpler view. English words have meaning, which we are not modeling. Instead the we regard a symbol to be an atomic (i.e. indivisible) unit. We will only be interested in the structure of the strings, in other words, the pattern of the symbols.

Example 7.1

Let $\Sigma = \{a, b, c\}$ be the set of symbols. Some strings over the alphabet Σ are ab, bbc and $abcba$. A language over Σ is $L = \{ab, abab, ababab\}$.

Example 7.2

Let $\Sigma = \{0, 1, +\}$ be the set of symbols. Some strings over Σ are 0, 1+1 and 10+11+10101. Such strings can be *interpreted* as sums of binary numbers, but other strings like +000+ are structurally problematic.

The **length** of a string is the number of symbols in it. In Example 7.1, the length of *abcba* is 5. Vertical bars, which in arithmetic denote the absolute value of a number, are used with strings to denote length, so we can write $|abcba| = 5$. A string can have length one: $|b| = 1$. Notice that *b* can mean either the symbol *b* or the string of length one consisting of the one symbol, *b*. Just as it is useful to have a symbol for the empty set, so here it is useful to have a symbol for a string with no symbols, the **empty string**, Λ, where $|\Lambda| = 0$. Note that Λ is a string and *not* a symbol in any alphabet.

Example 7.3

The set of strings over $\Sigma = \{a, b\}$ of length ≤ 2 is $\{\Lambda, a, b, aa, ab, ba, bb\}$.

Example 7.4

The set of strings over $\Sigma = \{0, 1, +\}$ that represent sums of 0's and 1's is $\{ 0+0, 0+1, 1+0, 1+1, 0+0+0, 0+0+1, \ldots\}$.

An important difference between these two examples concerns size: the language in Example 7.3 has a finite number of strings, 7 to be precise. In contrast the language described in Example 7.4 has infinitely many strings, so we had to resort to the use of ellipsis ("...") when attempting to list the strings. Many useful languages are infinite, such as the set of sentences of English and the set of permissible statements of C++. Even though a language may be infinite, recall each of its (infinitely many) strings is finite in length. Also the set of symbols is always finite.

There is one infinite language that we use repeatedly. For a given Σ there is an infinite language, Σ^*, associated with it:

$$\Sigma^* \text{ is the language consisting of all possible}$$
$$\text{strings over the symbol set } \Sigma.$$

For example, $\{a, b\}^*$ represents all strings over the specific symbol set $\Sigma = \{a, b\}$. Here is a list of them in order of increasing length.

$$\{a, b\}^* = \{\Lambda, a, b, aa, ab, ba, bb, aaa, aab, aba, abb, baa, \ldots\}.$$

Any language over $\{a, b\}$ is a subset of $\{a, b\}^*$. We will typically use letters near the end of the alphabet, like x and y, to stand for strings. We might have, for example, $x = abba$, in which case $x \in \{a, b\}^*$. It is now possible to restate the contents of Example 7.3 using set notation as follows.

Example 7.5

$$\{\Lambda, a, b, aa, ab, ba, bb\} = \{x \mid x \in \{a, b\}^* \wedge |x| \leq 2\}.$$

Since a language is a set of strings, like any set, we can represent it using extensional or intensional formats. Consider the language in Example 7.5; call it L. At this point, we have seen three different ways to represent L, written below as (i)-(iii). The first is simply an explicit list of elements, the *extensional* format. This format can only be used for small finite sets, otherwise we must use an ellipsis and sacrifice a rigorous definition. By contrast, (ii) and (iii) are *intensional* specifications of the same language. The first, (ii), is a loose description in English, while the other, (iii), uses standard terminology of formal languages, sets, logic and arithmetic. Increasingly, we will be using this last kind of specification, because it is compact, precise and versatile.

(i) $L = \{\Lambda, a, b, aa, ab, ba, bb\}$.
(ii) $L =$ the set of strings over $\{a, b\}$, of length no more than two.
(iii) $L = \{x \mid x \in \{a, b\}^* \wedge |x| \leq 2\}$

7.3   Language Operators

As just noted, languages can be specified extensionally, intensionally
and by description. It is also possible, and indeed useful, to be able
to build up new languages in terms of existing ones by making use
of various *operations on languages*. First, because languages are sets
(of strings), they can undergo all of the usual set operations. Given
two languages, L_1 and L_2, one can form their *intersection* $(L_1 \cap L_2)$,
union $(L_1 \cup L_2)$, and *set difference* $(L_1 \setminus L_2)$. Each language L has
a *complement* $\overline{L} = \Sigma^* \setminus L$ with respect to the universe of all possible
strings over its alphabet. Speaking of sets, note that just as there is
an empty set, there is also an *empty language*, which in fact is the
same thing as the empty set, written $\emptyset$, as usual. It is important to
distinguish between the empty language, $\emptyset$, and the empty string, Λ.

Example 7.6

$\emptyset$ is the empty language. It has no strings. The language $\{\Lambda\}$ has
one string, though that string is the empty string, having length 0.
The language $\{\Lambda, a, aa\}$ has three strings, of lengths 0, 1 and 2.

Another operation on languages, besides the set operations, is *concatenation of languages*, which is based on concatenation of *strings*,
introduced in Section 1.5. Remember that, for example, the concatenation of a and b is ab; the concatenation of ab and edc is $abedc$.
The order in which strings are concatenated can be (and usually is)
significant, so concatenation is not commutative.

Definition 7.1

Concatenation of strings.
If x and y are strings, xy is the concatenation of x and y. Occasionally
we will need a symbol for concatenation. We will use $\bullet$, so $x \bullet y$ is
the same as xy. For any string x, we have $x\Lambda = x = \Lambda x$; thus the
empty string is the identity element for concatenation. A string can
be concatenated with itself. The concatenation of x with x is xx,
sometimes denoted as x^2, and concatenating x with x^k gives x^{k+1}.
Also, $x^0 = \Lambda$ for any x.

Definition 7.2

Concatenation of languages
The concatenation of two languages L_1 and L_2 is written L_1L_2 (or $L_1 \bullet L_2$). It contains every string that is the concatenation of a member of L_1 with a member of L_2. That is,

$$L_1L_2 = \{xy \mid x \in L_1 \land y \in L_2\}.$$

Superscripts for languages behave analogously to those for strings. That is, for any language L, $L^0 = \{\Lambda\}$ and, for any integer k, $L^{k+1} = LL^k$. It then follows that $L^1 = L$, $L^2 = LL$, $L^3 = LLL$, and so on.

Since the concatenation of individual strings is not commutative, neither is the concatenation of languages. That is, L_1L_2 can — and usually does — differ from L_2L_1.

Example 7.7

Let $L_1 = \{a, aa\}$ and $L_2 = \{b, bb, bbb\}$. Then the concatenations L_1L_2 and L_2L_1 are as follows:

$$L_1L_2 = \{ab, abb, abbb, aab, aabb, aabbb\}$$
$$L_2L_1 = \{ba, bba, bbba, baa, bbaa, bbbaa\}.$$

Notice that there are 6 (the product of 2 and 3) possible ways to select strings to concatenate for L_1L_2 in Example 7.7, and all 6 results differ from each other. However, although the language L_2^2 has 9 (3×3) ways to select strings, the resulting overlap leads to L_2^2 having only 5 members: $L_2^2 = \{bb, bbb, bbbb, bbbbb, bbbbbb\}$.

Definition 7.3

Closure for languages
The *closure* of L is L^*, where $L^* = L^0 \cup L^1 \cup L^2 \cup L^3 \cup \cdots$; that is,

$$L^* = \bigcup_{i=0}^{\infty} L^i$$

Example 7.8

Let $L = \{a, bb\}$. Then $L^0 = \{\Lambda\}$, which is true for any language. Also,

$$L^1 = L = \{a, bb\},$$
$$L^2 = LL = \{aa, abb, bba, bbbb\}$$
$$L^3 = LL^2 = \{aaa, aabb, abba, abbbb, bbaa, bbabb, bbbba, bbbbbb\}$$
$$L^* = \{\Lambda, a, bb, aa, abb, bba, bbbb, aaa, aabb, abba, abbbb, bbaa, ...\}$$

The "$*$" or closure operator in Definition 7.3 is also sometimes called the (*Kleene*) *star operator*. The use of this symbol is consistent with the definition of Σ^* earlier. In each case, the operator produces a set of strings formed by concatenating any number (zero or more) of instances of its operand. That operand may be the alphabet Σ, a set of symbols, or L, a set of strings. If we regard a and b as strings of length 1 (as opposed to just symbols), then $\{a, b\}$ is a language, since it is a set of 2 strings, each of length 1. In that case the two definitions are in agreement that $\{a, b\}^*$ is the set of all strings over $\{a, b\}$. Definition 7.3 here implies that "$*$" is a unary operator on languages; that is, it operates on one language to produce another. For practically any language L (any except $\emptyset$ or $\{\Lambda\}$, to be precise) the language L^* has infinitely many strings.

We will assume certain precedence rules if parentheses are omitted with language operators. In particular closure will have the highest precedence, followed by concatenation, followed by ordinary set operators. So $L_1 \cup L_2 L_3^* = (L_1 \cup (L_2(L_3^*)))$.

7.4 Two Views of Alphabets and Language

For both human languages and programming languages, matters are complicated by the fact that we use symbols to represent two different kinds of things. For a human language, we might take the symbols to be the individual words. In that case we often call the symbol set a *vocabulary* (rather than "alphabet") and the strings of the language are its sentences, regarded as sequences of words. However, at a finer-grained level of detail, it is also true that each word can be regarded as a string composed of letters. (At least this is true in many human languages, though by no means all of them.) When we work at this lower level of analysis, the letters become the members of the symbol set, which is now more appropriately called an *alphabet*.

The situation is similar for programming languages, where symbols standing for two different kinds of things also prove useful for different purposes. Strings of (ASCII) characters make up what are called the **tokens** of a programming language. Tokens correspond to words of human languages and can serve as symbols. Some examples of multi-character tokens in C++ are for, <= and cout. The tokens in turn combine to form statements. But a token that is, say, a decimal integer is itself a string using the alphabet of decimal digits.

This dual nature can be confusing, but we never operate at two levels at the same time. To make this clear consider how a compiler processes, say, a C++ statement. It *first* reads it as a sequences of individual ASCII characters finding the strings that are the tokens and replaces each such string with a single newly-minted symbol. (This is called "lexical analysis" or "tokenization.") The *second* disjoint action is to process the statement as a whole with the tokens serving as single symbols.

Hereafter we will be working in more abstract domains so this dual nature will not arise.

7.5 The Questions of Formal Language Theory

It is easy to define a language to be a "set of strings," but that seems to be too general to be useful. How does a Computer Scientist use this theory? What sort of questions are we going to ask? Answering this will help us understand how we are going to proceed in the next few chapters and will motivate the choice of topics.

How is a language specified? The discussion of Example 7.5 emphasizes that languages are sets and can therefore be presented in extensional or intensional formats. The extensional form, which explicitly enumerates the elements, can only be used for small finite languages (though one may sometimes successfully communicate a simple infinite language to another person informally using a few sample strings and '...'). The intensional format uses a specification of the properties of the strings it contains. That statement may be informal or formal; here is an example of each.

$$L = \{x \mid x \text{ contains an equal number of } as \text{ and } bs\}$$

$$L = \{x \mid x \in \{a, b\}^* \wedge N_a(x) = N_b(x)\}.$$

With $N_a(x)$ denoting the number of occurrences of the symbol a in the string x, the informal and the formal versions specify the same language here. Note that the informal definition only indirectly implies a two-letter alphabet. Thus for each of them $abababba \in L$ and $aabaab \notin L$. Formal intensional specifications enable us to prove things about a language, and in that way can be more helpful than informal descriptions and partial listings of strings. However, none of these kinds of representation is suitable for answering the computational questions about language. In subsequent chapters we will therefore be introducing a variety of formal representations specifically devised for language, that do enable us to deal with such questions.

What are the key computational questions about language? Arguably the central questions are how to generate the strings and how to recognize them.

Generation: How can we generate the strings of a language? The interesting and useful languages are usually of unlimited size, in other words, infinite. Therefore we can *not* define them extensionally, simply by listing their strings. Rather, we need a finite — indeed compact — way to represent infinite languages. Then, once we have such a representation, the generation question arises: how can we use that representation to *generate* or display an unlimited number of strings of the infinite language in such a way that any particular string would ultimately be generated? This is a computational question. To answer it, we will need to specify our languages in a way that enables us produce, step-by-step, strings of the language. The formal rules for the steps needed to produce strings of a language are often presented as a *grammar* for that language.

Recognition: How can we recognize the strings of a language? The recognition problem is as follows: Given a language L and any string x over the alphabet for L, can we always correctly determine whether or not $x \in L$? This is a *decision problem*, where the output is "yes" or "no." For a particular language L, it may seem reasonable to think in terms a computer program that can take any string as input and tell whether it is in L. Such a program is said to *recognize* the language L. However we will not describe recognition in terms of a computer program but rather in terms of a simple *computing machine*, or *automaton*, which is built specifically for L. This allows us to calibrate how much "power" is needed for L.

What is the best way to specify a language? There is no best approach. We can define and represent a language L by giving an automaton that recognizes it *or* we can give a grammar that generates it *or* we can give an intensional format definition. The choice among these styles of representation depends on what we are trying to accomplish. We also want to show correspondences among them. We often translate one definition of a language to another dissimilar definition of it. For example, we will want to take a grammar that generates a language L and use it to produce an automaton that recognizes L. These translations will often be described in terms of *simulations*. These will be done mechanically, and are discussed in the coming chapters. The details will depend on the language class being discussed.

What is a language class? If Σ contains even a single symbol, then Σ^* contains an infinite number of strings, and so there are an infinite number of different languages over Σ. Some of these are more "complex" than others. How? Consider, for example,

$L_1 = \{x \mid x \in \{a\}^* \text{ and } x \text{ contains an even number of symbols}\}$

$L_2 = \{x \mid x \in \{a\}^* \text{ and } x \text{ contains a prime number of symbols}\}$

so that $aaaaa \in L_2$ but $aaaaa \notin L_1$. These look equally complex to the mathematician, since evenness or primality are just properties of integers. But they are quite different computationally. An automaton for L_2 will work harder than one for L_1, and a grammar for L_1 is easy but it is not even clear how to produce one for L_2.

One of the great achievements in the theory of formal languages, was the discovery that we *can* clearly state how and why some languages are more complex than others and that leads to the definition of a language class. We will impose some strong restrictions on how an automaton can be built — if we were still speaking in terms of computer programs those restrictions might be on the number and types of variables allowed. There will be some languages that can be recognized by these restricted machines, and other languages that are so complex that no such restricted automaton exists which can recognize them. Therefore a *language class* is a set of languages, each of which can be recognized by some automaton that abides by the restrictions. In other words, a language class corresponds to a type of restriction on how an automaton can be built!

In parallel to this, we will put restrictions on how grammars can be specified. We can define a language class in terms of the type of restriction on the form of the grammar — a language is in the class if there is a grammar for it of the restricted type. What is surprising is that we will find that exactly the same language classes can be defined in terms of automata and in terms of grammars!

We will encounter two major language classes: regular languages and context-free languages. This figure shows what is known about these classes. (Recall that a "class" is just a set so we can talk about one language class being contained in another language class.) It indicates that every regular language is also a context free language, but not vice versa. Also there are languages that are not context-free; these languages are more complex, in some sense, than context-free languages. We will demonstrate these relationships in the following chapters.

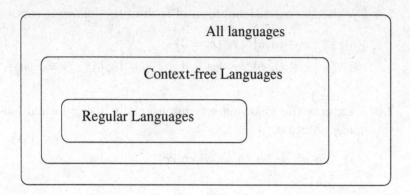

Figure 7.1: Containment of some language classes.

Exercises

7.1 – Give the length of each of the following strings.

   (a) b^3c^4

   (b) $(a\Lambda a\Lambda b\Lambda b)^2$

   (c) Λ^5

7.2 – How many of the strings over the symbol set $\Sigma = \{a, b, c\}$ are of length exactly 5?

7.3 – How many strings are there in the set $\{x \mid x \in \{a,b\}^* \land |x| \le k\}$? Notice that your answer should be a function of k.

7.4 – Let L be the language $\{a, bb\}$ and consider its closure, L^*.

   (a) How many strings in L^* are of length 4?

   (b) How many strings in L^* are of length 5?

7.5 – Write the extensional form of each of the following sets.

(a) $\{x \mid x \in \{a, b\}^* \land |x| = 3\}$.

(b) $\{x \mid x \in \{a, b\}^* \land |x| = 4 \land \exists y \in \{a, b\}^* : (x = aya)\}$.

7.6 – Express the following sets intensionally, using formal language notation.

(a) $\{aa, ab, ac, ba, bb, bc, ca, cb, cc\}$

(b) $\{aa\}^*$

7.7 – Use the notation of formal languages, sets, logic, and arithmetic to express in intensional form each of the following sets, using no English.

(a) The set of strings of length 5 over the alphabet $\{0, 1\}$.

(b) The set of strings over the alphabet $\{0, 1\}$ that begin with 1 and that represent, as binary numbers, the integers with values from 1 to 31.

7.8 – Let b and c signify the names of variables and let $+$ have its usual meaning of addition. Write an intensional definition, using your choice of either English or formal language terminology, of the set of all strings over $\{b, c, +\}$ that legally represent sums.

7.9 – Give a formal recursive definition of the language over $\Sigma = \{a, b\}$ where a string is in the language if it is a palindrome, like $abbbabbabbba$.

7.10 – Is concatenation of strings associative? Explain.

7.11 – Prove that concatenation distributes over union. Also give a counterexample to the conjecture that union distributes over concatenation.

7.12 – If L is the language of Example 7.5 and L_1 and L_2 are as specified in Example 7.7, give the extensional form of (a) $(L_1 L_2) \cap L$ and (b) $L_1(L_2 \cap L)$.

7.13 – Prove that if $L_1^0 \subseteq L_1 L_2$ then $L_2^1 \subseteq L_1 L_2$.

7.14 – Let L be any language. Is it true that $(L^*)^* = L^*$? That is, can applying the closure operator a second time ever yield anything not already obtained by applying it once?

7.15 – Show by means of a counter-example that the following statement is false: For any language L, the languages $(LL)^*$ and $L^* L^*$ are the same.

Chapter 8

Generative Models of Regular Languages

We argued in the early chapters that recursively defined expressions had a dual nature. The definition indicates that membership in the set is certified by recursively *decomposing* expressions into simpler subexpressions, until reaching some base cases. But computer scientists and most people have the more commonplace view of *building* an expression up from smaller ones. This building process need not be guided by some previous decomposition; anything that *can* be built up by the rules is an expression. In this chapter we explore this in more detail.

We will present two generative definitions of languages classes and show that they are the same class. We will call this class the class of regular languages. We will show they are equivalent by showing each is contained in the other. In the process we will need to introduce the concept of nondeterminism because of its close relationship to generative methods.

8.1   Generative Models

The recursive definitions of expressions found in Chapters 1 and 2 essentially specify how to generate expressions (from simpler

165

expressions). Since expressions are strings the corresponding sets of expressions are actually languages.

Example 8.1

Let L be defined as

- If $x \in B$ then $x \in L$,
- If $x \in L$ and $y \in L$ then $f_1(x, y) \in L$ and $f_2(x, y) \in L$,
- The first two rules define every element of L.

Assume B is some finite set of base case strings and f_1 and f_2 are two new string operators.

To see the parallelism recall the example of R the set of simple arithmetic expressions, in Chapter 1. Let B be the strings representing the variables, let $f_1(x, y)$ be the string "$(x+y)$," — a left parenthesis concatenated with x concatenated with a plus symbol concatenated with y concatenated with a right parenthesis — and let $f_2(x, y)$ be the string "$(x \times y)$".

There are two ways to "use" a recursive generative definition, that are computationally quite distinct. The first is *enumerative*. The definition allows us to systematically generate longer and longer stringers out of shorter strings. With care we can construct an exhaustive looping approach to combine all strings in all possible to create new longer strings. Such approaches have their subtleties and typically strings are generated repeatedly. However we are not concerned with this as it is so slow and repetitive as to be impractical.

However, the basic enumerative idea of building strings is the basis of this example which is focused on generating one string, not all strings. We use the recursive definition to specify a forward-building generative approach. This is called a "bottom-up" approach.

Example 8.2

This pseudo-code describes how to generate an w where $w \in L$, as defined in the previous example. The process verify-1(w), given a w, continues until it discovers that $w \in L$. In particular, if $w \in L$ it will "succeed" to discover it after a finite number of iterations, but if $w \notin L$ the process is doomed to an infinite loop.

> verify-1(w)
> $L' \Leftarrow B$;
> **while** $w \notin L'$ **do**
>   **choose** $x \in L'$
>   **choose** $y \in L'$
>   **choose** $i \in \{1, 2\}$
>   add $f_i(x, y)$ to L'
> **succeed**

Notice this pseudo-code makes use of a "**choose** $z \in A$" statement. To many readers this is intuitively correct but they would be unable to describe *how* the choices are made. The next section explains in detail what this means.

Next we briefly mention the second way to use a recursive definition.

Example 8.3

Below we describe a "top-down" recursive variation of the previous example. Given a w, it chooses how to decompose w and verifies it works. Note that this "fails" if it *can not* choose an appropriate x and y. (However, now it does not fail by going into an infinite loop.)

This top-down approach is confusing and unwieldy since there is no guidance on how to make the choices, especially since they are verified in the black-box of a recursive call. Top-down methods are good when there is guidance (such as in our discussion of parsing later) but we will avoid it for the most part. The thrust of our methodology is based on bottom-up motivations.

verify-2(w)
if $w \in B$ then
　　succeed
else
　　choose $x \in \Sigma^*$
　　choose $y \in \Sigma^*$
　　choose $i \in \{1, 2\}$
　　if $w = f_i(x, y)$ then
　　　　verify-2(x)
　　　　verify-2(y)
　　　　succeed
fail

Computation that relies on choices is the defining feature of **nondeterminism**. What matters is that the choices *can* be made, rather than discussing how they are made.

8.2　Nondeterminism: The General Idea

The good news about nondeterminism is that it is a powerful concept that enables us to simplify the way we represent some computations. The not-so-good news is that the idea itself can be a bit puzzling. In this section we introduce the notion of nondeterminism using further examples with pseudo-code. We use pseudo-code to ease into the topic; the pseudo-code will soon be replaced with other models.

Example 8.4

Let us start with a deterministic solution to a simple problem. Let J be a finite set of integers and let t be a "target" integer. This pseudocode decides if exactly 3 integers drawn from J add up to t. The summands need not be distinct.

```
for each a ∈ J do
    for each b ∈ J do
        for each c ∈ J do
            if a + b + c = t then succeed
fail
```

This code is simple and exhaustive.

We explicitly introduce the radical idea of an algorithm making choices. We do this by allowing this type of statement:

$$\textbf{choose } x \in S.$$

This next example shows that this type of statement does *not* make choices deterministically.

Example 8.5

We revisit the previous example. Here is a nondeterministic solution to the problem:

```
choose a ∈ J
choose b ∈ J
choose c ∈ J
if a + b + c = t then succeed
fail
```

But how do you choose each summand? And what if you choose the wrong ones? While these seem like reasonable questions we will not answer them. Instead we will say that there is no "how" behind the choice. And there is no "wrong" choice, in the sense of a mistake. We merely assert that if there are three such integers then this will succeed and it will only fail if three such integers can not be found. In other words, if the three numbers *can* be chosen then we assume they will be chosen and it will succeed. If there is more than one way to choose three such integers any of those would lead to success and there is no way to tell which one.

Notice, the process described by the pseudocode has the somewhat mystical ability to make choices that will turn out, in combination, to give a correct answer if it is at all possible to do so. This is the key idea of nondeterminism. Since it seems completely unrealistic, what, you may ask, is the value of even discussing it?

A nondeterministic approach should be regarded as a bare-bones description of *what* is being accomplished, but omits details of *how* it is being carried out. In fact, the nondeterministic approach can actually be implemented in some totally realistic ways, but — since they lack the magic described above — they are more complex and require more resources. We will describe two such implementations in the context of our numerical problem: parallel computation and backtracking.

The **parallel computation** approach assumes that we have as many parallel processors (multiple CPUs) as we will need. Let $j = |J|$. One processor is responsible for exploring each possible first number in a word, j processors in all. Each of these processors will use j additional processors to explore the various second numbers. And each of these will use j more processors to try out different third letters, for a total of $j + j^2 + j^3$ processors! If any of the third tier processors finds a sum of t then the entire computational effort stops successfully (even if other ways could also be found — it does not matter who wins such ties); if no such sum is found by any processor the entire collective computational effort fails.

The **backtracking** approach is used when you have a single processor, but want to exhaustively explore what would be possible with more.[1] Let $J = \{7, 12, 20\}$ and $t = 31$ For this problem, the code would tentatively choose a first number from the j possibilities, say 7. Then, in after recording that choice it picks a second number, say 7; so that now it is looking for sums starting with $7 + 7$. Then it tries various third numbers. But since $7 + 7 + 7$, $7 + 7 + 12$ and $7 + 7 + 20$ are not 31 it realizes that it must abandon the first two choices The algorithm now backtracks one step: it gives up on its most recent choice

---

[1]R. Floyd said "nondeterministic algorithms are conceptual devices to simplify the design of backtracking algorithms by allowing considerations of program bookkeeping required for backtracking to be ignored." *JACM*, 1967, p. 636.

and makes a new choice at that point. If all choices at that point are used up, it backtracks further. In the current context this means that it gives up on the 7 in second position (but at least for now keeps the 7 in first position) and tries a different second number 12 Now it once again tries different third numbers — getting $7 + 12 + 7$, $7 + 12 + 12$ and so on. These first one is bad but when $7 + 12 + 12$ is tried it is found to be t and the procedure succeeds. If there were no such three summands then the procedure would eventually fail, after an exhaustive search, that is, after trying all possibilities.

Both the parallel and backtracking approaches succeed when it possible to do so and fail otherwise. They differ greatly in details but they share the same nondeterministic characterization. The nondeterministic specification is thus a *model* of a solution in that it provides a relatively simple and succinct description of what is to be done, while ignoring those aspects of the implementation that do not currently interest us.

A "computation of code S" will mean any one of the many possible computational paths that S can following by exercising its choices. We say the code S is successful if there exists a computation of S that halts with a **succeed**, otherwise the computation of S fails, either with a **fail** or by being unable to succeed. The code S is unable to succeed if it goes into an infinite loop, or it is asked to choose from A and $A = \emptyset$.

Example 8.6

Consider a string oriented example. Let L^* be the closure of a given language L. Note that there is a recursive definition of L^* that will guide us: (1) $\Lambda \in L^*$, (2) if $x \in L$ then $x \in L^*$, (3) if $x \in L^*$ and $y \in L$ then $xy \in L^*$. This code fragment produces an $x \in L^*$.

```
x ⇐ Λ
choose continue ∈ {TRUE, FALSE}
while continue do
        choose y ∈ L
        x ⇐ xy
        choose continue ∈ {TRUE, FALSE}
```

Note that the decision to build further is itself a nondeterministic choice.

We demonstrate the power of **choose** by rewriting this code.

$$x \Leftarrow \Lambda$$
choose $k \in \mathcal{N}$
repeat k times **do**
    choose $y \in L$
    $x \Leftarrow xy$

Notice that it makes two types of choices: an integer to dictate the number of iterations, and the (sub-)strings used to build x. Observe that no matter how the choices are made x will be in L^*. Further note that for any specific $x \in L^*$ then *there exist* choices so that x can be built. (Of course, the body of the **repeat** loop is not executed if $k = 0$.) The first approach did not explicitly choose k, but the value of k was, so to speak, an emergent value made by a series of choices.

8.3   Regular Languages

In the previous chapter we saw many examples of "language opera-tors," operators that have languages as operands and languages as results. We can can use these operators to build up a class of lan-guages. In particular, in this chapter, we do this for a small fixed set of operators. We define the *regular operators* as these three: union, concatenation, and closure. Why these three? It is because the cor-responding class is of practical and theoretical interest. Of course we will need base cases, starting points from which to build larger lan-guages. Our base cases will just be singleton languages, those with just one string, and that string will be the empty string or a string of a single symbol.

Definition 8.1

Regular languages

Let $\mathcal{R}$ be the set of all *regular languages* over the symbol set Σ.

1. $\emptyset \in \mathcal{R}$.
   $\{\Lambda\} \in \mathcal{R}$.
   For every $\sigma \in \Sigma : \{\sigma\} \in \mathcal{R}$.

2. If $L \in \mathcal{R}$ then $L^* \in \mathcal{R}$.
   If $L_1 \in \mathcal{R}$ and $L_2 \in \mathcal{R}$, then $L_1 L_2 \in \mathcal{R}$.
   If $L_1 \in \mathcal{R}$ and $L_2 \in \mathcal{R}$, then $L_1 \cup L_2 \in \mathcal{R}$

3. There are no other regular languages over Σ.

In other words any set expression built from these bases cases and these three operator denotes a regular language

---

Example 8.7

Recall the precedence rules, so that $L_1 \cup L_2 L_3^*$ has these implicit parentheses: $(L_1 \cup (L_2(L_3^*)))$. Suppose L_1 is the base case $\{a\}$, a language of a single string of one symbol. Similarly, let $L_2 = \{b\}$ and $L_3 = \{c\}$. We can write this set expression as $\{a\} \cup \{b\}\{c\}^*$ which denotes a regular language. The shortest few strings in this language are $\{a, b, bc, bcc, bccc, \ldots\}$.

8.4 Regular Expressions

As defined regular languages are unwieldy, so we will find other more useful definitions ways to define them. Our first approach is with *regular expressions* (REs). REs represent regular languages directly, by just simplifying the set expressions. When we take languages like this

$$(\{a\}\{b\}^* \cup \{c\}^*\{d\})^*\{e\}.$$

they are difficult to read, even using precedence to suppress parentheses. It is for this reason that REs were devised. For the previous
set expression we will introduce this RE:

$$(ab^* + c^*d)^*e$$

which will *denote* the same language. Similarly

$$(\{a\}\{b\}\{b\} \cup \{c\})^* \cup \{a\}(\{b\}\{c\})^*.$$

will be denoted by the RE

$$(abb + c)^* + a(bc)^*.$$

These follow from this definition.

Definition 8.2

Regular expressions (REs) and their languages

Let R be the set of all REs over the symbol set Σ and for any $r \in R$,
let $\mathcal{L}(r)$ be the language that r denotes.

1. $\emptyset \in R$ and $\mathcal{L}(\emptyset) = \emptyset$.
   $\Lambda \in R$ and $\mathcal{L}(\Lambda) = \{\Lambda\}$.
   For every $\sigma \in \Sigma : \sigma \in R$ and $\mathcal{L}(\sigma) = \{\sigma\}$.

2. If $r \in R$, then $(r^*) \in R$ and $\mathcal{L}(r^*) = (\mathcal{L}(r))^*$.
   If $r_1 \in R$ and $r_2 \in R$, then $(r_1 r_2) \in R$ and $\mathcal{L}(r_1 r_2) = \mathcal{L}(r_1)\mathcal{L}(r_2)$
   If $r_1 \in R$ and $r_2 \in R$, then $(r_1 + r_2) \in R$ and $\mathcal{L}(r_1 + r_2) = \mathcal{L}(r_1) \cup \mathcal{L}(r_2)$

3. There are no other REs over Σ.

Definition 8.3

Equality of regular expressions

The notation $r_1 = r_2$ is used to indicate $\mathcal{L}(r_1) = \mathcal{L}(r_2)$.

The use of "expression" when talking about REs might suggest that we will present an algebraic approach. There are some algebraic laws, such as $r_1(r_2 + r_3) = (r_1r_2 + r_1r_3)$, for any three REs. However there are so few laws, and no powerful laws involving the closure operator, that we will not pursue that approach. We will, though, use the following identities to simplify some REs:

$$(\Lambda + r)^* = r^*, \quad \Lambda r = r = r\Lambda, \quad \text{and} \quad \Lambda^* = \Lambda. \qquad (8.1)$$

Example 8.8

What strings are in $L = \mathcal{L}((a + bb)^*)$? L is the language that the RE $(a + bb)^*$ denotes. This language contains all strings over $\{a, b\}$ in which all the blocks of bs must be of even length. Recall a block is a maximal substring, i.e. one that can not be made longer.

Notice that in part 2 of Definition 8.2, each new RE introduces a new set of parentheses. Therefore all the REs formed according to this definition will be fully parenthesized. The outermost parentheses are always unnecessary. Additional pairs of parentheses are unnecessary in some REs because of precedence. The precedence rules correspond to those for language operations: closure is highest, then concatenation and finally union, with lowest precedence. Moreover, their resemblance to ordinary algebraic expressions suggests the correct precedence, making them easy to read and understand. Further, associative operators group left-to-right.

It is worth noticing that "b" now has three related but distinct meanings. Within the symbol set "$\Sigma = \{a, b, c\}$" it is a symbol. In the phrase "the language $\{b\}$," it must be a string, since a language is a set of strings. The length of this particular string is one. Finally, to say "b is an RE" is to claim (correctly) that b is an RE, specifically the RE denoting the language $\{b\}$. The symbol Λ is the regular expression that represents the language $\{\Lambda\}$, while the expression $\emptyset$ represents itself, so to speak. Taken together, Λ and the symbols in

Σ are the building blocks of REs. (The RE $\emptyset$ does not happen to be used in this book's examples.)

The symbol "+" corresponds directly to the union of sets. Historically it is used since $\cup$ is not on the keyboard. It is often called the **alternation** operator, since it provides for alternatives. For example, $a + b$ is the RE for $\{a\} \cup \{b\}$, that is, the language $\{a, b\}$. Unlike concatenation, alternation is commutative; for example, $a + b = b + a$.

Example 8.9

The following table gives some REs and their languages. The expressions that use closure have infinite languages, so one can not list all their strings. In these cases we may list several of the shorter strings followed by "..." or we may specify an infinite set intensionally, as in the last row of the table.

RE	Corresponding Language
$a + bc$	$\{a, bc\}$
$a(b + c)$	$\{ab, ac\}$
$(a + b)(a + c)(\Lambda + a)$	$\{aa, ac, ba, bc, aaa, aca, baa, bca\}$
$a^*(b + cc)$	$\{b, cc, ab, acc, aab, aacc, aaab, aaacc, \ldots\}$
$a + bb^*$	$\{a, b, bb, bbb, bbbb, bbbbb, \ldots\}$
$(a + bb)^*$	$\{\Lambda, a, bb, aa, abb, bba, bbbb, aaa, \ldots\}$
a^*b^*	$\{\Lambda, a, b, aa, ab, bb, aaa, aab, abb, bbb, \ldots\}$
$((a + b)(a + b))^*$	$\{x \mid x \in \{a, b\}^* \wedge \lvert x \rvert \text{ is even.}\}$

A good way to improve understanding of REs is to try to translate back and forth between them and either English or set notation. In one direction, you would start with either a description in ordinary English for some set of strings or else with an intensional set specification for such a set. In either case you would try to write a corresponding RE, one that represents the given set. Alternatively, you could try to do the opposite. In the next few examples, we start from English.

Example 8.10

Find an RE for the language of all strings over $\Sigma = \{a, b\}$.

Since strings in the language are formed by zero of more choices we get the RE $(a + b)^*$. In fact, since "+" is commutative, as noted earlier, we could just as well give $(b + a)^*$.

Example 8.11

Find an RE that is simpler than $(a^*b^*)^*$ but represents the same language.

Example 8.9 shows that $\mathcal{L}(a^*b^*)$ is a superset of $\mathcal{L}(a + b)$. Taking the closure of each, it follows that $\mathcal{L}((a^*b^*)^*)$ must surely contain everything in $\mathcal{L}((a + b)^*)$. It can not contain more, since $\mathcal{L}((a + b)^*)$ contains everything over the two letter alphabet. So $\mathcal{L}((a^*b^*)^*) = \mathcal{L}((a+b)^*)$. Getting back to the original question: to simplify $(a^*b^*)^*$, write $(a + b)^*$.

Example 8.12

Find an RE for all strings of bs with at least two bs.

Since a string here can have any length except 0 or 1, the language is infinite, which suggests the use of closure. To get lengths of "at least 2" we start with lengths of "at least 0," for which we can use b^*, and then increase all lengths by 2, by adding bb. That is, b^*bb is an RE for the strings of at least two bs. The extra bs could have been added anywhere: $bbb^* = bb^*b = b^*bb$ are all correct answers. Note that each "*" applies only to the b right before it, according to the precedence rules.

Definition 8.4

An extension to the syntax for REs
Let r be any RE. Define $r^0 = \Lambda$ and for all $k \geq 0$, $r^{k+1} = rr^k$. Note this is a convenience but does not extend REs, in the sense of allowing new languages to be expressed.

An RE for all strings of length exactly 4 is $(a + b)^4 = (a + b)(a + b)(a+b)(a+b)$. Sometimes, as in the next example, we will use them to simplify the REs.

Example 8.13

Using the notation of Definition 8.4:

  (i) $(a + b)^k$ represents all strings of length k over $\{a, b\}$.
  (ii) $(a + b + \Lambda)^k$ represents all strings of length $\leq k$ over $\{a, b\}$.

Definition 8.5

Another extension of REs
Let r be any RE. The notation r^+ is called the "positive closure" and is defined as $r^+ = rr^*$. Therefore $r^* = \Lambda + r^+$. Another way to describe r^+ is to say that it stands for one or more repetitions of r, while r^* is zero or more repetitions of r.

Example 8.14

Write an RE for real numbers in binary notation as follows: one or more binary digits followed by a period (".") followed by one or more binary digits.
$$(0 + 1)^+.(0 + 1)^+$$

Example 8.15

Find an RE for all strings over $\Sigma = \{a, b\}$ in which the number of bs is: (i) exactly 2; (ii) at least 2; (iii) even; (iv) odd.

(i) For exactly two bs, just write them down and then allow for arbitrarily many as anywhere: $a^*ba^*ba^*$.

(ii) The case of at least 2 bs can be handled similarly, replacing each a in the preceding expression by $(a + b)$ to get $(a + b)^*b(a + b)^*b(a + b)^*$. However, some simpler expressions work too, such as $a^*ba^*b(a + b)^*$.

(iii) Since the even numbers are the multiples of 2, we might think of applying closure to the expression for 2 bs, to get $(a^*ba^*ba^*)^*$. However, this expression omits all strings with zero bs except Λ. A slightly simpler expression works: $a^*(ba^*ba^*)^*$.

(iv) By adding one more b (and any number of as) we get $a^*ba^*(ba^*ba^*)^*$ for strings with an odd number of bs.

Example 8.16

Describe the regular language represented by the RE $\Lambda + b + bbbb^*$.

Here we go in the direction opposite to that of the preceding examples: from an RE to English. By analogy with Example 8.12, $bbbb^*$ represents the strings of 3 or more bs. The rest of the expression takes care of lengths 0 and 1. A description of the language is "all strings of zero or more bs, except bb."

Example 8.17

Describe the regular language represented by the following RE.

$$0 + (1+2+3+4+5+6+7+8+9)(0+1+2+3+4+5+6+7+8+9)^*$$

Ignoring the "0+" out front, we have an expression that represents one or more decimal digits in which the first of them is not zero. Thus we have all the positive decimal numbers, without leading zeroes. The "0+" at the beginning allows the digit zero to appear alone. Our description of the language is "the set of nonnegative decimal integers."

8.5   Regular Expressions and Nondeterminism

Regular expressions are, by definition, a notation for defining sets of strings, that is languages. But as we discussed in Section 8.1 these recursive definitions can be turned around and be regarded as building processes. In fact we want to present the idea that an RE is nondeterministic "code" for generating strings! This section can be skipped. It is meant only to to broaden your scope, to see something in a different way.

To "execute" the code r we have to return to the recursive definition. Here we do not allow the RE to include a $\emptyset$.[2] Any r is either a base case or is built from smaller REs. If r is a base case we define the execution(s) this way:

$$\text{execute } r \quad \begin{array}{ll} \text{if } r = a \text{ this means} & \textbf{print } a \\[1em] \text{if } r = \Lambda \text{ this means} & \textbf{print } \Lambda \end{array}$$

For the more general cases we have recursive executions of subexpressions

---

[2]We omitted the rarely used base case $r = \emptyset$, since including it would have meant dealing with a confusing asymmetry (because $L \cup \emptyset = L$ but $L\emptyset = \emptyset$) and obscuring the point of this section.

if $r = r_1 + r_2$ this means	**choose** $i \in \{1, 2\}$
	execute r_i

if $r = r_1 r_2$ this means	execute r_1
execute r	execute r_2

if $r = r_1^*$ this means	**choose** $k \in \mathcal{N}$
	repeat k times **do** execute r_1

It is assumed that the symbols "printed" will be concatenated to the end of a single output string, which is initially Λ. If nothing is printed then the resulting string will be Λ. If a Λ is printed it will be undetectable, since it does not alter the output.

The main point of this section is that if we regard an RE as code for generating strings then it is nondeterministic code. Our comments about nondeterminism still apply here. In particular, regardless of what choices are made, the code r will always generate an x such that $x \in \mathcal{L}(r)$. Further, for any $x \in \mathcal{L}(r)$, r *can* make choices so that it will generate x.

Example 8.18

Recall that $r = a^*(ba^*ba^*)^*$ has $\mathcal{L}(r)$ equal to the language of strings over $\Sigma = \{a, b\}$ with an even number of bs. If we "execute" r it will begin by printing zero or more as. Then it will execute the ba^*ba^* code k times for some integer $k \geq 0$. Each of the k executions are independent; each will print a b followed by zero or more as followed by a b followed by zero or more as.

8.6   Grammars: The General Idea

The primary approach to language generation is to use *grammars*. Special generative techniques like REs, while useful, will not generalize in later chapters. A grammar is basically a set of rules, *grammatical rules*, that specify how to build up longer and longer strings in the language. These rules for specifying what is and is not in a language are more precise than the statements in traditional grammars of English and other "natural languages." However the basic ideas of natural language grammars inspired some of the formalisms.

A grammar begins with an enriched alphabet, which we call Φ. All the symbols of the alphabet that we use to form strings are included, $\Sigma \subset \Phi$. But we also include "metasymbols" that are not found in strings, but serve only during the building process to represent categories of strings. These metasymbols will be called *variables*. During the building process we will use strings over the alphabet Φ, so they will contain a mixture of variables and symbols from Σ.

A grammar will also have a set of substitution rules, called *productions*. A production specifies two strings, α and β, over Φ and is written $\alpha \to \beta$. We require $\alpha \neq \Lambda$. The intent of the rule is to specify how to transform a string γ_1 over Φ that contains α as a substring into a new string γ_2. When such a transformation occurs we call it a *derivation* step and it is denoted $\gamma_1 \Rightarrow \gamma_2$. The definition is:

$$(\gamma_1 \Rightarrow \gamma_2) \text{ if } (\gamma_1 = \mu_1 \alpha \mu_2 \text{ and } \gamma_2 = \mu_1 \beta \mu_2)$$

relative to a given production $\alpha \to \beta$. We also define the closure of the derivation step:

$$(\gamma \overset{*}{\Rightarrow} \mu) \text{ if } (\gamma = \mu \text{ or } \gamma = \mu_1 \Rightarrow \mu_2 \Rightarrow \cdots \Rightarrow \mu_k = \mu, \text{ for some } k > 1).$$

Example 8.19

Consider a grammar with $\Phi = \{a, b, A, B\}$ that contains these productions, among others:

$$ab \to AB$$
$$bab \to a$$
$$A \to bb$$

This grammar will allow these successive derivation steps to the string $ababAA$.

$$a\underline{bab}AA \Rightarrow aa\underline{A}A \Rightarrow a\underline{a bb}A \Rightarrow aABbA$$

so $ababAA \overset{*}{\Rightarrow} aABbA$.

The process of deriving a string with a grammar inherently involves choices, since more than one production might possibly be invoked at every step. Therefore we can cast the definition of $\gamma \overset{*}{\Rightarrow} \mu$ as non-deterministic code, using P for the set of productions.

$\mu \Leftarrow \gamma$
choose $k \in \mathcal{N}$
repeat k times **do**
$\qquad A \Leftarrow \{x \mid (\mu = \mu_1 \alpha \mu_2) \wedge (\alpha \to \beta \in P) \wedge (x = \mu_1 \beta \mu_2)\}$
$\qquad$ **choose** $\mu \in A$
return μ

We now have the concept that grammars can be used to specify a rule-based approach for transforming strings. However we now need to explain how this idea can be used generate languages. The basic idea is simple. One variable $S \in \Phi$ (so $S \notin \Sigma$) is designated as being a special *start symbol*. Suppose $S \overset{*}{\Rightarrow} \gamma$. Now γ may contain variables or it may not. In the latter case, $\gamma \in \Sigma^*$, we say that γ is in the language generated by the grammar.

Definition 8.6

The language generated by a grammar
A string x belongs to $\mathcal{L}(G)$ the language of G — also called the language that G *generates* — if and only if there exists a derivation $\psi_0 \Rightarrow \cdots \Rightarrow \psi_n$ such that

- $\psi_0 = S$ the start symbol of G,
- each step uses a rule of G and
- ψ_n contains only terminal symbols of G.

In other words $\mathcal{L}(G) = \{x \mid S \overset{*}{\Rightarrow} x \text{ and } x \in \Sigma^*\}$.

These basic notions of grammar will be sharpened in the next section. In later chapters we will alter the details to give two new and distinct types of grammars. The motivation from natural language can be found in some textbooks where such productions can be found:

$\langle sentence \rangle \rightarrow \langle noun - phrase \rangle \langle verb - phrase \rangle$

$\langle noun - phrase \rangle \rightarrow \langle article \rangle \langle noun \rangle$

$\langle noun - phrase \rangle \langle auxillary \rangle \rightarrow \langle auxillary \rangle \langle noun - phrase \rangle$

However the connections to natural languages are beyond the scope of this book.

8.7　Regular Grammars

In this section we present a specific family of grammars that are related to regular languages. We will do this by severely restricting the very general notion of grammars in the preceding section.

Definition 8.7

Regular grammars

A regular grammar G is a quadruple, (V, Σ, S, P), where

V　is the finite set of nonterminal symbols (also called variables);

Σ　is the finite set of terminal symbols, the symbol set for the strings of $\mathcal{L}(G)$;

S　is the start symbol, where $S \in V$; and

P　is a finite set of rules, each of the form $A \rightarrow \Lambda$ or $A \rightarrow bC$ where $A, C \in V$, and $b \in \Sigma$.

The restriction is on both the left-hand and right-hand sides of productions.[3] We will adopt the following *convention* to make it easier to read examples: elements from V will be upper-case letters and elements from Σ will be lower-case. Note that the complete alphabet in the previous section is $\Phi = V \cup \Sigma$. Lower case letters near the

---

[3] These are also known as "right-regular" or "right-linear" grammars. Minor variations on the restrictions allow regular grammars to have other types of productions, without changing them fundamentally.

end of the alphabet, like x, will be strings over Φ. The ideas about derivations and how a language can be generated from a start symbol are the same.

Definition 8.8

The language generated by a regular grammar
For ease of reference we repeat this definition here

$$\mathcal{L}(G) = \{x \mid S \stackrel{*}{\Rightarrow} x \text{ and } x \in \Sigma^*\}.$$

Example 8.20

Let $G_1 = (\{S, A\}, \{a, b\}, S, \{S \to aA, \ S \to \Lambda, A \to bS\})$. An example of a derivation is

$$S \Rightarrow aA \Rightarrow abS \Rightarrow abaA \Rightarrow ababS \Rightarrow ababaA \Rightarrow abababS \Rightarrow ababab.$$

The final step was where the variable S was erased by replacing it with Λ. The pattern in which this grammar builds strings is so restrictive that it is apparent that the language is easily described. In fact it can be described by a RE: $\mathcal{L}(G_1) = \mathcal{L}(r)$, where $r = (ab)^*$.

The convenient fact about regular grammars — it is not true of other grammars — is that all derivations have a simple structure.

> **Lemma 8.1** – For any regular grammar G if $S \stackrel{*}{\Rightarrow} x$ then
> either $x \in \Sigma^*$ or $x = yB$, where $y \in \Sigma^*$ and $B \in V$.

Proof: We prove this by induction on k, the length of the derivation $S \stackrel{*}{\Rightarrow} x$. If $k = 0$ then $x = S$, so $B = S$ and $y = \Lambda$ proves the basis of the induction. Assume that it is true of every derivation of length k. A derivation of length $k + 1$ must have been of the form $S \stackrel{*}{\Rightarrow} yB$ after k steps, otherwise it would have been unable to continue to step $k + 1$. If step $k + 1$ used the production $B \to \Lambda$ then $x \in \Sigma^*$. If step $k + 1$ used the production $B \to aC$ then $x = y'C$, where $y' = ya$. $\square$

Definition 8.9

Unit productions

A unit production is one of the form $A \to B$, that is when both A and B are variables. Normally a regular grammar cannot have any such productions. A *regular grammar with unit productions* allows the inclusion of these.

We will allow unit productions very briefly, to simplify our proof, and then show that they can be eliminated. Theorem 8.1 below will be a direct consequence of the next two lemmas.

> **Lemma 8.2** – If $L = \mathcal{L}(r)$ for any RE r then there exists a regular grammar G with unit productions, such that $L = \mathcal{L}(G)$.

Proof: Algorithm 8.1 finds such a G; we only need to establish the algorithm is correct. We prove this by strong induction on k, the number of operators in r. The basis is $k = 0$. There are three simple sub-cases which easily verified.

Assume the theorem is true for any RE with fewer than k operators, $k > 0$. Let r by any RE with k operators; the kth operator is either $+$, $\bullet$, or $*$. We argue that in all three cases the algorithm correctly computes G for r. By the inductive hypothesis the recursive calls on r_1 and r_2 will correctly compute the corresponding grammars.

Consider the case when $r = r_1 + r_2$. If $x \in \mathcal{L}(r)$ then either $S_1 \stackrel{*}{\Rightarrow} x$ or $S_2 \stackrel{*}{\Rightarrow} x$. The new grammar is essentially the union of the two computed grammars with the addition of two unit productions that permit either $S \Rightarrow S_1 \stackrel{*}{\Rightarrow} x$ or $S \Rightarrow S_2 \stackrel{*}{\Rightarrow} x$ Further it is clear that if $x \in \mathcal{L}(G)$ the first step of the derivation is one of the two unit productions and so $x \in \mathcal{L}(G_1)$ or $x \in \mathcal{L}(G_2)$; therefore $x \in \mathcal{L}(r)$.

Consider the case when $r = r_1 r_2$. If $x \in \mathcal{L}(r)$ then $x = x_1 x_2$ where $S_1 \stackrel{*}{\Rightarrow} x_1$ and $S_2 \stackrel{*}{\Rightarrow} x_2$. By Lemma 8.1 we know $S_1 \stackrel{*}{\Rightarrow} x_1 A \Rightarrow x_1$ for

Algorithm 8.1

Constructing a regular grammar from an RE
Input: A RE r such that $\mathcal{L}(r) \subseteq \Sigma^*$.
Output: A regular grammar $G = (V, \Sigma, S, P)$ with unit productions,
$\qquad \mathcal{L}(r) = \mathcal{L}(G)$

if r has no operators **then**
$\qquad$ **if** $r = a$ **then return** $(\{S, A\}, \Sigma, S, \{S \to aA, A \to \Lambda\})$
$\qquad$ **if** $r = \Lambda$ **then return** $(\{S\}, \Sigma, S, \{S \to \Lambda\})$
$\qquad$ **if** $r = \emptyset$ **then return** $(\{S\}, \Sigma, S, \emptyset)$
else
$\qquad$ **if** $r = r_1 + r_2$ **then**
$\qquad\qquad (V_1, \Sigma, S_1, P_1) \Leftarrow$ Algorithm 8.1 (r_1)
$\qquad\qquad (V_2, \Sigma, S_2, P_2) \Leftarrow$ Algorithm 8.1 (r_2)
$\qquad\qquad$ **return** $(V_1 \cup V_2 \cup \{S\}, \Sigma, S, P_1 \cup P_2 \cup \{S \to S_1,\ S \to S_2\})$
$\qquad$ **if** $r = r_1 r_2$ **then**
$\qquad\qquad (V_1, \Sigma, S_1, P_1) \Leftarrow$ Algorithm 8.1 (r_1)
$\qquad\qquad (V_2, \Sigma, S_2, P_2) \Leftarrow$ Algorithm 8.1 (r_2)
$\qquad\qquad$ **for** each $A \to \Lambda \in P_1$ **do**
$\qquad\qquad\qquad$ replace $A \to \Lambda$ by $A \to S_2$ in P_1
$\qquad\qquad$ **return** $(V_1 \cup V_2 \cup \{S\}, \Sigma, S, P_1 \cup P_2 \cup \{S \to S_1\})$
$\qquad$ **if** $r = r_1^*$ **then**
$\qquad\qquad (V_1, \Sigma, S_1, P_1) \Leftarrow$ Algorithm 8.1 (r_1)
$\qquad\qquad$ **for** each $A \to \Lambda \in P_1$ **do**
$\qquad\qquad\qquad$ replace $A \to \Lambda$ by $A \to S$ in P_1
$\qquad\qquad$ **return** $(V_1 \cup \{S\}, \Sigma, S, P_1 \cup \{S \to \Lambda, S \to S_1\})$

some A and that $A \to \Lambda \in P_1$. Therefore the new grammar permits either $S \overset{*}{\Rightarrow} x_1 A \Rightarrow x_1 S_2 \overset{*}{\Rightarrow} x_1 x_2$. Further it is clear that if $x \in \mathcal{L}(G)$ the derivation begins with S_1 and must contain a unit production $A \to S_2$ for some A at the point $S_1 \overset{*}{\Rightarrow} x_1 A \Rightarrow x_1 S_2$ where $x_1 \in \mathcal{L}(G_1)$ and that the S_2 will go to generate some x_2 where $x_2 \in \mathcal{L}(G_2)$; therefore $x \in \mathcal{L}(r)$. Note that $x_1 = \Lambda$ does not need to be handled as a special case.

Finally consider the case when $r = r_1^*$. If $x \in \mathcal{L}(r)$ then $x = \Lambda$ or $x = x_1 x_2 x_3 \ldots x_k$, for some $k > 0$, where $S_1 \overset{*}{\Rightarrow} x_i$ for each x_i. By Lemma 8.1 we know $S_1 \overset{*}{\Rightarrow} x_1 A \Rightarrow x_1$ for some A where $A \to \Lambda \in P_1$. Therefore the new grammar permits a derivation of x when $k > 0$:

first you follow the derivation $S \overset{*}{\Rightarrow} x_1 A$ using P_1, where A can be erased using P_1, but now you derive $x_1 S$ using the unit production; next you continue by following the derivation of x_2 using P_1 ending up with $x_1 x_2 S$, and so on, until S erases itself. It follows $x \in \mathcal{L}(G)$. We leave it as an exercise to show that if $x \in \mathcal{L}(G)$ then $x \in \mathcal{L}(r)$. $\square$

Example 8.21

Consider the RE $r = ab^* + c$. To allow this example to avoid renumberings we use this consistent numbering: $r_1 = a$, $r_2 = b$, $r_3 = b^*$, $r_4 = ab^*$, $r_5 = c$ and $r_6 = r = ab^* + c$.

$P_1 = \{S_1 \to aA_1, A_1 \to \Lambda\}$
$P_2 = \{S_2 \to bA_2, A_2 \to \Lambda\}$
$P_3 = \{S_2 \to bA_2, A_2 \to S_3, S_3 \to \Lambda, S_3 \to S_2\}$
$P_4 = \{S_1 \to aA_1, A_1 \to S_3, S_2 \to bA_2, A_2 \to S_3, S_3 \to \Lambda, S_3 \to S_2,$
$\qquad S_4 \to S_1\}$
$P_5 = \{S_5 \to cA_5, A_5 \to \Lambda\}$
$P_6 = \{S_1 \to aA_1, A_1 \to S_3, S_2 \to bA_2, A_2 \to S_3, S_3 \to \Lambda, S_3 \to S_2,$
$\qquad S_4 \to S_1, S_5 \to cA_5, A_5 \to \Lambda, S_6 \to S_4, S_6 \to S_5\}$

In each case $\mathcal{L}(r_i) = \mathcal{L}(G_i)$, where G_i is specified by its productions P_i, with start symbol S_i.

Lemma 8.3 – If $L = \mathcal{L}(G)$ for any regular grammar G with unit productions, then there exists a regular grammar G' such that $L = \mathcal{L}(G')$.

Proof: Algorithm 8.2 finds such a G'; we only need to establish the algorithm is correct. The **while** loop ensures that the set of unit productions exhibits transitivity.

Suppose $y \in \mathcal{L}(G)$ and a derivation of y uses k unit productions. We will argue that $y \in \mathcal{L}(G')$ by creating a derivation of x by removing the k unit productions, one at a time, from the original derivation of x. Suppose that we use $A \to B$, i.e., $S \overset{*}{\Rightarrow} xA \Rightarrow xB \Rightarrow x\alpha \overset{*}{\Rightarrow} y$, where α could be Λ, or C, or aC. In all cases with G' we can have $S \overset{*}{\Rightarrow} xA \Rightarrow x\alpha$ removing a unit production. By repeated application

Algorithm 8.2

Constructing a regular grammar without unit productions
Input: A regular grammar $G = (V, \Sigma, S, P)$ with unit productions
Output: A regular grammar $G' = (V, \Sigma, S, P')$, with $\mathcal{L}(G) = \mathcal{L}(G')$

$P' \Leftarrow P$
while $(A \to B \in P') \wedge (B \to C \in P') \wedge (A \to C \notin P')$ **do**
    add $A \to C$ to P'
for each $A \to B \in P'$ **do**
    for each $B \to \Lambda \in P'$ **do** add $A \to \Lambda$ to P'
    for each $B \to aC \in P'$ **do** add $A \to aC$ to P'
remove all unit productions from P'
return (V, Σ, S, P')

---

we create a derivation free of unit productions. We leave it as an exercise to show that if $x \in \mathcal{L}(G')$ then $x \in \mathcal{L}(G)$. $\square$

Example 8.22

Consider the final grammar, P_6, in example 8.21, but relabeled for readability:

$$\{B_1 \to aB_2, B_2 \to B_3, B_4 \to bB_5, B_5 \to B_3, B_3 \to \Lambda,$$

$$B_3 \to B_4, B_6 \to B_1, B_7 \to cB_8, B_8 \to \Lambda, S \to B_6, S \to B_7\}$$

The **while** loop will add the unit productions $B_2 \to B_4$, $B_5 \to B_4$ and $S \to B_1$. The first nested **for** loop will add $B_2 \to \Lambda$ and $B_5 \to \Lambda$. The second nested **for** loop will add these:

$$B_6 \to aB_2, B_5 \to bB_5, B_3 \to bB_5, B_2 \to bB_5, S \to aB_2 \text{ and } S \to cB_8.$$

After removing the unit productions, which are now unnecessary, we get:

$$\{B_1 \to aB_2, B_4 \to bB_5, B_3 \to \Lambda, B_7 \to cB_8, B_8 \to \Lambda, B_2 \to \Lambda, B_5 \to \Lambda,$$

$$B_6 \to aB_2, B_5 \to bB_5, B_3 \to bB_5, B_2 \to bB_5, S \to aB_2, S \to cB_8\}.$$

Notice that productions $B_6 \to aB_2$ and $B_3 \to bB_5$ can not be used by any derivation. This is because B_6 and B_3 are unreachable from S; they are now by-passed by transitivity.

Theorem 8.1 – If $L = \mathcal{L}(r)$ for any RE r then there exists a regular grammar G such that $L = \mathcal{L}(G)$.

Proof: It follows immediately from Lemma 8.2 and Lemma 8.3. $\square$

8.8   Unifying the Approaches

To prove the next theorem we introduce the concept of a *generalized regular grammar* that is forgotten as soon as the proof ends.

Definition 8.10

A **generalized regular grammar** G extends the definition of regular grammar so that each production is of the form $A \to \Lambda$ or $A \to rB$ where r is a regular expression over Σ. The latter is interpreted to mean that the variable A can be replaced by the string xB for any $x \in \mathcal{L}(r)$. A unit production indicates x is the empty string; we might write $A \to B$ as $A \to \Lambda B$ to emphasize this.

Note that every normal regular grammar is, without change, already a simple generalized regular grammar.

Theorem 8.2 – If $L = \mathcal{L}(G)$ for any regular grammar G then there exists a regular expression r such that $L = \mathcal{L}(r)$.

Proof: The proof follows from the correctness of Algorithm 8.3 which itself follows from this loop invariant claim. (The second **for** loop is used to simplify the later "each triple" test, since r_2 exists for every variable B. For that triple test we assume $A \neq B$ and $B \neq C$.)

Algorithm 8.3

Constructing an RE from a regular grammar
Input: A regular grammar $G = (V, \Sigma, S, P)$.
Output: A regular expression r over Σ, such that $\mathcal{L}(r) = \mathcal{L}(G)$.

Let V' be $V \cup \{S', H\}$, where S' is the new start variable
Add $S' \to \Lambda S$ and $H \to \Lambda$ to P
for each $A \to \Lambda \in P$ **do**
    Replace $A \to \Lambda$ by $A \to \Lambda H$ in P
for each $B \in V$ **do**
    if no $B \to aB$ in P **then** add $B \to \Lambda B$ to P
while $V \neq \emptyset$ **do**
    Remove some B from V
    for each triple from P: $A \to r_1 B, B \to r_2 B, B \to r_3 C$ **do**
        Add $A \to (r_1 (r_2)^* r_3) C$ to P
    for each pair from P: $D \to r_1 E, D \to r_2 E$ **do**
        Replace the pair by $D \to (r_1 + r_2) E$ in P
    Remove all productions using B from P
The only remaining productions are $S' \to rH$ and $H \to \Lambda$
return (r)

Claim: The loop invariant for the **while** loop is that the (currently modified) grammar generates the same language as the original grammar G.

The first thing that needs to be shown is that invariant holds when arriving at the loop, i.e. the preprocessing modifications do not change the language. Next we observe that if a derivation uses the variable B (which can not be the start variable or H) it must be that the derivation includes these three steps $A \to r_1 B, B \to r_2 B, B \to r_3 C$, for some A and C (possibly $A = C$). In the modified grammar grammar these can be simulated by one step, $A \to (r_1 (r_2)^* r_3) C$. Similarly any derivation of the modified grammar corresponds to an original derivation. (Note that if the last **for** loop simplifies a grammar with "parallel" productions; it can be done at anytime but must be done before returning.) □

Example 8.23

We convert the grammar with productions P into an RE:

$$P = \{S \to aA, A \to aB, A \to bA, A \to bB, B \to aS, B \to bB, B \to \Lambda\}.$$

First we add these productions $S' \to \Lambda S, H \to \Lambda, B \to \Lambda H$ and remove $B \to \Lambda$. Since there is no production that starts and ends with S we also add $S \to \Lambda S$. We now need to remove the original variables, which we will do in this order: A, B and then S.

Removing A will introduce two new productions: $S \to (ab^*a)B$, $S \to (ab^*b)B$. These two will immediately be replaced by $S \to (ab^*a + ab^*b)B$. At this point $S \to aA, A \to aB, A \to bA$ and $A \to bB$ will be removed. Removing B will introduce two new productions:

$$S \to ((ab^*a + ab^*b)b^*\Lambda)H \text{ and } S \to ((ab^*a + ab^*b)b^*a)S$$

and $B \to aS, B \to bB, B \to \Lambda H$ and $S \to (ab^*a + ab^*b)B$ will be removed. At this point $S \to \Lambda S$ and $S \to ((ab^*a + ab^*b)b^*a)S$ will be replaced by $S \to (\Lambda + (ab^*a + ab^*b)b^*a)S$. Removing S will introduce this production:

$$S' \to (\Lambda(\Lambda + (ab^*a + ab^*b)b^*a)^*(ab^*a + ab^*b)b^*\Lambda)H$$

and $S' \to \Lambda S$, $S \to ((ab^*a + ab^*b)b^*\Lambda)H$ and $S \to (\Lambda + (ab^*a + ab^*b)b^*a)S$ will be removed. At this point there are only two productions, the above and $H \to \Lambda$.

However by the identities in equation 8.1, we can simplify the Λs and we get

$$((ab^*a + ab^*b)b^*a)^*((ab^*a + ab^*b)b^*$$

as the RE. Typically we would simplify the REs as we go along. Note that if we removed the variables in a different order we would get a different but equally correct RE.

8.9 Deterministic Regular Grammars

To motivate this discussion consider this example.

Example 8.24

Using the grammar from the previous example, generate $x = aabaabb$ and $y = aabaab$. Recall

$$P = \{S \to aA, A \to aB, A \to bA, A \to bB, B \to aS, B \to bB, B \to \Lambda\}.$$

Starting off, reading the target string from left to right, we see the first symbol must be an a and must be derived from the start symbol, so the first derivation step must be $S \Rightarrow aA$. Now the A must produce the next a and so the next step must be $aA \Rightarrow aaB$. Continuing in this way the derivation of either x or y is forced to start

$$S \Rightarrow aA \Rightarrow aaB \Rightarrow aabB \Rightarrow aabaS \Rightarrow aabaaA.$$

Now there is a problem. For both x and y we need to generate a b but there are two productions to choose from: $A \to bA$ and $A \to bB$. Since there is a choice, nondeterminism suddenly arises. For x we must choose the first production and for y we must choose the second one.

Clearly by "looking ahead" in such examples we can see which choice is the right one. However we can construct examples where looking ahead becomes more and more complex. In this section we show that instead we can always change the grammar so that you can derive any given string in the language without ever making a choice, and so no look-ahead is needed.

Definition 8.11

A deterministic regular grammars
A deterministic regular grammar G is a regular grammar but it is not allowed to have two productions $A \to aB$ and $A \to aC$, where $B \neq C$, for any $a \in \Sigma$ and any $A, B, C \in V$.

The grammar in Example 8.20 is deterministic.

Lemma 8.4 – If $L = \mathcal{L}(G)$ for any regular grammar G then there exists a deterministic regular grammar G' such that $L = \mathcal{L}(G')$.

Proof: Let $G = (V, \Sigma, S, P)$. We define $G' = (V', \Sigma, S', P')$ as:

$$V' = \{V_{\mathcal{B}} \mid \mathcal{B} \in 2^V\}$$
$$S' = V_{\{S\}} \in V'$$
$$P' = \{V_{\mathcal{A}} \to aV_{\mathcal{B}} \mid \mathcal{B} = \bigcup_{A \in \mathcal{A}} Z_{a,A} \text{ for all } a \in \Sigma, A \in V \text{ and } \mathcal{A} \neq \emptyset\} \cup$$
$$\{V_{\mathcal{A}} \to \Lambda \mid \text{ there exists an } A \in \mathcal{A} \text{ where } A \to \Lambda \in P\}$$

where

$$Z_{a,A} = \{Y \mid A \to aY \in P\} \text{ for every } a \in \Sigma \text{ and } A \in V.$$

Note that the elements of V' are subscripted with sets of elements drawn from V. (So V' can be exponentially larger than V.) Clearly G' is a deterministic regular grammar, by construction. What remains to be shown is that it generates the same language. The key idea is that any derivations with G and G' are closely linked, as detailed by this claim.

Claim: For every $x \in \Sigma^*$ and $A \in V$, $S \overset{*}{\Rightarrow} xA$ with G iff $S' \overset{*}{\Rightarrow} xV_{\mathcal{A}}$ with G' where $A \in \mathcal{A}$.

Proof of claim: This is proved by induction on k, the length of the derivation. It is true for $k = 0$ because of the definition of S'. Assume it is true for all derivations of length k, $k \geq 0$. Suppose that using G step $k + 1$ used $A \to bC$, so $S \overset{*}{\Rightarrow} xA \Rightarrow xbC$. And, by the inductive hypothesis we can say using G' we have $S' \overset{*}{\Rightarrow} xV_{\mathcal{A}}$, with $A \in \mathcal{A}$. Since $C \in Z_{b,A}$ we know that the deterministic next derivation step $xV_{\mathcal{A}} \Rightarrow xbV_{\mathcal{B}}$ will have $C \in \mathcal{B}$. For the second half of the proof (the "if" part), suppose that using G' step $k + 1$ used $V_{\mathcal{A}} \to bV_{\mathcal{B}}$, so $S' \overset{*}{\Rightarrow} xV_{\mathcal{A}} \Rightarrow xbV_{\mathcal{B}}$. Again, by the inductive hypothesis we can say using G we have $S \overset{*}{\Rightarrow} xA$, for any $A \in \mathcal{A}$. Since for every $C \in V_{\mathcal{B}}$ we know $A \to bC \in P$ for some $A \in \mathcal{A}$ we know that with G the next step $xA \Rightarrow xbC$ is valid for any $C \in \mathcal{B}$. The claim follows.

The claim shows that derivations with the two grammars are synchronized as long as there are no erasing productions used. To complete the proof of the theorem we observe that the second half of the definition of P' ensures that a derivation with G can halt if and only if a derivation with G' can halt. $\square$

Example 8.25

We convert the grammar from the previous example, into a deterministic grammar. It is $G = (\{S, A, B\}, \{a, b\}, S, P)$ where

$$P = \{S \to aA, A \to aB, A \to bA, A \to bB, B \to aS, B \to bB, B \to \Lambda\}.$$

For G' we have

$$V' = \{V_{\{S\}}, V_{\{A\}}, V_{\{B\}}, V_{\{S,A\}}, V_{\{S,B\}}, V_{\{A,B\}}, V_{\{S,A,B\}}, V_{\emptyset}\}.$$

and $S' = V_{\{S\}}$. The set of productions P' includes:

$$
\begin{array}{lll}
V_{\{S\}} \to aV_{\{A\}} & V_{\{B\}} \to aV_{\{S\}} & V_{\{S,A\}} \to aV_{\{A,B\}} \\
V_{\{S\}} \to bV_{\emptyset} & V_{\{B\}} \to bV_{\{B\}} & V_{\{S,A\}} \to bV_{\{A,B\}} \\
V_{\{A\}} \to aV_{\{B\}} & V_{\{A,B\}} \to aV_{\{S,B\}} & V_{\{S,B\}} \to aV_{\{S,A\}} \\
V_{\{A\}} \to bV_{\{A,B\}} & V_{\{A,B\}} \to bV_{\{A,B\}} & V_{\{S,B\}} \to bV_{\{B\}}
\end{array}
$$

as well as $V_{\{S,A,B\}} \to aV_{\{S,A,B\}}$ and $V_{\{S,A,B\}} \to bV_{\{A,B\}}$ but these last two can be omitted, since $V_{\{S,A,B\}}$ "unreachable" and can not appear in any possible derivation. We also include in P'

$$V_{\{B\}} \to \Lambda, V_{\{A,B\}} \to \Lambda, V_{\{S,B\}} \to \Lambda$$

as well as the unreachable $V_{\{S,A,B\}} \to \Lambda$, which can be omitted. Note that $V_{\emptyset}$ will never appear in any valid derivation, so productions involving it can also be omitted.

Finally consider this alternative definition of $\mathcal{L}(G)$.

Definition 8.12

Language generate by a regular grammar
Let $G = (V, \Sigma, S, P)$. Let $G_A = (V, \Sigma, A, P)$, the same grammar but using the variable A as the start symbol. We can define $\mathcal{L}(G_A)$ recursively:

1. If $A \to \Lambda \in P$ then $\Lambda \in \mathcal{L}(G_A)$.

2. If $A \to aB \in P$ and $x \in \mathcal{L}(G_B)$ then $ax \in \mathcal{L}(G_A)$.

3. There are no other strings in $\mathcal{L}(G_A)$.

Of course, $\mathcal{L}(G) = \mathcal{L}(G_S)$.

This definition is the same regardless of whether G is deterministic or nondeterministic. This helps explain the close relationship between deterministic and nondeterministic grammars, and their utility i.e., how to generate a target string. The reason for emphasizing this is to contrast it with the regular expression situation. Regular expressions do *not* admit such an analogous deterministic model. ("Deterministic regular expressions" can be defined but they are not analogous in the way grammars are. Further questions about them are computationally challenging and beyond the scope of this book.) This explains, in part, why REs will not be extended in later chapters and grammars will be. It also explains why in the next chapter our discussion of automata is based on grammars and not on REs.

8.10   Summary

The theorems in this chapter, taken together, prove that the following statements are true:

L is regular iff there exists a regular expression r such that $L = \mathcal{L}(r)$.

L is regular iff there exists a regular grammar G such that $L = \mathcal{L}(G)$.

L is regular iff there exists a deterministic regular grammar G such that $L = \mathcal{L}(G)$.

The first is true since the definitions are the same, just using different notation. The second follows from first and Theorems 8.1 and 8.2. The third follows from the second and Lemma 8.4 and the fact a deterministic regular grammar is still a regular grammar.

The proofs in this chapter have a common character, which we chose to emphasize with the last two proofs. The theorems are all of the type "If a language exists relative to model A then the language also exists relative to model B." Such theorems are usually paraphrased as "model B is as powerful as model A." The proofs are constructive, actually showing how, given an instance of model A, we can construct an equally expressive instance of model B. Such newly constructed instances are said to "simulate" the instance of model A.

The notion of **simulation** is made explicit when we can prove a claim of the type that shows exactly how the second instance is keeping track of the behavior of the first instance. In the last two proofs these claims are explicit. In the earlier proofs we used a series of piecewise claims. This technique is well-known in the theory of computation and will be revisited in later chapters.

Exercises

8.1 – Write down all strings of length 3 in each of the following regular languages, where $S_1 = \{a\}$, $S_2 = \{b\}$ and $S_3 = \{c\}$.

(a) $S_1 \cup S_2 S_3^*$

(b) $(S_1 \cup S_2) S_3^*$

(c) $(S_1 \cup S_2 S_3)^*$

8.2 – In each case, write the set of strings of length 5 in the language of the RE.

(a) $a^*(b + cc)$

(b) $a + bb^*$

(c) $a^* b^*$

8.3 – For each of the following REs, r, give the language $\{x | x \in \mathcal{L}(r) \wedge |x| = 3\}$.

(a) $a + bc^*$

(b) $(a + b)c^*$

(c) $(a + bc)^*$

8.4 – Simplify each of these REs by writing another RE with fewer operators that represents the same language.

(a) $a + a^*$

(b) $a + aa^*$

(c) a^*a^*

(d) $(a^*b^*c^*)^*$

8.5 – Let $L = \mathcal{L}((aaa + aaaa)^*)$. List all the strings over $\Sigma = \{a\}$ that are *not* in L.

8.6 – What is the shortest string over $\{a, b\}$ that is *not* in the language corresponding to $(a + ba)^*b^*$?

8.7 – Write REs for the following languages over $\{a, b\}$. In each case, the language your RE represents should contain all and only the strings described.

(a) The strings that do not end in bb.

(b) The strings in which there is no b followed immediately by b.

(c) The strings containing exactly one occurrence of bb.

8.8 – Give an RE for these languages over the alphabet $\Sigma = \{0, 1\}$:

(a) $L_1 = \{x \mid x \text{ contains } 010\}$.

(b) $L_2 = \{x \mid x \text{ does not contain } 010\}$.

(c) $L_3 = \{x \mid x$ contains exactly one 010$\}$.

8.9 – Give an RE for $L = \{x \mid x$ does not contain *baba*$\}$, where $\Sigma = \{a, b\}$.

8.10 – Write an RE for the strings used to represent real numbers. Use a minus sign for negatives and an optional plus sign for positives.

(a) Start by allowing any such string of digits with at most one decimal point, such as 1.2, -00.5, +.0, and 10.

(b) Continue part (a) but disallow extra leading zeroes but allow trailing zeroes to the right of the decimal point; a single leading zero before a decimal point is allowed. The language of your RE should include these examples, +3.77, 200.0, -3.000, -33.0007, -.666, and 0.01, but it should exclude 000.1.

(c) Continue part (b) by restricting the representations of zero to: 0, 0., 0.0, 0.00, etc.. Note that zero should not have a sign.

(d) Now include scientific notation, so that each number allowed in part (a) can be immediately followed by an E, an optional plus or minus and an integer, such as 2.3E-45.

8.11 – Convert each of the following REs into a regular grammar.

(a) $a + bc^*$

(b) $(a + b)c^*$

(c) $(a + bc)^*$

8.12 – Give a regular grammar for each of these languages, over $\Sigma = \{a, b\}$.

(a) the language of all strings ending in $abab$ or baa.

(b) the language of all strings that contain aaa.

(c) the language of all strings $x = yz$, where y contains an odd number of as and z contains an odd number of bs.

8.13 – Give a regular grammar for the language corresponding to the RE $a + b^*c$.

8.14 – Convert each of these regular grammars into a regular expression.

(a) $\{S \to aA, S \to aB, A \to bS, A \to \Lambda, B \to bA, B \to aA\}$

(b) $\{S \to aA, S \to \Lambda, A \to bS, A \to bB, B \to aS, B \to aA\}$

8.15 – Convert each of the regular grammars in the previous exercise into a deterministic regular grammar.

8.16 – Prove by mathematical induction that if L is a regular language then $\forall k \in \mathcal{N} : L^k$ is a regular language.

8.17 – Complete the last step in the proof of Lemma 8.2.

8.18 – Complete the last step in the proof of Lemma 8.3.

8.19 – Argue that Definition 8.12 agrees with Definition 8.8.

8.20 – $P = \{S \to aA, S \to aB, A \to bA, B \to bS, A \to \Lambda\}$, convert to a regular expression, removing S then A then B.

8.21 – $P = \{S \to A, S \to bB, B \to S, B \to bA, A \to bS\}$, convert to a regular grammar without unit productions.

Chapter 9

Finite Automata and Regular Languages

In Chapter 7 we stated that a fundamental computational problem for formal languages was *recognition*. The goal is to design mechanisms that can answer questions of the form: for a given language L and string x, is it true or false that $x \in L$? We will approach the problem by designing special-purpose "hardware" for each language, with no operating systems and no software. Each language L is to have its own machine whose only task is to take arbitrary input strings over the alphabet of L and for each such string decide whether or not it is a member of L. We call such a machine design an *automaton* (plural: automata). Therefore, each language that has an automaton has a complete computational model of a recognition process for that language.

In this chapter we introduce a simple way to specify a category of automata and we determine what class of languages such automata can recognize. In fact, it will be the class of regular languages. In later chapters these automata will be enhanced by extra mechanisms, to get more complex categories of automata that recognize broader — and equally important — classes of languages. One interesting and important aspect of this machine-design approach is that it allows us to compare the complexity (or simplicity) of language classes by comparing the complexity of the corresponding classes of automata.

Even though we speak only in terms of *design* and not about actual machines, these designs could readily be implemented as real circuitry. Electrical engineers routinely begin the design of hardware with the specification of an automaton. A computer scientist, in contrast, is more likely to translate an automaton into a computer program, which simulates its behavior. In fact, some theories of software engineering, specify a program's actions with an automaton. In either case, this formal theory is crucial in understanding the computational aspects of languages.

9.1   Finite Automata: The General Idea

An **automaton** is a specification for a *symbol processing machine*. It differs from the real-life machines in at least three important ways. First, it is only a *specification*, something we design but do not expect to build. Second, it operates on *symbols*, mathematical objects with no properties. Finally, it has a relatively simple internal structure allowing us to *prove* statements. In later chapters we will see more powerful formulations but in this chapter we will focus on the simplest finite model.

Informally, we can think of an automaton for any language L as a "black box." As input, such a box can be given any string x over the alphabet of its language. The input will be processed one symbol at a time, from left to right, with no ability to return to earlier symbols; i.e., like streaming input. For output purposes it has something like a green light that is on when — but only when — the portion of the string processed so far is a string in L. Consequently, the light may go on and off at various times as the string is processed. If the light is on when the end of x is reached, $x \in L$. The automaton's user understands that it recognizes (the strings of) L, even though the automaton itself is unaware of when the string ends. The mechanism of a black box can be quite complicated but for finite automata the internal mechanism is remarkably simple.

As an automaton executes, various changes occur in its internal configuration. Each possible internal configuration is called a **state**.

We do not ask about the details of the internal machinery that make one state different from another, but rather simply give names (like A, B, ... or q_0, q_1, ...) to the different states. The states can be regarded as a kind of internal memory for an automaton, inasmuch as it knows what state it is in. A **finite automaton** (**FA**) has a finite number of states and moreover has no other form of memory. Hence an FA can only remember a finite number of things and this finiteness places some limits on what it can do. (In later chapters, we will look at two other kinds of automata — pushdown automata and Turing Machines — that have state memory along with additional forms of memory.)

We begin by illustrating the operation of a finite automaton with a simple diagram, called a state transition diagram. Then the formal notation of finite automata is introduced to provide a rigorous way of talking about the diagrams. With this notation in hand, it is easy to write a short straightforward algorithm for how FAs work. Ultimately, it is this algorithm that provides the solution to the recognition problem.

A finite automaton can either be a deterministic model or a non-deterministic variant. These are referred to as a DFA or a NFA, respectively. We will start with the deterministic DFA model because it is more intuitive.

9.2 Diagrams and Recognition

We approach the study of DFAs by introducing the idea of a simple processing diagram called a **state transition diagram**. When DFAs are defined formally later, it will be clear that every DFA can be expressed as one of these diagrams. Moreover, the diagram has all the information needed to get back to a complete formal specification of its DFA. Therefore the two representations, one visual and the other formal, are completely equivalent.

A state transition diagram specifies a process that receives a string as its input and either **accepts** it or not. The set of strings that a diagram accepts is considered to be its language. Consider the state transition diagram used as the figure for Example 9.1. This diagram accepts precisely the two strings a and bc, as we shall prove below, but for now just have a look at its general appearance. The name "state transition diagram" comes from the circles in the diagram called **states** and the labeled arrows called **transitions**.

The rules for using these diagrams for recognition are similar to the King of Heart's reading instructions to the White Rabbit: "Begin at the beginning, and go on till you come to the end: then stop."[1] The beginning point in a state transition diagram is the **start state**. There is always just one of these, indicated by a short arrow pointing to it, not coming from any other state. The first symbol of the input is initially the "current" symbol.

At each step of the process, follow a labeled arrow, called a transition, that leads out of the current state, that is labeled with the current input symbol. The new current state is the one to which the arrow points, possibly the same as before if the arrow curves back to the state it comes from. Carrying out this step moves past the current symbol of input, making the next one current. The process then repeats. A double circle signifies an **accepting state**. A string that leads us from the start state to such a state is **accepted** by the diagram. When the machine is in an accepting state then, as described in the previous section, we can regard a green light as being illuminated. That is, if the end of input and an accepting state are reached simultaneously, the string is in the language corresponding to the state transition diagram. Unless this occurs, the string is not in the language.

These processing instructions, like the King of Heart's, go to the end of input and stop there. Where in the *diagram* one stops, however, is less easy to say. A state transition diagram can have more than one accepting state (see the diagram for Example 9.3). Also, accepting states are not "final" in the sense that if there is more input, the process will continue. Thus in Example 9.1 with input aa, after

---

[1]Quoted from *Alice's Adventures in Wonderland*, by Lewis Carroll.

going from state A to state C processing continues with a transition to state D, so the string is *not* accepted, even though we pass through an accepting state.

For each state in Example 9.1 we provided exactly one transition out of that state for each symbol in Σ. This important property can be restated as follows: for each state-and-symbol pair, there is exactly one transition. This is a required property for every deterministic FA.

Example 9.1

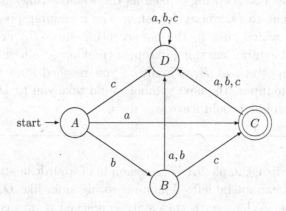

Let L be the language accepted by the 4-state diagram in the above figure. Input strings must be over the alphabet $\Sigma = \{a, b, c\}$. Prove that $L = \{a, bc\}$.

To prove equality of the sets L and $\{a, bc\}$, we need to show that each is a subset of the other. We first need to show that $a \in L$ and that $bc \in L$.

The initial state is A. If the first input symbol is a there is a transition to the accepting state C, so $a \in L$. When the first input symbol is b the machine makes a transition to the state B. Then if the second input symbol is c, there is a transition from B to the accepting state C, so $bc \in L$.

Next we need to show that $x \in L \to x \in \{a, bc\}$ or its contrapositive, $x \notin \{a, bc\} \to x \notin L$. In other words, we need to show that all strings *other than a* and *bc* are *not* accepted. We need to consider those other strings, and since there are infinitely many of them, we better not try them one at a time, but rather divide them into a few broad (indeed infinitely large) categories on the basis of some properties, like what member of the alphabet is the first symbol.

If the first input symbol is c then we go to state D. The state D has only a transition to itself, so all future transitions stay at D, which is nonaccepting. It follows that all input strings beginning with c end up stuck at D, like c, cab, $cccbac$, ... Strings that begin with a and continue (that is, excepting a itself as the whole string) go to state C and continue to D, where they stay. The remaining possible first symbol is b, which goes to the nonaccepting state B. From there if the second symbol anything except c (making bc altogether) you would end up stuck at D. Finally, if you reached state C before the end of the input, the next symbol would take you to D and any additional symbols would leave you there.

The state D in Example 9.1 is an example of a **sink**, a state which once entered cannot be left. A non-accepting sink, like D, is called a **trap state**. Whenever a trap state is reached it means that the input seen so far is enough to disqualify the entire string from being accepted. A single trap state in a diagram is always enough. There are accepting sinks as well; see Examples 9.6 and 9.7 a bit further on. Unfortunately a trap state, and especially all the transitions to it, clutter up our diagrams. We will therefore use *trap-free* diagrams, like in Example 9.2, where the trap state is not shown and any missing transitions are assumed to be to the trap state.

Example 9.2

Redraw the diagram of Example 9.1 without the trap state.

We omit not only the trap state but also all transitions to it. The resulting diagram accepts the same language, $\{a, bc\}$. Note, for example, the transition for symbol b from state B is implicitly to a trap state that is not drawn.

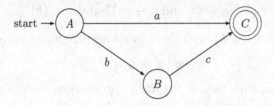

Since we are discussing DFAs, the omitted trap state and any missing transitions as implicitly present, and they can always be unambiguously reinstated. In fact it will hold for all the DFAs in this chapter.

Example 9.3

Draw a state-transition diagram for an automaton that recognizes the language L, where

$$L = \{x \mid x \in \{a, b\}^* \text{ and every } a \text{ precedes every } b\}.$$

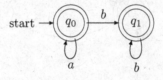

It is drawn without a trap state (the transition from q_1 on input a is to a trap state). Note that "every a" and "every b" can reference the empty set, so $\Lambda \in L$, $aaa \in L$ and $bb \in L$

In the set specification of Example 9.3, "every" is used twice to express universal quantification. As stated at the end of Section 4.4, the universal quantifier is always true over an empty set, so L includes all strings that contain no as and/or no bs. We could have given many other equivalent intensional descriptions of the language recognized by this machine, for example

$$L = \{x \mid x = yz \text{ and } y \in \{a\}^* \text{ and } z \in \{b\}^*\}.$$

$$L = \{x \mid x \in \{a, b\}^* \text{and there is no occurrence of } ba \text{ in } x\}.$$

$$L = \{x \mid x \in L(a^*b^*)\}.$$

The last description uses a regular expression, a technique that is explored further below.

Example 9.4

Draw a state-transition diagram for an automaton that recognizes the language

$$L = \{x \mid x \in \{a, b\}^* \text{and there is no odd block of } bs \text{ in } x\}.$$

where an "odd block of bs" means an odd number of consecutive bs (not contained in a longer block of bs). In other words, for x to be accepted by the machine, consecutive bs must be paired up, or else it ends up at a non-accepting state (possibly the trap state).

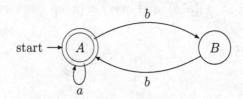

The opposite of acceptance is **rejection**. Now that we are omitting trap states, it might appear that there are two different ways for a diagram to reject strings. One results from a transition to an implicit trap state. This occurs for the string *abab* in Example 9.4 when trying to process its third symbol. The other is not new: if the end of the string is reached in a state that is not an accepting state, the string is not accepted. This occurs for the string *abbab* with the diagram of Example 9.4. Of course, if the trap state were made explicit we would see that these are the same idea.

Example 9.5

Give a state-transition diagram for the language L over $\Sigma = \{a, b, c, d\}$ which contains exactly the strings x such that (i) x begins with dc; (ii) x ends in a substring cd (but $x \neq dcd$); and (iii) the only occurrence of cd in x is at the end.

In the first of the two diagrams shown here, the straight arrows make it clear that all accepted strings must satisfy conditions (i) and (ii). After an opening dc takes us to the middle state, the self-loop keeps us there for any number of input symbols in $\{a, b, d\}$. This enforces rule (iii), so that the language of this diagram has *only* strings of L. However, the diagram does not accept *all* the strings of L, since it does not include such strings as $dcaaacbbbcd$, $dcccd$, and many other strings that meet the requirements.

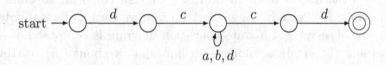

The trouble with the first diagram is that it assumes that from the middle state the occurrence of c takes us to a state that *must be* one symbol from the end of the string. That is fine if the next symbol is d, but if the next symbol is a, b or c, it is still possible to end up with an accepted string. The next diagram takes these additional possibilities into consideration.

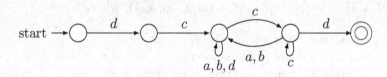

This section has introduced the idea of a state transition diagram. Back in the introduction to Chapter 1, we mentioned the broad applicability of a graph. As noted in Section 1.8, a graph is just a set of vertices and a set of edges, where the edges connect pairs of vertices. You could have taken the idea of vertices and used it here for what we have called states. Similarly the arrows that represent state transitions are also familiar to anyone who has studied graphs: they are just directed edges. In fact, they are labeled directed edges, with labels coming from the alphabet Σ. So from a graph theoretic viewpoint, these diagrams can be called labeled, connected, directed graphs in which each path corresponds to a string. But we do introduce something more: start and accepting states.

9.3   Formal Notation for Finite Automata

The diagrams that we have been using up to this point have the advantage of being easy to understand at a glance, but expressing precise ideas about them in ordinary English can lead to clumsy discussions. To remedy these shortcomings we turn to formal notation. We observe that a state-transition diagram is composed of (i) states and (ii) symbols, along with information about (iii) starting the recognition process, (iv) continuing it, and (v) accepting or not, when done. Formally, a **deterministic finite automaton** (DFA) is a model of these five things, so we say it is quintuple (or 5-tuple). We typically call it M, for "machine."

Definition 9.1

Deterministic finite automaton
A DFA M is a quintuple, $M = (Q, \Sigma, q_0, \delta, A)$, where

> Q is a finite set of states,
> Σ is a finite set of symbols,
> $q_0 \in Q$, where q_0 is the start state,
> $A \subseteq Q$, where A is the set of accepting states, and
> $\delta : Q \times \Sigma \to Q$.

The last line states that δ is a function from $Q \times \Sigma$ to Q. Recall $Q \times \Sigma$ is the set of all ordered pairs (q, σ) such that $q \in Q$ and $\sigma \in \Sigma$. One writes $\delta(q, \sigma)$ to express the result of applying δ to these arguments. The function δ is understood to be the **transition function** of the DFA, specifying the transitions in the corresponding state-transition diagram. That is, if the current state of the DFA is q and the current input is σ, then the DFA's next state is the value of $\delta(q, \sigma)$.

Recall for deterministic automata, the choice of next state is uniquely determined at each step; there is never more than one possibility. Moreover, there is never less than one possibility; that is, δ is a *total function*, with $\delta(q, \sigma)$ defined for all q and σ. While a trap state is omitted from diagrams, it is included in Q and used in δ to ensure δ is total.

Example 9.6

Specify a DFA $M = (Q, \Sigma, q_0, \delta, A)$ for the language $\{a\}^*$ and also draw the corresponding diagram.

$$Q = \{q_0\},$$
$$\Sigma = \{a\},$$
$$A = \{q_0\} \text{ and}$$
$$\delta(q_0, a) = q_0.$$

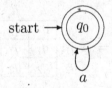

Note that Λ is a string accepted by this machine, as it should be.

The next example is motivated by the format of names like X1, TEMP, X3A and so on, that are used for variables, arrays and functions in programming languages. Typically such names are required to begin with a letter and to continue with letters and digits, as well as possibly some other characters, which we ignore for simplicity. As a further simplification, let $\Sigma = \{a, d\}$; think of a as standing for any letter of the alphabet and d for any digit. Then the accepted strings are those that begin with a. This readily leads to this diagram:

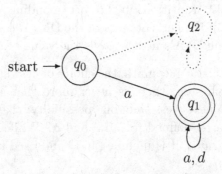

Notice that state q_2 in this DFA, shown with a dotted circle, is a trap state. The transitions to and from it are also shown in dotted form.

Example 9.7

Let $M = (\{q_0, q_1, q_2\}, \{a, d\}, q_0, \delta, \{q_1\})$, where δ is specified by the table below. Justify the claim that M accepts exactly the strings over $\{a, d\}$ beginning with a.

$$
\delta = \quad
\begin{array}{c|cc}
 & a & d \\
\hline
q_0 & q_1 & q_2 \\
q_1 & q_1 & q_1 \\
q_2 & q_2 & q_2 \\
\end{array}
$$

By Definition 9.1, the start state is found in the third position in the quintuple; as usual, it is denoted q_0. The fifth (last) element of M is always the set of accepting states; it is $\{q_1\}$ in this case. From the middle row of the table for the transition function, δ, you can see that q_1 is a sink, since both of its transitions are to itself. The same can be seen for q_2 in the bottom row. In addition to being a sink, q_2 (but not q_1) is a trap state, because it is also non-accepting. Clearly the first symbol of the input is crucial here. If it is d, the automaton M goes into the trap state and the string will be rejected. If the first symbol is a, M goes to the accepting sink, so it will accept the string, no matter what else follows. Thus, the language accepted by M consists of exactly the strings beginning with a, as intended.

One way to view the transition function, δ, of an DFA is that it tells us the state-to-state movement for each individual input symbol. To discuss state-to-state movement resulting from *strings* of symbols, we introduce a new function, δ^*, that works by using as many applications of δ as needed, one for each symbol in the string. In Example 9.7, the string ad can make M go from q_0 (via q_1) to q_1, so we write $\delta^*(q_0, ad) = q_1$. Sometimes called the **closure** of δ or the generalized transition function, δ^* has the following formal definition.

Definition 9.2

The closure of the transition function, δ^*
For a given DFA $M = (Q, \Sigma, q_0, \delta, A)$, δ^* is a function that takes a state and a string as input and produces a resulting state. That is, $\delta^* : Q \times \Sigma^* \to Q$ and

  (i) For any $q \in Q$, $\delta^*(q, \Lambda) = q$ and

  (ii) For any $q \in Q$, any $\sigma \in \Sigma$ and any $x \in \Sigma^*$, $\delta^*(q, x\sigma) = \delta(\delta^*(q, x), \sigma)$.

Part (i) of Definition 9.2 states that the empty string, Λ, has no effect on the DFA, simply leaving it at its current state, q. Part (ii) is for non-empty strings. First notice that x and σ are both variables, but they differ in that σ is a member of Σ and so stands for a single symbol, whereas x has a value in Σ^*, making it a string. Also worth noting is that part (ii) is recursive; it defines δ^* in terms of itself. To avoid circularity it defines the behavior of δ^* for each string, $x\sigma$, in terms of what happens with a slightly shorter string, x. Part (ii) says that to know what δ^* does with input $x\sigma$, first figure out what it does with x and then apply δ (whose behavior is known from the specification of M) to the resulting state and the one remaining symbol, σ. Next comes a simple but useful result, following directly from Definition 9.2, for applying δ^* to strings of length 1.

> **Lemma 9.1** – $\delta^*(q, \sigma) = \delta(q, \sigma)$, for any state, q, and any string σ of length 1. That is δ^* gives the same value that δ gives when applied to singleton strings.

Proof

$$
\begin{aligned}
\delta^*(q, \sigma) &= \delta^*(q, \Lambda\sigma) && \text{Substitution: } \sigma = \Lambda\sigma \\
&= \delta(\delta^*(q, \Lambda), \sigma) && \text{Part (ii) of Definition 9.2, with } x = \Lambda \\
&= \delta(q, \sigma) && \text{Part (i) of Definition 9.2}
\end{aligned}
$$
$\square$

Example 9.8

It was noted above that from the start state q_0 in Example 9.7, the input string ad should take the automaton M to state q_1. Show how Definition 9.2 formally confirms this result.

$$
\begin{aligned}
\delta^*(q_0, ad) &= \delta(\delta^*(q_0, a), d) && \text{Definition 9.2 with } x = a \text{ and } \sigma = d \\
&= \delta(\delta(q_0, a), d) && \text{Lemma 9.1} \\
&= \delta(q_1, d) && \text{Evaluating the inner } \delta \\
&= q_1 && \text{Evaluating } \delta
\end{aligned}
$$

The foregoing definitions — of an automaton, the transition function, δ, and its closure, δ^* — now make it easy to define the language recognized by an DFA as the set of strings that take the DFA from its start state to an accepting state using δ^*.

Definition 9.3

The language recognized by a finite automaton

The language $\mathcal{L}(M)$ **recognized** by a DFA $M = (Q, \Sigma, q_0, \delta, A)$ is the set of all strings $x \in \Sigma^*$ such that $\delta^*(q_0, x) \in A$. One says that M **accepts** the strings of $\mathcal{L}(M)$ and that it **rejects** those of its complement, $\Sigma^* \setminus \mathcal{L}(M)$.

Algorithm 9.1

Recognizing the language of a finite automaton.
Consider a DFA M processing an input string. The function *read* gets the next symbol from the input. This recognition algorithm returns **succeeds** for acceptance and **fails** for rejection. Note it correctly handles an empty input.

$$q \Leftarrow q_0$$
while more input **do**
$$read(\sigma)$$
$$q \Leftarrow \delta(q, \sigma)$$
if $(q \notin A)$ **then fail**
succeed

Writing a recognition algorithm is now remarkably simple if we allow ourselves to use the generalized transition function δ^*. Following Definition 9.3, to determine whether or not the input string x is accepted, one would just compute $\delta^*(q_0, x)$ and check whether or not it is a member of A. This approach assumes that we can implement δ^*. Although Definition 9.2 tells us exactly how to write a recursive function for δ^*, we will instead use the simple iterative Algorithm 9.1.

9.4 Relationship to Regular Languages

We have defined regular languages and given equivalent generative characterizations in the last chapter. We now show that the class of regular languages is exactly what DFAs can accept.

> **Lemma 9.2** – If $L = \mathcal{L}(G)$ for any deterministic regular grammar G then there exists a DFA M such that $L = \mathcal{L}(M)$.

Proof: Let $G = (V, \Sigma, S, P)$. We define the DFA $M = (Q, \Sigma, q_0, \delta, A)$ as follows: $Q = V$, $q_0 = S$, $A = \{p \mid p \to \Lambda \in P\}$ and

$$\delta(p, \sigma) = q, \text{ when } \{p \to \sigma q\} \in P$$

for every $p \in Q$ and $\sigma \in \Sigma$. If δ is not a total function we can add a trap state to Q; we leave this as an exercise. Note that δ is well-defined, since G is deterministic. The key observation is:

Claim: For every $x \in \Sigma^*$ and $A \in V$, $S \overset{*}{\Rightarrow} xA$ iff $\delta^*(q_0, x) = A$.

Proof of claim: This is proved by induction on k, the length of x. It is true for $k = 0$ because of the definition of q_0. Assume it is true for all x of length k, $k \geq 0$. Suppose when using G step $k + 1$ used $A \to bC$, so $S \overset{*}{\Rightarrow} xA \Rightarrow xbC$. And, by the inductive hypothesis, we can say when using M we have $\delta^*(q_0, x) = A$. Since $\delta(A, b) = C$ we know that $\delta^*(q_0, xb) = C$. For the second half of the proof, suppose when using M step $k + 1$ was $\delta(A, b) = C$, so $\delta(\delta^*(q_0, x), b) = C$. Again, by the inductive hypothesis we can say when using G we have $S \overset{*}{\Rightarrow} xA$. Since $A \to bC \in P$ we know $S \overset{*}{\Rightarrow} xbC$. The claim follows.

The claim shows that derivations and the machine's transitions are synchronized as long as there are no erasing productions used. To complete the proof of the theorem we observe that the DFA can accept x exactly when the derivation of x can end with an erasure.

□

Example 9.9

Consider the grammar $G = (\{C, D, E, F\}, \{a, b\}, C, P)$, with start symbol C and these production in P:

$$
\begin{array}{lll}
C \to a\,D & C \to b\,E & F \to \Lambda \\
D \to a\,C & D \to b\,F & \\
E \to a\,F & E \to b\,C & \\
F \to a\,E & F \to b\,D &
\end{array}
$$

Convert this into a DFA as described in the proof of the Lemma. The following transition diagram results:

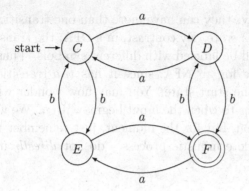

You should verify the claim for various x; for example $\delta^*(C, aab) = E$ and $C \overset{*}{\Rightarrow} aabE$.

Lemma 9.3 – If $L = \mathcal{L}(M)$ for any DFA M then there exists a deterministic regular grammar G such that $L = \mathcal{L}(G)$.

Proof: This a rare example of when a simulation techniques is reversible. For example it is obvious in the Example 9.9 that if we were given the DFA we could uniquely reconstruct the grammar. The same claim and proof still hold for this inverse mapping. $\square$

These lemmas taken with the characterizations in the last chapter immediately give this result.

Theorem 9.1 – L is regular iff there exists a DFA M such that $L = \mathcal{L}(M)$.

9.5 Nondeterministic Finite Automata

Nondeterministic finite automata (NFAs) share several aspects and properties of the DFAs formally defined in Section 9.3. Despite substantial similarity in the definitions, NFAs do differ from DFAs in one crucial way: they can have more than one transition for a single symbol out of a state. By contrast, in a DFA, the transitions leaving a state must all be labeled with different symbols. Thus the diagram below must be for an NFA, since it has *two* transitions labeled *a* both leaving the start state. You may now wonder what state this automaton goes to when the input begins with *a*. We will come back to that question, but for the moment, just remember (from Section 8.2) that nondeterministic processes do not *directly* model real-life processes.

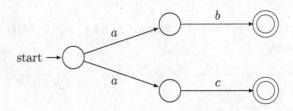

This NFA is a natural, straightforward representation of the language $L = \{ab, ac\}$. However this automaton presents a dilemma by having two transitions with the same label departing from some state. To have a chance of acceptance by this machine, of course, a string must begin with *a*. After the processing of the *a*, there are, momentarily, two possible current states. The next symbol then forces a resolution between them, assuming that it is *b* or *c*. Of course, the string *aa* is rejected. The crucial idea here is that we have introduced a *choice* of transitions.

We need to introduce formal definitions to state clearly how an NFA works. The only difference between the two kinds of automata involves the transition function, δ. For DFAs, the (output) value of δ was an element of the set Q, that is, it had to be exactly one state. For NFAs, however, a value of δ can be any subset of the states. For a particular state and input symbol, the number of possible next states may be zero, one, or more than one.

To be more precise about this difference between DFAs and NFAs, we can say that the difference concerns the *codomain* of δ. The codomain of any function is the set from which its outputs are chosen. Thus for DFAs the codomain of δ is Q. Since δ for NFAs has values that are *sets* of states, its codomain must be all the subsets of Q, that is, the power set, 2^Q (see Section 1.1).

Definition 9.4

Nondeterministic finite automata
A nondeterministic finite automaton, M, is a quintuple, $(Q, \Sigma, q_0, \delta, A)$, where Q, Σ, q_0 and A are just as for DFAs, that is, Q is a finite set of states, Σ is a finite alphabet, q_0 is the start state and A is the set of accepting states, but where

$$\delta : Q \times \Sigma \to 2^Q.$$

For various values of $q \in Q$ and $\sigma \in \Sigma$, the value of $\delta(q, \sigma)$ may be a set of zero, one, or more states. Cases of $\delta(q, \sigma)$ containing more than one state present a choice of what the next state will be. There will be at least one such case in each of the NFAs we present, to make the machine genuinely nondeterministic. However, a machine for which each of the $\delta(q, \sigma)$ contains zero or one state never has any real choices to make. Although such a machine can formally satisfy the definition of an NFA, it has a decidedly deterministic flavor and is readily rewritten as a deterministic automaton; see Exercise 9.1.

What strings are accepted by an NFA? Informally, a string x is accepted if there exists some choice of transitions, while reading the symbols of x left-to-right, that will take us from the start state to an accepting state. To make this formal we need to adapt the definition of δ^* to the case of an NFA.

Definition 9.5

δ^*, the generalized transition function extended to NFAs
For NFA $M = (Q, \Sigma, q_0, \delta, A)$, δ^* is a function that takes a state and a string as input and produces a resulting set of states. That is, $\delta^* : Q \times \Sigma^* \to 2^Q$, such that:

(i) For any $q \in Q$, $\delta^*(q, \Lambda) = \{q\}$ and

(ii) For any $q \in Q$, any $\sigma \in \Sigma$ and any $x \in \Sigma^*$,

$$\delta^*(q, x\sigma) = \bigcup_{p \in \delta^*(q,x)} \delta(p, \sigma).$$

Part (i) of Definition 9.5 is straightforward. In part (ii), the left side, $\delta^*(q, x\sigma)$, *means* the set of all states you can reach from state q by processing $x\sigma$, while the right side spells out how to *find* all these states: first find what states x can take you to (subscript on the union operator) and then, continuing from each of those, find the union of the states that you can get to in one more step with σ. For the case in which q is the initial state and $\delta^*(q, x)$ includes some accepting state, the machine accepts the string x. This leads to the definition of the language recognized by an NFA.

Definition 9.6

The language recognized by an NFA
The language $\mathcal{L}(M)$ **recognized** by an NFA $M = (Q, \Sigma, q_0, \delta, A)$ is the set of all strings $x \in \Sigma^*$ such that $\delta^*(q_0, x) \cap A \neq \emptyset$. One says that M **accepts** the strings of $\mathcal{L}(M)$ and that it **rejects** those of its complement, $\Sigma^* \setminus \mathcal{L}(M)$.

Example 9.10

Consider the language $L = \{x \mid x \in \{a, b\}^*$ and x ends with $ab\}$. This language contains, for example, the string $bbab$ but not $abba$. Draw simple state-transition diagrams for both a DFA and an NFA to recognize L.

First, here is a DFA for L. Although the machine is small — just 3 states — it is not straightforward to see how one might have thought of it. Even after it has been presented, it might be a challenge to characterize each state.

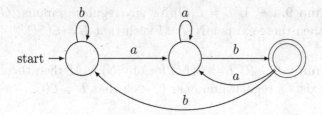

Compare the DFA to the following NFA that also recognizes L. Again we have three states, but now the diagram looks simpler and it is easier to see how it works.

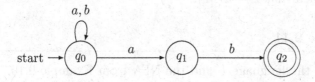

This machine simply loops until, nondeterministically, it chooses to verify that the final two input symbols are ab. The formal notation for this machine is

$$M = (\{q_0, q_1, q_2\}, \{a, b\}, q_0, \delta, \{q_2\}),$$

where δ is specified by the table below.

	a	b
q_0	$\{q_0, q_1\}$	$\{q_0\}$
q_1	$\emptyset$	$\{q_2\}$
q_2	$\emptyset$	$\emptyset$

with $\delta = $ at the left.

We have already seen the equivalence of deterministic regular grammar and DFA representations of regular languages by way of a simple two-way mapping between the representations. What is remarkable is that *exactly* the same mapping works in the nondeterministic case. Exactly the same proofs given for Lemma 9.2 and Lemma 9.3 work for these lemmas!

Lemma 9.4 – If $L = \mathcal{L}(G)$ for any regular grammar G then there exists a NFA M such that $L = \mathcal{L}(M)$.

Lemma 9.5 – If $L = \mathcal{L}(M)$ for any NFA M then there exists a regular grammar G such that $L = \mathcal{L}(G)$.

These lemmas, again, taken with the characterization in the last chapter immediately give this result.

Theorem 9.2 – L is regular iff there exists a NFA M such that $L = \mathcal{L}(M)$.

Example 9.11

Consider the language L and the NFA from Example 9.10. We can convert back and forth from this NFA and the regular grammar $G = (\{A, B, C\}, \{a, b\}, A, P)$ where the states q_0, q_1 and q_3 are identified with the variables A, B and C, respectively, and

$$P = \{A \to aA, A \to bA, A \to aB, B \to bC, C \to \Lambda\}.$$

The crux of the role of nondeterminism is highlighted in the above lemmas. Nondeterministic machines very mysterious when viewed as hardware, but they are very natural in this context. That is, regular grammars are related to NFAs in exactly the same way deterministic regular grammars are related to DFAs. If we regard regular languages in light of the essentially nondeterministic characterizations of the last chapter we might conclude that NFAs are the more natural machine model. And perhaps they are! But the real-life utility of a deterministic machine model gives primacy to DFAs.

Algorithm 9.2 gives another approach to define $\mathcal{L}(M)$. It is instructive to see just how similar this approach is to the deterministic Algorithm 9.1.

We conclude with a consequence of these theorems.

Algorithm 9.2

Recognizing the language of a nondeterministic FA.
Let M be an NFA and let x be the input string. This nondeterministic pseudo-code completes successfully exactly when $x \in \mathcal{L}(M)$. Thus the algorithm succeeds when $q \in A$ is true. Note it can also fail if every possible computation involves trying to make a transition using an empty set of states (because the **choose** would fail).

$$q \Leftarrow q_0$$
while more input **do**
     $read(\sigma)$
     choose $q \in \delta(q, \sigma)$
if $(q \notin A)$ **then fail**
succeed

Theorem 9.3 – $L = \mathcal{L}(M_1)$ for some DFA M_1 iff $L = \mathcal{L}(M_2)$ for some NFA M_2.

Proof: This is immediate since L is regular, regardless of the machine model. But we can give more constructive details.

If we start with M_1 we observe it is already an NFA; an NFA with singleton sets for all values of the transition function, corresponding to the single values of the DFA's transition function. If we start with the NFA M_2 we can convert it into a regular grammar, the regular grammar can be converted into a deterministic regular grammar, and that can be converted into a DFA. $\square$

It is instructive to recall that converting a regular grammar into a deterministic can result in an exponential blow-up in the number of reachable variables. (Only reachable variables need be used in the construction of the DFA.) Hence the number of states resulting from the method given in the proof can be exponentially larger than the number in the original NFA. It can be shown, by example, that sometimes a corresponding DFA must be exponentially larger; see exercise 9.26.

9.6   Properties of Regular Languages

Recall that at this point if a language is known to be regular it follows that it can be generated by a RE, a regular grammar and a deterministic regular grammar, and it can be recognized by a DFA and NFA. Further we have algorithmic techniques to translate from one format to any other. In this section we will use these representations to explore closure properties of the class of regular grammars.

An language operator is said to be closed for a language class if applying it to languages in that class produces a language in the same class. For example, if we take any regular languages L_1 and L_2 then their intersection $L_1 \cap L_2$ is also a regular language, as shown below. Example 9.12 indicates the potential applicability of the closure properties.

Example 9.12

We want to design an FA for the following language over $\Sigma = \{a, b\}$:

$$L = \{x \mid x \text{ is an } a \text{ followed by zero or more } bs \wedge x \text{ is a } b \\ \text{ preceded by zero or more } as\}.$$

It is easy to see that $L = L_1 \cap L_2$ where

$$L_1 = \{x \mid x \text{ is an } a \text{ followed by zero or more } bs\}.$$

$$L_2 = \{x \mid x \text{ is a } b \text{ preceded by zero or more } as\}.$$

Perhaps if we can design FAs for L_1 and L_2 we can use those to design one for L.

Theorem 9.4 – If L_1 and L_2 are regular languages then $L = L_1 \cup L_2$ is a regular language.

Proof: Since they are both regular we know that $L_1 = \mathcal{L}(G_1)$ and $L_2 = \mathcal{L}(G_2)$, for some regular grammars $G_1 = (V_1, \Sigma, S_1, P_1)$

and $G_2 = (V_2, \Sigma, S_2, P_2)$. Without loss of generality we can assume the variables of the two grammars are disjoint Consider $G = (V, \Sigma, S, P)$ where $V = V_1 \cup V_2 \cup \{S\}$, S is a new variable and $P = P_1 \cup P_2 \cup \{S \to S_1, S \to S_2\}$. Note G is a regular grammar with unit productions, but, by Lemma 8.2, it can be converted into a regular grammar, so $L = \mathcal{L}(G)$ is regular.

We need to show that $x \in \mathcal{L}(G)$ iff $x \in \mathcal{L}(G_1) \cup \mathcal{L}(G_2)$. If $x \in \mathcal{L}(G)$ then either $S \Rightarrow S_1 \stackrel{*}{\Rightarrow} x$ or $S \Rightarrow S_2 \stackrel{*}{\Rightarrow} x$. So $x \in \mathcal{L}(G_1)$ or $x \in \mathcal{L}(G_2)$. If $x \in \mathcal{L}(G_1) \cup \mathcal{L}(G_2)$ then G can derive it by either $S \Rightarrow S_1 \stackrel{*}{\Rightarrow} x$ or $S \Rightarrow S_2 \stackrel{*}{\Rightarrow} x$. $\square$

Next we consider the complementation operation, which has a proof that uses DFAs.

Theorem 9.5 – If L is regular language then $\overline{L} = \Sigma^* \setminus L$, the complement of L with respect to Σ, is a regular language.

Proof: Since it is regular $L = \mathcal{L}(M)$ for some DFA $M = (Q, \Sigma, q_0, \delta, A)$, from which we will construct a new $\overline{M}$, such that $\overline{L} = \mathcal{L}(\overline{M})$. In particular, $\overline{M} = (Q, \Sigma, q_0, \delta, Q \setminus A)$. In other words, $\overline{M}$ differs from M in that the set of accepting states is complemented. Therefore, x is accepted by $\overline{M}$ iff x is not accepted by M. $\square$

This next result about intersection can not be proven using the technique we used for union.

Theorem 9.6 – If L_1 and L_2 are regular languages then $L = L_1 \cap L_2$ is a regular language.

Proof: Recall one of the deMorgan Laws for sets: $\overline{A \cap B} = \overline{A} \cup \overline{B}$ which can be rewritten as $A \cap B = \overline{\overline{A} \cup \overline{B}}$. It follows from Theorems 9.4 and 9.5 if L_1 and L_2 are regular then all $\overline{L_1}$, $\overline{L_2}$, $\overline{L_1} \cup \overline{L_2}$ and $\overline{\overline{L_1} \cup \overline{L_2}}$ are regular. $\square$

Because concatenation and closure (*) are regular operators the next theorems are straightforward.

Theorem 9.7 – If L_1 and L_2 are regular languages then their concatenation $L_1 L_2$ is a regular language.

Proof: If L_1 and L_2 are regular languages then there exist REs r_1 and r_2 such that $L_1 = \mathcal{L}(r_1)$ and $L_2 = \mathcal{L}(r_2)$. Since $r = r_1 r_2$ is a RE it follows that $\mathcal{L}(r)$ and therefore $L_1 L_2$ are regular. $\square$

Theorem 9.8 – If L_1 is regular language then its closure L_1^* is a regular language.

Proof: If L_1 is regular then there exist an RE r_1 such that $L_1 = \mathcal{L}(r_1)$. Since $r = r_1^*$ is a RE it follows that $\mathcal{L}(r)$ and therefore L_1^* is regular.$\square$

9.7   Limitations of Regular Languages

In this section we show that the class of regular languages does not contain all languages. We will give a technique to show some languages are non-regular. The technique will also lead to a method for reducing the complexity of DFAs. The starting point for both is this definition.

Definition 9.7

Distinguishability
Let L be a language over Σ and $x, y \in \Sigma^*$. Then x and y are *distinguishable with respect to L* if for some $z \in \Sigma^*$ one of the strings xz and yz is in L but the other is not in L. Otherwise x and y are *indistinguishable*. A set S of strings is pairwise distinguishable with respect to L, if any two distinct strings drawn from S are distinguishable.

The next theorem has a long history and is part of the **Myhill-Nerode** theorem.

Theorem 9.9 – Let L be a language over Σ. If there exists a finite set S of strings that are pairwise distinguishable with respect to L, then if a DFA recognizes L then it must contain at least $|S|$ states.

Proof: Let $|S| = n$. Suppose, to the contrary, that some DFA, M, accepts the language L but M has $m < n$ states. We invoke the pigeonhole principle: to fit $k + 1$ pigeons into k pigeonholes, some pair must share a pigeonhole. As pigeonholes we take the m states of M. As pigeons, for each of the n strings of $S = \{x_i \mid 1 \le i \le n\}$, we take the state, $p_i = \delta^*(q_0, x_i)$, to which x_i leads, from the start state. By the pigeonhole principle, two of the latter states must be the same state; in particular $p_i = p_j$, where $i \ne j$. This is impossible, since from that state, on any input string z, a fixed path will be taken. Hence the two strings x_i and x_j can not be distinguished. $\square$

With this theorem we can prove certain languages require a certain number of states. In this sense it is possible to show that some regular languages are more complex than others. However we will use this theorem in a more dramatic way, to show some language is too complex for any DFA to exist that accepts it.

Corollary 9.1 – Let L be a language over Σ. If there is an infinite set S of strings over Σ that are pairwise distinguishable with respect to L, then L is not regular.

Proof: Suppose, to the contrary, that L is regular, so that some DFA, M, accepts L. Being a finite automaton, M has a finite number of states; let m be that number. Let $S' \subset S$ be any subset with $|S'| = m+1$. Obviously the strings in S' are pairwise distinguishable. But Theorem 9.9 guarantees that M does not have enough states to do the job. $\square$

A simple example of an aspect of computer languages that is beyond the representational capacity of regular languages is the balancing of parentheses, as used in algebra, logical expressions and programming languages. We get a simple *model* of parentheses by taking the language formed by ignoring everything else in these expressions. Thus for the expression $\log(a(b + c)(d + e))$, we are left with the string "(( ) ( ))". The alphabet for this language is $\{(,)\}$. Another string of balanced parentheses is "(( ) (( ) ( )))". We will define balanced parentheses more precisely in Chapter 10. However the following example simplifies this motivation further and substitutes a for "(" and b for ")".

Example 9.13

We will show $L = \{a^n b^n | 0 \leq n\}$ is not regular. Strings in L include Λ, ab, and $aaaabbbb$. We choose $S = \{a^n \mid 0 \leq n\}$. Consider the strings aaa and $aaaaa$. Using the continuation string $z = bbb$, we have $xz \in L$ but $yz \notin L$. Therefore these two strings are distinguishable with respect to L.

This reasoning extends to any two sequences of as that are of different lengths. For any distinct values of i and j, the strings a^i and a^j are distinguishable with respect to L, using $z = b^i$ as the continuation ($z = b^j$ would also work).

To summarize, when building a FA for a language, we need *distinct states* for strings that are (pairwise) distinguishable with respect to the language. The full Myhill-Nerode theorem goes further: if S is the largest set of pairwise distinguishable string with respect to a regular language L then there exists a DFA accepting L with only $|S|$ states. However this is not proven here. We will instead look at a practical consequence of this fact. We will show how to simplify a DFA be reducing the number of states.

Theorem 9.9 identifies the strings in the set S with the states of a DFA. We can go a step further and say that the set of all strings Σ^* is partitioned into m blocks, where m is the number of states. For each state there is a block of the partition contains all the strings that go to that state from the start state. Clearly all the strings in one block must be pairwise indistinguishable.

We give an algorithm based on these insights. We start with a very coarse partition of the states and repeatedly refine it by splitting blocks apart until each block consists of states that are indistinguishable. Each block will then collapse into one new state.

Definition 9.8

Distinguishability of states
Let M be a DFA. Two states p and q are *distinguishable with respect to M* if for some $z \in \Sigma^*$ exactly one of the states $\delta^*(p, z)$ and $\delta^*(q, z)$ is accepting. Otherwise p and q are indistinguishable.

Definition 9.9

Indistinguishability of states
Let $M = (Q, \Sigma, q_0, \delta, A)$ be a DFA. Two states p and q are indistinguishable with respect to M for strings of length at most k, written $p \overset{k}{=} q$, if for all $z \in \Sigma^*$, with $|z| \le k$,

$$\delta^*(p, z) \in A \text{ iff } \delta^*(q, z) \in A.$$

This is an equivalence relation that induces a partition Π_k of the set of vertices Q.

Clearly Π_0 has just two blocks initially, the sets of accepting and non-accepting states, since the only z is Λ. Algorithm 9.3 computes the series of partitions for increasing values of k. Each partition is a refinement of the previous partition. That is, when more strings are considered (as k increases) strings that were in the same block may be discovered to be distinguishable; this will cause a block to be divided into sub-blocks for the next partition. When $\Pi_k = \Pi_{k-1}$ no block was subdivided on that pass. It follows that no further refinements will occur for larger values of k, since the body of the loop will repeat the same behavior. The algorithm must halt since the number of blocks in any partition can not exceed the number of states.

Algorithm 9.3

Refining the partition of indistinguishable states.
Input: $M = (Q, \Sigma, q_0, \delta, A)$.
Output: the final partition Π_k

> Initialize Π_0
> $k \Leftarrow 0$
> **repeat**
>   **for** every $p \in Q$ and $q \in Q$ **do**
> $(p \stackrel{k+1}{=} q)$ iff $((p \stackrel{k}{=} q) \wedge (\forall a \in \Sigma^* : \delta(p,a) \stackrel{k}{=} \delta(q,a)))$
> $k \Leftarrow k + 1$
> **until** $\Pi_k = \Pi_{k-1}$

When the algorithm halts we construct a DFA $M' = (Q', \Sigma, q'_0, \delta', A')$ as follows. Let $[q]$ be the block that q ended up in. Let $Q' = \{[q] \mid q \in Q\}$, so each state of M' is a block produced from M. Let $q'_0 = [q_0]$ and $A' = \{[q] \mid q \in A\}$. Finally, $\delta'([q], a) = [\delta(q, a)]$ for all q and a. We leave it as exercise to prove $\mathcal{L}(M) = \mathcal{L}(M')$.

It follows that M' has the minimum number, m, of states for any DFA that accepts $L = \mathcal{L}(M)$. To see this, find one string that reaches each state of M' and construct the set S of these m strings. Suppose two strings x and y in this S are indistinguishable with respect to L, they must be indistinguishable with respect to M. But they are distinguished by a string z since at some point the algorithm put the $\delta^*(q_0, y)$ and $\delta^*(q_0, x)$ into separate blocks. Therefore Myhill-Nerode theorem implies that m states are also required.

This algorithm can be presented in many ways using a variety of notations. Some presentations emphasize how to translate it into code. We only mention that the partitions can be represented by $m \times m$ matrices.

9.8   Pattern Matching

Pattern matching is an important application. Web searching is just one example of the need for techniques for finding occurences of patterns in text. Pattern matching algorithms are a well-studied topic. What is interesting is that some of the best known algorithms are based on finite automata! The whole story is beyond the scope of this book, but we will introduce the connection. This will also give us some practice designing FAs.

The standard pattern matching problem begins with two strings: the *pattern* $P = p_1 p_2 \ldots p_m$ and the *text* $T = t_1 t_2 \ldots t_n$. The simplest goal is to find an occurence of P in T, typically the first occurrence. For example, if $P = aaba$ and $T = baabbaabab$ then first (and only) occurrence of P in T begins at the 6th character of T, $p_1 p_2 p_3 p_4 = t_6 t_7 t_8 t_9$.

What is the connection with FAs? Suppose we designed an FA M to accept the language

$$L(P) = \{x \mid x \text{ contains the string } P\}.$$

When processing the input we know that M must enter an accepting state when it has just finished seeing the first occurrence of P and that thereafter it must remaining in some accepting state or other. In other words M essentially solves the pattern matching problem when given T as input. Further M provides an efficient way to search for P; it processes the characters of T very quickly. The main problem is how do we get the FA M?

We will use the example of $P = ababb$ to motivate an approach. An FA looking for P does not know, when it sees an a in the input, if that a is the beginning of an occurrence of P or not. So when it (first) encounters an a it must go to a state that corresponds to the fact that has seen the first character of P. Now if we are in this new state and encounter a b we can go to another state that corresponds to the fact we have just encountered the first two characters of P. Continuing in this fashion we can motivate the set of states $\{q_1, q_1, \ldots, q_m\}$, where reaching q_i corresponds to the fact that we have just encountered the first i characters of P. We introduce the state q_0 to correspond to the fact that no progress towards forming P has been made up to this point.

We have to be very careful. Suppose that we have just processed these 6 input characters: *ababab*. Should we be in state q_2 (because the last two characters were *ab*) or state q_4 (because the last four characters were *abab*). Clearly we need to be in state q_4, otherwise if the next input character were a *b* and we were in state q_2 we would not realize we had just encountered the fifth character of *P*. In general, you would never be in state q_i if you could be in state q_j, where $j > i$.

What if you were in state q_4 and you encountered an *a* in the input. It follows that the last five characters of the input were *ababa*. We appear to have a choice between q_1 and q_3, but using the above observations we see that we must make a transition to state q_3. This sort of example can be generalized into a single rule: if we are state q_i and the input is σ then we make a transition to state q_j where

$$j = \max\{k \mid (k = 0) \vee (1 \leq k \leq m \wedge p_1 p_2 \ldots p_k = p_{i-k+2} \ldots p_i \sigma)\}.$$

We know that we have just encountered all the characters leading up to the ith character of *P*, and we try use as many of those as possible in choosing j. It is important when interpreting this rule to realize there are two degeneracies, when $j = 1$ and $j = 0$. When $j = 1$, none of the prior characters match up but we do keep track of the fact that the new input α does match up with the first character of *P*. When $j = 0$ we go to the state q_0 which means that we have currently made no progress at all towards finding *P*.

We are now ready to build an FA using only the states $Q = \{q_0, q_1, \ldots, q_m\}$. We will make q_m an accepting sink, for the same reason we did in the NFA above. Using the rule above we can generate all the other transitions we will need. For $P = ababb$, we get this machine:

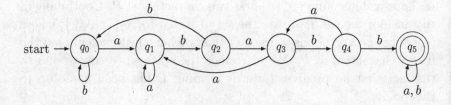

This gives a general technique for building FAs to solve the pattern matching problem. It is rare that we are able to find such a general technique; most FAs are found less systematically.

9.9 Designing Finite Automata

If the problem given is to build a FA for the language of all strings having a certain property, then no general technique can be expected. Occasionally, as in the pattern matching section, if the property is quite specific and simple then a special-purpose technique may be possible. However, there are several general observations we want to make in this section.

First, a property is simply a logical predicate $p(x)$ of a string x; it is true or false that x belongs to the language defined by that property. Suppose $p(x)$ is complex but can be decomposed as $p(x) = q(x) \vee r(x)$, then the language is the union of the two languages corresponding to the predicates $q(x)$ and $r(x)$. The constructive proof of the closure property of union allows you to build the desired machine mechanically from two simpler machine. Similar remarks hold for intersection, complementation and other operators with closure properties.

Second, implicit in the proof in Section 9.7 is the following principle: You need one state for each distinct memory you need to encode about the past. Recall since we do not rewind our input that *everything* that is remembered about the portion of the string that has been processed is remembered solely by virtue of being in one state, rather than another. Turning this around, when building an FA you should create each new state only when you can specify what memory of the past does arrival at that state represent.

Third, there is more than one FA for any language. There is an urge to find the FA that has the fewest state. If you followed the advice in the preceding paragraph you will probably not generate excess states. But what if you do? In this textbook the focus is entirely on correctness and extra states are a minor issue. However in some applications there is an economic incentive to have no extra states. In those cases you could use the state minimization algorithm, given at the end Section 9.7, that will transform a machine with extra states into an equivalent machine with the minimum number of states.

Finally, a powerful design technique is to begin your building process with a nondeterministic formulation and convert it into a deterministic FA.

Exercises

9.1 – Let $M = (Q, \Sigma, q_0, \delta, A)$ be an NFA with no genuine choice. In other words, for every q in Q and σ in Σ, the value of $\delta(q, \sigma)$ either has one element or is empty. Formally specify a new *deterministic* FA, M' that accepts the same language as M. That is, formally specify the 5 parts of the quintuple for M', so that $\mathcal{L}(M') = \mathcal{L}(M)$.

Hint: Introduce a trap state, q'_t, and then specify δ by formally specifying what must happen (i) when $\delta(q, \sigma) = \emptyset$ and (ii) when $\delta(q, \sigma) = \{p\}$, that is, when δ yields the one-element set containing only state p.

9.2 – For both the DFA and the NFA in Example 9.10, evaluate $\delta^*(q_0, x)$ for each of the following strings, x.

    (a) a

    (b) b

    (c) ab

    (d) ba

    (e) a^k, where $k \geq 1$

9.3 – Redraw the diagram of Example 9.3 including its trap state and all the transitions associated with that state.

9.4 – Draw a state transition diagram for each of the languages specified, omitting trap states. The languages are the sets of all strings over $\Sigma = \{a, b, c\}$ that

    (a) start with c.

    (b) end in c.

    (c) contain exactly one c.

    (d) contains at least one c.

    (e) contain at least one c and are of length exactly 2.

    (f) are of length at most 2.

9.5 – Argue that every finite language is regular.

9.6 – Give an NFA for each of these languages, over $\Sigma = \{a, b\}$.

    (a) the language of all strings ending in *abab* or *baa*.

    (b) the language of all strings that contain *aaa*.

    (c) the language of all strings $x = yz$, where y contains an odd number of as and z contains an odd number of bs.

9.7 – Express the language L of Example 9.3 as $L = L_1 L_2$ by specifying L_1 and L_2 formally.

9.8 – Give the formal specification of a FA that recognizes the language of binary strings that contain at least one odd block of ones, $\Sigma = \{0, 1\}$; e.g., 00110001001 is in the language.

9.9 – Draw a state-transition diagram for comments in C or C++. These are the strings that (i) begin with /*, (ii) end in */ without overlap (so /*/ is excluded) and (iii) have no other occurrence of */. Hint: Look at Example 9.5.

9.10 – Formally specify a machine $M = (Q, \Sigma, q_0, \delta, A)$ by giving the values of Q, Σ, q_0, A and δ corresponding to the state-transition diagram in Example 9.4. Since δ is a total function you must first add the trap state and the transitions associated with it.

9.11 – Let $M = (\{q_0, q_1, q_2, q_3\}, \{a\}, q_0, \delta, \{q_1, q_3\})$, where δ is specified by the table below.

$$
\delta = \quad
\begin{array}{c|c}
 & a \\
\hline
q_0 & q_1 \\
q_1 & q_2 \\
q_2 & q_3 \\
q_3 & q_0 \\
\end{array}
$$

(a) Draw the state-transition diagram for this finite automaton.

(b) Very briefly describe the language $\mathcal{L}(M)$ in English.

(c) Using (b) give a formal specification of a 2-state automaton that accepts $\mathcal{L}(M)$. (Note the relevance of this exercise to state minimization, even though no algorithm was invoked here.)

9.12 – Specify just the transition function of the second state-transition diagram in Example 9.5. Label the states q_0, q_1, q_2, q_3, q_4 and q_5, where the latter is the trap state.

9.13 – For your DFA in Exercise 9.12, give the values of δ^* for the arguments shown here.

(a) $\delta^*(q_0, dcba)$

(b) $\delta^*(q_1, \Lambda)$

(c) $\delta^*(q_1, dcba)$

(d) $\delta^*(q_2, dcba)$

(e) $\delta^*(q_0, dcd)$

(f) $\delta^*(q_0, dccccd)$

9.14 – Following the technique in Example 9.8 in its use of Definition 9.2, *prove* that for the DFA of Example 9.7, $\delta^*(q_0, dad) = q_2$.

9.15 – Build an DFA for $L(P)$ for these patterns, using $\Sigma = \{a, b\}$:

   (a) $P = aaab$

   (b) $P = abba$

9.16 – Build an DFA for $L(P)$ for these patterns, using $\Sigma = \{a, b\}$:

   (a) $P = ababab$

   (b) $P = ababaa$

9.17 – Give an DFA for the language L over $\Sigma = \{a, b\}$, in which each string

   (a) contains the substring aa and at some later point the substring bb. Thus for example, $bbaaababba \in L$ but $bbaa \notin L$.

   (b) consists of an even number of as followed by an even number of bs, such as $aabbbb$. Recall that zero is even.

9.18 – Give an DFA for the language L, over $\Sigma = \{a, b, c\}$, in which each string

   (a) contain the substring ab and at least two cs after that point. Thus for example, $baaababcbca \in L$.

   (b) contains an aba before any bb. Note that strings like aab are in the language!

   (c) contains an a and a b before some c, such as $bcac$.

9.19 – Show that the regular languages are closed under set difference. In particular, show that if L_1 and L_2 are regular then $L_1 \setminus L_2$ is also regular.

9.20 – You can often see a direct connection between REs and DFAs without invoking algorithms. Draw the state-transition diagrams for DFAs that recognize the languages denoted by:

(a) $(aa + ab)^*$

(b) $(aaa + abb)^*b$

(c) $(a + aab)^*b$

9.21 – Give the regular grammars corresponding to the two FAs in Example 9.10.

9.22 – Give the FAs corresponding to the regular grammars in Exercise 8.15.

9.23 – Give an DFA for the language of strings that do not contain the substring aba, over $\Sigma = \{a, b\}$. Solved this by building a pattern matching machine and "complementing" that machine.

9.24 – Let L_1 be the set of strings of equal numbers of left and right parentheses in arbitrary order. Let $L_2 = \{(^n)^n \mid 0 \leq n\}$ and let L_3 be the language of balanced parentheses (such "(())()"). Let $\Sigma = \{(,)\}$.

(a) Specify the subset relationships among the languages L_1, L_2, L_3 and Σ^*. Use $\subset$ and/or $\subseteq$ as appropriate. Wherever you specify $\subset$, give an example of a string in the relevant set difference.

(b) Show that L_1 is not regular.

9.25 – Show each of these languages over $\Sigma = \{a, b, c\}$ is not regular:

(a) $\{x \mid x$ is a palindrome $\}$

(b) $\{x \mid x = yy$ for some $y \in \Sigma^*\}$

(c) $\{x \mid x = a^i b^j c^k$ where $j = i + k\}$

9.26 – Consider the language $\{x \in \{a, b\}^* \mid$ the kth symbol from the end of x is $a\}$.

    (a) Show that the language requires a DFA with at least 2^k states.

    (b) Show that only a NFA for the same language exist with $k + 1$ states

9.27 – Complete the proof of Lemma 9.2 by addressing the details of a trap state.

9.28 – Prove Theorem 9.4 use REs instead grammars.

9.29 – We can extend the definition of regular grammars by permitting a string of terminals where the definition allows a single terminal. Even with this extended definition, any regular grammar can still be converted to a DFA. Consider the grammar

$$G = (\{S, T\}, \{a, b, c\}, S, \{S \to a\,b\,S \mid a\,b\,c\,T, \;\; T \to b\,c\,T \mid a\}).$$

    (a) What aspect(s) of the grammar make it regular according to this extended definition.

    (b) Write a (possibly nondeterministic) state-transition diagram that has $\mathcal{L}(G)$ as its language.

    (c) Give a normal regular grammar for $\mathcal{L}(G)$. Indicate how this might be done in general.

9.30 – Write a DFA for L, $\Sigma = \{a, b, c\}$, $L = \{x \mid$ if x has an a and a b then x has a $c\}$, $bca \in L$, $bc \in L$.

9.31 – Write an NFA for L, $\Sigma = \{a, b\}$, $L = \{x \mid$ the 3rd character is the same as the 3rd from the end$\}$, $abbababba \in L$.

Chapter 10

Context-Free Grammars

Context-free grammars can express important languages including many that are *non-regular* and they can assign a useful *structure* to individual strings. These two important capacities combine to give CFGs a central role in both formal models of language and the practical modeling of computer languages.

With the class of regular languages we began with a definition of the class relative to a machine model. After that we showed its equivalence to classes defined by nondeterministic models, specifically generative models such as grammatical models. In this chapter we will define a new class of languages and we will start with a nondeterministic grammatical model. In the next chapter we will establish its equivalence to a machine model (push-down automata).

The motivation for introducing a new class of language models was given in Section 9.7, where we showed the models we have seen so far are *inadequate*. We exhibited languages that they are non-regular for which there can be no finite automaton that accepts the language. Nor can these languages be represented by regular grammars. (Regular expressions are also inadequate but the generative model exemplified by REs will not be extended.)

Besides specifying the strings for a wide range of languages, context-free languages also provide an account of the *structure* of each string in their languages. These structures are the focus of Section 10.3, where we show how they can play a role in extracting the *meanings* of statements in programming languages. Some grammars provide more than one structure for some strings. This somewhat awkward result is known as *structural ambiguity* and although it turns up frequently in human languages, it is usually regarded as something that can and should be avoided when designing programming languages.

10.1   Introduction to Context-Free Grammars

Context-free grammars (CFGs) are an important formalism for representing both programming languages and human languages. Since we have been introduced to the general idea of grammars when we introduced regular grammars this new type of grammar is easily defined.

Definition 10.1

Context-free grammars
A context-free grammar G is a quadruple, (V, Σ, S, P), where

V a finite set of nonterminal symbols (also called variables);
Σ a finite alphabet of terminal symbols
S the start symbol, $S \in V$; and
P a finite set of productions, each of the form $A \to \alpha$, where $A \in V$
  and $\alpha \in (V \cup \Sigma)^*$. That is, the left side of a production is a
  nonterminal and the right side is any sequence of terminals
  and/or nonterminals.

Definition 10.2

The language generated by a context-free grammar
A string x belongs to $\mathcal{L}(G)$ — the language that G *generates* — if

and only if there exists a derivation of x from the start symbol and x is composed entirely of terminal symbols.

$$\mathcal{L}(G) = \{x \mid S \overset{*}{\Rightarrow} x \text{ and } x \in \Sigma^*\}.$$

This is defined the same as for regular grammars; we repeat it for completeness.

Example 10.1

Consider the $G_1 = (\{S\}, \{a, b\}, S, \{S \to a\,S\,b, \ S \to \Lambda\})$. Here is a derivation of *aaabbb* from S, the start symbol of G_1.

$$S \Rightarrow a\,S\,b \Rightarrow a\,a\,S\,b\,b \Rightarrow a\,a\,a\,S\,b\,b\,b \Rightarrow a\,a\,a\,b\,b\,b.$$

It is easily seen (and can be proven by induction) that if the first production is used $k \geq 0$ times that the string $a^k S b^k$ will be derived. Further if the other production is used the derivation halts. It follows that $L_1 = \mathcal{L}(G_1)$ is the non-regular language $\{a^n b^n \mid n \geq 0\}$ studied in Section 9.7.

Definition 10.3

Conventions

1. A capital roman letter will denote a variable from V.

2. A lower-case roman letter from the beginning of the alphabet will denote a terminal from Σ.

3. A lower-case roman letter from the end of the alphabet will denote a terminal string from Σ^*.

4. A lower-case Greek letter will denote a string over from $(V \cup \Sigma)^*$.

Combined with the convention of using S as a start symbol these allow us to specify a CFG by only presenting P, the set of productions. These are the same conventions as earlier, but we state them here for ease of reference.

Example 10.2

What language is generated by the following grammar?

$$G_2 = (\{S\}, \{(,)\}, S, \{S \rightarrow (S), S \rightarrow \Lambda\})$$

It is important to note that "(" and ")" are just ordinary terminal symbols. Since this grammar is just like G_1 except for replacing a and b by left and right parentheses, the same is true of the resulting language: $\mathcal{L}(G_2)$, is the language $L_2 = \{(^n)^n \mid n \geq 0\}$

Next we will look for a CFG for *all* strings of balanced parentheses, not just those of L_2. Recall that we discussed this language in Section 9.7 where we established it was a non regular language However, except for giving some examples, we have never really said what strings of balanced parentheses *are*. Since there are infinitely many of them, a recursive definition is appropriate.

Definition 10.4

Strings of balanced parentheses

If B is the language of strings of balanced parentheses, then,

1. $\Lambda \in B$.
2. If $s_1 \in B$ and $s_2 \in B$, then $s_1 s_2 \in B$.
3. If $s \in B$, then $(s) \in B$.
4. Nothing else is in B.

Of course, when parentheses appear in ordinary mathematical expressions, there are other things mixed in with the parentheses, both within and between balanced pairs, as well as before and after, but here we are ignoring everything else.

Example 10.3

The language of balanced parentheses, B, is generated by the grammar G_3, with the following productions:

$$S \to \Lambda \qquad S \to S\,S \qquad S \to (\,S\,)$$

In other words, we claim that $B = \mathcal{L}(G_3)$ is the language of balanced parentheses. The following derivation shows that the string $(\,(\,)\,(\,)\,)$ is in $\mathcal{L}(G_3)$. The symbol which is replaced next is underlined.

$$\underline{S} \Rightarrow (\,\underline{S}\,) \Rightarrow (\,\underline{S}\,S\,) \Rightarrow (\,(\,S\,)\,\underline{S}\,) \Rightarrow (\,(\,\underline{S}\,)\,(\,S\,)\,) \Rightarrow (\,(\,)\,(\,\underline{S}\,)\,) \Rightarrow (\,(\,)\,(\,)\,)$$

The proof of the claim that $\mathcal{L}(G_3)$ is the language of balanced parentheses is straightforward, using mathematical induction and drawing on the similarity of the three productions of G_3 to, respectively, lines 1, 2 and 3 of Definition 10.4. Line 4 of that definition corresponds to the parenthesized comment "and only" in Definition 10.2, for the language of any CFG.

The key reasons for our interest in the language B is not just that it is non-regular. The language serves as a model of how parentheses, and delimiters in general, behave. Recall that models simplify yet retain essential features. In this case, the simplification is to remove all other material, while the essential feature that is retained is described in line 3 of Definition 10.4 and echoed in the third production of G_3 in Example 10.3: parentheses *surround* expressions. There are theoretical characterizations of CFLs, that are beyond the scope of this book, that point out that the *nested balance* of parentheses, is found in all non-regular CFLs.

Definition 10.5

Context-free languages
The class of context-free languages contains exactly those languages for which a context-free grammar exists that generates it.

The CFGs are more powerful than the various models of regular languages, in the sense that the CFGs can represent all of the regular languages and also some non-regular languages. We have demonstrated the second part by example. The first part is easily proved.

Theorem 10.1 – Every regular language is a context-free language.

Proof: This follows immediately since every regular language is generated by a regular grammar and every regular grammar, by definition, is a context-free grammar. □

10.2   An Example

A palindrome is a string that reads the same forwards and backwards; it is the reverse of itself. The empty string and all strings of length one are palindromes. A string of length two is a palindrome if and only if its two symbols are the same. Among the words of English, some palindromes are "a", "gag", "eke", "deed", "noon", "level", "tenet", "redder" and "reviver". Here is a more precise definition of palindromes:

Definition 10.6

Palindromes over Σ

- Λ is a palindrome.
- For any $a \in \Sigma$, a is a palindrome.
- If x is a palindrome and $a \in \Sigma$, then axa is a palindrome.
- No other strings are palindromes.

Notice that a new palindrome axa is longer by 2 than x, so Λ in the first line of the definition gets us started only on the even-length palindromes. We also need all the $a \in \Sigma$ (all the strings of length 1) in the second line to get started on the odd-length palindromes. We focus on the even-length palindromes, leaving the odd-length case as an exercise.

Example 10.4

These are the productions for G_4, a grammar for the even-length palindromes over $\Sigma = \{a, b\}$:

$$S \to a\,S\,a \qquad S \to b\,S\,b \qquad S \to \Lambda$$

To save space we sometimes combine productions with the same left-hand side using "|", the *alternation* symbol. So our three productions can be written:

$$S \to a\,S\,a \mid b\,S\,b \mid \Lambda$$

A derivation of $a\,b\,b\,b\,b\,a$ using G_4 is

$$S \Rightarrow a\,S\,a \Rightarrow a\,b\,S\,b\,a \Rightarrow a\,b\,b\,S\,b\,b\,a \Rightarrow a\,b\,b\,b\,b\,a$$

We can prove properties of $\mathcal{L}(G_4)$ which we state formally for the practice.

Claim: G_4 can only derive string with an even number of terminals.

Proof. We prove it by induction on the length of the derivation of an x such that $S \overset{*}{\Rightarrow} x$. The basis is a zero step derivation so $x = S$ still. Since x has *no* terminal symbols and zero is an even number. Suppose it is true for any k step derivation. The $k + 1$st step either uses the first or the second production As each production either increases the number of terminals by 2 (for $S \to a\,S\,a$ or $S \to b\,S\,b$) or by zero (for $S \to \Lambda$), an even number results. So the claim follows.

We introduced palindromes above with the informal statement that each one is the reverse of itself. Presumably this means that in a string $x = x_1 x_2 \ldots x_n$, we have $x_1 = x_n$, $x_2 = x_{n-1}$, and more generally $x_i = x_{n+1-i}$ for every i such that $1 \le i \le n$. (Note that each x_i is a symbol, not a substring). However, Definition 10.6 and grammar G_4 do not mention reverses. The next example relates reverses to G_4.

Example 10.5

We prove the following claim.

Claim: Every string $x_1 x_2 \ldots x_n \in \mathcal{L}(G_4)$ is the reverse of itself, so $x_i = x_{n+1-i}$ for every i such that $1 \leq i \leq n$. We also regard Λ as its own reverse.

Proof. We show that it is true for any $x \in \Sigma^*$ such that $S \overset{*}{\Rightarrow} x$ with k derivations steps, by induction on k. The basis again is a zero-step derivation of Λ. Assume it is true for any derivation of k steps. Consider a terminal derivation with $k+1$ steps and look at its first derivation step. There are two cases. (If the first step produced Λ there is no second step.)

The first case is when the first derivation step is $S \to a\,S\,a$. By the inductive hypothesis, the new S will derive $x_1 x_2 \ldots x_n$, which is its own reverse. The resulting string is $y = a x_1 x_2 \ldots x_n a$. If $n = 0$ we are done. Using the same convention for y as for x, we write $y = y_1 y_2 \ldots y_m$, where $m = n + 2$. To show that y is its own reverse, first we note that $y_1 = a = y_m$. For $2 \leq i \leq m - 1$, we have

$$y_i = x_{i-1} = x_{n+1-(i-1)} = x_{n+2-i} = x_{m-i} = y_{m+1-i}.$$

The second case, where the first step is $S \to b\,S\,b$, is analogous.

10.3   Structure, Meaning and Ambiguity

We will model the structure of the derivation of a string and show how that structure can have an effect on the meanings of the string. In this section we introduce various concepts by using a continuing example: the design of a grammar for simple algebraic expressions.

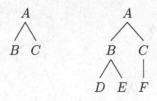

Figure 10.1: A derivation tree using the productions: $A \to B\,C$, $B \to D\,E$, and $C \to F$.

A **derivation tree** is a diagram of a derivation. For example, the left side of Figure 10.1 shows the derivation tree for a one-step derivation using the production $A \to B\,C$. We say in such a case that we have *expanded* the node A. The derivation tree in the right side of the figure starts the same way and then expands B and C, using the two additional productions $B \to D\,E$ and $C \to F$. In general, a parent in the tree must be labeled by the left side of some production and its children must be labeled by, in order, the symbols on the right side of the same production.

The second tree in Figure 10.1 can be regarded as a non-linear *model* of the linear derivation

$$A \Rightarrow B\,C \Rightarrow D\,E\,C \Rightarrow D\,E\,F,$$

in the sense that it focuses on only certain aspects of it. In particular, the tree does not specify in what order B and C are expanded, and often we will not care.

The derivation tree is a model of structure in the sense that it emphasizes certain structural relationships. For example, the lines in the derivation tree that descend from B to its children D and E show that B is composed of D and E. This information is in the linear derivation, but one has to infer it by looking at what has changed from before the arrow to after it, in the derivation step $B\,C \Rightarrow D\,E\,C$.

The kind of structural information that is present in derivation trees plays a crucial role in figuring out the **semantics** (roughly speaking, the meanings) of strings in useful CFGs. To *understand* an expression like $a + b \times c$ one must at least know that "+" calls for adding, that

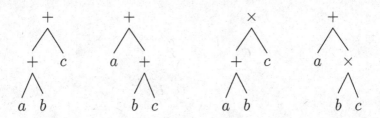

Figure 10.2: Expression tree structures that indicate order of the applications of operators.

"×" calls for multiplying and that the multiplication is to be done first. This last point, the issue of which operator to apply first, is what concerns us here. More generally, we want the derivation trees in our grammar for algebraic expressions — which we will be designing below — to provide an answer to the question: When an expression has two or more operators, in what order should they be executed? *You* know the answer, but the question has to be answered by compiler software.

So, we seek a grammar whose derivation trees always suggest the correct order for applying operators. We will do this for a simplified language of algebraic expressions, using just the two operators "+" and "×", parentheses and a few variables. Informally

$$L = \{x \in \{a, b, c, +, \times\}^* | x \text{ represents a simple arithmetic expression}\}$$

Examples of such expressions $a+b+c$ and $a \times b+c$. Our example will illustrate the ideas are broadly applicable to algebraic expressions for programming languages with numbers, variables, parentheses, functions, arrays and a wide range of other operators. Our goal will be a grammar for which the derivation trees always imply the correct order of application for the operators, taking into account four concepts: recursion, ambiguity, precedence and parentheses.

Consider the expressions and tree structures in Figure 10.2. These trees are *not* derivation trees; they are the expression trees from Chapter 1. Each branching in these trees associates an operator with its two operands. In the case of $a + b \times c$, For example, in the last tree the lower three-way branching groups "×" with b and c to form $b \times c$. Then the upper branching groups the "+" with this result and a. The tree as a whole correctly reflects the fact that "×" takes **precedence** over "+" and should be performed first. The third tree violates precedence and implies the use of *parentheses*, e.g. $(a+b) \times c$. We will deal with parentheses later.

The expressions $a + b + c$ and $a \times b \times c$ are also of some interest. Recall from Chapter 1 that such associative operators imply left-to-right evaluation. Therefore the first tree is the default and the second tree implies the use of *parentheses*, e.g. $a + (b + c)$. The branching structures for these expressions also suggests the repeatable nature of these operators, the fact that a single expression can use these operators as many times as a programmer needs. We will achieve this repetition by **recursion** in CFGs.

Definition 10.7

Recursive productions, grammars and symbols
A *recursive production* in a CFG has the form $A \to \alpha A \beta$, so that the symbol on the left side also appears on the right. (By convention, α and β are arbitrary sequences, possibly empty, of terminal and/or nonterminal symbols.) A *recursive grammar* has some nonterminal for which there is a derivation $A \overset{*}{\Rightarrow} \alpha A \beta$ with at least one step. The symbol involved in either case — here A — is a *recursive symbol*.

Example 10.6

Write a grammar for simple algebraic expressions, that is for the language L.

Out first attempt is the grammar G_5. It is based on a recursive definition of simple arithmetic expressions: an expression is one or more expressions added (multiplied) together or it is just a variable. E, standing for "expression," is the start symbol of the grammar and its only variable. The terminal symbols are a, b, c, $+$ and $\times$. However, this grammar has the undesirable property of being ambiguous, according to the next definition, as we will see.

Productions for G_5: $E \rightarrow E\ +\ E$
                           $E \rightarrow E\ \times\ E$
                           $E \rightarrow a \mid b \mid c.$

Recall that a derivation is *leftmost* if at every step the variable that is replaced by a production is the leftmost variable in the string derived up to that point.

Definition 10.8

Ambiguity

An *ambiguous string* with respect to a CFG is one that the grammar can generate with at least two different derivation trees. An *ambiguous grammar* is one that generates at least one ambiguous string.

Example 10.7

Draw derivation trees that shows the ambiguity G_5.

See Figure 10.3. Repeated use of the production $E \rightarrow E + E$ occurs in each, and further repetition would yield larger trees and longer strings, as needed, without limit. Since there are two trees for the string $a + b + c$, that string is ambiguous and so is the grammar, G_5, that generated them. (Recall that associative operators should associate left-to-right.)

Note that the left tree in the figure corresponds to this leftmost derivation

$E \Rightarrow E + E \Rightarrow E + E + E \Rightarrow a + E + E \Rightarrow a + b + E \Rightarrow a + b + c$

and the right tree corresponds to this leftmost derivation of the same string:

$E \Rightarrow E + E \Rightarrow a + E \Rightarrow a + E + E \Rightarrow a + b + E \Rightarrow a + b + c$

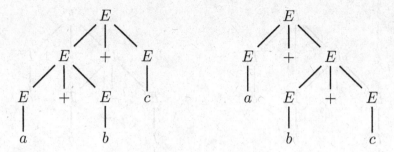

Figure 10.3: Trees for Example 10.7.

The previous example illustrates a general result: a string is ambiguous for a grammar if and only if that string has two distinct leftmost derivations. We leave it as an exercise to show the equivalence.

Example 10.8

Can we produce another grammar for L that is not ambiguous?

The ambiguity of G_5 arises from having two Es on the right side of the recursive productions. (Using one repeatedly causes the tree to lean to the left or the right.) So we will use productions with no more than one E on the right, as shown below. The production set for G_6, shown next, does indeed give us an unambiguous grammar. The production $E \to T$ is necessary to have a non-recursive production.

productions for G_6:
$$E \to E + T$$
$$E \to E \times T$$
$$E \to T$$
$$T \to a \mid b \mid c.$$

Why is G_6 unambiguous? All the branching in the derivation trees of G_6 is to the left, as shown in each of the trees in Figure 10.4. For strings of a given length, there is only one tree shape, or branching pattern. This makes ambiguity impossible.

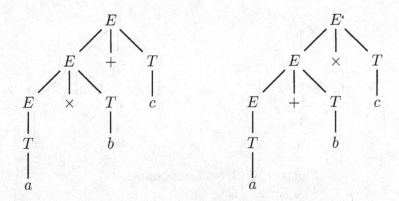

Figure 10.4: Trees for Example 10.8.

Despite being unambiguous, G_6 has a flaw. Unfortunately, some derivation trees generated by G_6 violate precedence. We mean, the derivation tree for the string $a + b \times c$ on the right side of Figure 10.4 incorrectly suggests applying "+" before "×". (The grammar G_5 has a similar shortcoming.)

Example 10.9

Give a grammar for L that generates derivation trees trees respect precedence.

The trees in Example 10.8 reveal a flaw in the productions of G_6: that grammar makes no distinction in the way it handles the two operators, but instead treats them identically, so it can generate them in any order. As is often the case, we are having difficulties because we have not been precise enough in our initial definitions. Define a simple *expression* as one or more terms added together, a *term* as one or more factors multiplied together, and *factor* as a variable. (This definition is familiar to all elementary schools students.)

The grammar below fixes things by hewing closely to the recursive definition.

productions for G_7: $E \to E + T \mid T$
$T \to T \times F \mid F$
$F \to a \mid b \mid c.$

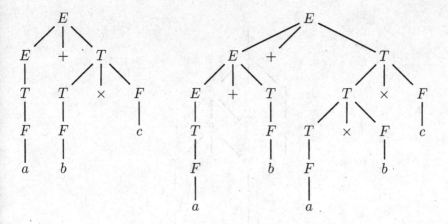

Figure 10.5: Trees for Example 10.9.

Figure 10.5 shows some derivation trees for G_7. For example, in the tree for $a + b + a \times b \times c$ on the right, both multiplications are performed before the result, $a \times b \times c$, is added to $a + b$ at the top level.

The grammar G_7 is unambiguous and handles precedence correctly. However, suppose G_7 has been designed to generate a programming language and a programmer using that language needs addition to occur before multiplication in some computation. The programmer might like to write $(a + b) \times c$, but is unable to do so since G_7 has no parentheses.

Example 10.10

How can we modify G_7 to allow derivation trees that respect precedence but let parentheses override it?

We return to the recursive definition, but notice that our definition of factor was lacking. A factor can be either a variable, but it also can be an entire parenthesized expression. This leads to grammar G_8.

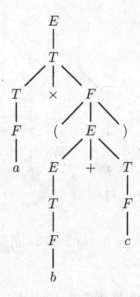

Figure 10.6: Tree for Example 10.10.

productions for G_8: $E \to E + T \mid T$
                          $T \to T \times F \mid F$
                          $F \to (E)$
                          $F \to a \mid b \mid c$

We give the derivation tree for $a \times (b + c)$ using G_8 in Figure 10.6.

The examples in this section are meant to illustrate that CFGs, properly posed, can convey not only syntactic characterization of the strings in a language but also structural/semantic information about the strings.

10.4 Chomsky Normal Form

In a CFG any production $A \to \alpha$, where $\alpha \in (V \cup \Sigma)^*$, is allowed. However we can put severe restrictions on α without limiting the expressive power of CFGs. Such restrictions force the grammar into so-called "normal forms." We will see one in this section and another later.

Definition 10.9

Chomsky normal form

A CFG in which every production is of the form $A \to BC$ or $A \to a$ is in Chomsky normal form (CNF), where $A, B, C \in V$ and $a \in \Sigma$. In particular $A \to \Lambda$ is not allowed.

Definition 10.10

Λ-free language

A language that does not happen to contain Λ is said to be Λ-free.

If a language L is generated by a grammar in Chomsky normal form then clearly L is Λ-free. This is because every derivation starts with one symbol (the start symbol) and no production will ever reduce the number of symbols derived; we can not derive zero symbols.

This theorem shows that constraining ourselves to CNF does not restrict what we can express.

> **Theorem 10.2** – For any Λ-free context-free language L there exists a CFG G in Chomsky normal form, where $L = \mathcal{L}(G)$.

Before proving this we state various lemmas that allow us to "clean up" our grammars.

Definition 10.11

Useless variables

A variable $A \in V$ is *useful* if $A \overset{*}{\Rightarrow} x$, for some $x \in \Sigma^*$; otherwise the variable is *useless*. A production is *useless* if any of its variables are useless. Clearly no derivation of a string of terminals will ever include any useless variables.

> **Lemma 10.1** – For any CFG G there exists a CFG G'
> such that G' contains no useless variables and $\mathcal{L}(G) = \mathcal{L}(G')$.

Proof: First it is trivially true that such a G' exists. Since no useless variable can be used in derivation of any $x \in \mathcal{L}(G)$ we can construct G' by simply removing every useless production from G. We will go a little further and explain how to distinguish the useless variables in practice.

We give an algorithm to compute $\mathcal{A}$, the set of useful variables, which is enough to compute G'. Algorithm 10.1 computes $\mathcal{A}$ using this function:

$$useful(A) = \{A \to \alpha \mid \text{every variable in } \alpha \text{ is in } \mathcal{A}\}.$$

The correctness of the algorithm is seen by strong induction on the length needed to justify the inclusion of a variable in $\mathcal{A}$. The initialization provides the basis of the proof; one-step derivations. If an A needs k steps then for some $A \to \alpha$ every variable in α requires $k-1$ or fewer steps. $\square$

Definition 10.12

Erasable variables

A variable $A \in V$ is *erasable* if $A \overset{*}{\Rightarrow} \Lambda$.

Algorithm 10.1

Computing the set of useful variables in a CFG
Input: A context-free grammar $G = (V, \Sigma, S, P)$
Output: The set of useful variables $\mathcal{A}$

$\mathcal{A} \Leftarrow \{A \mid A \to a \in P\}$
while $A \notin \mathcal{A} \wedge |useful(A)| > 0$ **do**
     add A to $\mathcal{A}$
return $\mathcal{A}$

Lemma 10.2 – For any CFG G if $\mathcal{L}(G)$ is Λ-free there exists a CFG G' such that G' contains no erasable variables and $\mathcal{L}(G) = \mathcal{L}(G')$.

Proof: We give an algorithm which first computes $\mathcal{B}$, the set of erasable variables. Algorithm 10.2 computes $\mathcal{B}$ using this function:

$$erasing(B) = \{B \to \alpha \mid \text{ every symbol in } \alpha \text{ is in } \mathcal{B}\}.$$

The correctness of the computation of $\mathcal{B}$ follows since any derivation $A \overset{*}{\Rightarrow} \Lambda$ cannot contain a single terminal or non-erasable variable.

The remainder of the computation, of P', creates productions that obviate the need for a variable that will later be erased. It creates parallel productions where such variables do not appear. Note that if some production has several erasable variables on it is right-hand side then several iterations of the second **while** loop will produce productions that remove those erasable variables in various combinations. Since P' can more directly derive any string x that was previously derived via the introduction of variable that generated no terminal symbols, the erasing productions are no longer needed. If there are no erasing productions there are no erasable variables. □

Algorithm 10.2

Computing a CFG with no erasable variables
Input: A context-free grammar $G = (V, \Sigma, S, P)$
Output: A CFG $G' = (V, \Sigma, S, P')$, with no erasable variables and
$\qquad \mathcal{L}(G) = \mathcal{L}(G')$

$\mathcal{B} \Leftarrow \{B \mid B \to \Lambda \in P\}$
while $B \notin \mathcal{B} \land |erasing(B)| > 0$ **do**
$\qquad$ add B to $\mathcal{B}$
$P' \Leftarrow P$
while $(B \to \alpha A \beta \in P') \land (A \in \mathcal{B}) \land (B \to \alpha \beta \notin P')$ **do**
$\qquad$ add $B \to \alpha\beta$ to P'
for each $B \to \Lambda \in P'$ **do**
$\qquad$ remove $B \to \Lambda$ from P'
return (V, Σ, S, P')

Definition 10.13

Unit productions
A production of the form $A \to B$ is a *unit production*, where $A, B \in V$.

> **Lemma 10.3** – For any CFG G there exists a CFG G'
> such that G' contains no unit productions and $\mathcal{L}(G) = \mathcal{L}(G')$.

Proof: The proof is analogous to the proof of Lemma 8.3. We leave it as an exercise. $\square$

We are now able to prove Theorem 10.2.

Proof of Theorem 10.2: The three previous lemmas allow us to assume that the language L has a CFG $G = (V, \Sigma, S, P)$ that does not have any useless variables, nor any erasing productions, nor any unit productions. Therefore every production is either just $A \to a$, where $A \in V$ and $a \in \Sigma$ or

$$A \to \alpha = \alpha_1 \alpha_2 \ldots \alpha_k$$

where $k > 1$, $A \in V$, and each $\alpha_i \in (V \cup \Sigma)$. For each symbol $a \in \Sigma$ create a new variable B_a and add the production $B_a \to a$ to P. Now *replace* each such production $A \to \alpha$ in P with

$$A \to \beta = \beta_1 \beta_2 \ldots \beta_k$$

where $\beta_i = \alpha_i$ if $\alpha_i \in V$, and $\beta_i = B_a$ if $\alpha_i = a \in \Sigma$. At this point every production in P is either just $A \to a$, where $A \in V$ and $a \in \Sigma$ or $A \to \beta$ where $A \in V$ and $\beta \in V^*$ and $|\beta| \geq 2$. To complete the proof we need to show that if $|\beta| > 2$ then the production can be replaced by a series of short productions. If $A \to \beta_1 \beta_2 \ldots \beta_k$ and $k > 2$ we replace this by $A \to \beta_1 A'$ and $A' \to \beta_2 \ldots \beta_k$, where A' is new variable. Repeated use of this replacement will yield CNF. $\square$

Example 10.11

Reconsider the CFG of Example 10.3 modified to be Λ-free:

$$P = \{S \to (S), \ S \to SS, \ S \to ()\}$$

Let the terminals now be produced by their own variables:

$$P = \{S \to LSR, \ S \to SS, \ S \to LR, \ L \to (, \ R \to)\}$$

And finally break up the right-hand side of length three:

$$P = \{S \to LA, \ A \to SR, \ S \to SS, \ S \to LR, \ L \to (, \ R \to)\}$$

This is in Chomsky normal form.

10.5   Greibach Normal Form

In this section we introduce a second normal form for context-free languages. Each normal form is introduced to make proofs and algorithms simpler and more natural in its own way.

Definition 10.14

Greibach normal form

A CFG in which every production is of the form $A \rightarrow a\alpha$ is in Greibach normal form (GNF), where $A \in V$ and $a \in \Sigma$ and $\alpha \in V^*$. In particular $A \rightarrow a$ is allowed, but $A \rightarrow \Lambda$ is not allowed.

There is a certain familiarity with this type of grammar. In particular, if every $A \rightarrow a\alpha$ has $|\alpha| = 1$ then it would be like productions in a regular grammar. Clearly the power comes from allowing longer αs. (It will turn out that we will only need αs of length up to two variables.) The following lemma is analogous to Lemma 8.1.

> **Lemma 10.4** – For any leftmost derivation using a CFG
> G in Greibach normal form, if $S \overset{*}{\Rightarrow} \gamma$ then $\gamma = x\beta$,
> where $x \in \Sigma^*$ and $\beta \in V^*$.

Proof: The proof is analogous to the proof of Lemma 8.1 $\square$

> **Theorem 10.3** – For any Λ-free context-free language L
> there exists a CFG G in Greibach normal form, where
> $L = \mathcal{L}(G)$.

Proof: We assume, without loss of generality, that L is given as a CFG $G = (V, \Sigma, S, P)$ in Chomsky normal form. Let $V = \{A_1, A_2, \ldots, A_n\}$, $P_1 = \{A \rightarrow a \in P \mid A \in V, a \in \Sigma\}$ and $P_2 = \{A \rightarrow BC \in P \mid A, B, C \in V\}$; $P = P_1 \cup P_2$. We begin by noting that a rightmost derivation using a grammar in CNF implies this property:

$$A_j \overset{*}{\Rightarrow} x \in \Sigma^* \text{ iff } x = ay, A_j \overset{*}{\Rightarrow} A_i y, \text{ and } A_i \rightarrow a \in P \qquad (10.1)$$

In other words, when deriving a string of terminals, we can delay producing the first terminal until the last step.

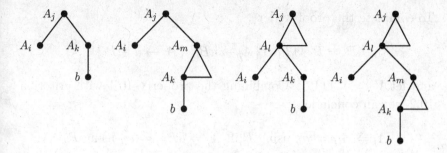

Figure 10.7: Possible derivations trees.

We will produce our new GNF grammar $G' = (V', \Sigma, S, P')$ in parts. Define $V'' = \{B_{i,j} \mid 1 \leq i, j \leq n\}$ to be a set of new variables. We want to discover a set of productions P'' for these variables that satisfies this criterion:

$$B_{i,j} \overset{*}{\Rightarrow} y \text{ using } P_1 \cup P'' \text{ iff } A_j \overset{*}{\Rightarrow} A_i y \text{ using } P_1 \cup P_2 \qquad (10.2)$$

Observe that the CNF grammar using P has the four types of derivation trees of $A_j \overset{*}{\Rightarrow} A_i y$ shown in Figure 10.7. The first tree is the case where $y = b$. The second tree correspond to the case when the first derivations step was $A_j \Rightarrow A_i A_m$. The third tree is the case, where the derivation step that produced A_i, $A_l \Rightarrow A_i A_k$, was not the first but was constrained so that $A_l \overset{*}{\Rightarrow} A_i b$ only. The fourth tree is the most general unconstrained case.

By appealing to the criterion recursively we can build P'' this way:

$$\{B_{i,j} \to b \mid A_j \to A_i A_k \in P_2 \text{ and } A_k \to b \in P_1\} \cup$$
$$\{B_{i,j} \to b B_{k,m} \mid A_j \to A_i A_m \in P_2 \text{ and } A_k \to b \in P_1\} \cup$$
$$\{B_{i,j} \to b B_{l,j} \mid A_l \to A_i A_k \in P_2 \text{ and } A_k \to b \in P_1\} \cup$$
$$\{B_{i,j} \to b B_{k,m} B_{l,j} \mid A_l \to A_i A_m \in P_2 \text{ and } A_k \to b \in P_1\}$$

It can be shown inductively (on the length of x) that the criterion does indeed hold for this P''. It follows since the four sets of productions given correspond to the four types of derivations trees.

To complete the proof we let

$$P' = P'' \cup P_1 \cup \{A_j \to aB_{i,j} \mid A_i \to a \in P_1\}$$

and let $V' = V \cup V''$. Combining the property 10.1 with criterion 10.2 we can conclude

$$A_j \overset{*}{\Rightarrow} A_i y \Rightarrow ay \text{ using } P \text{ iff } A_j \Rightarrow aB_{i,j} \overset{*}{\Rightarrow} ay \text{ using } P'$$

for all $A_j \in V$ and $y \in \Sigma^*$ and so it is true for the case when $S = A_j$.

□

Example 10.12

Reconsider the CFG in CNF of Example 10.11:

$$P = \{S \to LA, \; A \to SR, \; S \to SS, \; S \to LR, \; L \to (, \; R \to)\}$$

with the variables renamed as in our proof:

$$P = \{A_1 \to A_2 A_3, A_3 \to A_1 A_4, A_1 \to A_1 A_1, A_1 \to A_2 A_4, A_2 \to (, A_3 \to)\}$$

where A_1 is the start symbol. So $P_1 = \{A_2 \to (, \; A_3 \to)\}$. First we create V''. For brevity we will omit all productions that contain useless variables.) We get these contributions to P''

$\{B_{1,3} \to), \; B_{1,2} \to)\} \cup$
$\{B_{2,1} \to (B_{2,3}, \; B_{2,1} \to)B_{4,3}, \; B_{1,3} \to (B_{2,4}, \; B_{2,1} \to (B_{2,4}, \; B_{2,1} \to)B_{4,4}\} \cup$
$\{B_{1,j} \to)B_{3,j} \mid 1 \le j \le 4\} \cup \{, B_{2,j} \to)B_{1,j} \mid 1 \le j \le 4\} \cup$
$\{B_{2,j} \to (B_{2,3} \mid 1 \le j \le 4\} \cup \{B_{2,j} \to)B_{4,3}B_{1,j} \mid 1 \le j \le 4\} \cup$
$\quad \{B_{2,j} \to (B_{2,4}B_{1,j} \mid 1 \le j \le 4\} \cup \{B_{2,j} \to)B_{4,4}B_{1,j} \mid 1 \le j \le 4\}$

and finally

$$P' = P'' \cup P_1 \cup \{A_j \to (B_{2,j} \mid j \in \{1,3,4\}\} \cup \{A_j \to)B_{4,j} \mid j \in \{1,3,4\}\}$$

This is in Greibach normal form.

10.6   Beyond Context-Free Languages

Canonical examples of context-free languages, such as the set of strings of balanced parentheses, exhibit two-way balance — a later symbol (or symbols) being paired up with an earlier symbol (or symbols). However, if the notion of structure in the language is more complex than two-way balance we might find that context-free grammars are not powerful enough.

Consider the language L which has *three-way* balance:

$$L = \{a^n b^n c^n \mid n > 0\}.$$

To appreciate why there is no context-free grammar for L, you might pause and try to devise one. We know that a language (which is Λ-free) is context-free iff there exists a CFG for it in Chomsky normal form (CNF). We begin by establishing simple properties of CFGs.

> **Lemma 10.5** – For any infinite context-free language L,
> if a CFG G in CNF generates L, there is no bound
> on the height of the derivation trees required of G by
> strings of L.

Proof: Note that derivation trees for CNF are binary trees, with single edges reaching the leaves. Consequently, a derivation tree of height h can only generate a string of length at most 2^{h-1}. Therefore L, being an infinite language, has strings longer than any bounded tree size can accommodate. $\square$

> **Lemma 10.6** – For any infinite context-free language L,
> if G is a CFG in CNF that generates L then some
> derivation tree that G generates has a path from the
> root to a leaf with two occurrences of the same non-
> terminal symbol.

Proof: Since L is an infinite language, by Lemma 10.5, there are derivation trees of unbounded height corresponding to G. In particular, we must have derivation trees for some strings in L that have

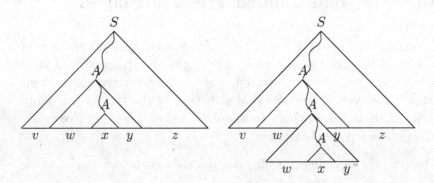

Figure 10.8: In tree T at the left, replace the lower A-rooted subtree by a *copy* of the upper A-rooted subtree to get tree T' at the right.

heights exceeding $n = |V|$, the number of nonterminal symbols in G. By the pigeon-hole principle a tree with a path of length greater than n must have the same nonterminal appearing twice. (The left side of Figure 10.8 depicts the situation, with a path running down from S through two occurrences of A.) □

Theorem 10.4 – $L = \{a^n b^n c^n \mid n > 0\}$ is not a context-free language.

Proof: Suppose that there is a context-free grammar $G = (V, \Sigma, S, P)$ in CNF such that $\mathcal{L}(G) = L$; we will find that this assumption leads to a contradiction.

Since L is an infinite language, by Lemma 10.6, G generates some derivation tree with the same nonterminal occurring twice on some path; call it A, as shown in the left-hand diagram of Figure 10.8. Let x be the string that the lower A generates. Then the upper A generates a string that *contains* x, that is, wxy, for some w and y. We know that either w or y is not Λ; since G is in CNF the upper A will generate a non-empty subtree that does not include the lower A. The entire string generated by the S at the root is $u = vwxyz$, for some v and z. Since $u \in L$ we know $u = a^m b^m c^m$ for some m.

Now a copy of the whole subtree rooted at the upper A can replace the subtree rooted at the lower A, creating a new valid derivation tree T'; this is shown in the right-hand diagram of Figure 10.8. The string generated by the root of T' is $u' = vwwxyyz$. Clearly T' is a valid derivation tree using G, so $u' \in \mathcal{L}(G)$ or equivalently $u' \in L$. Therefore $u' = a^l b^l c^l$ for some l.

A string is *homogeneous* if it is composed of only one symbol, possibly repeated. We claim that w is homogeneous, for suppose, to the contrary, that w contained two different symbols, say an a and a b. In that case ww would have a b before an a, and so would u', in violation of the requirement that $u' = a^l b^l c^l$. Similarly y is homogeneous. Now u' must be longer than u so $l > m$, but since the only increase in the number of symbols in going from u to u' comes from an extra occurrence of each of the two homogeneous strings w and y, there must be one terminal symbol among the three — an a, b or c — that is not in w or y and hence still appears only m times in u'. Consequently, the string u' — which is generated by G — cannot be in L. This result contradicts the assumption that there exists a grammar G generating $L = \{a^n b^n c^n \mid n \geq 0\}$). □

The proof just given was not devised just for the given language. The proof technique is well-known and can be generalized to most (but not all!) non-context-free languages. The technique is known by the nickname "The Pumping Lemma" (since we can repeatedly pump the upper-A subtree to create larger legitimate trees).

The proof also illustrates why these grammars are called "context-free." The mechanics of the proof relies on the observation that any time a variable like A occurs in a derivation it can generate, by itself, anything an A can generate in any other context, and still be valid.

Exercises

10.1 – What is the language generated by: $S \to SSS \mid a$?

10.2 – Using G_3, write derivations for the following strings and give the corresponding derivations trees:

   (a) ( ) (( ))

   (b) ((( ) ( )))

10.3 – Write a CFG for the language of balanced braces and balanced angle brackets. Your grammar should permit nesting and concatenation but not arbitrary permutations. For example, "{ < > { } } < { } >" is in this language, but not "{ < } >". (Hint: Start with a recursive definition.)

10.4 – Give examples of languages that satisfy the following conditions:

   (a) L_r is regular and infinite, L_n is non-regular and $L_r \subset L_n$.

   (b) L_r is regular, L_n is non-regular and $L_n \subset L_r$.

   (c) L_1 and L_2 are non-regular but $L_r = L_1 \cap L_2$ is regular.

10.5 – For the grammar G_4,

   (a) Prove by mathematical induction that it is possible to derive from S any string of the form $x\ S\ x^R$, where x is any string over $\{a, b\}$ and x^R is its reverse. You may assume a recursive definition of reverse: (i) $\Lambda^R = \Lambda$, and (ii) $(x\,a)^R = a\,x^R$

   (b) Use the result of part (a) to prove that $\mathcal{L}(G_4)$ is the set of even-length palindromes.

10.6 – What productions can be added to the grammar G_4 for even-length palindromes to yield a grammar for all palindromes (including odd lengths)?

10.7 – Give a CFG for these languages:

   (a) $\{x \mid x = a^i b^{2i},\ i > 0\}$.

(b) $\{x \mid x = a^i b^j c^k, \; j = i + k\}$.

(c) $\{x \mid x = a^i b^j c^k, \; (i = j \lor j = k)\}$.

(d) $\{x \mid x = a^i b^j, \; i \neq j\}$.

10.8 – The set of balanced parentheses, B, was specified by Definition 10.4. There is another way to characterize B. First, for any string x, let $m(x)$ be the number of left parentheses and $n(x)$ the number of right parentheses. Also, recall that y is a *prefix* of x iff there is a string w (possibly empty) such that $yw = x$. Let

$$B = \{x \mid x \in \{(,)\}^* \land m(x) = n(x) \land \forall y : y \text{ a prefix of } x \to m(y) \geq n(y).\}$$

To put it another way, as we process a string from left to right suppose we keep track of the difference between the number of left and right parentheses. Then that difference ends up at zero and never goes negative along the way. Show that the two definitions of B are equivalent.

10.9 – Let L_e be the set of strings of equal numbers of as and bs in arbitrary order. Devise a grammar, G_e, for this language, such that $\mathcal{L}(G_e) = L_e$. (Hint: Find a natural way to pair the as and bs with nested balance.)

10.10 – Give a CFG for the expressions of propositional logic, including all three operators. Recall that, even though the formal definition of proposition did not rely on precedence, that expressions are rarely fully parenthesized and rely on precedence productions to be interpreted. Negation has the highest precedence and and conjunction has the lowest Make use of the techniques introduced for the grammar of algebraic expressions to create a grammar that deals with all the issues raised there. In particular, your grammar should be unambiguous and should create structures that reflect the way that precedence and parentheses group the propositions during correct evaluation.

10.11 – Prove that every regular language is context-free in a different way. Give an algorithm to convert an RE into a CFG. (Hint: Recursively build grammars from sub-grammars as guided by how a regular expression is built from subexpressions.)

10.12 – As follow up to the previous exercise, write a context-free grammar for the language corresponding to the regular expression $((a + b^*c)d)^*$

10.13 – Prove that if a string has two distinct leftmost derivations then it follows the string is ambiguous for the grammar.

10.14 – Prove Lemma 10.1.

10.15 – Show that $L = \{a^i b^j c^k \mid i < j < k\}$ is not a CFL using the same proof technique as in Theorem 10.4.

10.16 – Show by example that the intersection of two CFLs not necessarily context-free.

Chapter 11

Pushdown Automata and Parsing

In earlier chapters you learned about an important class of languages — the regular languages — and about a class of automata, the finite automata, that can recognize all of those languages and no others. You might therefore wonder whether there is some category of automata that is precisely suited to recognize the broader class of languages introduced in Chapter 10, those that can be generated by context-free grammars (CFGs). There is indeed a type of automaton for this task, the *nondeterministic pushdown automaton* (NPDA). NPDAs, along with their cousins the deterministic PDAs (DPDAs), are the topic of this chapter. We will write simply "PDA" when determinism or its absence is not the focus of discussion.

NPDAs are of interest for computer science mainly because of their relationship to CFGs: that for every CFG, G, there is an NPDA that recognizes $\mathcal{L}(G)$. In the course of demonstrating a simple way to find such an NPDA, we will see where the nondeterminacy comes from. We will find that nondeterminism is not only convenient but necessary. That is, for some CFGs and their languages, there is no DPDA that recognizes them. It follows that the class of NPDAs is larger than the class of DPDAs. This situation is different from what we found with NFAs and DFAs, which are equivalent with respect to the class of languages they accept.

271

We already know — from several suggestive examples in Chapter 10 — that CFGs play a key role in specifying programming languages. If G is a CFG specifying the grammar of some programming language, then $\mathcal{L}(G)$ *is* that programming language, from the formal language viewpoint. In other words, each correct computer program in that language is a string in $\mathcal{L}(G)$, typically a very long one. Now, that is not the whole story, since the strings of a programming language have meanings. However, it also turns out — as you will see in detail if you take a compiler course — that grammars can also provide a structural basis for meanings in programming languages; recall Section 10.3.

When compiling a program expressed as a string s, the compiler must analyze whether and how G could have generated s. This key phase in compiling, of inferring how the string was derived, is called *parsing*. In Section 11.5, we will construct NPDAs that mimic some crucial aspects of parsing and thus qualify as *models* of parsing. Despite the absence of some details of true parsers, we will see how different PDA construction techniques correspond to different parsing strategies.

11.1   Motivating PDAs

It is now time to see just what a PDA actually is. PDAs have states, like FAs and will make transitions from state to state in response to a stream of input symbols. However, a PDA is different in that it maintains a memory mechanism called a (pushdown) stack. Symbols can be **PUSH**ed onto the stack and later removed by an action called **POP**ping. **POP**ping the stack removes the most recently added (**PUSH**ed) symbol. Because there is no limit on the **PUSH**ing, the stack provides unbounded — infinite, one might say — memory.

Example 11.1

This pseudocode is for a stack-based approach to recognizing the language $L = \{0^n 1^n \mid n > 0\}$

> *read*(c)
> **while** $c = 0$ **do**
> > *push*(0)
> > *read*(c)
> **if** $c = 1$ and stack not empty **then** $d \Leftarrow pop()$
> **else fail**
> **while** stack not empty **do**
> > *read*(c)
> > **if** $c = 1$ **then** $d \Leftarrow pop()$
> > **else fail**
> **succeed**

There is a single unnamed stack where *push*(0) pushes the character 0 on the stack and $d \Leftarrow pop()$ pops the stack top and assigns it to the variable d. (In this example the variable d is not used.) The *read*(c) command reads the next character from the input stream into the variable c; it will "fail" if there is no further input.

Clearly this approach counts the number of 0s in the input by pushing n times if there are n 0s in the initial input. When the first 1 arrives it switches over and starts popping a 0 for each 1 it encounters. But in what sense does this recognize L? An input string is in the language L if and only if the last input character had just be read when the stack becomes empty; that is we successfully terminate the algorithm exactly when the input is exhausted.

Consider what else could have happened. If the input was 00111 then the stack would be empty, leading to termination when there was one more 1 to read. (It "accepted" the string that was the first four characters of the input.) Alternatively, if the input was 00011 the input would have been exhausted before the stack was empty, leading to a read error and no successful termination. Further if the input was not of the form $0^i 1^j$ then there would also have been no successful termination.

Example 11.2

Consider this pseudocode for a stack-based approach to recognizing the language L of even-length palindromes over $\Sigma = \{a, b\}$, of length at least two.

$$read(c)$$
$$mid \Leftarrow \text{false}$$
while $\neg\, mid$ **do**
    $push(c)$
    $read(c)$
    choose $mid \in \{\text{true, false}\}$
$d \Leftarrow pop()$
if $c \neq d$ **then fail**
while stack not empty **do**
    $read(c)$
    $d \Leftarrow pop()$
    if $c \neq d$ **then fail**
succeed

Unlike the previous example this pseudocode is nondeterministic. It chooses mid and when mid first becomes true it believes the first character after the midpoint was just read and proceeds to verify that the input is palindromic. A stack is a very natural mechanism for verifying that a string is a palindrome; if the first half of the string is pushed on the stack then the second half, read left to right, should match the first half as it is being popped off.

As in the previous example, an input string is in the language L if and only if the last input character had just be read when the stack becomes empty. Why use the power of nondeterminism? It is because the input is stream input and can not be rewound; so as we go forward, if we want to use the stack as described, then we need to act when we reach the middle of the input. Since there is nothing near the middle of a long string to give us a clue, we guess nondeterministically.

These two examples will guide and motivate decisions as we give a formal definition of a PDA. First is the decision to start with nondeterminism as part of the model. The first example was deterministic but the the palindrome example used choices in a very natural way. We will discover there are languages for which there is no deterministic PDA but simple nondeterministic PDAs do exist. The palindrome language is such a language. Notice that this is fundamentally different from the situation with finite automata, where nondeterminism did not confer superior expressive power.

Second is the observation that strings can be recognized as being in a language by virtue of the fact that the stack is empty exactly when the last symbol of the input is read. This is called "acceptance by empty stack". We will define PDAs to accept in this way. This is also at variance with the way finite automata accept input, which is by arrival at an accepting state. It turns out that PDAs *can* be defined, instead, to recognize input using accepting states; we will discuss the two approaches in Section 11.7.

Next we will decide to have every transition depend on the stack top value. The alternative is that sometimes we will use it and sometimes we will ignore it and that will make our model unnecessarily complicated. A consequence of this decision is that we will insist that when we turn a PDA on, in its initial state it will start with a non-empty stack; otherwise it will not be able to even make a first transition. It will start with exactly one stack symbol and we will know what this symbol is. This symbol will allows us to do several things: we can use it to test if the stack has only one symbol on it (almost empty) and we can use to initiate something (if it is immediately replaced). Another consequence of this decision is the fact that *we will not allow the empty string to be accepted by a PDA*; since we accept by empty stack and the stack starts out non-empty.

We pause to consider how the stack will be regarded. It might be regarded as a special-purpose memory in hardware or it might be regarded as a data structure in software. Instead we will steer to a more formal notion of a stack: the stack is a string S. For example if the stack has three elements — an a on top of a b on top of a c —

then it will be represented by the string $\mathcal{S} = abc$. In particular the stack "read from top to bottom" is the same as the string version read from left to right. Note that the stack top symbol will be the first symbol of the string. The stack is empty if $\mathcal{S} = \Lambda$. To **PUSH** a symbol on the stack is to append it to the beginning of $\mathcal{S}$ and to **POP** it is to remove the first symbol.

The fourth decision is the most unexpected. We will not use **PUSH** and **POP** operations. In an effort to simplify PDAs researchers have discovered that it is best to use only one "stack action", rather than two operators. This decision will simplify everything that follows, though you might not be able to see that now.

What is our single stack action? It is to specify a string α of stack symbols and ask for the first symbol of $\mathcal{S}$ to be replaced by α. Suppose, again, that $\mathcal{S} = abc$ and we wish to **PUSH**(d); we will do this by specifying $\alpha = da$ so that the a at the beginning of $\mathcal{S}$ is replaced resulting in $\mathcal{S} = dabc$. Suppose instead we wanted to **POP** the stack top off of $\mathcal{S} = abc$; we will do this be making $\alpha = \Lambda$ which result in $\mathcal{S} = bc$. Therefore the two stack operations are subsumed by one stack action. However this stack action is actually even more flexible since there is no restriction on α. In general, if α has length k then a single stack action is the same as a **POP** followed by k **PUSH**es.

11.2   Standard Notation for PDAs

This section describes our model for PDAs. We will begin with the formal model and then describe PDAs with state-transition diagrams. The motivations which we discussed in the previous section are found here.

The general definition of NPDAs involves six items. Four of these are the ones in the quintuples (5-tuples) used in Chapter 9 to represent FAs. Not surprisingly, NPDAs require additional items involving the stack, specifically, a set of stack symbols and the special stack symbol, S. Because we are adopting acceptance by empty stack there is no set of accepting states.

Definition 11.1

Nondeterministic Pushdown Automata

A pushdown automaton is a sextuple (6-tuple), $M = (Q, \Sigma, \Gamma, q_0, S, \delta)$, where

> Q is a finite set of states;
> Σ is a finite set of input symbols;
> Γ is a finite set of stack symbols;
> $q_0 \in Q$, where q_0 is the start state,
> $S \in \Gamma$, where S is the start symbol for the stack;
> δ is a transition function,

$$\delta : Q \times \Sigma \times \Gamma \to 2^{Q \times \Gamma^*}.$$

Note that codomain of this δ function shares an important characteristic with the δ used for NFAs: δ is a set-valued function. The key difference is that here each transition in the set is an ordered pair, specifying the new state and the stack action. Here, δ will have three arguments: a state and an input symbol as in FAs, and also a stack symbol, which will be the stack top symbol. The output of δ will be a set of ordered pairs. For example if

$$(q, \alpha) \in \delta(p, a, b)$$

then if the PDA is in state $p \in Q$, the next input symbol is $a \in \Sigma$ and the stack top symbol was $b \in \Gamma$ then one of the choices will be to transition to state q and perform stack action α to the stack. The choices presented by δ are processed nondeterministically.~

We introduce a formal description of the current snapshot of the PDA in action. A **configuration** is the ordered pair of the state and the stack. We will adopt the $\vdash$ operator to indicate when one configuration can lead to another. In particular:

$$(p, \mathcal{S}_1) \vdash (q, \mathcal{S}_2)$$

when a is the next symbol on the input, $\mathcal{S}_1 = b\beta$ and $\mathcal{S}_2 = \alpha\beta$, and when $(q, \alpha) \in \delta(p, a, b)$. We let $(p, \mathcal{S}_1) \vdash^* (q, \mathcal{S}_2)$ indicate that zero or more transitions of the PDA can take you from the first to the second configuration, for some input. Further we let

$$(p, \mathcal{S}_1) \vdash^*_x (q, \mathcal{S}_2)$$

indicate that the transitions of the PDA processing the input $x \in \Sigma^*$ can take you from the first to the second configuration.

Definition 11.2

Language accepted by NPDA $M = (Q, \Sigma, \Gamma, q_0, S, \delta)$

$$\mathcal{L}(M) = \{x \mid (q_0, S) \vdash^*_x (p, \Lambda)\}.$$

In other words, if M, starting in state q_0 with a stack consisting of the single symbol S, *can* choose a sequence of transitions ending up with an empty stack, after reading the input x. (The state p is unconstrained.)

In order to present readable examples we discuss how these machines can be presented as state-transition diagrams. The basic ideas are the same as with FAs, but now we need to accommodate the new type of transitions. An arc representing an transition is labelled with the two symbols, input and stack top, that enable the transition, as well as the stack action that takes place during the transition. So when $(q, \alpha) \in \delta(p, a, b)$ the transition is drawn as:

Example 11.3

Give a PDA for the language addressed in Example 11.1, $L = \{0^n 1^n \mid n > 0\}$, based on the pseudocode.

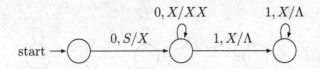

Figure 11.1: A stack-augmented state-transition diagram.

The diagram for a PDA M is given in Figure 11.1. The PDA starts by immediately overwriting the stack start symbol S with the symbol X. Thereafter we push an X for each successive 0 in the input. (The pseudocode pushes 0s on the stack instead of Xs. Since symbols from Σ can also be in Γ our PDA could do that. We have elected to push Xs just to emphasize that Γ allows us to use new, possibly more general symbols.)

When the first 1 arrives we transition to the rightmost state while popping off one X symbol. Thereafter M pops Xs for each 1 on the input. If the last input input symbol results in an empty stack then the input is accepted. Note that the machine has no way of detecting that the input is exhausted, nor does it detect an empty stack.

It is easy to see that even though we are using the stack memory to serve as a counter, we continue to use the states as a memory mechanism just as any FA would. With the states we insure the input is of the form 0^i1^j, and with the stack we insure $i = j$.

Example 11.4

Give a PDA for the language addressed in Example 11.2, the language of even-length, palindromes over $\Sigma = \{a, b\}$, based on the pseudocode.

The diagram for a PDA M is given in Figure 11.2. The PDA starts by immediately overwriting the stack start symbol S with the symbol X or Y. Thereafter we push an X for each a in the input and a Y for each b. Again, we have elected to push Xs and Ys instead of as and bs.

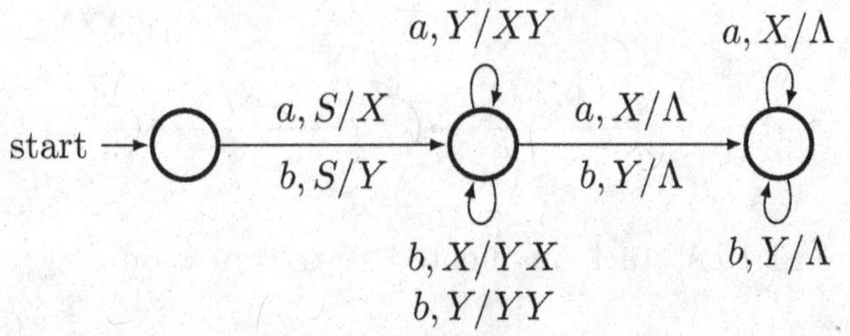

Figure 11.2: A state-transition diagram for even-length palindromes.

We use the full power of nondeterminism choosing to move to the rightmost state as we are reading the first symbol of the second half. We pop during this and every successive transition. While there were no restrictions on the first half of the input, when reading the second half our PDA keeps going only as long as each new input symbol matches each new stack to symbol. If the last input input symbol results in an empty stack then the input is accepted.

Example 11.5

Express the diagram in Figure 11.2 as the 6-tuple.

Calling the states, left to right, q_0, q_1, and q_3 we get

$$(\{q_0, q_1, q_2\}, \{a, b\}, \{X, Y, S\}, q_0, S, \delta),$$

where δ still needs to be specified. In the following table we present just three of the transitions needed for δ and leave it as an exercise is to provide the rest of the δ table.

from state Q	input symbol Σ	stack symbol Γ $\rightarrow$	to state Q	stack action Γ^*
q_0	a	S	$\{(q_1,$	$X)\}$
q_1	b	Y	$\{(q_1,$	$YY), (q_1, \Lambda)\}.$
q_2	b	X	$\emptyset$	

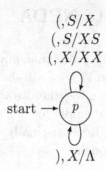

$$(,S/X$$
$$(,S/XS$$
$$(,X/XX$$

start $\rightarrow$ p

$$),X/\Lambda$$

Figure 11.3: A state-transition diagram for balanced parantheses.

Example 11.6

A PDA for the language of balanced parentheses can be based on the recursive definitions used for the grammar in Example 10.3. Instead we will give a design based on Exercise 10.8, which uses a counter-based approach. A stack can use pushes and pops to simulate increment and decrements of a counter.

Unfortunately testing for zero is problematic if zero corresponds to an empty stack, since a PDA with an empty stack can not make a transition. For this language consider when a right parenthesis is read and the counter goes to zero. If that was the final input character the stack could go empty leading to acceptance. However if there is another character — necessarily a left parenthesis — the PDA should have an S on the stack, because in a strong sense the PDA is starting all over afresh. However the S will only be on the stack if the PDA nondeterministically guessed there would be more input when the counter next went to zero and pushed an S when the counter was last zero in anticipation of the need to continue. On the other hand if there was no more input the PDA would have guessed that and not pushed an S, hence allowing the PDA to accept when the stack next went empty. This is summarized in Figure 11.3, where the only state is p.

11.3   From CFG to NPDA

This section will essentially prove that any CFG can be converted into a NPDA. In the Section 11.4 we will show that any NPDA can be converted into a CFG. Taken together we will conclude that NPDAs could be used as a machine model for defining the class of context-free languages, even though we originally defined the class with a grammatical generative model.

> **Theorem 11.1** – If G is a CFG for a Λ-free language
> then there exists an NPDA M, such that $L(G) = L(M)$

Proof: We will assume the CFG grammar is in Greibach normal form. If it is not, the proof of Theorem 10.3 shows that there is an effective procedure to convert it into that form. We will also assume that all derivations are leftmost and therefore each derivation is of the form indicated by Lemma 10.4. So $G = \{V, \Sigma, S, P\}$, where each production in P is of the form $A \to b\alpha$, where $A \in V$, $b \in \Sigma$, and $\alpha \in V^*$. We define the NPDA $M = (\{q_0\}, \Sigma, V, q_0, S, \delta)$, where the stack alphabet is the same as the set of variables in G. Further the stack start symbol is the same as the grammar's start symbol. Notice that M has only one state! The transition function is defined by:

$$\delta(q_0, b, A) = \{(q_0, \alpha) \mid A \to b\alpha \in P\}$$

The key idea is that derivations with G and computations with M are closely linked, as detailed by this claim.

Claim: For every $x \in \Sigma^*$ and $\beta \in V^*$, $S \overset{*}{\Rightarrow} x\beta$ iff $(q_0, S) \vdash^*_x (q_0, \beta)$.

Proof of claim: Recall each step of the derivation increases the length of x by one. We prove the claim by induction on k the length of x. When $k = 0$, $x = \Lambda$ and β is still just S, so the basis follows.

In general assume $x = yb$ and $S \overset{*}{\Rightarrow} yA\gamma \Rightarrow yb\alpha\gamma = x\beta$, where $\beta = \alpha\gamma$. By the inductive hypothesis $(q_0, S) \vdash^*_y (q_0, A\gamma)$ and $(q_0, A\gamma) \vdash (q_0, \alpha\gamma) = (q_0, \beta)$ after processing the final b of x. The second half of the proof (the if-part) is similar. So the claim follows.

The derivation of a string x ends with $\beta = \Lambda$, so from the claim it follows that x is generated by G iff x is accepted (by empty stack) by M. □

Example 11.7

Consider this CFG, in Greibach normal form, for the language of balanced parentheses.

$$P = \{S \to (R, \ S \to (RS, \ S \to (SR, \ S \to (SRS, \ R \to)\}$$

The transition function δ is:

Q	Σ	Γ	$\to$	Q	Γ^*
q_0	(	S		$\{(q_0,$	$R),$
				$(q_0,$	$RS),$
				$(q_0,$	$SR),$
				$(q_0,$	$SRS)\}$
q_0	)	R		$\{(q_0,$	$\Lambda)\}$

11.4 From NPDA to CFG

Theorem 11.2 – If M is a NPDA then there exists a CFG G, such that $L(M) = L(G)$

Proof: The NPDA is $M = (Q, \Sigma, \Gamma, q_0, S', \delta)$. We will create $G = \{V, \Sigma, S, P\}$. The grammar will have a complex set of variables. In particular, $V = Q \times \Gamma \times Q'$, where $Q' = Q \cup \{\diamond\}$. We use the special symbol $\diamond$ to stand for any member of Q, a "don't care" symbol. We will write the elements of V using angle brackets to make them easier to read, i.e. $\langle p, A, q \rangle \in V$.

The set of productions P might be a large but finite set. When α has $k > 0$ symbols we use $\alpha = \alpha_1 \alpha_2 \ldots \alpha_k$, where each α_i is one symbol.

For each $p \in Q$, $a \in \Sigma$, $A \in \Gamma$, and $(q, \alpha) \in \delta(p, a, A)$ we include these productions in P:

$$\langle p, A, r \rangle \to a \langle q, \alpha_1, r_1 \rangle \langle r_1, \alpha_2, r_2 \rangle \langle r_2, \alpha_3, r_3 \rangle \ldots \langle r_{k-1}, \alpha_k, r \rangle$$

for every $r \in Q'$ and for every $r_i \in Q$, $1 \leq i < k$. So, for each (q, α) there are many productions added to P because of the various choices for r and the r_is. In addition P will contain

$$\langle p, A, q \rangle \to a \text{ and } \langle p, A, \diamond \rangle \to a$$

if $(q, \Lambda) \in \delta(p, a, A)$.

These productions are consistent with the definition of Greibach normal form. Since Lemma 10.4 holds, a (leftmost) derivation of l steps will derive the string $x\alpha$, where $|x| = l$, $x \in \Sigma^*$ and $\alpha \in V^*$. Let $head(\langle p, A, q \rangle) = p$ and $tail(\langle p, A, q \rangle) = q$. Further, let $head(\alpha) = head(\alpha_1)$ and $tail(\alpha) = tail(\alpha_k)$, where $|\alpha| = k$. Also let $core(\alpha) = A_1 A_2 \ldots A_k$ when $\alpha_i = \langle p_i, A_i, q_i \rangle$.

Claim 1: If $\langle p, A, q \rangle \overset{*}{\Rightarrow} x\alpha$ and $|\alpha| = k > 1$ then for every $1 \leq i < k$, $tail(\alpha_i) = head(\alpha_{i+1})$. Further $tail(\alpha_k) = q$.

Proof of Claim 1: A proof by induction on the length of x, follows from the definition of P.

This next claim helps explain the strange definition of V and our choice of productions.

Claim 2: For every $\langle p, A, q \rangle \in V$, $\langle p, A, q \rangle \overset{*}{\Rightarrow} x\gamma$, $x \in \Sigma^*$, $\gamma \in V^+$ iff $(p, A) \vdash^*_x (head(\gamma), core(\gamma))$. Notice M starts with a singleton stack A. Further $\langle p, A, q \rangle \overset{*}{\Rightarrow} x$, $x \in \Sigma^+$ iff $(p, a) \vdash^*_x (q, \Lambda)$.

Proof of Claim 2: We will prove it by induction on the length of x. The basis is $x = \Lambda$, when $\gamma = \langle p, A, q \rangle$ so $(head(\gamma), core(\gamma)) = (p, A)$.

Let $x = ya$, where $a \in \Sigma$, and $\langle p, A, q \rangle \overset{*}{\Rightarrow} ya\gamma$. By the inductive hypothesis $\langle p, A, q \rangle \overset{*}{\Rightarrow} y\beta$ while $(p, A) \vdash^*_y (head(\beta), core(\beta))$. There are two cases.

First $\beta_1 = \langle head(\beta), A, r \rangle \to a\tau$, $\tau \in V^+$ and $\alpha = core(\tau)$. So $(q, \alpha) \in \delta(head(\beta), a, A)$ and $head(\tau) = q$. Since $\gamma = \tau\beta_2 \ldots \beta_k$, $(p, A) \vdash^*_x (head(\gamma), core(\gamma))$.

Second $\beta_1 \to a$ is used , so $(q, \Lambda) \in \delta(head(\beta_1), core(\beta_1))$. There are two subcases. First $\beta = \beta_1$, when the derivation halts with x and the machine will be in configuration (q, Λ). (Note that it does not matter what q is when the stack is empty, so if $tail(\beta_1) = \diamond$ it is still correct.) The second subcase is $|\beta| = k > 1$. Now $\gamma = \beta_2 \ldots \beta_k$ and by Claim 1, $q = tail(\beta_1)$ and $tail(\beta_1) = head(\beta_2) = head(\gamma)$ so we will be in configuration $(q, core(\gamma))$. So Claim 2 follows.

To complete the proof we complete our specification of G, by giving the start symbol $S' = \langle q_0, S, \diamond \rangle$. By Claim 1 and the definition of P we can infer that if $S' \overset{*}{\Rightarrow} x\gamma$, $\gamma \in V^+$, then the symbol $\diamond$ occurs exactly once in γ and $tail(\gamma) = \diamond$. From Claim 2 we conclude $S' \overset{*}{\Rightarrow} x$, $x \in \Sigma^*$ iff $(q_0, S) \vdash_x^* (q, \Lambda)$ for some q. $\square$

Example 11.8

Consider the PDA in Example 11.6. Since it only has one state, p, and four transitions the constructions will be of a manageable size. The first transition, where S is replaced by X gives:

$\langle p, S, p \rangle \to (\langle p, X, p \rangle$ and $\langle p, S, \diamond \rangle \to (\langle p, X, \diamond \rangle$

The second transition, where S is replaced by XS gives:

$\langle p, S, p \rangle \to (\langle p, X, p \rangle \langle p, S, p \rangle$ and $\langle p, S, \diamond \rangle \to (\langle p, X, p \rangle \langle p, S, \diamond \rangle$

The third transition, where X is replaced by XX gives:

$\langle p, X, p \rangle \to (\langle p, X, p \rangle \langle p, X, p \rangle$ and $\langle p, X, \diamond \rangle \to (\langle p, X, p \rangle \langle p, X, \diamond \rangle$

The fourth transition, where X is replaced by Λ gives:

$\langle p, X, p \rangle \to)$ and $\langle p, X, \diamond \rangle \to)$

The start state is $\langle p, S, \diamond \rangle$.

11.5 Parsing

In Section 7.5 we discussed using machine models to define languages by giving mechanisms for *deciding* if a string x was in language L. In other words the machine gives "Yes"/"No" answers. What if we want more information? It turns out to be fairly common when the answer is "Yes" to ask for a proof of the answer.

When a string x is generated by a CFG G we now know how to build
a PDA that will recognize x. When a string x is accepted by that
PDA it is because $x \in \mathcal{L}(G)$, so if asked to prove that it was correct
to accept x all we need to do is exhibit a derivation of x using G.
The process of computing the actual derivation of a given string x is
called **parsing**.

In some sense this is a problem we have already solved. The machine
produced by the constructive proof of Theorem 11.1 makes a series
of transitions on input x that mirror the corresponding derivation of
x. Therefore by simply outputting the successive configurations of
that PDA we will recover the derivation.

Example 11.9

Reconsider Example 11.7 with this CFG:

$$P = \{S \to (R,\ S \to (RS,\ S \to (SR,\ S \to (SRS,\ R \to)\}$$

and the transition function δ given there. Consider the processing of
the input $x = ()(())$.

Input seen	Stack	Derived string
Λ	S	$S \Rightarrow$
$($	RS	$(RS \Rightarrow$
$()$	S	$()S \Rightarrow$
$()($	SR	$()(SR \Rightarrow$
$()((%)$	RR	$()((RR \Rightarrow$
$()(()$	R	$()(()R \Rightarrow$
$()(())$	Λ	$()(())$

You should observe that input seen so far concatenated with the
current stack is exactly the currently derived string. This follows
directly from the Claim in the proof of Theorem 11.1. Therefore we
can say that as the PDA accepts any x it exhibits the derivation
of x.

However this is very unsatisfying since the parsing is done by a non-deterministic machine. While this is theoretically interesting the problem of parsing is a very practical problem. Parsing is the basic process in any approach to exploring the *semantics* of the strings of a language generated by a grammar. Why do we parse English sentences in high school? Because that is how we analyze the structure and meaning (i.e. the relationship of the constituent parts) of a sentence. (Natural language grammars have inspired context-free grammars, but do not be misled; natural language grammars are far more subtle that the grammars in this chapter.)

There are many applications familiar to computer scientists that involving parsing. Primarily the applications involve artificial languages — especially computer programming languages — that are typically defined with context-free grammars. The prototypical application is the design of compilers for artificial languages. The material in this chapter is a preamble to the PDA-based parsing techniques discussed in every textbook for compiler theory.

If the parsing is so important how can we tolerate nondeterministic solutions? Surely there are deterministic solutions! Unfortunately the situation is: yes and no. There are context-free languages for which we will escape the NPDA approach. However there will be context-free languages for which deterministic parsing with a PDA is impossible. These are the subjects of the next three sections.

11.6 Deterministic Pushdown Automata and Parsing

With FAs we began by discussing deterministic machines because they were simple and realistic. Moreover it turned out that NFAs were no more powerful than DFAs in terms of the class of languages recognized. In contrast, for PDAs we began with the *non*deterministic ones principally because they *are* more powerful, and we need that power to recognize all context-free languages. We will show that that there are context-free languages that cannot be recognized by any deterministic PDA. The proof is deferred until the Section 11.8.

Definition 11.3

Deterministic Pushdown Automata (DPDA)

A DPDA is a sextuple (6-tuple), $M = (Q, \Sigma, \Gamma, q_0, S, \delta)$, where the parts are the same as in Definition 11.1 except that the δ function does not provide any choices. In particular,

$$\delta : Q \times \Sigma \times \Gamma \to Q \times \Gamma^*,$$

so that the codomain of δ is ordered pairs, not sets of ordered pairs.

The challenge now is to parse deterministically. The approach for parsing with NPDAs was to simulate a leftmost derivation for the grammar. When there was a choice, because the grammar allowed more than one production to be invoked, the NPDA sidestepped the issue by nondeterministically choosing between those possibilities. DPDAs confront such choices when they try to deterministically simulate a derivation process that is inherently nondeterministic. A DPDA has to get the right answer every time. There two aspects to the solving this problem.

First a context-free language might be generated by many different CFGs and some are easier to work with than others. To get the choices deterministically correct we have DPDAs use input symbols as a guide. The resulting **look-ahead** methods pay attention to the next symbol in the current input and let it influence the choice of which right-hand side to use, when more than one is available. When the grammar is in a form, like Greibach normal form, this is simpler for the PDA trying to guess the next production of the derivation. This is because the the next input symbol must match up with the first symbol of the right-hand side.

To see why, we need to recall the idea of a **recursive** rule, that is, one whose left-side symbol also appears on the right side. Recursive rules come in different varieties. Our immediate concern is with **left-recursive** rules, those in which the left-side symbol appears *first* on the right, for example, $S \rightarrow S\,a$.[1] The next example shows how left-recursion frustrates look-ahead.

Example 11.10

The grammar $(\{S\}, \{a, b\}, S, \{S \rightarrow S\,a, S \rightarrow b\})$ generates the language of the regular expression ba^*. Since every string begins with b, looking (ahead) at the first symbol never helps to decide between the two right-hand sides for S.

However as seen in Example 11.9 even in Greibach normal form there can still be choices of productions and so a NPDA needs stricter guidance on how to build the derivation.

Another difficulty is that a grammar can be **right recursive**. This means that the left-hand variable also appears as the last symbol of the right-hand side, like $S \rightarrow aS$. If a grammar had both $S \rightarrow aS$ and $S \rightarrow a$ as productions and a was the last character in the input how could a PDA deterministically choose between these in its effort to build a derivation. Both production are consistent with the a seen in the input stream, but waiting for the next character will not disambiguate the situation when there is no next character. The problem lies with the inability of PDA to detect the end of the input!

We can finesse the issue in order to build a DPDA by changing the problem. Detecting the end of input should not be a big deal. Since ordinary programs have things like end-of-file markers, it seems fair enough to allow ourselves the same kind of technique with automata. In particular, we can augment each string in any language L by appending a new symbol that is not in the original alphabet of L.

---

[1]There are cases like $X \rightarrow Ya$ and $Y \rightarrow Xd$. This means that X is *indirectly left-recursive* (and so is Y), but this not readily observed. These can all be found by modifying an algorithm for finding cycles in graphs.

Any new symbol will do; we choose $\lhd$.

$$L^{\lhd} = \{x \mid x = y\,\lhd \ \wedge \ y \in L\}.$$

The new symbol is called a *sentinel* since it should be the final symbol of any valid input, and so it can alert the machine that the input is finished.

Example 11.11

Again reconsider Example 11.7 with this CFG:

$$P = \{S \to (R, \ S \to (RS, \ S \to (SR, \ S \to (SRS, \ R \to)\}.$$

Notice that when it produces a '(' it has to decide if this is mated with the final symbol, or if its mate is followed another '('. We wish to modify it so that it uses the sentinel to decide whether there is not another symbol.

Consider this grammar for $L^{\lhd}$, where L is the set of non-empty balanced parentheses:

$$\begin{aligned}
S &\to (AB \\
A &\to (AA \mid) \\
B &\to (AB \mid \lhd.
\end{aligned}$$

This grammar was *newly conceived*, not a modification of the P above. The explanation is based on these assertions: a) S will generate any string in $L^{\lhd}$, b) A will generate anything in L with the first symbol missing, and c) B will generate any string in $L^{\lhd}$ as well as just the symbol $\lhd$. These assertions can be proven by induction on the length of the derivations. (Notice that if L contained the empty string then we could have just used B as the start symbol.)

The key observation is that with the new grammar the next symbol allows the PDA to deterministically decide which production is next used in a derivation. Again, consider the processing of the input $x = ()(())$.

Input seen	Stack	Derived string
Λ	S	$S \Rightarrow$
(	AB	$(AB \Rightarrow$
()	B	$()B \Rightarrow$
()(	AB	$()(AB \Rightarrow$
()((	AAB	$()((AAB \Rightarrow$
()(()	AB	$()(()AB \Rightarrow$
()(())	B	$()(())B \Rightarrow$
()(())◁	Λ	$()(())◁$

As Example 11.11 illustrates, the key in building a deterministic parser is to begin, when necessary, by rewriting the grammar to remove the effects of left and right recursive rules. We have not given a clear algorithmic method for accomplishing this. Such methods are beyond the scope of this book and are covered at length in texts on compiler theory.

A language is called a **deterministic context-free language** if there exists a DPDA that accepts it. However there are variations of the PDA definition, that keep us from exploring a grammatical definition here.

11.7 A Variation of the Pushdown Automata Model

A principal variation in the definition of PDAs in the literature is between the PDAs we have defined, which "recognize by empty stack," and PDA models that "recognize by accepting states." After all FAs use accepting states. Indeed we *can* define a PDA model that uses accepting states. Regardless of how recognition is decided, the models remain fundamentally nondeterministic, with determinism as the exception. In this section only we call the old and new models PDA-E and PDA-A respectively.

We will not give a new formal definition of the PDA-A model, since it is completely analogous with how NFAs recognize inputs with accepting states. There is an interesting consequence of this change. The PDA-E machines could only be used for Λ-free languages. However a PDA-A machine will not require the languages to be Λ-free. This is a small change theoretically but for somebody building a PDA it makes things more natural, since the empty string is often the expected base case in a recursive definition.

The reason we chose to use the PDA-E model is because our focus is on theoretical issues. The proofs we have given are much simpler than the corresponding proofs with the PDA-A model. There is an ineffable sense in which the ideas behind the proofs are tied to the PDA-E model.

11.8   Limitations on Deterministic Pushdown Automata

We will now show that deterministic PDAs are less powerful than nondeterministic PDAs. This might not seem surprising, except that there was no such distinction for FAs. The proof will exhibit a particular CFG language for which there can *not* be a DPDA. The existence of such a language is all we need, since for *any* CFG we know how to construct a corresponding nondeterministic PDA.

> **Theorem 11.3** – There exists a context-free language that is not recognized by any DPDA.

Proof: This will follow from the fact that a DPDA accepts by empty stack. A PDA with an empty stack must halt since the transition function δ requires a stack top variable as an argument to compute the next state and stack action. So if a language contains two distinct strings x and y and x is prefix of y (i.e. $y = xz$) then a deterministic PDA for that language must have an empty stack after reading x and halt; it can not continue reading input in order to accept y. Many context-free languages have such an x and y, like the language of balanced parentheses. □

This proof is somewhat unsatisfying. There is a suspicion that if our PDA was not forced to accept by empty stack then deterministic PDAs might have more scope. As described in the previous section there are variant PDA models that allow recognition by accepting states. But that does not change any conclusions.

Theorem 11.4 – There exists a context-free language that is not recognized by any DPDA that uses accepting states.

Proof: We exhibit a specific language and show that it cannot be recognized by a DPDA. In particular, consider the following context-free language over the alphabet $\Sigma = \{a, b\}$:

$$L = \{x \mid x = a^i b^i,\ i > 0\} \cup \{x \mid x = a^i b^{2i},\ i > 0\}$$

so that, for example, $a^3 b^3 = aaabbb \in L$ and $a^3 b^6 = aaabbbbbb \in L$. To fix ideas, we will argue in terms of these two specific strings, though the arguments are valid in general. We leave it as an Exercise to show that L is a CFL, i.e. there is a CFG G such that $L = \mathcal{L}(G)$.

Assume (for the sake of contradiction) that there exists a DPDA M such that $L = \mathcal{L}(M)$, where $M = (Q, \Sigma, \Gamma, q_0, S, \delta, A)$, where A is the set of accepting states. Consider the behavior of M on the 9-symbol string $a^3 b^6$. After the first six symbols, M has seen $a^3 b^3$ which is in L so M must be in one of its accepting states. Moreover the deterministic nature of M means that there is no choice about which state this will be. From there the remaining symbols (the 7th, 8th and 9th) take M to a state (possibly the same one) that also is accepting. We will use this M to construct another PDA M' that accepts the language $L = \{a^n b^n c^n \mid n \geq 0\}$. But that is impossible according to Theorem 10.4, so M' cannot exist, and hence neither can M from which it is built.

From M we construct M' by first making two equivalent but disjoint copies of M, called M_1 and M_2, by relabeling states so that corresponding states in the two copies can be distinguished. To complete

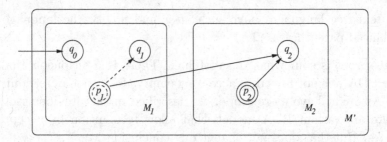

Figure 11.4: The construction of M' that could recognize the language of Theorem 10.4 if M could recognize the language of Theorem 11.4.

the construction of the single machine M', we then modify and augment the components so that:

- The start state of M' is the start state of M_1.

- The accepting states of M' are those of M_2 (but *not* those of M_1).

- The new transitions to get from M_1 to M_2 are formed from a special set of M_1 transitions: those that go out from an *accepting* state on input b (with any stack symbol). For such a transition, say from p_1 to q_1 (where p_1 must be accepting but q_1 can be any state, possibly even p_1), M' also has a transition on input c (instead of b) from p_1 to q_2, where q_2 is the state in M_2 that corresponds to q_1.

- In M_2, change all bs to cs.

Figure 11.4 is a schematic illustration of M'.

Consider what happens when $x = a^3b^3$ is the input to M'. Of course x takes us to a state of M_1 corresponding to an accepting state of M. Now what about the input $y = a^3b^3c^3$? After processing the first six symbols we will make a transition into M_2 on the first c (and will continue within M_2 on the next two cs). What is the state q_2 where we first reach M_2? It is the state corresponding to the state in M arrived at after processing a^3b^4. Further, the state in M_2 that is reached after processing $a^3b^3c^2$ corresponds to the state we would have reached in M on the input a^3b^5. Finally, y takes us to a state corresponding to the state M reached on a^3b^6; this must be an accepting state of M so it is an accepting state of M'. Therefore $y \in \mathcal{L}(M')$.

The above example can easily be generalized. We find that $a^ib^ic^j$ reaches a state in M' (specifically in M_2) that corresponds to the state reached in M on the input a^ib^{i+j}. Further, since M' must reach the states of M_2 to accept a string, any string accepted by M' must begin with a^ib^i, and therefore the behavior outlined above is not only possible, it is forced. It follows that $a^ib^ic^j$ is accepted exactly when $j = i$. So M' is a PDA that accepts the language of Theorem 10.4. However, that language is not context-free and therefore cannot be accepted by any PDA. Hence we have a contradiction to the assumption that M exists. □

There are, of course, many other context-free languages that could have been used to prove the above theorem. A notable example is the set of palindromes (see Definition 10.6). Informally, the language of palindromes is not deterministic because a DPDA can not know when it has reached the middle of an input string.

11.9   More on Parsing

The goal of parsing is to find a derivation of a string in a language. Since the derivation can be exhibited as derivation tree, some people say that the goal is to provide the derivation tree, which is called a **parse tree** in this context. The parsing technique we presented earlier is called **top-down parsing** because, to the external observer, the tree is built by first expanding the root, then a child of the root, etc. This is straightforward theoretically, but this is not how practical parsers are built.

The stack-based method used by compiler builders is called **bottom-up parsing**. This method has both deterministic and nondeterministic versions; we will focus on the deterministic version often called "shift-reduce parsing." This method reads forward in the input stream pushing the input on a stack. When it has read enough

to have just seen the right-hand side of some production, it pauses
and removes the right-hand side from the stack and replaces it on
the stack with the variable on the left-hand side of that production.
(If the right-hand side had k characters, then the top k stack elements would spell out the right-hand side; there would be k "pop"s
and one "push.") Then it goes back to reading input and pushing
it on the stack. Moving input onto the stack is a "shift" step and
removing a right-hand side from the stack is a "reduce" step. We
will not describe the method further but the next example hints at
the generality of the scheme.

Example 11.12

Use the bottom-up parsing method on strings of $\mathcal{L}(G)$, where $G = (\{S\}, \{a, b, f, (,), ,\}, S, P)$ and P contains the rules

$$S \rightarrow f\ (\ S\ ,\ S\ )\ |\ a\ |\ b.$$

Note the use of the comma (",") here as one of the terminal symbols
of G. It is printed in boldface to make it look slightly different from
the ordinary commas. Strings in $\mathcal{L}(G)$ includes b, $f(a,b)$, $f(b,f(a,a))$.

We will show how the stack changes as this method processes the
input $f(f(b,a),b)$. It is clearer in this context to show the stack as a
string with bottom on the left and the top on the right.

Stack	Reason	Stack	Reason
f	shift	$f(f(S,S$	$S \rightarrow a$
$f($	shift	$f(f(S,S)$	shift
$f(f$	shift	$f(S$	$S \rightarrow f(S,S)$
$f(f($	shift	$f(S,$	shift
$f(f(b$	shift	$f(S,b$	shift
$f(f(S$	$S \rightarrow b$	$f(S,S$	$S \rightarrow b$
$f(f(S,$	shift	$f(S,S)$	shift
$f(f(S,a$	shift	S	$S \rightarrow f(S,S)$

Note that when the input is exhausted the stack has been reduced
to the start symbol.

The reason the method is called "bottom-up" is that the reduce step is interpreted as building a subtree of the parse tree. Initially the subtrees have elements of Σ as the leaves, but later the roots of previously built subtrees can be the children of the new roots. It terminates with the start symbol at the root. Hence it is fully-formed parse tree.

Even though this method is stack-based it is not easily explained with the PDA model. PDAs only see the topmost symbol on a stack, but a reduce step needs to know about larger clusters at the top of the stack. We can use PDAs to implement bottom-up parsing but the method loses its clarity and elegance.

11.10   Notes on Memory

The stack provides memory, but it is not the only kind of memory we have seen. Recall that an FA has memory too: it "remembers" which of its states it is in. Although many FA examples use only a few states, real devices — even relatively simple ones — have huge numbers of states. A 16-bit register, for example, has $2^{16} = 65536$ states, while for a single 32-bit register there are over 4 billion states. Strictly speaking, a large modern computer with large but fixed memory could be regarded as an FA with an astronomical number of states. Given that it is easy to have an incredibly large number of states in a real FA, what is the point of introducing the extra memory that the stack provides?

One answer is that PDA memory is not finite, but infinite. In the world of mathematics, the difference between finite and infinite is clear and crucial. We have seen that an unlimited supply of memory is important, since we have proved that without it, FAs can not recognize important context-free languages. But what about in the world of real computers? As a practical matter, computers of modest size by current standards can — despite their finiteness — carry out the recognition of long strings from useful CFGs. Do not let the large size of real machines blind you to the conceptual significance of the distinction between the finite and the infinite. Of course, as seen in this chapter, we never use an infinite amount of memory; instead we require an *unbounded* amount of memory. Alternatively, we insist that all requests for memory will be filled, which can not be true if we start with some finite amount of memory.

Further, while the PDA has extra memory beyond that of FAs, it constrained to behave like a stack. Such last-in-first-out storage allows the automaton to consult only the most recently added symbol (but not the ones below it on the stack). With such a constraint on how it can access its memory, we should not be too surprised to find that there are automata even more powerful than PDAs. That turns out to be true, as we will see in the next chapter on Turing Machines.

Exercises

11.1 – For each of the following strings, show what happens when it is provided as an input to the diagram of Figure 11.1. Give the sequence of configurations that describe the PDA's behavior, using q_0, q_1 and q_2 for the states, left-to-right.

   (a) 0011

   (b) 001

   (c) 00111

11.2 – Express the PDA in Figure 11.2 formally.

11.3 – For each of the following strings, show what happens when it is provided as an input to the diagram of Figure 11.2. Give the sequence of configurations that describe the PDA's behavior.

   A nondeterministic PDA has choices of sequences of configurations. Give a sequence so that the PDA either accepts the input or "accepts" the longest prefix of the input it can (ending with an empty stack) when possible.

    (a) *abaaba*

    (b) *aab*

11.4 – Modify the PDA in Figure 11.2 to recognize all palindromes.

11.5 – For each of the following strings, show what happens when it is provided as an input to the PDA of Example 11.7. Give the sequence of configurations that describe the PDA's behavior.

    (a) $(()())$

    (b) $((())))$

11.6 – The table in Example 11.5, specifies the transition function δ for three of the ten transitions. Complete the table by specifying δ for the remaining transitions.

11.7 – Repeat Exercise 11.5, with sentinels, using the deterministic PDA of Example 11.11.

11.8 – Consider the CFG $G = (\{S, T\}, \{a, b\}, S, \{S \to b\, T, T \to a\, T, \quad T \to \lhd\})$. Give a deterministic PDA, M, that parses top-down with lookahead and that recognizes the language $\mathcal{L}(G)$.

11.9 – Let $L = \{x \mid x = a^i b^j c^k, i < k\}$. For the language $L^\lhd$:

    (a) Informally describe a DPDA.

    (b) Formally describe a DPDA.

11.10 – As requested in the proof of Theorem 11.4 show $L = \{x \mid x = a^i b^i, i > 0\} \cup \{x \mid x = a^i b^{2i}, i > 0\}$ is a context-free language by exhibiting a CFG for it.

11.11 – Given a CFL L_1 and a regular language L_2 show that the intersection $L_3 = L_1 \cap L_2$ is a CFL. (Compare to Exercise 10.16.)

11.12 – Consider the language

$$L' = \{x \in \{a, b, c\}^* \mid x \text{ contains an equal number of}$$
$$a\text{s}, b\text{s}, \text{ and } c\text{s } \}.$$

Prove that L is not context-free, using Exercise 11.11.

Chapter 12

Turing Machines

When we discovered that there are non-regular languages, this led to the discussion of context-free grammars and their languages. Similarly, the fact that there are languages beyond the representational power of CFGs, leads us to consider a more powerful formulation of grammars. On the machine model side we will need a more powerful automaton than pushdown automata.

Specifically we will introduce *unrestricted grammars* and the *Turing Machine* (TM) model. These are advanced topics, so we confine our attention to a few key ideas, illustrated by a continuing example. By skipping directly to TMs we come to end of the storyline of Automata Theory since they are the most powerful. Paradoxically, since they were formulated in 1936, TMs were the beginning of the story historically. Since then the landscape has become complicated with hundreds of languages classes based on as many models. Some are well-known, like *context-sensitive languages*, which we briefly mention.

Turing Machines are the most versatile category of automata. The most important thing about this category is the following assertion: *For every possible algorithm, no matter how complex, there is a Turing Machine that implements it.* Although this assertion is not provable, no counter-example has been found, as is discussed in Section 12.7. For this and other reasons, the assertion is widely believed. In fact, the TM model is used as a definition of computability. The determination of what is computable and what is not is in the realm of theoretical computer science, but the practical value of knowing that something is impossible — that for some problem there is no algorithm that always solves it — should not be underestimated. It tells us that we must reformulate the problem, perhaps restricting the scope of what we hope to accomplish.

12.1 Unrestricted Grammars

The **unrestricted grammar** (UG) class gets its name from the fact that the constraints on productions are relaxed.[1] In particular, we drop the CFG constraint of using a single symbol on the left-hand side of rules. This modification yields a significant gain in the power to generate languages. The definition of a UG looks familiar; it is a quadruple $G = (V, \Sigma, S, P)$, where P is finite and each production in P is of the form:

$$\alpha \to \beta, \quad \alpha, \beta \in (V \cup \Sigma)^*.$$

The four parts here correspond directly to those of CFGs, and derivation steps are defined the same way (with any production $\alpha \to \beta$ permitting the derivation step $\phi\alpha\psi \Rightarrow \phi\beta\psi$). The difference is that where CFGs allowed just a single nonterminal on the left, UGs allow any sequence of terminals and nonterminals. (Note that we have essentially return to the original presentation of grammars in Section 8.6.)

Theorem 10.4 made clear the need for a formulation of grammars more powerful than CFGs if we are going to generate $L = \{a^n b^n c^n \mid n \geq 0\}$. One view of CFG shortcomings is that the left-hand side of the production $A \to \alpha$ can be applied *any* time A appears during a derivation. To control of the use of a replacement — so that it can occur in some contexts but not others — is something that context-*free* productions can not do.[2]

---

[1] These are also known as Type-0 grammars, and by other names.

[2] The so-called context-*sensitive* grammars (CSGs) overcome this shortcoming of CFGs. They give rise to *context-sensitive languages* and their corresponding class of machines, the *linear-bounded automata*. (See Exercise 12.5.)

Example 12.1

The UG production $aAb \rightarrow aCb$ permits an A to be replaced by a C, but only when, at some point in a derivation, it has the surrounding context a_b. So a possible derivation step would be $abaAbAc \Rightarrow abaCbAc$, replacing the first A. The string $abaAbCc$ could *not* be derived instead because the second A does not have the required context.

Example 12.2

Show that the unrestricted grammar G with productions shown here generates exactly the strings of the language $L = \{a^n b^n c^n \mid n \geq 0\}$, which we know is not context-free.

$$
\begin{aligned}
S &\rightarrow WDZ \mid \Lambda \\
D &\rightarrow ABCD \mid ABC \\
CA &\rightarrow AC \\
CB &\rightarrow BC \\
BA &\rightarrow AB \\
WA &\rightarrow aW \\
WB &\rightarrow bX \\
XB &\rightarrow bX \\
XC &\rightarrow cY \\
YC &\rightarrow cY \\
YZ &\rightarrow \Lambda
\end{aligned}
$$

First observe that the second production permits the derivation $D \overset{*}{\Rightarrow} ABCABCABC$ and more generally $D \overset{*}{\Rightarrow} (ABC)^n$ for any $n \geq 1$. So S clearly can derive an intermediate string beginning with a W, ending with a Z, and containing an equal number of As, Bs and Cs in between. Unfortunately the As, Bs and Cs are all mixed up, so if we just made them lower case, with productions like $A \rightarrow a$, we would fail to have all the as before all the bs before all the cs.

The third, fourth and fifth productions can be used to rearrange the As, Bs and Cs, putting all the As before all the Bs before all the Cs.

Consider this example:

$$S \Rightarrow WDZ \Rightarrow WABCDZ \Rightarrow WABCABCZ$$

$$\Rightarrow WABACBCZ \Rightarrow WABABCCZ \Rightarrow WAABBCCZ$$

These interchanges of adjacent As, Bs and Cs constitute a *sorting* process – sorting the As, Bs and Cs. This example clearly generalizes to longer strings.

However, just because a rule *can* be used does not mean it *will* be. Therefore we must examine what happens if the above sorting process is not fully carried out. We will see that it becomes impossible to complete a derivation. First note that any nonempty string $x \in \mathcal{L}(G)$, must have a derivation in which the first replacement introduces an instance of Z (as well W and D). Since Z is a nonterminal it must ultimately be removed. Note that the only production that can remove a Z is the last one, $YZ \to \Lambda$. In other words, for x to be derived we must find Z in the context of a preceding Y. Looking at G we see that the appearance of such a Y must have been triggered by the appearance of an X, which was itself triggered by a W. Consider the following continuation of the above derivation:

$$WAABBCCZ \Rightarrow aWABBCCZ \Rightarrow aaWBBCCZ \Rightarrow aabXBCCZ$$

$$\Rightarrow aabbXCCZ \Rightarrow aabbcYCZ \Rightarrow aabbccYZ \Rightarrow aabbcc$$

This illustrates how the grammar dictates the behavior of the derivation. In particular, the W symbol sweeps across the As (and only As) leaving as behind. When the W reaches a B it changes to an X which then sweeps across Bs (and only Bs) leaving bs in its wake. Finally, the X becomes a Y which changes the Cs it encounters into cs. In other words, in order for a Y to reach the Z we must have all the As before all the Bs before all the Cs. In this way the grammar forces any valid derivation to begin with the sorting process. Hence any string derived with G is in L.

The above example illustrates how much more powerful an unrestricted grammar is than a context-free grammar. The grammar above has a distinct *algorithmic* flavor. It forces three phases: a building phase, a sorting phase, and then a checking phase. There are mechanisms which can force certain productions to be applied before others. Although checking can begin before sorting is completed (or building is completed for that matter), no *part* of a string can be checked until it is sorted.

Given the above grammar, with its algorithmic flavor, it is perhaps not surprising that we will next propose a machine model with mechanisms that allow local changes in a string and the ability to sweep back and forth across a string.

12.2   The Turing Machine Model

Alan Turing in the 1930s devised a model of computation, now called a **Turing Machine** (**TM**), in order to explore questions about the limits of computability. Remarkably, his investigations predate the design of the first modern digital computers (which later Turing was to help design). Because it is a model of what must be true of *any* computational device, the TM is far simpler (and less efficient) than our current notion of what a computer is. Moreover, for proving things, it helps to make the model as simple as possible. Despite its simplicity, however, the TM model has been shown to be every bit as powerful — in terms of what TMs can ultimately compute — as any more realistic model of a computer that has been proposed to date.

A Turing Machine shares characteristics of FAs and PDAs. It has a finite control unit with a finite number of internal *states*. The distinction between the models is in the amount of memory and how it can be accessed. For an FA the input is considered to be in read-only memory that can only be processed left-to-right; the only other "memory" is the implicit knowledge of what each state encodes about the past. For a PDA the input is still found in read-only memory, processed left-to-right, but there is an additional read-write memory, of unbounded size, that is constrained to behave like a stack. A TM also allows an unbounded amount of read-write memory, but without the stack constraint on its use. Further, to simplify the model, the input is assumed to be found in the same read-write memory that is used for the rest of the computation.

The memory of a TM consists of a set of consecutive cells. At each step the machine looks at the symbol in a cell. On the basis of what it sees there, along with its internal state, the TM writes a symbol in the cell, makes a transition to a state and moves to another cell. The movement must be to an adjacent cell. This access mechanism has suggested to some that we call the memory a **tape**; a tape is a read-write storage mechanism accessed by a **tape head** that can move back and forth on the tape. The cells are *not* given addresses, so there is no notion of random access. To get the TM to access a distant cell you have to arrange for it to move there one cell at a time.

More formally, a TM consists of a finite control with a tape that is unbounded in one direction; that is, it has a first cell and a second and so on, indefinitely. Initially the TM is in a designated initial state and the input string x is found right next to the start of the tape, beginning in the second cell. The first cell is "blank." The **blank symbol**, denoted Δ, is a distinguished element of the *tape alphabet*. The infinitely many tape cells beyond the input string are also blank (contain Δ) at the outset. The Δ symbol is not part of the *input alphabet*. Because Δs surround the input, but cannot be part of it, a TM can detect where the input string begins and ends. The input can be the empty string, in which case the second cell is a blank. Initially the tape head is at the first cell. The machine makes a sequence of state transitions.

Since the input is already loaded into memory TMs have a different mechanism for accepting a string that FAs and PDAs. When a TM has decided whether to accept or reject an input it halts and announces its answer. It halts by making a transition to one of two sink states, the **halt states**, q_a and q_r. If the machine halts in state q_a it accepts the input, if it halts in state q_r it rejects the input. Unfortunately a TM may never reach a halt state, instead going into an *infinite loop*.

Like FAs, TMs have transitions that depend on a state and a symbol. Here the symbol is the one in the tape cell that the tape head is currently positioned at. Based on these two values the TM decides three things:

1. what state to be in next (possibly unchanged; possibly a halt state)

2. what symbol to write in the current tape cell (possibly the same symbol), and

3. where to go (move one cell left or right).

We express TMs with transition diagrams that are similar to those for FAs and PDAs, but with information corresponding to the above specifications of what happens during a transition. Suppose there is a transition from state p to state q (which may be the same, in the case of a self-loop), with the label "$X/Y, \mu$", where X and Y are tape symbols and μ ("mu") is the *move*, which can be L = left, or R = right. Then this transition can be used when the machine is in state p and the current tape cell contains the symbol X. As a result the machine enters state q and, after overwriting the X with Y, makes the move that μ specifies. Since a transition to q_r is functionally equivalent to a transition to a trap state, we adopt the same convention as we used with FAs: transitions missing from a diagram are considered to be transitions to q_r.

Definition 12.1

Turing Machines

Formally we define a Turing Machine M by a 7-tuple $M = (Q, \Sigma, \Gamma, q_0, q_a, q_r, \delta)$ where

Q is a finite set of states

Σ is a finite input alphabet, where $\Delta \notin \Sigma$

Γ is a finite tape alphabet, where $\Sigma \subseteq \Gamma$ and $\Delta \in \Gamma$

$q_0 \in Q$ is the initial state,

$q_a \in Q$ is the accepting halt state,

$q_r \in Q$ is the rejecting halt state, and

δ is the transition function, where
$$\delta : Q \setminus \{q_a, q_r\} \times \Gamma \to Q \times \Gamma \times \{L, R\}.$$

Note that the two halt states can only be the possible *result* of δ and they can not be used as inputs. This is because a halt state can have no outbound transitions. The set $\{L, R\}$ in the definition corresponds to the two possible tape head movements: Left or Right. Also note that the TM is a *deterministic* model. The transition described above, from p to q with label "$X/Y, \mu$" is denoted $\delta(p, X) = (q, Y, \mu)$.

The **language accepted by a Turing machine** M, $\mathcal{L}(M)$, is the set of all input strings that cause the TM to halt in state q_a. This creates an unanticipated asymmetry because an input string can be rejected in two ways: it can be rejected by entering state q_r, or it can be rejected by going into an infinite loop (and hence not be accepted)! We would prefer it if every TM always halted, whatever its input. Unfortunately, as we will show below, there are languages that require both ways of failing to accept strings!

Definition 12.2

A language that is accepted by some TM that always halts is a **recursive language**. A language that is accepted by some TM — even a TM that does not halt on all inputs — is a **recursively enumerable language**.[3] Note that a recursive language is necessarily recursively enumerable, but not the necessarily the other way.

Example 12.3

Show that $L = \{a^n b^n c^n \mid n \geq 0\}$ is recursive; that is, give a TM M that always halts and for which $\mathcal{L}(M) = L$.

The state transition diagram for such a TM M is given in Figure 12.1. The accepting halt state is shown, but the rejecting halt state is omitted. This machine is supposed to verify that the input x is in L. In particular, M enters q_a in those cases (and no others) when the

---

[3]This terminology comes from the mathematics of Recursive Function Theory, which was a rival theory of computation in the 1930s.

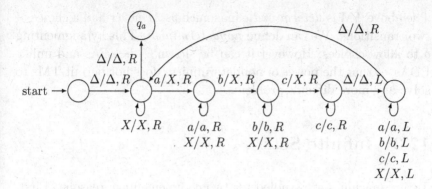

Figure 12.1: A Turing Machine for $L = \{a^n b^n c^n \mid n \geq 0\}$.

tape started out with "$\Delta a^n b^n c^n \Delta$" as the symbols in the first $3n+2$ cells, for some $n \geq 0$. M does its work by making repeated passes across the input. Passing left-to-right it changes one a, one b and one c, each into the symbol X. The pass ends when it encounters a blank, at which point it turns and faces left, so to speak. Passing right-to-left it searches for the Δ at the very beginning, and then turns around to start the next left-to-right pass. A rightward pass skips over any Xs left from earlier passes. If a rightward pass encounters only Xs before encountering the trailing Δ then it accepts the input.

What if this M finds itself unable to make a transition found in the diagram? Suppose we halt in the third state. In that case we have already encountered an a on a rightward pass and, after possibly skipping some Xs, we expect to find a b to pair up with the a we have already seen. If we encounter, say, a c instead there is no indicated transition since the input is ill-formed and so not in L. As indicated above, what actually happens is a transition to the rejecting halt state q_r.

The above example demonstrates typical behavior for a TM: running up and down the tape looking for symbol patterns to initiate certain activities. As a result, TMs have a reputation for being tediously slow. (Actually, while slow, they are not *too* slow, but that is beyond the scope of this discussion.) What is important to us is: *can* a TM recognize some language L?

The above TM is *deterministic* inasmuch as M never had a choice of two transitions. We can define *nondeterministic* TMs by augmenting δ to allow choices. However it can be shown — like FAs and unlike PDAs — that the power of nondeterminism does not permit TMs to solve any more difficult problems.

12.3   Infinite Sets

Turing machines are studied for two complementary reasons. First, they allow us to describe succinctly what any computer *can* do; we return to this topic in Section 12.7. Second, they allow us to explore what a computer can *not* do. The idea of a computational task that no computer can perform may seem counter-intuitive and the work of *proving* that such tasks exist may seem daunting. Indeed it must be admitted that the proofs are indirect and somewhat complicated even when treated informally. To get a handle on them, we need to begin with a better understanding of infinite sets. (This material could have been in the first chapter, but it is better to present/review it this context.)

Recall that a finite set is a set with a cardinality that is an integer. So $\{a, b, c\}$ is a finite set since its cardinality is 3. Also recall that two sets have the same cardinality if and only if there is a one-to-one correspondence between them. So $\{a, b, c\}$ and $\{1, 2, 3\}$ have the same cardinality because of this mapping:

$$
\begin{array}{ccc}
1 & 2 & 3 \\
\updownarrow & \updownarrow & \updownarrow \\
a & b & c
\end{array}
$$

This use of mappings to determine that two sets have the same cardinality carries over to infinite sets. The most important infinite set is the set of non-negative integers, $\mathcal{N} = \{0, 1, 2, 3, 4, \ldots\}$. We can define $\mathcal{N}$ formally, but that would take us beyond the scope of this book. Informally, $\mathcal{N}$ is defined by starting with 0 and using the rule that if i is in $\mathcal{N}$ then $i + 1$ is also in $\mathcal{N}$; clearly there is no largest element of $\mathcal{N}$. Consider the following one-to-one correspondence between $\mathcal{N}$ and

$\mathcal{E}$, where $\mathcal{E}$ is set of even non-negative integers:

$$
\begin{array}{cccccc}
0 & 1 & 2 & 3 & 4 & \cdots \\
\updownarrow & \updownarrow & \updownarrow & \updownarrow & \updownarrow & \\
0 & 2 & 4 & 6 & 8 & \cdots
\end{array}
$$

This mapping shows that the two infinite sets can have the same cardinality, even though one is a proper subset of the other! This is just one of many counter-intuitive properties of $\mathcal{N}$. We must be careful using the word "infinite," as will become clear soon. A set with the same cardinality as $\mathcal{N}$, such as $\mathcal{E}$, is said to be *countably infinite*.[4] This makes sense because the mapping explicitly shows how we "count" the elements; every element is eventually reached and counted. Are there sets with so many elements that they have more elements than $\mathcal{N}$? The answer is "yes." Moreover — and equally important here — *the set of all languages over an alphabet is uncountable.*

First consider the idea of an infinite string. Recall that by definition a "string" is composed of a finite number of symbols, so let us define a new term ω-**string** for strings with a countably infinite number of symbols. The *occurrences* of symbols of an ω-string can be put in one-to-one correspondence with the elements of $\mathcal{N}$; we can speak of the ith symbol in an ω-string. An example of an ω-string is the decimal representation of a irrational real number, such as $\pi = 3.141592653589\ldots.$

Recall that in an infinite language, even though there is no limit on how long a string can be, each string must be finite. So *no* language we have studied so far — even though most of them have been infinite — has contained an ω-string. So as not to disturb this terminology, we will say "sets of ω-strings" when that is what we mean, and not call them languages. In particular, let $\mathcal{W}$ be the set of all ω-strings over the alphabet $\{0, 1\}$. Although the remainder of this section uses only this alphabet, the results can be generalized to any alphabet with more than one symbol.

---

[4]Such a set is said to be *denumerable*.

A finite binary string can regarded as the binary representation of an integer; in this sense every language we have discussed can be regarded as a set of integers and is therefore a subset of $\mathcal{N}$ (ignoring the empty string for the present argument). As with $\mathcal{E}$ above, every infinite subset of $\mathcal{N}$ is countable, so it follows that every infinite language is composed of a countably infinite number of (finite) strings.

We will want to build an ω-string ν_L from a given language L. Let the ith symbol of ν_L be 1 if the string which corresponds to the integer i is in L; otherwise the ith symbol is a 0. Each $\nu_L \in \mathcal{W}$. Also every element of $\mathcal{W}$ is ν_L for some L; if L is finite then there will only be a finite number of 1 symbols in ν_L. It is immediately apparent that there is a one-to-one correspondence between languages over the binary alphabet and the elements of $\mathcal{W}$.

Theorem 12.1 – If $|\Sigma| \geq 2$, the set of all languages over Σ is uncountable.

Proof: We will show that $\mathcal{W}$ is uncountable by contradiction. We assume Σ is the binary alphabet; other alphabets are analogous. Assume $\mathcal{W}$ is a countably infinite set, so that its elements can be put in one-to-one correspondence with $\mathcal{N}$. This is equivalent to saying that we can make a numbered list of all the elements of $\mathcal{W}$. Once the correspondence is chosen we can unambiguously talk about the ith element of $\mathcal{W}$. By hypothesis this list contains every possible binary ω-string, but we will show that there must be an ω-string that cannot be on the list. Define the ω-string ν as follows: the ith bit of ν is 0 if the ith bit of the ith string in $\mathcal{W}$ is 1, and vice versa. (We are using a 0-based indexing.) An illustration of this construction is

$$\nu = \quad 1 \quad 1 \quad 0 \quad 1 \quad \cdots$$

0th	$\underline{0}$	1	1	0	0	1	$\cdots$
1st	0	$\underline{0}$	1	0	1	1	$\cdots$
2nd	1	1	$\underline{1}$	1	0	1	$\cdots$
3rd	1	0	1	$\underline{0}$	0	1	$\cdots$
$\vdots$			$\ddots$				

The key observation is that ν is an ω-string and hence should be on the list of all ω-strings. On the other hand, for any ν the construction prevents ν from being the ith string on the list, since it differs from that string in the ith bit. Hence a contradiction. $\square$

This proof is an example of the technique called **diagonalization** and is well-known in the history of set theory. We will use it again soon. (It is worth remarking that the above argument is almost identical to the proof that the number of real numbers between 0 and 1 is uncountably large. To see the relationship, note that any such real can be represented in binary notation as a ω-string preceded by a "binary point". There are some additional technical details since some reals have more than one representation.)

12.4 Universal Turing Machines

We have promised that the Turing machine is a general model of computation (Section 12.2). The prospects for such a claim seem dubious so far, though, since a general-purpose computer can run all kinds of software, but the TM in Example 12.3 — the only TM we have seen — can do only one thing: determine whether each input string is in the language L. The goal of this section is to dispel this appearance of TM rigidity by presenting a design strategy for a TM that can accept as input a description of any other TM — much as a real computer accepts software — and then carry out the behavior of that other TM on whatever data is provided as a second input. Such a TM is called a **Universal Turing Machine (UTM)**.

If one TM is to be input to another (the UTM), that first TM is going to have to be expressed in terms of symbols that are allowed to appear on the tape of the second. In particular, if the UTM uses $\Sigma = \{0, 1\}$, there has to be an **encoding scheme** that will represent any TM M in 0s and 1s. The encoding of a machine M will be denoted $\langle M \rangle$. It needs to be emphasized that there is no single correct encoding scheme. Various schemes could be used that agree in spirit but differ in details. To get a clearer understanding of encoding schemes, it's best to look at one.

Example 12.4

Give an encoding scheme for converting a given TM $M = (Q, \Sigma, \Gamma, q_0, \delta)$ into a binary string, $\langle M \rangle$.

The encoding of each TM element will be a string of 1s (possibly empty), with each string separated from the next by a single 0. First we represent the states $Q = \{q_0, q_1, \ldots, q_n\}$ by the strings $\{\Lambda, 1, 11, 111, \ldots, 1^n\}$, where q_i corresponds to 1^i. Similarly we can represent the symbols in the tape alphabet $\Gamma = \{x_0, x_1, x_2, \ldots, x_m\}$ by the strings $\{\Lambda, 1, 11, 111, \ldots, 1^m\}$, where x_i corresponds to 1^i. This takes care of Σ, since $\Sigma \subseteq \Gamma$. If we let $\Delta = x_0$ then the blank symbol will be $\Lambda = 1^0$. Finally, for the tape head movements $\{R, L\} = \{\mu_0, \mu_1\}$ represent the move μ_i by the string 1^i.

Consider a generic transition of the TM, $\delta(q_i, x_l) = (q_j, x_k, \mu_m)$. We encode this transition by the string $1^i 0 1^l 0 1^j 0 1^k 0 1^m 0$. We represent all of δ by concatenating together the representations of each and every transition to form one long string, w. In fact w represents a complete description of M, so we let $\langle M \rangle = w$.

Although there may be wide variations among rule encodings with respect to the number of 1s, the number of 0s for the encoding of each transition is always five, a fact that helps the UTM keep track of where it is. For example, moving from the beginning of the tape past 5 0s brings the tape head to the second transition rule.

Since an encoding scheme makes a string out of each TM, the set of TM encodings is a language. Now consider a TM encoding, followed by a extra 0 symbol, followed by an input string that that TM accepts. This too is a string and the set of all *these* strings is a language. We will denote this language L_U and call it the "universal language." It is universal in that it represents all TM computations that succeed in halting. Formally, we write

$$L_U = \{\, \langle M \rangle 0 x \mid \text{TM } M \text{ accepts } x \}$$

where the 0 is used only as the divider, allowing any string in L_U to be broken down unambiguously into an encoding of M and another string taken to be the input to M. (Note that reading an encoding $\langle M \rangle$ from the the left we will never see two adjacent 0s, so the 0 separator will be recognized as not being part of $\langle M \rangle$.) We assume, without loss of generality, that input strings, like encodings, use the alphabet $\{0, 1\}$. Thus L_U has a binary alphabet.

We now claim that there exists a TM M_U that accepts L_U. Such a TM is a *universal Turing Machine* or UTM because it has the behavior discussed above. That is, it accepts the encoding of any TM with its data and simulates that TM's behavior. In this way it is analogous to a general-purpose computer running a program. The strongest way to support this claim would be to give the details of a UTM. Even though some very compact UTMs have appear in the literature, the task of specifying one requires many TM design techniques. An example of such a technique is the one used in Example 12.3: a self-loop with the label $X/X, R$ lets us "move rightward across Xs." A slight extension of this would be to "find the 0 divider" by moving rightward across 0s and 1s with a self-loop labeled both $0/0, R$ and $1/1, R$ until two adjacent 0s are found. Rather than develop and deploy a bag of TM tricks, we content ourselves with a rough and informal — but we hope reasonably convincing — description of M_U.

Given the input $\langle M \rangle 0x$, a UTM simulates the execution of M on the input x and accepts its input iff the simulation indicates that M accepts x. It works on the portion of the tape to the right of the 0 divider as if it were the tape used by M itself. (Note that tape alphabet can be much richer than the underlying binary alphabet which will allow symbols that can be interpreted as, say, "a zero with an accent mark on it.") It also needs to allocate a portion of the tape to hold the encoding of the current state that M would be in, as the simulation progresses. Thereafter, the UTM simulates M by scanning down to find what symbol is currently being scanned by the simulated M (assuming that position is marked in some way) and then it scans to find within $\langle M \rangle$ the transition that M must make at this time (it needs to use the current state of M to determine this). It then executes that transition, by changing the encoding of M's current state, the currently scanned symbol, and moving the tape-head (by moving the "mark") as appropriate. The details of M_U and its operation are messy but have been worked out in various ways in the literature. The above discussion of the design strategy provides some confidence that M_U exists. The existence of M_U establishes the next theorem.

Theorem 12.2 – The language L_U is recursively enumerable.

Note that the proof of this theorem, only sketched above, involves the simulation of M. If M does not halt on the input x then our M_U will not halt on the input $\langle M \rangle \diamond x$. Hence we have *not* established whether L_U is recursive.

In the following section we will need to talk about the "ith TM." To see that such a notion is meaningful, note that for any TM M its encoding, $\langle M \rangle$ is a bit-string (a string over $\{0,1\}$) which in turn can be read as a unique integer i in binary (base 2). In this way, the TMs map into the integers. Now consider the mapping in the other direction, from integers to bit strings to TMs. Disallowing leading 0s — which never occur in our encodings — every i has its own unique bit-string, call it $bin(i)$. (For example, if $i = 9$ then $bin(i)$ is the string 1001, not 0001001.) Now this bit-string may be a valid encoding of a TM but it may not, because the encoding process imposes constraints on what strings it can produce. Still, for simplicity, we make the "ith TM" the one that maps to i, so $\langle M_i \rangle = bin(i)$. For any i where $bin(i)$ is not a valid encoding, we may think of M_i as being ill-formed and accepting no strings, so that its language is empty.

12.5   Limits on Turing Machines

The Turing Machine model has been presented as the most powerful model of computation, a point to which we return in Section 12.7. Still, there are limits to what this class of machines can do. For some languages there is no TM at all; such a language is not recursively enumerable. Other languages, though they are recursively enumerable, are not recursive; for these there is no TM that reliably halts.

Theorem 12.3 – There exists a language that is not recursively enumerable.

Proof: Theorem 12.1 states that the number of languages is uncountable. On the other hand we showed in Section 12.4 that each TM can be encoded as an integer, so it immediately follows that the set of all TMs is only countably infinite. Thus there are "more" languages than TMs, so after you map TMs to the languages they accept, there must be languages left over that do not correspond to any TM. □

This proof is not very satisfying. It shows that such a language must exist without exhibiting it. We can get a specific language that is not recursively enumerable by applying the diagonalization technique used Section 12.3 directly to TMs. Recall that M_i is the ith TM, as defined in Section 12.4.

$$L_D = \{ \, bin(i) \mid i \in \mathcal{N} \text{ and TM } M_i \text{ does not accept } bin(i) \}$$

Even though this is a peculiar language, since M_i is uniquely defined there is no ambiguity as to whether some string x is in L_D or not. Since $\langle M_i \rangle = bin(i)$, a string $x \in L_D$ iff the machine whose encoding is x does not accept x. This is the sense in which this is a "diagonalization" argument.

Theorem 12.4 – The language L_D is not recursively enumerable.

Proof: Suppose, for the purpose of contradiction, that L_D is accepted by some TM M, so that $L_D = \mathcal{L}(M)$. Since $\langle M \rangle = bin(i)$ for some i it follows that $M = M_i$. Now consider whether M accepts $x = bin(i)$. If M accepts x then $x \in \mathcal{L}(M)$ and so $x \in L_D$. On the other hand, if M accepts x then x can not be in L_D, by the definition of L_D. This contradiction implies that M can not exist. □

There are many properties of recursive and recursively enumerable languages that can be proven. We will only need the following one. Recall that the complement of a language L over an alphabet Σ is $\overline{L} = \{x \in \Sigma^* \mid x \notin L\}$.

Lemma 12.1 – If a language L is recursive then $\overline{L}$ is also recursive.

Proof: Let L be a recursive language. Then by definition there is an M that accepts L and halts on all inputs. We can build a new TM $\overline{M}$ for $\overline{L}$ by modifying M. The modification simply interchanges the states q_a and q_r. For any input x, $\overline{M}$ halts and further, $\overline{M}$ accepts x iff M does not accept x. □

Corollary 12.1 – The language $L_A = \overline{L}_D$ is not recursive.

Proof: By Lemma 12.1 if L_A were recursive then L_D would be recursive, but we know, by Theorem 12.4 that it is not even recursively enumerable. □

With these results we are now prepared to give an example of a language that is recursively enumerable but not recursive. Recall that in Section 12.4 we showed that L_U, the universal language, was recursively enumerable.

Theorem 12.5 – The language L_U is not recursive.

Proof: Suppose, for the purpose of contradiction, that there exists a TM M_U that accepts L_U and halts on all inputs. We will use M_U to build a TM M_A that accept L_A and halts on all inputs (which we now know is impossible by Corollary 12.1). First the TM M_A checks whether the first symbol is a 0 (if it is not it cannot begin a $bin(i)$

for any $i > 0$, or $i = 0$; in either case it is in L_A and M_A can halt). If the input starts with a 1 then M_A begins, when given $x = bin(i)$ as input, by making a duplicate of x while placing the 0 divider between the two copies of x. Since $\langle M_i \rangle = bin(i)$, the tape now contains the string $\langle M_i \rangle 0x$. At this point M_A switches over and starts behaving like M_U. Since, by hypothesis, M_U always halts, it follows that M_A always halts, which gives us a contradiction. □

Why is recognizing L_U so difficult? Recall that we argued that $\langle M \rangle 0x$ can be accepted by M_U simulating M on input x. Now if M halted on all inputs the M_U would halt on all inputs. On the other hand if our TM M_U could determine if the simulation would not halt it would know that M did not accept x and could halt without accepting its input. Hence, the underlying reason that L_U is not recursive is because it is too difficult, in general, to decide whether a TM will halt or not! This is pursued in the next section.

12.6 Undecidability

In this chapter we have been concerned with question of testing whether we can find a machine that will recognize a given language. This is an example of a **decision problem**. Informally a decision problem is a problem for which we need to compute "yes/no" answers. This decision problem has been discussed at length:

- Is string x in language L?

However we could add many others to such a list:

- Does a given string contain an even number of symbols?

- Is a given number prime?

- Does TM M halt on input x?

- For a given context-free grammar G, is $\mathcal{L}(G)$ regular?

They seem different in character, but it is important to realize that these, and all other decision problems, are special cases of the first example "Is string x in language L?"

We need to recast each decision problem as a language recognition problem. For each problem we specify how instances of the problem can be regarded as strings and then define the set of strings which correspond to instances for which the answer is "yes." This set of strings is a language and testing membership in that language is tantamount to answering the decision problem. For example, the examples above can be recast as:

- $L_1 = \{x \mid x \text{ is of even length}\}$

- $L_2 = \{bin(i) \mid i \text{ is prime}\}$

- $L_3 = \{\langle M \rangle 0x \mid \langle M \rangle \text{ is an encoding of a TM } M \text{ and } M \text{ halts on } x\}$

- $L_4 = \{\langle G \rangle \mid \langle G \rangle \text{ is an encoding of a CFG } G \text{ and } \mathcal{L}(G) \text{ is regular}\}$

where $\langle G \rangle$ is some encoding of the grammar G into a (binary) string; by analogy with $\langle M \rangle$, we can concatenate together encodings of each of the productions of G.

It is the ability to cast diverse problems as language tasks that gives the study of formal languages its crucial role in computation theory. Many of the languages in this text may seem artificial, but that is only because we need to start with simple examples. In fact, the power of languages is in their ability to capture the essence of "natural" problems.

Some decision problems are fairly straightforward. The decision problem corresponding to L_1 can be solved by a simple FA; it can therefore be solved by a TM that always halts. It is also possible to give a TM that accepts L_2, that always halts. However L_3, which corresponds to the decision problem known as the **Halting Problem** is more difficult. In Section 12.5 after we proved that L_U is not recursive we gave an argument showing that L_3 is also not recursive. (If it were recursive then L_U would be recursive.)

A decision problem is said to be **undecidable** if the corresponding language is *not recursive* (even if it is recursively enumerable). We can say the "Halting Problem is undecidable." (Sometimes we say the "language L is undecidable" but properly we should refer to the corresponding decision problem.) Note that undecidability refers to our inability to design a single computer (Turing Machine) that will correctly solve the problem for all inputs. In other words, you might be able to build a TM that almost always gets the right answer, but if the problem is undecidable then your TM must give the wrong answer for at least one input!

Some undecidable problem are artificial but many, such as the Halting Problem, have direct impact on computer scientists. If someone tells you they have a program that can do a complete analysis of, say, C++ code then you should doubt them. After all, their program can not always decide if some given C++ code even halts, so how can they decide if it works. (This is the reason we stressed the notion of proofs of "partial correctness" in Chapter 6.) Sometimes the most innocent problems turn out to be undecidable. For example, the problem of determining if a CFG corresponds to a regular language – L_4 above – is undecidable! Unfortunately the proof is too complicated to give here.

12.7 Church-Turing Thesis

Alonzo Church and Alan Turing simultaneously defined models of computation. Church's model, called the λ-*calculus*, was later found to be equivalent to TMs. Both researchers contended that their models were truly universal models of computation. In other words, they were sure that any other model, including specifications for real computers, would not be any more powerful than theirs, with respect to the question of which computations succeed. This was a bold and unprovable thesis, since it makes a statement about any model of computation that will ever be devised in the future. The **Church-**

Turing Thesis can be paraphrased as: any computational task can be accomplished by a Turing Machine.

In order to appreciate this claim we need to expand slightly our notion of what a TM does; so far a TM can only solve decision problems. A TM can be thought of as computing a function f, where if x is the input then whatever is on the tape when the machine halts is $f(x)$. The Church-Turing Thesis has been verified to the extent that there is no known function f that can be computed by some other model, but not by a TM. This has remained true since the 1930s, despite the fact that many alternate models have been proposed, often with the intent of falsifying the thesis.

Will the thesis continue to hold? Perhaps not, if we are willing to push the limits of the notion of "computation." For example, people have seriously investigated to what extent brain functions are not computable by a TM. Alternatively, researchers into so-called *quantum computers*, that make use of the uncertainties of subatomic reactions, raise important questions (even though so-called "quantum TMs" can be simulated by normal TMs). These ideas are very speculative. For all practical purposes we can rely on the thesis.

It is because of the general support for the Church-Turing Thesis that the TM has a central role in theoretical Computer Science. Another entire textbook could be written to explore what is known about TMs. We mention one such topic in the next section.

12.8   Computational Complexity

So far in the second part of this book we have dealt exclusively with questions of what can or can not be done. For example, $L = \{a^n b^n \mid n > 0\}$ is a language for which we can not give a regular grammar, but we can give a context-free grammar. In practice, computer scientists wish to go beyond whether they *can* solve a problem, to how hard it is to solve the problem. By sorting problems into language classes, we can gauge how hard a problem is; after all if one problem can be solved with an FA and another requires a TM there is a sense in which the first problem is easier. However, if a regular language requires an FA with a number of states exponentially larger than a TM would require to recognize the same language, then the simplicity of the FA is moot.

In computer science we have traditionally evaluated the difficulty of a problem by how much resources are consumed by the (optimal) computer program that solves that problem. Typically the resource that is studied the most is execution time, but memory usage is also important. In an Algorithms course, these issues are studied extensively. However, there are important issues about efficiency that can be studied theoretically with Turing Machines.

We will confine our attention to decision problems in this section, which is equivalent to concentrating on language recognition tasks. In Chapter 7 we discussed sorting languages into "language classes," as dictated by various models of computation, grammars, etc. Now, instead, we wish to sort languages into **complexity classes** according to how much resources a TM must use in order to recognize that language, as defined below. This leads to a whole field of study known as *computational complexity*, which would require a semester to survey. In this section we indicate some directions that can be pursued in that field.

Example 12.5

What resources — that is, how much time and space — are required by the TM in Example 12.3, when it begins with the input $a^n b^n c^n$?

The TM repeatedly scans the tape, back and forth, until it eventually halts. In particular it will scan all $3n$ symbols plus the two bracketing blanks (Δs), n times left-to-right and n times right-to-left, plus a final left-to-right pass. Careful counting show that it takes the TM $(2n + 1)(3n + 1) + 1$ steps to accept x; generally we are looser and simply state that the number of steps it takes is a quadratic function, $O(n^2)$. It can also be seen that it could take a quadratic number of steps to reject an input of n symbols. The TM does not use any additional tape cells beyond the $3n + 2$ already mentioned; we say it uses a linear amount of space.

We need more formal definitions. Recall that the $O(\cdot)$ notation was defined in Section 1.7. We say a TM M "accepts a language L in time $T(n)$" if for every $x \in L$, of length n, M accepts x in $O(T(n))$ steps. Further, we say a TM M "accepts a language L in space $S(n)$" if for every $x \in L$, of length n, M accepts x using $O(S(n))$ tape cells.

We have stated (without proof) that nondeterminism does not allow a TM to accept a language that is not accepted by some deterministic TM. However nondeterminism may allow a TM to accept the strings of a given language, using fewer resources than any deterministic TM. Of course, this sort of speed-up is only of theoretical interest since only deterministic machines exist. Surprisingly, the theory of nondeterminism turns out to lead to some practical insights. Let DTM stand for deterministic TM and let NTM stand for a nondeterministic TM. Here are two types of time complexity classes:

$$DTIME(T(n)) = \{L \mid L \text{ is accepted by a DTM in time } T(n) \}$$

and

$$NTIME(T(n)) = \{L \mid L \text{ is accepted by a NTM in time } T(n) \}.$$

Note that a complexity class is a set of languages, that share the property of being equally difficult to recognize, in some sense. The space complexity classes $DSPACE(S(n))$ and $NSPACE(S(n))$ are defined analogously.

There are literally thousands of theorems known about various complexity classes, most depending on the growth rates of $T(n)$ and $S(n)$. A simple example of such a theorem is

$$DTIME(f(n)) \subseteq DSPACE(f(n)).$$

To prove this you need only observe that if a DTM uses $f(n)$ steps it will use at most $f(n)$ cells, but a DTM using $f(n)$ cells could use far more time. These results ultimately inform us about the relative difficulty of the various decision problems.

The best known area of complexity theory concerns the two complexity classes $\mathcal{P}$ and $\mathcal{NP}$:

$$\mathcal{P} = \{L \mid L \text{ is accepted by a DTM in polynomial time }\}$$

$$\mathcal{NP} = \{L \mid L \text{ is accepted by a NTM in polynomial time }\}$$

which can defined more formally as

$$\mathcal{P} = \bigcup_{k=0}^{\infty} DTIME(n^k)$$

$$\mathcal{NP} = \bigcup_{k=0}^{\infty} NTIME(n^k).$$

Even though, these are defined in terms of language recognition we will continue to interpret them as pertaining to decision problems. A decision problem is in $\mathcal{P}$ if it can be solved deterministically in $O(n^k)$ time, for some integer k.

When k is small, say $k = 2$, then we have a runtime of a reasonably efficient machine, but if $k = 1,000,000$ then such an implementation is incredibly impractical. So why is polynomial time central to these definitions? There are three reasons. First, even if membership in $\mathcal{P}$ does not guarantee a practical implementation, it is certainly true that *not* belonging to $\mathcal{P}$ means that the decision problem has no practical solution, for large n. We label a decision problem *intractable* if it is not in $\mathcal{P}$. Second, even though a DTM seems tediously slow, it is known that a DTM can simulate a single step of a normal modern random-access computer in polynomial time. (In fact there is whole literature on the complexity of various machine simulations.) Third, polynomials have simplifying closure properties; for example, a polynomial number of steps, each taking polynomial time to execute/simulate, takes a cumulative time that is also polynomial. (Experience tells that for natural problems when a polynomial time algorithm exists that the value of k is small. However we can easily invent problems that require larger values of k.)

Membership in $\mathcal{NP}$ is of no *direct* practical significance. In fact nondeterminism appears to be be very helpful in allowing unrealistically fast implementations. A NTM can guide the computation by making shrewd guesses, whenever it has a choice of transitions, and so avoid having to search for evidence that a string should be accepted. It is obvious that

$$\mathcal{P} \subseteq \mathcal{NP}$$

since the power of nondeterminism can only improve the time needed to accept a language. In fact it seems plausible that there would be problems solvable in polynomial time nondeterministically, that can not be solved by any polynomial time DTM. Any such problem is, of course, intractable.

In fact, $\mathcal{NP}$ is of great indirect practical significance, because of the class of $\mathcal{NP}$-complete languages. The definition of $\mathcal{NP}$-**complete** languages is too technical to give here, but the upshot is that these are the languages in $\mathcal{NP}$ that are the hardest to solve. In particular, if *any* language in $\mathcal{NP}$ is intractable then *every* $\mathcal{NP}$-complete language is intractable.

The class of $\mathcal{NP}$-complete problems is quite unusual, considering its very abstract definition. This class contains tens of thousands of decision problems that people have actually needed to solve in real life. A few examples of $\mathcal{NP}$-complete decision problems are:

- **Partition** – Given a set of integers, can it be partitioned into two disjoint sets, such that the sum of the elements in each set is the same?

- **Hamiltonian Cycle** – Given a graph, is there a subset of the edges that forms a cycle that goes through every vertex exactly once? (The related **traveling salesperson** problem, uses an edge-weighted graph and asks for the hamiltonian cycle of least total weight.)

- **Scheduling** – Given a set of tasks, with their durations and deadlines, is there a schedule for two (or more) processors that will complete all the tasks by their deadlines?

- **Satisfiability** – Given a boolean formula, is there a truth assignment to the boolean variables such that the formula is true?

This short list begins to illustrate the fact that the class of $\mathcal{NP}$-complete problems is diverse and of practical interest. It is worth pointing out (given the emphasis on logic in this text) that the satisfiability problem is the problem on which all of the rest of the theory is based! Why is satisfiability so important? Briefly, it is because boolean expressions can "express" that certain problems are as hard as some other problems.

The thousands of $\mathcal{NP}$-complete problems have an interesting property in common. While they have attracted much attention by people trying devise efficient algorithms (because of their real life importance) no researcher has ever devised a polynomial time implementation that solves any such problem! And as we said, if any $\mathcal{NP}$-complete problem can be solved in polynomial time, then every $\mathcal{NP}$-complete problem can be solved in polynomial time. These observations provide strong *circumstantial evidence* that none of the $\mathcal{NP}$-complete problems have polynomial time solutions.

In summary:

- If any problem in $\mathcal{NP}$ is intractable (not in $\mathcal{P}$) then every $\mathcal{NP}$-complete problem is intractable. Alternatively, if any $\mathcal{NP}$-complete problem is tractable (in $\mathcal{P}$) then every problem in $\mathcal{NP}$ is tractable.

- Every $\mathcal{NP}$-complete problem appears to be intractable because the combined efforts of thousands of researchers has failed to show even one such problem is in $\mathcal{P}$.

Taken together these strong observations lead people to *expect* these problems, like the satisfiability and the partition problem, will have no polynomial time algorithms that solve them. However there is no known proof of this conclusion.

Exercises

12.1 – Show that each of the following sets is countably infinite by providing a one-to-one mapping between that set and $\mathcal{N}$.

   (a) the perfect squares

   (b) the set of all integers (including the negatives)

12.2 – Design a Turing Machine that recognizes $\{ww^R \mid w \in \{a, b\}^*\}$, the language of even-length palindromes like *aabaabaa*. Recall w^R is the reversal of w.

12.3 – Design a Turing Machine that recognizes $\{ww \mid w \in \{a, b\}^*\}$, the language of repeated strings like *aabaaaba*. Hint: The most difficult part is locating the first symbol of the second half.

12.4 – Specify a finite automaton that accepts exactly the strings that are valid encodings of Turing Machine transition functions, according to the encoding scheme used in Section 12.4.

12.5 – A *context-sensitive grammar* (CSG) is a grammar in which each production $\alpha \to \beta$ has the property that $|\alpha| \le |\beta|$; no step in a derivation results in a shorter string of terminals and nonterminals.

   (a) Explain why any language generated by a CSG does not contain the empty string.

   (b) Give a CSG for $L = \{a^n b^n c^n \mid n \ge 1\}$.

Bibliography

1. Alfred V. Aho, Brian W. Kernighan and Peter J. Weinberger, *The AWK Programming Language*, AT&T, 1988.

    The manual for the language AWK.

2. Alfred V. Aho and Jeffrey D. Ullman, *Foundations of Computer Science*, Computer Science Press, 1995.

    A comprehensive introduction to many areas of theoretical Computer Science.

3. Alfred V. Aho, Ravi Sethi and Jeffery D. Ullman, *Compilers: Principles, Techniques, and Tools*, Addison-Wesley, 2006.

    A classic text that extends and applies formal language concepts in the domain of compiling.

4. Mordechai Ben-Ari, *Mathematical Logic for Computer Science*, Springer, 2012.

    A sophisticated, readable account that includes but goes well beyond the logic portion of this text.

5. George Boole, *An Investigation of the Laws of Thought*, Dover, 1958.

   A reprint of the original work on the mathematical approach to logic, originally published in 1854. Many details are no longer used though.

6. Ivan Bratko, *Prolog: Programming for Artificial Intelligence*, Addison-Wesley, 2000.

   A good treatment of Prolog that makes a strong connection to the field of artificial intelligence.

7. Michael R. Garey and David S. Johnson, *Computers and Intractability: A Guide to the Theory of NP-Completeness*, Freeman, 1979.

   Still the standard reference work on $\mathcal{NP}$-completeness, even though it was published in 1979.

8. Andrew Hodges, *The Imitation Game: Alan Turing, The Enigma*, Princeton University Press, 2014.

   A new edition of the biography that puts Turing's many contributions in perspective. This book was adapted into the Oscar winning script for *The Imitation Game*.

9. John E. Hopcroft, Jeffery D. Ullman, and Rajeev Motwani, *Introduction to Automata Theory, Languages, and Computation, second edition*, Pearson, 2006.

   An advanced but readable book on languages and automata.

10. Efim Kinber and Carl Smith, *Theory of Computing: A Gentle Introduction*, Prentice Hall, 2001.

    A text that gives a "gentle" treatment of the topics in Part II.

11. Peter Linz, *An Introduction to Formal Languages and Automata*, Jones and Bartlett, 2006.

> An excellent text that goes beyond this one in Turing machines and related topics.

12. James Martin, *Introduction to Languages and the Theory of Computation: Second Edition*, McGraw-Hill, 1997.

> An excellent text for those already motivated that goes well beyond the formal language and automata portion of this text.

13. Ernest Nagel and James R. Newman, *Gödel's Proof*, New York University Press, 2008.

> A remarkably simple introduction to the very complex subject, with a new preface by Douglas Hofstadter.

14. Charles Petzold *The Annotated Turing*, Wiley, 2008.

> A readable line-by-line explanation of Alan Turing's original paper.

15. Rudy Rucker, *Infinity and the Mind*, Princeton University Press, 2004.

> An introduction to the broad mathematical, scientific and philosophical implications of infinity.

16. Raymond Smullyan, *Forever Undecided: A Puzzle Guide to Gödel*, Knopf, 1987.

> A lively puzzle-oriented approach to undecidability and related concepts.

17. Raymond Smullyan, *Satan, Cantor and Infinity*, Knopf, 1992. (Dover, 2009)

> A recreational look at the relationship between logic and infinity.

18. A. B. Tucker, A. P. Bernat, W. J. Bradley, R. D. Cupper, and
    G. W. Scragg, *Fundamentals of Computing I*, McGraw-Hill,
    1995.

    Provides a good introduction to program verification.

19. Friedrich J. Urbanek, "On Greibach normal form construc-
    tion." *Theoretical Computer Science*, **40** (1985) 315-317.

    The source of our proof.

Appendix A

Logic Programming

A good way to appreciate the precision and power of predicate calculus as a system for representing ideas is to watch it in action as the basis of a **logic programming language**, such as Prolog. This appendix focuses on parts of Prolog inspired by logic, but also touches on some other capabilities, like data structures, arithmetic and input/output, that are needed for practical programming.

Prolog lets you make assertions in predicate logic. These can be particular facts about individual objects, or general statements about relationships among concepts. Then you can pose questions to the Prolog processor and it will provide answers on the basis of what it can figure out or infer from what you have asserted. It does so by a **deductive inference** procedure consistent with what you have learned about predicate calculus. We will touch lightly on how this process is carried out.

A.1 The Essence of Prolog and its Relation to Logic

Three unusual and significant characteristics of Prolog are its relationship to logic, its **interactive** style and its **declarative** nature. Though distinct, the three properties are related in a way that makes

Prolog a powerful tool for rapid prototyping. That is, they can help a Prolog programmer to get a working initial version of a program that represents complex concepts.

A Prolog interaction begins with a question—called a **query**—typed in by the user. This might be an end-user but here we envision a developer testing a piece of a new program. Then Prolog (strictly speaking, the Prolog interpreter) provides an answer to the query on the basis of some code that has been loaded for testing. This is a particularly convenient approach to informal testing.

Moreover, the code itself is simple in appearance because of its logical and declarative nature. Prolog is a declarative language in that you just state—or **assert**—what you know, in a form equivalent to expressions of predicate logic. In the old imperative languages like Fortran and C, it is necessary to write many procedures to get things done. This is true even for languages like C++ that support some object-oriented techniques. In contrast, a Prolog program does not need to specify the procedure that puts its logical facts and rules to use. Instead, the Prolog processor supplies an **inferencer**, that is, a procedure for carrying out logical inferencing. (The programmer does exert some control over procedure by specifying rule ordering and by some advanced techniques.) The programmer, relieved of the need to write a procedure, can then focus on the concepts in the subject matter of the application.

Now let's have a look at the language itself. The assertions you can make in Prolog are of two varieties, **facts** and **rules**. Facts describe the properties of particular objects—which may be things, people, institutions, etc.—and the relationships between/among those objects. Rules apply more broadly and are used to infer new information. Consider an example with both facts and rules.

Example A.1

Here are three facts about specific individuals and two rules about family relationships in general.

```
parent(mary,john).
parent(ann,mary).
female(mary).
mother(X,Y) :- parent(X,Y), female(X).
grandparent(X,Z) :- parent(X,Y), parent(Y,Z).
```

The first fact is intended to mean that someone named Mary is a parent of someone named John, and the third that Mary is female. These two facts together with the rule for **mother** will allow Prolog to tell us — when we ask it — that Mary is the mother of John. Of course, as in other programming languages, the use of English words to name the symbols has no significance to Prolog, though it may be helpful to human beings who read your program. Thus the constant symbol **mary** can represent someone named Ma Ry or, for that matter, John. When typing Prolog facts and rules, be sure to avoid blanks between the predicate and the left parenthesis; blanks are ok elsewhere.

Each fact in Example A.1 consists of a predicate with suitable arguments. This notation is like that of predicate logic except that there must be a period (".") at the end. Prolog rules are also directly related to predicate logic, but the notation disguises that relationship quite a bit more than in the case of facts. First, variables like X, Y and Z here, are capital letters (or begin with a capital), while predicates, like **parent**, and constants, like **mary**, begin with lower case letters. Prolog's operator symbols differ considerably from those in logic. The symbol ":-" means implication, but from right to left, opposite to the direction for predicate logic. You might think of it as a backward implication with a "←" symbol. Also, you can read ":-" as the English word "if." Each of the above rules has two propositions to the right of the ":-", separated in each case by a comma. The comma can be read as "and" since it corresponds to " ∧ " in logic. Later we will use a semi-colon—read as "or"—to correspond to " ∨ " (in a restricted way).

Yet another way in which Prolog concepts resemble those of predicate logic but differ in notation is that each rule in Prolog is understood to begin with universal quantifiers on all of its parameters. Using the second rule in Example A.1 above as an example, we can reverse the implication and put in the quantifiers and $\wedge$ sign to get the corresponding statement in predicate logic:

$$\forall X : \forall Y : (\exists Z : \text{PARENT}(X, Z) \wedge \text{PARENT}(Z, Y))$$
$$\rightarrow \text{GRANDPARENT}(X, Y)$$

A good way to read the Prolog version of this rule is as follows: To prove that X is the grandparent of Y, one proves that X is a parent of some Z and also that the same Z is a parent of Y. Notice that the parameters of the rule are universally quantified; it is rule for all possible arguments. But notice the variable Z which is introduced on the right-hand side is understood to be existentially quantified.

Having examined assertions—both facts and rules—it is time to turn to the question-answer part of Prolog. The assertions in Example A.1 enable the Prolog inferencer to answer quite a variety of questions. For example, just the fact `parent(mary,john)` by itself lets us get answers not only to "Is Mary a parent of John?" but also to "Who is a parent of John?", "Who is Mary a parent of?", "Who is a parent of whom?", "Is Mary a parent?" and more. Using the rules of Example A.1, Prolog can also give the correct answer to the likes of "Who is the mother of John" and "Is anyone a grandparent?" We will soon see what such questions look like in a form that Prolog understands.

A.2 Getting Started Using Prolog

Using Prolog is easy. As mentioned above, an important aspect of Prolog is that it is typically used interactively, with an interpreter rather than a compiler. This section is intended to give you a sense of what a Prolog session is like. In a typical Unix system, you can enter Prolog by typing "`prolog`", but before you start anything, be sure you know how to stop! In many implementations, you can stop by using the input "`halt.`"—without quotes but you do need to include the period and the $\boxed{\text{return}}$ (or $\boxed{\text{enter}}$).

Example A.2

If the system prompt is "=>" and the Prolog prompt is "|?- " then
the shortest possible session looks like this.

```
=> prolog
   [startup message from the software company]
|?- halt.
=>
```

Before starting the Prolog interpreter, as above, you should prepare a
file containing some facts and rules, using your favorite editor. Then,
once you have started, you can get those facts and rules into the
session by means of the built-in predicate consult which takes a file
name as its one argument. This predicate is understood as a query
about whether the file is loadable and also as a request to load it. So
the Prolog response is "yes" and the loading of the file takes place,
as a side-effect. It is also possible to make assertions during a session,
using the special predicate, assert, but this is *not* recommended in
general. If the file named afile contains parent(mary,john)., the
following have the same effect.

```
|?- consult(afile).
|?- assert(parent(mary,john)).
```

So let us say you have created a file called family containing the
three facts and two rules in Example A.1. You have started a Prolog
session and loaded the file. Now you are ready—and able—to enter
queries and receive answers based on the facts and rules you have
loaded.

Suppose you start with the query, parent(mary,john). Since this is
identical to one of the three facts you just loaded, it is not surprising
that Prolog prints yes as its response, as shown in Example A.3
below. In contrast, when you enter parent(john,ann), Prolog prints
no, because it is not among the facts you loaded and your rules are
no help since they do not have the parent predicate on the left side.
The same can be said for the query, parent(bea,cal).

Example A.3

What do queries about facts look like within a session?

```
|?- consult(family).
yes
|?- parent(mary,john).
yes
|?- parent(john,ann).
no
|?- parent(bea,cal).
no
```

As you look at the short Prolog session in Example A.3, keep in mind that it is you, as the user, who has caused each new line to start by typing [return] (or [enter]). Some of these new lines come after your own query. (Remember that the period is part of your query.) Others come after Prolog's "yes" or "no" answer. All the material you type in must end with a period. Any time you hit [return] without remembering the period, just type a period and [return] again.

Example A.4

Can Prolog give correct affirmative answers about a predicate for which there are no facts?

Yes. For the predicate `mother`, there is a rule but no facts. When Prolog is given the query below, it initially fails to find a directly relevant fact, but then it proceeds to make use of the `mother` rule and gives the correct answer. Later we will see just how Prolog manages to arrive at answers to this and even more difficult queries.

```
|?- mother(mary,john).
yes
```

Example A.5

What happens when a variable appears in a query?

The Prolog inferencer tries to prove that there are answers by finding suitable values for the variable. In simple examples, the Prolog variables correspond to the question words "who" and "what" in English. The following queries mean "Who is the mother of John?" and "Who is Mary the mother of?" (or "Whose mother is Mary?").

```
|?- mother(X,john).
X = mary
yes
|?- mother(mary,X).
X = john
yes
```

Example A.6

Suppose you put variables in both positions?

Prolog again seeks suitable values for variables. With two variables, the corresponding English question is awkward but still understandable. For example the query below asks "Who is a mother of whom?" or "Who is whose mother?" (Note that we say "Is Mary *a* mother of John?", rather than "Is Mary *the* mother of John?", since the information given to Prolog does not rule out having more than one mother.) After receiving one answer, the user can request another by typing a semicolon (;) before return , as shown here. Typing additional semicolons will yield additional answers, if they exist. In order to get an example with multiple answers, we first assert the additional fact that Ann is female. If you keep typing semicolons until there are no more answers, Prolog utimately prints "no," meaning "no more."

```
|?- assert(female(ann)).
|?- mother(X,Y).
```

```
X = mary, Y = john
yes;
X = ann, Y = mary
yes;
no
```

Example A.7

Can I ask who is a grandparent, without asking for a grandchild?

Yes, you can. Prolog has **anonymous** variables, whose value is not reported. Anonymous variables have names that begin with the underscore character, "_", and need not have any additional characters. Thus the query grandparent(P,_) asks if any object P is a grandparent of any object "_" but reports only the value of P. Since grandparent (like mother) is a predicate for which no facts have been asserted, Prolog invokes the grandparent rule in order to get started. Ultimately it finds the correct answer, but prints a value only for the **named** variable, not the anonymous one. In English, this reads, "Who is a grandparent?"

```
|?- grandparent (P,_).
P = ann
yes
```

We have now seen that the Prolog processor responds to queries in the form of predicates with three different kinds of arguments: constants like "mary," ordinary named variables like "X" and anonymous variables, ("_"). A named variable in a query is printed out with its substitution value, so that it has the effect of English words like "who" and "what". In contrast, there is no output provided for anonymous variables. Another difference between named and anonymous variables is that a named variable must take the same

Prolog interaction	Paraphrase in English	Comments
`|?- female(X).` `X = mary`	Who is female?	Value of named variable is given.
`|?- female(_).` `yes`	Is anyone female?	Prolog is silent about "_".
`|?- parent(X,john).` `X = mary`	Who is a parent of John?	
`|?- parent(_,john).` `yes`	Is anyone a parent of John?	

Figure A.1: Prolog queries and the corresponding questions in English.

particular value throughout a clause, but each occurrence of "_" is treated as a different variable, so two occurrences of it do not necessarily have the same value, though they *may*, just as two different named variables *may* have the same value. Figure A.1 shows Prolog at work on queries with one or another of the two kinds variable. Then Figure A.2 moves to some more challenging examples querying two vaiables at once. Included with each query is a paraphrase in English. You should check that "who" always corresponds to a named variable. The answers are based on the rules and facts of Example A.1.

A.3 An Example Related to Databases

You have seen several of the most important aspects of Prolog: its facts and rules, their declarative form and its similarity to logic, how to interact in a Prolog session using queries in several formats and how these queries relate to varied and useful questions in ordinary English. To provide some practice with this knowledge and at the same time emphasize its significance, we now put it to work in the world of databases.

Prolog interaction	Paraphrase in English	Comments

`|?- parent(_,X).`
`X = mary;`
`X = john`
	Who has a parent?	Semi-colon to get another answer.

`|?- parent(X,Y).`
`X = ann, Y = mary;`
`X = mary, Y = john;`
 	
`no`
	Who is a parent of whom?	Prolog gives x and y values. On request, Prolog gives another answer
		Now there are no more answers.

`|?- parent(X,X).`
 	
`no`
	Who is his/her own parent?	

Figure A.2: Two-variable queries in Prolog and English.

Database management systems play a central role in the modern world, allowing individuals and organizations to store, manipulate, extract and report information with a convenience and volume that would have astounded most people a generation ago. In this section we will introduce the three fundamental operations of the dominant database model and show how to express each of them in Prolog. The ease with which this can be done reflects a conceptual tie between logic and databases. While Prolog may be good for prototyping a database it is to slow for the actual implementation of a full database system.

Although there are several ways to organize databases, we will confine attention to relational databases, which are by far the most widely used. The main construct for representing data in this type of database is the **relation**. It may seem obvious that a relational database would use something called a "relation," but it is perhaps a bit surprising that this word that is so familiar in a management context can be correctly understood here in terms of its mathematical definition. Define **tuple** to be a sequence, which may be a singleton, like (a), a pair, like (a, b), a triple, (a, b, c) and so on; the members of a cross-product. (This definition allows for a single set to be a "cross product.") Tuples will be represented as Prolog facts. They can also be interpreted as a Boolean functions, see Sections 1.1 and 1.2. A **database relation** is a set of tuples.

Example A.8

Let "EMPINFO," be a 3-place predicate for employee information. Its first argument is an employee's 5-digit identification number, the second is the year that employee joined the company and the third is the company work unit to which he or she belongs. Thus it might be the case that EMPINFO$(34567, 1998, unit23)$ is TRUE. Letting *Idnum* be the set of all possible identification numbers, *Year* the set of years and *Unit* the set of work units, we express this predicate's mapping as EMPINFO : $Idnum \times Year \times Unit \to \mathcal{B}$. Corresponding to this EMPINFO predicate there is also a *relation* that consists of all the triples that—like $(34567, 1998, unit23)$—are in the truth set of the EMPINFO predicate. Suppose that a relation has four such triples. It is usual and convenient to present the corresponding database relation in the form of a table as shown here.

Idnum	*Year*	*Unit*
34567	1998	*unit23*
34612	2000	*unit23*
33927	1991	*unit06*
33825	1987	*unit08*

We are now in a position to get specific about Prolog. The initial steps, creating a file of facts and loading that file into a Prolog session, are done in the usual way. Each fact is a predicate with constants as arguments; e.g., `empinfo(34567, 1998, unit23)`. As a warmup exercise, we access all relations in this database we can use this Prolog query:

```
empinfo(X,Y,Z).
```

Three fundamental operations on relational databases are called "select," "project" and "join." The **select** operation chooses some of the rows on the basis of their contents in particular columns. Suppose we wish to select and print out the rows having *unit*23 as the unit. Two Prolog queries for doing this are shown here

```
empinfo(X,Y,unit23).
empinfo(X,Y,Z), Z = unit23.
```

The first query plugs the desired value directly into the appropriate argument position of `empinfo`. In the second query, we achieve the same result by using a variable in that position and then explicitly constraining it to be equal to—actually, to *unify* with—the desired value.

As another example of the select operation, suppose we want all the rows with a year before 1995. The following query does this. Notice that to express a constraint other than having a specific value, we need a format like the second—not the first—of the two foregoing queries about *unit*23.

```
empinfo(X,Y,Z), Y < 1995.
```

It is also possible to write a rule that confines attention to these earlier years, yet retains information about all the columns of the database. The rule below for `early_empinfo` does exactly this. After the rule comes a query that uses it, followed by the response from Prolog.

```
early_empinfo(X,Y,Z) :- empinfo(X,Y,Z), Y < 1995.

|?- early_empinfo(X,Y,unit23).
no
```

The **project** database operation chooses columns. (To see why the choosing of columns is called "projection" think of a point (x, y, z) in three-dimensional space being projected vertically to the point (x, y)

in the two-dimensional plane.) Recall that the choice of rows was based on particular values in the table, but the choice of columns is based only on the labels at the top of the table. Below are Prolog rules for two projections. The rule for `year(Y)`, selects only the second column, which contains the years in which current employees have been hired. The query "`year(Y).`" (or "`year(X).`" for that matter) will then extract those entries one at a time if the user keeps hitting the semi-colon key. The second Prolog rule below selects the last two columns, thereby restricting attention to year-and-unit combinations. These can be printed out using the query "`year_unit(Y,Z).`" and then using semi-colons to continue.

```
year(Y) :- empinfo(_,Y,_).
year_unit(Y,Z) :- empinfo(_,Y,Z).
```

A relational database is a collection of relations, but up to now our database has contained just the one relation, EMPINFO. We will now introduce a second relation and show how relations can be used together. The new relation, MANAGES, will associate each work unit with its manager. (To avoid ambiguity, one should use managers' employee numbers rather than their last names, but the way we have done it here is easier to follow.)

Unit	Manager
unit06	Nguyen
unit23	Smith
unit17	Lee

We are now ready for the **join** operation. Actually, there are several related versions of joins, but we will not distinguish among them. Our one example will concern the so-called "natural join." Notice that our two relations have a field in common, the "*Unit*" field. Via this field we can relate other fields in the two relations, as shown in the next table. In effect the new table merges the two relations on the *unit* field, where possible, that is, wherever the two have the same value in that field. The new table has two rows for *unit23*, but none for *unit*08 and *unit*17, one of which lacks a manager and the other, employees.

Idnum	Year	Unit	Manager
34567	1998	unit23	Smith
34612	2000	unit23	Smith
33927	1991	unit06	Nguyen

The following Prolog rule expresses the same ideas. As with "EMP-INFO," we reuse the relation name "MANAGES" to name the Prolog predicate. More significant is how the requirement of identical values in the *unit* field is implemented by means of a shared variable (Y) in Prolog.

```
empinfo_aux(W,X,Y,Z) :- empinfo(W,X,Y), manages(Y,Z).
```

This concludes our brief demonstration of the similarity between predicate logic and the relational algebra that plays a key role in many database management systems. The latter field is of course much more complex than what appears here. Built on top of relational algebra are query languages designed to let a user request needed information without having to understand even the logical organization of the data. Beneath the level we have been discussing there are issues of storing the data in real physical devices and providing access to it for multiple users in overlapping timeframes. These are topics for a more specialized and comprehensive treatment of the subject.

A.4 The General Form and a Limitation of Prolog

To explore just what we can do with Prolog, we look at the general structure of rules. First, to broaden our range of examples, consider the rule for **ancestor**, presented in the next example. This rule is more complicated than the rules for **mother** and **grandparent** in Example A.1, in that it provides two ways, not just one, to prove that the predicate holds.

Example A.9

The first part of this ancestor rule says that anyone who is your parent is one of your ancestors. The second says that your ancestors also include the parents of your ancestors. Each part of the rule ends with a period and is called a **clause**. So `ancestor` is a two-clause rule, in contrast to the one-clause rules for `mother` and `grandparent`. Note that the rule also is accompanied by bits of explanation, each beginning with the Prolog comment symbol, "%".

```
ancestor(X,Y) :-      % First clause: X is an ancestor of Y if
     parent(X,Y).      %                X is a parent of Y.

ancestor(X,Y) :-      % Second clause:X is an ancestor of Y if
     parent(X,Z),      %                X is a parent of someone (Z)
     ancestor(Z,Y).    %                who is an ancestor of Y.
```

In general, a Prolog rule is a set of Prolog clauses, perhaps none or just one, sometimes two as in this case, and possibly more. Each clause has the form of a backwards implication with exactly one proposition on the left side of the ":-" symbol. The right side, however, is more flexible: it may have any number of propositions (0, 1, 2, 3, ...). For example, each of the earlier rules—`mother` and `grandparent`—is a single clause with two propositions on the right side, while one of the `ancestor` clauses has just one proposition on the right. A bit later on, we will see that one of the clauses for the `different` rule has *no* propositions on the right. Here is the general form of a Prolog clause:

$$P :- Q_1, Q_2, \ldots, Q_n.$$

The symbols P, Q_1, etc. are propositions, so each of them may actually stand for a predicate with one or more arguments, as in every example so far. For instance, to get the rule `mother` in Example A.1 above, the proposition P here in the general pattern would

be replaced by `mother(X,Y)`, that is, a predicate with two arguments, while Q_1 and Q_2 would be, respectively, `parent(X,Y)` and
`female(X)`. But here, to focus on what is true of all rules in general,
it is convenient to use the general form, ignoring the more detailed
level of specific predicates and arguments.

A clause in the general form may be read as "P is true if all of the Q_i
are true." Note that when $n = 0$ the list of Q_i disappears and for the
case of $n = 1$ it becomes just Q_1. For $n = 2$, it is Q_1, Q_2; and so on.
P is called the head of the clause and $Q_1, Q_2, \ldots, Q_n$ constitute the
body. Now translating this form into the usual symbols of logic, with
the implication symbol pointing to the right, we get the following
propositional form, called a **Horn clause**.

$$[Q_1 \wedge Q_2 \wedge \cdots \wedge Q_n \to P]$$

It is important to ask about the consequences of the restrictions in
the Prolog general form $P :- Q_1, Q_2, \ldots, Q_n$. On the face of things,
it looks like we are allowed conjunction operators but not disjunctions
on the right side (remember that the commas are really $\wedge$ signs), and
neither operator on the left. Note, however, that there is no limit on
the number of clauses, so we can write things like this:

$$P \quad :- \quad Q_1.$$
$$P \quad :- \quad R_1, R_2.$$

The effect of these two clauses together (which are exactly the form
of the rule `ancestor`) is that P can be inferred by Q_1 *or* by the
combination of R_1 and R_2. So we really do have the ability to express
disjunction on the right, at least implicitly. In fact, Prolog lets us do
so explicitly, using a semicolon ("`;`"), So the preceding clauses are
equivalent to $P :- Q_1 ; R_1, R_2$. In correspondence with propositional
logic, the semicolon (the $\vee$ operator) has lower precedence than the
comma (the $\wedge$ operator).

Example A.10

Here the `ancestor` rule from Example A.9 is rewritten using a semicolon to mean "or". This version of the rule is equivalent to the earlier one so far as Prolog is concerned.

```
ancestor(X,Y) :- parent(X,Y) ; parent(X,Z), ancestor(Z,Y).
```

Prolog's restriction to Horn clauses makes it fall short of expressing everything representable in predicate logic. That is, there are no rules corresponding to $Q_1 \wedge Q_2 \wedge \cdots \wedge Q_n \rightarrow P_1 \vee P_2$ and no facts of the form $P_1 \vee P_2$. This was a deliberate choice—for the sake of efficiency.

Finally, we rewrite the Horn clause shown above using the conditional law and then DeMorgan's law to get the forms shown below. The last form is a disjunction of propositions, of which all but one are negated. Since the various facts and rules of a program are all supposed to be true, they constitute one long conjunction of such disjunctions. Thus a Prolog program is very close to being in conjunctive normal form.

$$[Q_1 \wedge Q_2 \wedge \cdots \wedge Q_n \rightarrow P] \equiv [\neg(Q_1 \wedge Q_2 \wedge \cdots \wedge Q_n) \vee P]$$
$$\equiv [\neg Q_1 \vee \neg Q_2 \vee \cdots \vee \neg Q_n \vee P]$$

A.5 How Prolog Works

To understand how the Prolog processor does logical inference, we first need to look at the **scope** of the variables in Prolog rules. We then step through some examples of how the inference proceeds. Concluding this section is an introduction to the special operator **cut**, for which processing is quite unusual.

To begin our look at the idea of scope, recall the rule `mother(X,Y):-parent(X,Y),female(X)`. Clearly we want Prolog to require the X to mean the same person throughout one use of the rule. That is, we want it to find that Mary is the mother of John because *she* is female and is *his* parent, not because somebody else is a female parent of yet another person! Similarly when `grandparent(X,Z) :- parent(X,Y), parent(Y,Z)` is used to show that Ann is the grandparent of John, it is necessary to prove things about Ann and John, and not about some arbitrary X and Z. Moreover, it is necessary to find a single individual, Y, satisfying both parent relationships on the right side: someone whose parent is Ann and who also is the parent of John. On the other hand, when proving a `grandparent` relationship we certainly do *not* have to look at the variables in the rule for `mother`.

The foregoing considerations are part of the issue of the (lexical) **scope** of variable names. Since `grandparent` and `mother` are one-clause rules, it is hard to tell whether to say that scope extends to one clause or one rule. To make that determination, what we need is a two-clause rule, like the one for `ancestor`, repeated here.

```
ancestor(X,Y) :- parent(X,Y).
ancestor(X,Y) :- parent(X,Z), ancestor(Z,Y).
```

If you think of yourself as Y in this rule, what it says is that to prove someone is your ancestor, show that he or she is your parent (first clause) or is a parent of one of your ancestors (second clause). Although the two clauses work together, they do *not* need to share variables. In fact, we could change the variables in the first clause to U and V, making it `ancestor(U,V) :- parent(U,V)`, without changing the way it is processed by the Prolog inferencer. The clause would still mean "to prove that `ancestor` holds for two arguments, prove that `parent` holds for them." Therefore we conclude that in Prolog rules, the scope of variable names is one clause.

With scope in mind, we look in some detail at how Prolog carries out its deductive inference on some queries. To match the facts and rules in a program against the questions that are asked, Prolog uses a matching technique called **unification**, which makes sensible use of variables from both the assertion side and the query side. A variable from either side can be matched against a constant or variable from the other side (or even against a whole expression). The sequence of events in an inference is governed by a control strategy of depth-first search with backtracking, keeping track of proposed values for variables that arise from attempts at matching. The algorithm is not presented here, but we will run through descriptions of how Prolog works on some simple examples.

Example A.11

With the facts and rules of Example A.1 loaded, what does the Prolog interpreter have to do to handle the query `mother(mary,john)`?

Upon finding that there are no `mother` facts loaded, the processor will move on to trying the `mother` rule. First, the inferencer makes a substitution list for the rule's variables, associating X with `mary` and Y with `john`. Since substitutions have scope over the entire clause, the right side leads to the subtasks of proving `parent(mary,john)` and `female(mary)`, each of which is then established simply by looking them up among the available facts. Finally, Prolog prints `yes` as its answer.

Example A.12

Referring again to Example A.1, how does the Prolog interpreter handle the query `grandparent(ann,john)`, meaning "Is Ann the grandparent of John?"?

This query has the same form as the one in Example A.11: a predicate with two constants as its arguments. However, the interpreter's processing is a bit more complex here, because the rule it uses, for `grandparent`, has *three* variables, one of which must be associated with an entity other than the two in the input.

As in Example A.11, the variables on the left side of the rule are associated with the input arguments, here X with `ann` and Y with `john`. Because of scope, these substitutions are used on the right side, giving the subtasks `parent(ann,Z)` and `parent(Z, john)`. Now comes a more subtle use of scope. Since these subtasks came from the same clause, the inferencer must insure that Z gets the same value for each of them. Working on `parent(ann,Z)`, the inferencer now seeks a `parent` fact with `ann` as first argument, which it can do, since `parent(ann, mary)` fits this description. As a result, Z is now associated with `mary`. To obey scope, the inferencer now narrows the second subtask, requiring Z to be `mary` there too. The second subtask thereby becomes merely the confirmation that `parent(mary,john)` is a fact.

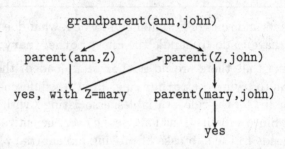

Before proceeding to a study of list operations, it will be helpful to examine the important idea of **recursion** in a familiar context. For this purpose, let's look back at the `ancestor` rule, repeated here. The second clause of the `ancestor` rule is recursive because it expresses `ancestor` in terms of itself.

```
ancestor(X,Y) :-          % First clause: X is an ancestor of Y if
    parent(X,Y).          %                X is a parent of Y.

ancestor(X,Y) :-          % Second clause:X is an ancestor of Y if
    parent(X,Z),          %                X is a parent of someone (Z)
    ancestor(Z,Y).        %                who is an ancestor of Y.
```

Example A.13

Suppose we ask Prolog to prove `ancestor(ann,john)`, having loaded the facts `parent(ann,mary)` and `parent(mary,john)`. To use the first clause of the `ancestor` rule, the inferencer would need to prove `parent(ann,john)`, which is *not* a fact. It must therefore try the second clause. By substituting **ann** for X and **john** for Y in the second clause and then consulting the right side of that clause, the inference procedure comes up with the subtasks of proving **parent(ann,Z)** and **ancestor(Z,john)**.

The inferencer succeeds at the first of these two subtasks by look-up, finding that Z can be **mary**, which alters the second subtask to **ancestor(mary,john)** and makes it the only remaining task. Notice that this is where recursion comes into play: we now have another **ancestor** task, that is part of the original one. In this new use of the **ancestor** rule, we are asking about a different pair of arguments than before (**mary** and **john** rather than **ann** and **john**), so its variables must now get fresh values. Keeping the new values of these variables separate and distinct from the original ones is a crucial aspect of Prolog's inference algorithm.

Using the first clause, the inferencer now processes **ancestor(mary, john)** by processing **parent(mary,john)**, which is confirmed by look-up. When it finishes, Prolog announces its success by print-ing **yes**. It does not report the value it used for Z (**mary**) since that variable is not used in the query. (However, Prolog has a **trace** fa-cility that allows you see its internal use of variables as you watch it step through a proof, discussed below.)

Our discussion of the Prolog search procedure would not be complete without a consideration of the so-called **cut** operator, denoted by the exclamation point: "!". The cut is a special operator for letting the programmer influence the procedure—in violation of Prolog's (mostly) declarative nature. Here's how it works. The inferencer regards a cut as logically true, so it continues to the next proposition on the right side of its clause. However, if a failure occurs later in this clause, after the cut, the inferencer will not go on to try the remaining clauses in the rule. (In particular, the backtracking feature is blocked by the cut.)

Here we shall use a cut for the indispensable purpose of insuring that two things are different from each other, using the Prolog code given next. This rule for the predicate **different** has two objectives: (i) to fail when given two identical arguments but (ii) to succeed in all other cases.

```
different(X,X) :- !, fail.
different(_,_).
```

Example A.14

How does Prolog achieve the twin objectives of the `different` predicate?

If you try `different(b,b)`, Prolog will match X to b on the left side, proceed to the right, succeed on the cut, continue to `fail` and then not try the second clause, because of the cut. The result is failure.

In contrast, if you try `different(c,d)`, Prolog will match the first X on the left side of the first clause to c and then it will try to match the second X on the left side to d. However, since X is already committed to c, this attempt fails. Processing then proceeds to the second clause, which succeeds with the first anonymous variable ("_") as c and the second one as d.

To see how the predicate `different` can be put to good use, consider the word "sibling," which means someone who shares at least one parent with you. If a pair of people have just one parent in common, they are "half-siblings". If they have two parents in common they are "full siblings". The next example introduces a predicate that covers both of these concepts, both full siblings and half-siblings. It takes care to avoid letting you be your own sibling. Please note: When using `different`, be sure to put it at the *end* of a rule, as in Example A.15.

Example A.15

Write a rule for the predicate `sibling`, that is true for two people who are siblings of each other.

```
sibling(X,Y) :- parent(Z,X), parent(Z,Y), different(X,Y).
```

There are four aspects that we have illustrated that we should make explicit. First the inferencer is a "search engine". That is essentially what Prolog is giving to the programmer—the programmer is giving facts and rules to guide a search. The more experienced Prolog programmer understands the search mechanism and how to order clauses, etc. to gain efficiency. Second, even though Prolog is a "logic" programming language there is no concept of true and false. These are replaced by "success" and "failure" of a search. The philosophical underpinnings of logic are completely absent, having been replaced by a mechanistic view of "true if verifiable." Third, there is no mechanism for even writing a general Boolean expression. There is a total reliance on Horn clauses. There is no "not" operator—it can only be approximated with the cut mechanism. (There *is* a **not** but it is only a hidden use of a cut and should be avoided by all beginners.) Fourth, the idea a matching a variable to a value (the key operation in unification) is a stronger concept than "assignment" in procedural languages. The programmer can not change the value that a variable has been matched to (some say "bound to"); that only happens within the backtracking mechanism controlled by the inferencer.

A.6 Structures

Like other languages, Prolog has built-in mechanisms for dealing simply with some important data structures. These include lists, which are the topic of the next section, and structured objects, or simply **structures**, taken up very briefly here. Prolog structures are very much like what are called structures or records in other programming languages. A Prolog structure consists of a name for a particular kind of structure, followed by parentheses that enclose one or more comma-separated elements. Each element may be a variable, a constant or another (sub)structure.

Example A.16

Suppose that `person` is a predicate and that it has a structure
for each of its arguments, like this: `person(names(john,smith),`
`date(december,3,1970))`, which we take to mean that John Smith
was born on December 3, 1970. Write Prolog queries that mean
"What is the birth year of anyone named John with a birthday in
December?" and "What are the first and last names of anyone born
in 1970?"

```
person(names(john,_), date(december,_,X)).
X = 1970
person(names(F,L), date(_,_,1970)).
F = john, L = smith
```

Notice the use of named variables in the positions about which our
English language questions specifically ask, in contrast to the anonymous variables ("_") for positions that our questions do not refer to.
(If facts had been loaded about several additional people, the user
could keep getting answers by typing semi-colon and ⎡return⎤ after
each answer until no more answers are forthcoming.)

A.7   Lists and Recursion

Another data structure, and one of great flexibility, is the **list**. Lists
are very important in a wide range of programming applications, especially in artificial intelligence (AI) programming where they were
first developed and extensively used, as early as the 1950s, in a pi-
oneering AI program for proving theorems in logic! The Lisp programming language, which is still the language of choice in much of
AI after 50 years, was actually named for *list* *p*rocessing. First we
look at list representation in Prolog. Then come some simple Prolog
programs for the basic list operations of membership, concatenation,
adding new elements, and deleting existing ones.

For input and output, a Prolog list consists of its elements separated
by commas and enclosed in brackets. The empty list appears as [ ],

while [a,b,c] is a three-element list. Another way to write lists comes from the recursive definition of what a list is. A list is a data structure that is either empty or consists of two parts: a *head* and a *tail*. The head of a non-empty list is its first element and the tail is the rest. The tail itself has to be a list (possibly the empty list). Therefore Prolog lets us write a list in general with brackets and a vertical bar, that is, as [H|T], where H is the head and T is the tail.

You can see this list notation at work by typing [H|T] = [a,b,c] to the Prolog interpreter. The equals sign in Prolog is the unification (matching) operator. Using only its own built-in capabilities Prolog will succeed with this unification by matching the variable H to a and T to the list [b,c]. This also means that [a,b,c] = [a|[b,c]]. Try it! A variant of the list notation that can be useful at times is where we put down the first few elements in the usual way, then a "|" and finally a symbol for whatever is left. Thus [a,b,c,d,e] matches [a,b|X] with X as [c,d,e].

Now we create some rules for lists as examples of the important interplay between the recursive definition of a list and the recursive search mechanism of Prolog. We start with the task of determining whether some item is a member of a given list. The 2-argument predicate member should have a rule that makes a query like member(c, [a,b,c,d]) yield a reply of "yes". A strategy for creating such a rule flows from the observation that for an item to be a member of a list it must be either (i) the first element or (ii) a member of the tail. Notice that part (ii) of this description is recursive: it defines member in terms of member. This is acceptable because the arguments will get shorter and shorter until we reach a simple successful case or fail.

Example A.17

In this rule for member, the first clause succeeds when the item in question is found first in the list. The second clause is a recursive test of whether the item occurs later in the list.

```
member(H,[H|_]).
member(X,[_|T]) :- member(X,T).
```

Notice that the foregoing definition uses named variables like H in some places and the anonymous variable in other places. For example, in the first clause of member the H appears in two places, thereby *linking* them, that is, requiring both to have the same value. On the other hand, the tail of the second argument does not need to be linked to anything, so it is appropriate to use the anonymous variable. You *can* use a named variable in that position; some Prolog processors will issue a warning if you do ("singleton variable"), but the rule will still work.

Example A.18

Suppose you want a predicate that can tell you whether or not its argument is a list. The first clause here looks for the empty list. If that fails, the second one looks for any other list, that is, an arbitrary non-empty list. The second clause will succeed on any list of length 1 by matching the first underscore to the list element and second underscore to the empty list. For lists of length 2 or more, the second underscore unifies with a list consisting of all elements of the input except the first.

```
list([ ]).
list([_|_]).
```

Whereas member and list are thought of as giving yes or no answers, the next few list-processing predicates—append, push and delete—are often be regarded as having two inputs in the first two argument positions and operating on them to produce a result that gets associated with a variable in the third argument position. Thus each of them is a 3-argument predicate and not, as you might have expected, a 2-argument function. Once defined, though, these predicates can be used in other ways, as shown below for append. We begin with the simplest, push.

Example A.19

Pushing an item X into the beginning of a list L can be accomplished with the following rule for the predicate **push**. The third argument of **push** is a list consisting of X followed by all the elements of L.

```
push(X,L,[X|L]).
```

The **append** predicate is built into some versions of Prolog; when it is not, the recursive rule given here will do the job.

Example A.20

For concatenation of two lists to give a third one, we define the relation **append(L1, L2, L3)** where L1, L2 and L3 are all lists, possibly empty, and L3 is the concatenation of the others. For example, we want the query **append([a,b], [c,d], Result)** to report success with the substitution **Result = [a,b,c,d]**. Interestingly, the rule given here can also be used in the other direction, so that the query **append(First, [g,h], [d,e,f,g,h])** succeeds and reports **First = [d,e,f]**.

```
append([ ],L,L).
append([X|L1],L2,[X|L3]) :- append(L1,L2,L3).
```

The first clause of this rule indicates that the concatenation of an empty list "[ ]" with a list L is L. The second shows that the concatenation of [X|L1] with list L2 is [X|L3] where L3 is the concatenation of L1 and L2.

Next we look at deletion. As with **append**, there are three argument positions. The item to be removed appears as the first argument and the list comes second. The third argument is the list that results from removing the designated element. Thus for the query

delete(a,[b,c,a,g,h],Result), Prolog's reply should be Result
= [b,c,g,h].

Example A.21

```
        delete(H,[H|T],T).
        delete(X,[H|T],[H|U]) :- delete(X,T,U).
```

Earlier, in Section A.5, we looked at the actual operation of the
Prolog processing mechanism in some detail. We now do the same
with delete.

Example A.22

The easiest case is when the element to be deleted appears at the
beginning of the list. Suppose the query is:

```
        |?- delete(a,[a,g,h],Result).
```

The Prolog interpreter tries to match the first clause of the rule with
H=a and T=[g,h] and it succeeds, giving as the value of the user's
variable Result = [g,h]. Now suppose the element to be removed
is *not* at the beginning of the list.

```
        |?- delete(a,[b,a,g,h],Result).
```

The Prolog processor begins by trying to match this query to the first
clause of the delete rule, delete(H,[H|T],T). The matching in the
first argument is H=a. For the second argument, matching requires
H to be the first element of the user's list, [b,a,g,h], that is, H=b.
But H is already required to be a, so this attempt at matching fails.
Prolog therefore moves on to try the next delete clause,

```
        delete(X,[H|T],[H|U]) :- delete(X,T,U).
```

Recall that the user's query is `delete(a,[b,a,g,h],Result)`. Prolog must first match the query to the head of the current clause. It succeeds with `X=a`, `H=b`, `T=[a,g,h]` and `Result=[H|U]`. Note this works because—unlike the situation with the first clause—`X` is assigned to `a` and `H` is assigned to `b`, so there are no conflicts. We are off to a good start, but this clause will only work if the Prolog processor can also manage to prove the right hand side, `delete(X,T,U)`. That is, plugging in the matched values of `X` and `T`, we need `delete(a,[a,g,h],U)`.

Prolog takes on the challenge of proving this proposition as if it had come from a user. It consults the first clause of the `delete` rule, and as in the earlier example, it succeeds immediately, with `U` matched to the tail of the second argument, that is, `U=[g,h]`. If you look back (really, as Prolog's recursion unwinds back to the original use of the rule) you will see that `Result=[H|U]` and that `H=b`. Thus, along with `U=[g,h]` just above, the Prolog interpreter concludes that `Result=[b,g,h]` which is exactly what we want in this case.

If the element to be deleted appears even later in the list, the processing will take longer, but the idea will be the same, with repeated recursive use of the second clause, and one use of the first clause.

A powerful ingredient of programming in any language is the idea of identifying fundamental concepts and building on them. In list processing, concatenation is a fundamental concept. Having defined `append`, we can use it in rules for other predicates.

Example A.23

Write a Prolog rule for the predicate `last(E,L)` for determining whether E is the last element in the list L.

```
last(E,L) :- append(_,[E],L).
```

The concept of reversal can apply to both strings and lists. Here we are interested in lists, but reversing a *string* is of some interest in the study of formal models of language. The next example is about a predicate called **reverse** with arguments that are lists. It checks whether each of these lists is in the reverse order of the other. The idea of a palindrome also applies to both strings and lists. A palindrome reads the same backwards and forwards. Examples of strings of letters that form palindromic English words are "pop", "deed", "radar", "redder" and "reviver." Here, we will be interested in lists that are palindromes.

Example A.24

Write a recursive rule for the predicate **reverse** that determines whether two lists are reverses of each other. Use that predicate to write a rule for **palindrome** that determines whether a list is the reverse of *itself*.

```
reverse([ ],[ ]).
reverse([H—T],Result) :- reverse(T,R), append(R,[H],Result).

palindrome(X) :- reverse(X,X).
```

A.8   Built-In Predicates and Operators

The logical core of Prolog has been augmented by its designers to make it a real programming language. This has been done by including a substantial number of built-in predicates and arguments that provide normal programming capabilities like the writing of output and that provide programming environment tools like tracing. You have already seen a few. This section briefly introduces a few more and then gathers them all into a couple of tables for convenient reference. Bear in mind, though, that the goal of this appendix is not a thorough treatment of Prolog, but rather to give a sense of how logic can be extended into a declarative approach to programming.

For substantial projects you should consult a Prolog text, which will introduce you to many features.

Several built-in predicates take a single argument and determine whether it has some particular type. In the section on lists, we wrote such a predicate ourselves, `list`. Prolog provides `integer` for integers, `float` for floating point numbers and `number` for either. The predicate `atom` succeeds for constant symbols like `a1` and `mary` as well as anything enclosed in a pair of single quotes like `'object-oriented design'` or `'New York'`. These are treated like strings in that they are appropriate arguments to `write`, which writes them to the output. The predicate `atomic` succeeds on all numbers and constant symbols. Example A.25 shows some simple queries with these predicates. Later, in Example A.27, we will use `atom` to avoid errors on the wrong kinds of input.

Example A.25

```
|?- integer(55).
yes
|?- float(55).
no
|?- float(55.0).
yes
|?- atom(55).
no
|?- atomic(55).
yes
|?- atom(abc).
yes
|?- atom(X).
no
|?- atom('X').
yes
|?- atom('Is this a string?').
yes
|?- atomic(particle).
yes
```

The predicate **name** has two arguments. The first argument is a constant symbol. (These were described in the preceding paragraph.) The second is the corresponding list of ascii codes. As with other Prolog predicates, information can flow in either direction between the two arguments, as the simple queries in Example A.26 show. This capability comes in handy for manipulations within a string (constant symbol), as in Example A.27: **name** is used to break up the string at the outset and reassemble it later.

Example A.26

```
|?- name(abc,X).
X = [97,98,99]
|?- name(Y,[97,98,32,99]).
Y = 'ab c'
|?- name(a,[97]).
yes
```

Example A.27

Implement a Prolog predicate called **upcase** that, when given a constant symbol as its first argument, will convert each lower case letter in it to the corresponding capital letter.

The ascii codes for the letters "a", "b", ... and "z" are 97, 98, ... and 122. First we create **upcasecode1** to take a single ascii code from lower to upper case, if it happens to be lower case. Notice the use of the cut (exclamation point). Without the cut, there would be two possible results for numbers from 97 to 122. Next, **upcasecodelist** handles all the codes in a list, using **upcasecode1** on the first and itself (recursively) on the rest. With these auxiliary rules in place, we take on the original task of creating **upcase**, using **name** to get at the codes and then reassemble them after **upcasecodelist** has done the main work.

```
low2up(X,Y) :- 96<X, X<123, !, Y is X-32.
low2up(X,X).
low2uplist([ ],[ ]).
low2uplist([Xh|Xt], [Yh|Yt]) :- low2up(Xh,Yh), low2uplist(Xt,Yt).
lower2upper(X,Y) :- atom(X),
                    name(X,Xcodes),
                    low2uplist(Xcodes, Ycodes),
                    name(Y,Ycodes).
```

Finally, we consider **setof** and **bagof**. To see the usefulness of these, suppose you have a Prolog-style database of **parent** facts and you want to know all the people that have our old friend **mary** as a parent. While it is true that you can do this interactively with the query **parent(mary, X)**, using the semi-colon as often as necessary, this approach will not let you do anything with the set of answers within a Prolog program. What we need is a way to collect those answers into a list. That is what **setof** and **bagof** let you do. The difference between them is that **setof** removes duplicates and sorts the list.

Example A.28

Interactively show some individual's children in two different ways. First, using **parent**, show them one at a time, as the multiple answers to a query. Then, using **setof**, produce a list containing all of them.

```
|?- parent(mary,X).
X = bea ;
X = cal ;
X = dot ;
no
|?- setof(X, parent(mary,X), Y).
X = _9398,
Y = [bea,cal,dot] ;
no
```

Example A.29

Write Prolog rules that take a string and produce a new string containing one instance of each vowel of the original string, in alphabetical order. Also write Prolog rules to yield the vowel substring of a string, that is, all the instances of vowels, in the order in which they appear in the original string.

We create Prolog rules vowelset and vowelbag, using setof and bagof, respectively. Each relies on the rule for member, repeated here, and on a list of the codes for the 5 vowels. Try each of them on inputs like mississippi and pneumonia.

```
member(H, [H|_]).
member(X, [_|T]) :- member(X,T).

vowelcode(X) :- member(X, [97,101,105,111,117]).
vowelset(X,Y) :- name(X,Xcodes),
          setof(U, (member(U,Xcodes), vowelcode(U)), Ycodes),
          name(Y,Ycodes).

vowelbag(X,Y) :- name(X,Xcodes),
          bagof(U, (member(U,Xcodes), vowelcode(U)), Ycodes),
          name(Y,Ycodes).
```

Here are the tables of built-in predicates and operators promised earlier. The operators are all binary, and each is used in infix position with one operand before and one after. Following the name of each predicate is a slash and the number of arguments it requires. The operators are all binary, and each is used in infix position with one operand before and one after.

Operator	What it does
is	tries to compute the value of an arithmetic expression on its right and unifies the result with the operand on its left.
=	tries to unify (or match) its two operands. This can be used to cause a variable to be associated with an appropriate value.
==	succeeds if it has two identical operands.
=:=	succeeds if it has two numerical expressions that are equal.
> and <	greater than and less than.
>= and =<	greater-or-equal and less-or-equal; note the placement of "=".
\=	the negation of =.
\==	the negation of ==.
=\=	the negation of =:=.

Predicate /arguments	What the predicate does
assert/1	is used to assert something during a Prolog session.
atom/1	is true if its one argument is an atom.
bagof/3	is good for collecting possibly repeated answers
consult/1	loads a file into a Prolog session. If the argument begins and ends with a single quote, it can be a path. Brackets around a filename is a substitute for consult.
fail/0	always fails
halt/0	terminates the Prolog session
integer/1	is true if its one argument is an integer.
name/2	succeeds if its two arguments are an atom and the corresponding list of ascii codes.
nl/0	writes a newline to the current output.
notrace/0	turns off tracing
read/1	reads the next Prolog expression in the current input.
setof/3	is good for collecting non-repeated answers. argument 1: a variable argument 2: an expression involving that variable argument 3: list of values of the variable for which the expression succeeds.
tab/0	has one argument, which specifies how many blanks to output.
trace/0	turns on the tracing operation.
true/0	always succeeds.
write/1	has one argument that is written to the current output. If there are blanks, enclose everything in single quotes.
!	"cut"; see text.

By the way, it is possible for a Prolog program to include a clause with *nothing* on the left side like this: " $:- Q_1, Q_2, \ldots, Q_n$". This is not a rule but is just used to get something done. As usual, the Prolog inferencer must prove the propositions on the right to establish what is on the left, even though in this case there is nothing on the left to establish. Notice the pre-defined predicates "nl", and "write".

Example A.30

Suppose file h contains two parent facts, parent(a,b) and parent(b,c), followed by ":- nl, write('parent data loaded from file h.'),nl.". What happens when this file is loaded?

In addition to the facts becoming available within your session, the "nl" starts a new line and the "write" causes the single-quoted material to appear on the screen.

```
=> prolog
    [startup message from the software company]
|?- consult(h).
parent data loaded from file h.
yes
```

A.9   Finite Automata in Prolog

This section should only be read after the chapter on finite automata (FA).

Implementing FAs in Prolog brings together key techniques from both halves of this book and is surprisingly easy to do. The idea is to get Prolog to carry out the acceptance of exactly the strings that are in a particular FA's language. We will do this in two ways. The first method straightforwardly converts the specification for a particular machine directly to a Prolog predicate. The second approach is a more general one involving a rule that is useful for any FA. In this method, Prolog *facts* express the structure of a particular machine, an organization that we will argue makes better sense.

To write a Prolog program for machine M by the first method, we create just one predicate, which we will call **accept**, to suggest that it will accept strings. We want it to succeed (that is, be true, and give a **yes** answer) when given a string that M accepts; it should fail on all other strings. We will assume that input strings are converted to lists; for example, the string *abc* becomes **[a,b,c]**. Conversion facilities from strings to lists and vice-versa are often available in implementations of Prolog.

The predicate **accept** will have two arguments that together express the current situation: the current state and what remains of the input string. We want to be able to see if a string is accepted, by entering a query with that string's list form as the second argument to accept, and with the start state, q_0, as first argument.

Example A.31

Consider the FA,

$$M = (\{q_0, q_1, q_2\}, \{a, b, c, d\}, q_0, \delta, \{q_2\})$$

where $\delta(q_0, a) = q_1$, $\delta(q_1, b) = q_1$, $\delta(q_1, c) = q_2$ and $\delta(q_2, d) = q_0$

To test a string, say, *abbcdac*, one would enter the query, **accept(q0,[a,b,b,c,d,a,c])**. In this case, the answer should be **yes**, since the string is in the language of the automaton. Here is a multi-clause rule for **accept**:

```
accept(q0,[a|Tail]) :- accept(q1,Tail).
accept(q1,[b|Tail]) :- accept(q1,Tail).
accept(q1,[c|Tail]) :- accept(q2,Tail).
accept(q2,[d|Tail]) :- accept(q0,Tail).
accept(q2,[ ]).
```

Look at the program in Example A.31 and begin by noticing that the first argument to the predicate `accept` is always a state of the FA and the second is always a list. In each clause, the list on the right side is shorter by one input symbol, exactly the one that causes the transition from the state on the right to the state on the left. In addition, the predicate `accept` succeeds when its first argument is q_2 and its second argument is the empty list. You can see this from the last line. This implements the fact that q_2 is a final state. It follows that with q_0 as first argument the program succeeds for any string in $\mathcal{L}(M)$, the language of the FA, and fails for any other string.

Now consider a more general approach to FAs in prolog. Although the Prolog rule in Example A.31 correctly implements the machine for which it was created, it does not give us any help with other FAs. We therefore now put the `accept` predicate into a form that is more abstract and therefore is also of more general use. In Example A.32, `accept` expresses the workings of FAs in general, so its rule can be used, unchanged, in any FA program.

The strategy is to express as Prolog *facts* the information about the transition function of a particular FA, while the *rule* is reserved for what is true of all FAs. It is appropriate to use `delta` as the name of the new predicate for fact about δ. The first and second arguments of `delta` are therefore the current state and input, while the third argument is the resulting new state, which is the value (output) of δ. (The technique of converting a function to a predicate with an extra argument for the result is a common one. You have seen it with `append`, a 3-argument predicate that corresponds to the 2-argument function of list concatenation.)

Example A.32

Transition information for the FA in Example A.31, now appears as facts about the predicate `delta`.

```
accept(Q,[S|Tail])   :- delta(Q,S,R), accept(R,Tail).
accept(Q,[ ])        :- acc(Q).
```

```
delta(q0,a,q1).
delta(q1,b,q1).
delta(q1,c,q2).
delta(q2,d,q0).
acc(q2).
```

Notice that in Example A.32, there are only two clauses for the accept rule. They reflect Prolog's declarative style in that each of the two clauses makes a statement about the nature of FAs, one dealing with transitions and the other with final states. Moreover, the facts about a particular FA are expressed as Prolog facts, using only delta, so there is a clean break between rules and facts, with rules used for general matters and facts used for the specifics of one machine.

The first clause for accept specifies how transitions work. Look at its right side. The first conjunct, delta(Q,S,R), means that this clause is useful only if there is a transition (an arrow, in terms of FA diagrams) that goes from state Q to state R and has S as the current input. Since Q, S and R are all variables, they can refer to any transition in any FA.

Now look at the whole first clause. It says that from state Q, with current input S, acceptance (success of accept) will occur provided that delta(Q,S,R) succeeds, where R is the new state, and also provided that acceptance occurs from R with a slightly shorter input list, diminished by the removal of S from the front of it.

The second clause of accept handles the idea of accepting states. It says that if you are in state Q and there is no more input, accept succeeds provided that Q is an accepting state of the FA. The idea of an accepting state is represented by the predicate acc. The last line of this Prolog program states that q_2 is an accepting state.

As already mentioned, the delta predicate corresponds directly to the δ function of the particular FA. Compare the four lines of the delta predicate with the four lines of the δ function. Notice that in each case the third argument of `delta` is the value (output) when δ is applied to the first two arguments.

A.10   Pushdown Automata in Prolog

This section should only be read after the chapter on push-down automata (PDA).

Implementing PDAs in Prolog brings together key techniques from both halves of this book. PDAs embody major concepts in programming language analysis which our Prolog program will express essentially as logic, while also bringing the computation into the real world. Our strategy for PDAs in Prolog builds upon the Prolog program for FAs in Section A.9 just as PDA concepts extend those of FAs. Once again we take advantage of Prolog's declarative nature and its rule-fact distinction to separate the general ideas of an automaton class, expressed as rules, from what is true of particular automata, expressed as facts.

To emphasize practicality, we choose for our Prolog implementation a PDA that is formed systematically from a given grammar to embody a useful parsing technique. This PDA comes from Example 11.7 in Section 11.3; it accepts balanced parentheses.

As with FAs, we will express the facts of a particular PDA transition function δ with the appropriately named predicate `delta`. As the PDA definition specifies in general – and as diagrams and tables for particular PDAs also show in various ways – each transition has five parts: a source state, an input symbol, a stack symbol, a destination state and a string of symbols (possibly empty) to push onto the stack. This string becomes a list in the Prolog implementation. In line 1 of Example 11.7, the five items are, respectively, q_0, (, S, q_0 and R. Correspondingly, we get the Prolog fact

```
delta(q0, (, S, q0, [R]).
```

All the Prolog facts that arise in this way from the transitions appear in Figure A.3(a).

(a) Transition facts:

```
delta(q0, (, S, q0, [R] ).
delta(q0, (, S, q0, [R,S] ).
delta(q0, (, S, q0, [S,R] ).
delta(q0, (, S, q0, [S,R,S] ).
delta(q0, ), R, q0, [ ] ).
```

(b) Acceptance rule:

```
accept(_,[ ],[ ]).
```

(c) Transition rule, using input:

```
accept(Q,[S|T1],[Z|T2])  :- delta(Q,S,Z,R,P),
                            append(P,T2,Y),
                            accept(R,T1,Y).
```

Figure A.3: A Prolog program for a PDA.

As with FAs, the operation of PDAs will be specified just once for an entire automaton class, and again we name the predicate "accept." PDAs, however, are a bit more complicated than FAs. The predicate accept now needs three arguments instead of two. The first two are the state and the remaining input, as for FAs. The third is the stack, represented as a list. For example, consider the query

```
accept(q0,[(,(,),(,),)], [S]).
```

The purpose of this query will be to ask what happens when processing begins at the start state, q_0, with input $(()())$, and with the stack holding its initial contents, S. For the PDA that we are going to try to implement, the Prolog program should answer "yes," since the language to be recognized is the balanced parentheses.

Let us now build the rule for accept so that this works out. We will need clauses for transitioning from state to state and for recognizing success in an accepting state. Acceptance is the easier of the two: we write accept(_,[ ],[ ])., as shown in Figure A.3(b). This says that acceptance occurs when the input has been used up, indicated by the empty list, [ ], when the stack is also empty.

We turn now to the clause of accept whose purpose is to deal with transition rules. In Figure A.3(c), look at the first conjunct on the right-hand side, delta(Q,S,Z,R,P). All the arguments of delta here are variables, so that this transition rule can be used for any PDA. In general such a PDA rule is supposed to permit going from state Q to state R (the first and fourth arguments) with input S and with the stack getting its top symbol Z replaced by the list P. To see that this is exactly what the clause does, compare the arguments of the two uses of accept in this clause. As we go from one to the other, state Q in the first argument position is replaced by state R. In the second position, symbol S is popped. Finally, in the third position Z is popped and replaced by the list P as can be ascertained by noting that the use of append requires Y to be the concatenation of P and the stack-tail, T2. (The predicate append is built into some versions of Prolog and is provided in Section A.7.)

This technique can be modified, using ideas from the previous section, to build a prolog implementation of a PDA that uses accepting states.

Exercises

A.1 – Suppose you have a database of people, with facts like those in Example A.1. Besides parent(X,Y) and female(X), we now include a third predicate for facts, male(X), used to express things like the fact that John is male. Add rules for the following predicates. Where appropriate, make use of a predicate for which a rule has already been specified, either in this appendix or within your solution to this problem.

   (a) father(X,Y)

   (b) grandmother(X,Y)

   (c) child(X,Y) (opposite of parent(X,Y))

   (d) grandchild(X,Y)

   (e) descendant(X,Y)

A.2 – Being careful to distinguish the conditional and biconditional operators,

> (a) Write the exact translation of the `mother(X,Y)` rule into logical notation.
>
> (b) Define "mother" in logical notation.

A.3 – Suppose that the family example (Example A.1) is extended to include facts about people being married, using the predicate `husband`. For example, `husband(bill,ann)` means that Bill is the husband of Ann.

> (a) Write a rule for `wife` in terms of `husband`.
>
> (b) Write a rule for `spouse` in terms of `husband` and `wife`. Do this both *with* a semi-colon and *without* one.
>
> (c) Write a rule for `spouse` using only `husband`.

A.4 – Write a rule for `aunt` that takes account of both kinds of aunt: sister of a parent and aunt via marriage to an uncle. Use a semi-colon.

A.5 – Write a Prolog rule for full siblings, that is, those who share two parents. You will now need to use the `different` rule in two ways: as in the `sibling` rule, in Example A.15, and also to require the two shared parents not to be the same person.

A.6 – Write a Prolog rule for first cousins, using a criterion that says we are first cousins if you have a parent who is a full sibling of one of my parents, but we ourselves are not full or even half siblings and of course first cousins must not the same person. Use cut twice to exclude these possibilities. It will simplify matters to use the sibling rule and/or the rule for full siblings, in Exercise A.5.

A.7 – Suppose we represent a world of stackable, cubical blocks of identical size by writing facts like `on(a,c)` to mean that block *a* is resting directly on block *c*, being in contact with it and supported by it. The predicate `higher` requires only that the first block be somewhere above the second, within the same stack. While allowing physical contact it does not require it, as `on` does. In the situation just described, suppose we add block j and have it sit directly on a. Then `higher(j,c)` holds, though not `on(j,c)`. Write a recursive rule that expresses `higher` using both itself and `on`.

A.8 – Numerical predicates like "$<$" are expressed in Prolog in the familiar infix order used in mathematics, so we can write, for example, "$x < 4$" rather than something like `lessthan(x,4)`. Suppose that `age(John,33)` means that John is 33 years old.

    (a) Write a rule for `olderthan(X,Y)` that is true whenever person X is older than person Y.

    (b) Write a rule for `bigsib(X,Y)` that is true if person X is an older brother or an older sister of person Y.

A.9 – Consider an employee database with facts of the form

$$\texttt{employee(730638,dee,hr,8,1998)}.$$

This particular Prolog example encodes the fact that the person with employee number 730638 is named Dee, works in the Human Resources division (expressed "`hr`" in this Prolog implementation) of the company and was hired in August (the 8th month) of the year 1998. Write queries that will extract the information specified below. Assume that the user will have to use repeated semi-colons to get multiple answers.

(a) the names (only) of the people who work in PP (Physical Plant)

(b) the name and division of each person who joined the company in 1998 or after

(c) the name of everyone hired in the 10 years ending June, 2000.

A.10 – With `employee` facts as in Exercise A.9, write rules that express the following concepts as Prolog rules related to the relational operators select and project.

(a) Confine attention to an employee's name and where in the organization he or she works.

(b) Confine attention to when people began work.

(c) Confine attention to (all information about) just those employees who are in the Payroll Office, which is expressed as `pay` in the Prolog facts.

(d) Confine attention to employees in Human Resources who joined the organization before 1997.

A.11 – In part (a) of the preceding problem, use the built-in Prolog operator `setof` so that all the answers are returned at once, so that you are not obliged to keep on typing semi-colons.

A.12 – Along with the Prolog facts of the form `employee(730638,dee,hr,8,1998).` introduced in Exercise A.9, assume that we now also have facts about the month and year of an employee's date of birth that look like this: `dob(730638,3,1968).`

(a) Write a Prolog rule for a new predicate — call it `all_info` — corresponding to a natural join of the `employee` and `dob` tables on the registration number. The result should have 7 fields.

(b) Use the predicate `all_info` from part (a) in writing a rule for a predicate that accepts an employee's number and is true if that employee joined the organization during or after the month in which he or she turned 50.

A.13 – With `employee` facts as in Exercise A.9, write rules for the following predicates.

(a) `later(W,X,Y,Z)`, meaning that the month W of year X is later in time than the month Y of year Z. This does not depend on `employee` facts so it may be useful not only in the next part but elsewhere as well.

(b) `senior_to(X,Y)`, meaning that the employee with number X has worked longer for this firm than the one with number Y. Use the predicate `later`.

(c) `senior_div_mate_of(X,Y)`, meaning that the employees with numbers X and Y are in the same division and X has worked longer for this firm than Y. Use the predicate `senior_to`.

A.14 – Let `employs(a,b)` mean that person a owns a firm that employs person b. Note that it is possible to work in your own firm. Write eleven Prolog queries, each having an argument pattern that differs significantly from all of the others. For each of your eleven queries, write down a question in English that expresses the idea of that query.

One kind of significant difference between argument patterns is having a different kind of argument — constant versus named variable versus anonymous variable ("_") — in one of the argument positions. When two argument positions both have a constant (or both have a named variable) there is a significant difference between the case in which those two constants (or named variables) are the same and the case of them being different.

A.15 – Implement and test Prolog rules for list predicates each having two arguments, as follows:

(a) In the predicate `delete_first2`, the second argument can be found be deleting the first two elements of the first argument. Thus Prolog should answer "yes" to `delete_last2([a,b,b,c,c],[b,c,c])`.

(b) In the predicate `delete_last2`, the second argument can be found be deleting the last two elements of the first argument. Thus Prolog should answer "Result = [a,b,b]" to `delete_last2([a,b,b,c,c],Result)`.

(c) In the predicate `delete22`, the second argument can be found be deleting the first two and the last two elements of the first argument. Thus Prolog should answer "yes" to `delete22([a,b,c,d,e],[c])`.

A.16 – Consider the Prolog rule `pal2(Z) :- append(X,Y,Z), reverse(X,Y)` for some, but not all, palindromes.

(a) For which palindromes does `pal2` fail?

(b) Why must `pal2` fail in these cases?

A.17 – All of the recursive examples in the text involved direct recursion, that is, a predicate calling itself. In this exercise you are asked develop two predicates that call each other, so that each calls itself not directly but indirectly via the other. Specifically, write predicates `evenlength` and `oddlength` that determine, respectively, whether the length of a list is even or odd, by calling each other on shorter and shorter lists — shorter by 1 each time. The resulting indirect recursion bottoms out when a call is ultimately made with the empty list, which should succeed for `evenlength`, since zero is an even number, but not for `oddlength`. Hint: use `evenlength([  ]).` as the base case.

Appendix B

The AWK Language

Having learned something about regular expressions, you are ready for AWK. AWK is a powerful software tool that uses regular expressions to simplify programming for some applications. The language was name for its inventors Aho, Weinberger, and Kernighan. It is the precursor to Perl, but where Perl has become large (due to "feature creep"), AWK has remained small. Its relative simplicity is what makes it suitable for us. We will study AWK because of it use of regular expressions to ease the programmer's job for certain problems.

AWK is a *data-driven* language in that the actions that are taken, over time, depend on the input stream; actions are selected by the input. However, the actions themselves are implemented in a familiar procedural style. (AWK is arguably the first scripting language, a language that can be used to program the flow of control of several tasks. However in this chapter we will not explore the advanced features that allows AWK to write scripts.)

This is not a complete discussion of AWK's features, but it is self-contained.

B.1 Overview of AWK

AWK is a Unix tool and as is standard for most such tools, it reads from standard input and writes to standard output. If a file name

is given on the command line then the input is read from that file
instead. A file consists of consecutive *records* and AWK operates on
one record at a time. By default a record is a single line of text.
A record consists of consecutive *fields*, separated by *field separators*.
By default a field separator is "white space", a sequence of spaces
and/or tabs (though a field separator can be redefined to be other
characters, such as colons).

An AWK program is a sequence of *rules*. Each rule is

> *pattern* {*action*}

and rules appear on separate lines. The braces are part of the syntax. While *pattern* is the standard term, "selector" might be more
descriptive. The pattern is used to select records from the input file
and then apply the corresponding action to each such record. It is
possible to omit the pattern or the action (along with its braces),
but not both. If there is no pattern given then every record will be
selected. If there is no action given then the default action of printing
the current record will be performed.

A pattern is often a regular expression. A regular expression corresponds to a set of strings and such a pattern is said to match a
record if any string in that set of strings appears within the record.
However a "pattern" can contain other tests for selecting a record,
such a boolean expressions involving numerical operators and string
expressions.

An action is a sequence of statements. The syntax of the statements
is described below. It is a very simple syntax similar to C, C++,
Java and related languages. Comments are indicated by a # and the
comment continues to the end of the line. (A # in a regular expression
does not start a comment.)

The basic idea of AWK code is simple. The file is read one record at a
time. For each record every rule is invoked, and for each record that
is selected by a rule's pattern the corresponding action is performed
using the current record. The same record can be selected by several
rules; their corresponding actions will be done in the order they
appear in the program.

An AWK program is often very short. Indeed many useful programs can be written in one line. We can always enter our AWK programs as a text file. However, when the program is short, and when it is only going to be used once, AWK allows the user to type the program directly into the command line! The latter option is called a "one-shot" program, and will be illustrated below.

B.2   Writing Expressions

There are predefined variables that can be used in AWK code. The variable NR is equal to the number of the current record (that is, the most recently read record). The variable NF is equal to the number of fields of the current record. The string variables $1, $2, $3, ... are the strings corresponding to each consecutive field of the current record. The variable $0 corresponds to the entire record, and $NF is the string corresponding to the last field.

User-defined variables are not declared. The type of such a variable is inferred by how it is used. Type conversion occurs as needed by the various operators. Numeric variables are automatically initialized to 0 and string variables are initialized to the empty string.

The operators are the standard operators of most languages. The assignment operator is = but variants like += are allowed. Arithmetic operators are normal and the relational operators are <, <=, ==, !=, >=, >. The string concatenation operator is just a blank. The logical operators are || (or), && (and), ! (not). There are several predefined functions; only three of them are mentioned here. First is the string length function: length(*string*) takes a string as its argument and returns its length. By convention it can be written with no argument at all, length, in which case it is the same as length($0). The function substr(*string, start, length*) returns the substring of *string* of *length* characters, starting in position *start*. Third, rand() returns a random floating point number, such that $0 \leq$ rand() < 1.

The *matching* operators are new and crucial to most AWK programs. The operators, ~ and !~, separate a string from a regular expression. Regular expressions are explained in the next section. An example is `stringa ~ /abc/`, where `/abc/` is the simple regular expression representing the string "abc" and the matching operator returns true if the string "abc" appears in the string `stringa`. A very common special case is when the string operand is $0, the entire record; by convention $0 ~ `/abc/` can be written simply as `/abc/`.

B.3   Writing Regular Expressions

A regular expression is enclosed in slashes. What comes between the slashes is a normal RE, but with several syntactic conventions that are explained below. This notation extends REs by permitting some useful operations that are not part of the core definition of REs. Yet this notation is only an extension and not a whole new kind of representational system inasmuch as practically any example can be rewritten as a normal RE. Still, in many cases of interest the use of the extra operators will allow a more compact expression than the corresponding RE.

See Figure B.1. While regular expressions are normally delimited by slashes, there are optional ways of designating a regular expression. For example, instead of `$2 ~/x[a-z]*f/` we could use double quotes: `$2 ~ "x[a-z]*f"`. Also we could set the variable var to the string `x[a-z]*f` and write `$2 ~ var`.

B.4   Writing Patterns

A pattern is essentially a boolean expression, using variables that refer to the current record. If the expression evaluates to true the corresponding actions is invoked. There are two special patterns, that must be used alone, BEGIN and END. BEGIN evaluates as true only once, before the first record is read. END evaluates as true only once, after the last record is read. Using the details above we can now write examples of interesting patterns.

Concatenation is the same as in REs.

| The vertical bar separates alternatives instead of the plus sign used in ordinary REs.

() Parentheses are used in the ordinary way, for grouping. They do not add any meaning.

* Star stands for zero or more occurrences of its operand, just as it does in REs.

+ Plus means one or more occurrences of whatever it is applied to. It is *not* used to separate alternatives. That role is taken by the vertical bar.

? A question mark after something makes it optional, so b? stands for the RE, $(b + \Lambda)$. This operator has the same high precedence as star and plus. For example, the expression ab?cd+e can match with *acde, abcde, acdde, abcdde, abcddde,* .... Another example is -?(0|1)+ which will match non-empty sequences of binary integers, with or without a preceding unary minus.

\ Backslash before an operator makes it behave like an ordinary character. For example, \+ matches an input plus sign and \. matches a period or decimal point. However, by convention, \t stands for the tab and \n means newline. Since regular expressions are delimited by slashes, if a slash appears in the regular expression it should be as \/.

[ ] Brackets denote a choice among characters, so [aeiou] means any vowel, just like (a|e|i|o|u). Inside brackets, most of the special symbols lose their special properties; for example, [*/] represents a choice between star and slash, [.?!] denotes a choice among sentence-ending punctuation marks, and [,] denotes a choice of comma or blank. To include a \,], - or a ^ you should precede it with a backslash. This [\t]+ matches whitespace within a line. See the next two entries.

- Characters with consecutive ASCII codes can be expressed with a hyphen within brackets; for example, [a-z] is a pattern for any lower-case letter, and [a-zA-Z] for any letter. However, a hyphen at the beginning or end of a bracketed choice behaves normally, so [-+]? stands for an optional sign character.

^ When caret ^ appears at the start of a bracketed pattern, it negates the remaining characters. Thus [^aeiou]+ means a sequence of one or more consonants. A further, unrelated use of the caret is when it appears at the beginning of a pattern: it matches no character but does match the beginning of the string.

$ When $ appears at the end of a pattern; it matches no character but does match the end of the string.

. A period matches any single character except newline. The pattern "b..b" matches any sequence of four characters starting and ending with a "b".

Figure B.1: AWK regular expression notation

- `$3 < 100 || $4 == "Bob"` selects a record in which either the third field is numeric and less than 100 or the fourth field is the string "Bob".

- `10*NR == $1` selects a record if the first field is 10 times the current record number.

- `($4 $5) !~ /Alice/` selects a record for which the string "Alice" does *not* appear in the string formed by concatenating the fourth and fifth fields.

- `/Alice/` selects a record that contains the string "Alice" anywhere (i.e., in `$0`).

- `/[-+]?[0-9]+\.[0-9][0-9]/` selects records that contain fixed-point optionally-signed numbers, such as -123.45, +0.12, or 1.00.

B.5   Writing Actions

Actions are written in a simple syntax, very similar to C, C++, Java and related procedural languages. An action is zero or more statements. The statements are separated by either a semicolon (;) or the end of the line. (Statements can be extended to multiple lines by ending lines with a backslash.) Some basic *statements*, among others, are:

`print` *expression-list*

`if (` *expression* `)` *statement*

`if (` *expression* `)` *statement* `else` *statement*

`while (` *expression* `)`*statement*

`for (` *expression* `;` *expression* `;` *expression* `)` *statement*

assignment statements, function calls, etc.

The `print` outputs a string terminated by a newline. The string can be built from several string expressions separated by commas. The commas introduce blanks as separators. For example, if $2 is "Bob" and $1 is "Alice" then `print $2, $4` prints the line "Bob Alice". Note that `print $2 $4` prints the line "BobAlice" since there is only a single string expression, the concatention of the strings $2 and $4. By convention, `print` by itself is the same as `print $0`. (There is a `printf` command available to do formatted output.)

B.6   Using Arrays

AWK uses *associative arrays*, arrays in which the subscripts are strings. The arrays are one-dimensional and brackets are used to delimit subscripts. The arrays elements can be strings and/or numbers. For example, suppose our input file has state abbreviations as the third field of each record. We could have an expression such as `table[$3] > table["VA"]`. Also note, because of type conversion, `item["4"]` can be written more naturally as `item[4]`.

Through usage the program learns the set of subscripts that correspond to entries. There is a form of the `for` statement for array processing:

> `for ( variable in array ) statement`

where the loop executes *statement* with *variable* set in turn to each different subscript in the array (in no particular order). Further, `in` is also a boolean operator, where (`variable in array`) is true if *variable* has been use as a subscript to the *array*. (A subscript can be removed the set of valid subscripts for an array with the function `delete array[subscript]`.)

Any string can be regard as a "record" that is itself composed of consecutive fields. The function `split (string, array, separator)` breaks up *string* into fields, separated by the string *separator*, and stores the fields in the array *array*. For example, `split`

("12/4/2003", date, "/") stores 12 in date[1], 4 in date[2], and 2003 in date[3].

Multidimensional arrays are not supported *but* they appear to be. This is because if you write matrix[i,j] it converts "i,j" into a single string and treats matrix as a one-dimensional array. In other words, in this context, the comma is an enhanced concatenation operator.

B.7　Sample Programs

Several complete (!) programs are given below.

1. Print the input lines numbered 15 to 20:

   ```
   NR >= 15 && NR <=20
   ```

2. Print the total number of input lines:

   ```
   END {print NR}
   ```

3. Print the last field of the last line:

   ```
   {x = $NF}
   END {print x}
   ```

4. Print the total of all the third fields:

   ```
   {sum = sum + $3}
   END {print sum}
   ```

5. Print the third field of every line in which the second field contains "xyz":

   ```
   $2 ~/xyz/ {print $3}
   ```

6. Print the fields of each non-empty input line in reverse order:

   ```
   NF > 0 {x = $NF; for(i = NF-1; i > 0; i = i-1) x
   = x " " $i; print x}
   ```

7. Print the longest input line:

```
{if (length > length(max)) max = $0}
END {print "The longest line is :", max}
```

8. Print the input lines where the second field is entirely digits:

```
BEGIN {digits = "^[0-9]+$"}
$2 ~ digits
```

9. Assuming the third field is a state abbreviation, print which states occurred and how often:

```
{count[$3] = count[$3] +1}
END {for (state in count) print state, count[state]}
```

10. Exchange the first two fields of each input line and then print it:

```
{x = $2; $2 = $1; $1 = x; print}
```

11. Assuming just three numerical fields, print the fields in sorted order:

```
$2>$3 {t=$3; $3=$2; $2=t}
$1>$2 {t=$2; $2=$1; $1=t}
$2>$3 {t=$3; $3=$2; $2=t}
{print}
```

B.8   Using AWK in Unix

What do you have to do to actually use AWK? First, of course, you have to gain access to it, but that is easy because it is widely available. In particular it is on nearly all computers that run some version of the Unix operating system. Since it is a Unix command, there is an entry for it in the online manual. You can get that documentation by typing "man awk" at the operating system prompt. Note the correct spelling is with lower-case letters, "awk", just like other Unix commands.

Note that there are many versions of AWK. On some systems you may get, say, GAWK if you enter the command awk. However, there is little dependence on the version.

At the Unix prompt you will type:

```
awk -f source input1 input2 ...
```

where *source* is file with your AWK program, and the other files are the input files. Typically there is only one input file; if there are more they are concatenated into one input stream. All files are text files. If there is no input file specified then the input comes from standard input. Of course AWK code can be piped with other Unix tools and filters.

An unusual and attractive variant syntax of the command line is permitted:

```
awk 'program' input1 input2 ...
```

where *program* is the entire text of the AWK program given right in the command line! This is called a one-shot program, since you need to retype it each time. An example given earlier could be invoked with:

```
awk '$2 ~/xyz/ {print $3}' data
```

where data is the input file. (Multiple rules can be used in one-shot programs, but are not discussed here.)

B.9   An Example

Assume that your input file is composed of lines such as:

```
Jim Smith 23.34
Bob G. Johnson 122.56
Jim Smith 5.21
```

where the number represents the payment to named individual, but the payments to an individual are not necessarily consecutive. Note that the name may be compose of two or three fields; we assume that names are consistent through the file.

Consider this code:

```
NF==3 {print $2 $1, $0}
NF==4 {print $3 $1 $2, $0}
```

This produces a file with a new field, a "key," at the beginning of each line:

```
SmithJim Jim Smith 23.34
JohnsonBobG. Bob G. Johnson 122.56
SmithJim Jim Smith 5.21
```

This output file can be sorted with the effect that the various records of each person will become contiguous. Assume that this new file has been sorted. Now we want to use the new file as input to a second AWK program:

```
NR==1 || $1==prevkey {total = total + $NF}
NR>1 && $1!=prevkey {print prevname, total; total = $NF}
{prevkey = $1; $1 = ""; $NF = ""; prevname = $0}
END {print prevname, total}
```

Assuming the data and the two programs are in the files **data**, **prog1**, and **prog2**, respectively, then this

```
awk -f prog1 data | sort | awk -f prog2 > outfile
```

produces the output file **outfile**:

```
Bob G. Johnson 122.56
Jim Smith 28.55
```

Appendix C

Answers to Selected Problems

Chapter 1: Mathematical Preliminaries

Ex: 1.1 (a) multiplication is commutative,

(b) concatenation is not commutative (if $x = abc$ and $y = def$ then $xy \neq yx$),

(c) union is commutative.

Ex: 1.2 (a) $A \cup B = B \cup A$ and $(A \cup B) \cup C = A \cup (B \cup C)$

(b) $A \cap B = B \cap A$ and $(A \cap B) \cap C = A \cap (B \cap C)$

(c) $A \cap (B \cup C) = (A \cap B) \cup (A \cap C)$

(d) $A \cup (B \cap C) = (A \cup B) \cap (A \cup C)$

Ex: 1.3 $|S_1 \times S_2| = |S_1| \, |S_2|$

Ex: 1.4 (a) $\emptyset$; $A \cup \emptyset = A$

(b) $\mathcal{U}$; $A \cap \mathcal{U} = A$

Ex: 1.5 (a) Yes, since if $A \subseteq B$ and $B \subseteq C$ then $A \subseteq C$. To see this note that if $x \in A$ then $x \in B$ (since $A \subseteq B$) and if $x \in B$ then $x \in C$ (since $B \subseteq C$) so $x \in A$ implies $x \in C$.

(b) No. Consider $S = \{T\}$, $T = \{a\}$ and $T \times T = \{(a, a)\}$. Since $T \times T$ is not in S it follows that S is not closed under cross-product. In fact only specially constructed sets would be expected to have the property.

Ex: 1.6 The cardinality is 13 since the language is this set of strings:

$$\{\Lambda, a, b, c, aa, ab, ac, ba, bb, bc, ca, cb, cc\}$$

Ex: 1.8 $f(n)$ is $O(n^3)$

Chapter 2: Propositional Logic

Ex: 2.1 (a) If p is TRUE, the second expression as a whole is TRUE. With p TRUE, the only way to make the other expression FALSE is for r to be FALSE. With p = TRUE and r = FALSE, the two expressions must have different values. To complete the answer set q = TRUE.

(b) The answer to (a) shows that the placement of parentheses can affect the value of a logical expression. Therefore, some means of ordering operations, such as parentheses or precedence, is essential to avoiding ambiguity in expressions.

(c) The remarks in part (a) hold without regard to q, we can leave p and r unchanged with q = FALSE.

Ex: 2.2 (a) Specifying a function for this domain and codomain is a matter of selecting TRUE or FALSE for each of the 4 states. Therefore there are 4 choices to be made, each having 2 options. Since all the choices are independent of each other they can be made in $2^4 = 16$ ways.

(b) Straightforward use of one or two negations always yields a correct expression. However, in the lower right, $\neg (p \vee q)$ has fewer operators than $\neg p \wedge \neg q$.

Location of TRUE	Simple Logic Expression
upper left	$p \wedge q$
upper right	$p \wedge \neg q$
lower left	$\neg p \wedge q$
lower right	$\neg (p \vee q)$

(c) Straightforward use of one or two negations always yields a correct expression. However, in the upper left, $\neg\,(p \wedge q)$ has fewer operators than $\neg\,p \vee \neg\,q$.

Location of FALSE	Simple Logic Expression
upper left	$\neg\,(p \wedge q)$
upper right	$p \rightarrow q$
lower left	$q \rightarrow p$
lower right	$p \vee q$

Ex: 2.3 (a) The $\vee$ operator yields TRUE when one or more of its operands is TRUE. Here a particular one of them is the constant TRUE.

p	TRUE	$p \vee$ TRUE
T	T	T
F	T	T

(b) It states that a proposition and its negation cannot both be TRUE.

p	$\neg\,p$	$p \wedge \neg\,p$	$\neg\,(p \wedge \neg\,p)$
T	F	F	T
F	T	F	T

(c) The only possible way to get false, the TRUE $\rightarrow$ FALSE case, is impossible.

p	$p \rightarrow p$
T	T
F	T

Ex: 2.4 (a)

p	q	$p \vee q$	$\neg(p \vee q)$	$\neg p$	$\neg q$	$\neg p \wedge \neg q$
T	T	T	F	F	F	F
T	F	T	F	F	T	F
F	T	T	F	T	F	F
F	F	F	T	T	T	T

(b)

p	q	r	$q \wedge r$	$p \vee (q \wedge r)$	$p \vee q$	$p \vee r$	$(p \vee q) \wedge (p \vee r)$
T	T	T	T	T	T	T	T
T	T	F	F	T	T	T	T
T	F	T	F	T	T	T	T
T	F	F	F	T	T	T	T
F	T	T	T	T	T	T	T
F	T	F	F	F	T	F	F
F	F	T	F	F	F	T	F
F	F	F	F	F	F	F	F

Ex: 2.5 (a)

p	q	$\neg p$	$\neg p \vee q$	$p \to q$
T	T	F	T	T
T	F	F	F	F
F	T	T	T	T
F	F	T	T	T

(b)

p	q	$p \to q$	$q \to p$	$(p \to q) \wedge (q \to p)$	$p \leftrightarrow q$
T	T	T	T	T	T
T	F	F	T	F	F
F	T	T	F	F	F
F	F	T	T	T	T

(c)

p	q	$\neg p$	$\neg q$	$\neg q \to \neg p$	$p \to q$
T	T	F	F	T	T
T	F	F	T	F	F
F	T	T	F	T	T
F	F	T	T	T	T

Ex: 2.6

$$\neg\,(\alpha \wedge \beta \wedge \gamma) \equiv \neg\,(\alpha \wedge \beta) \vee \neg\,\gamma \equiv \neg\,\alpha \vee \neg\,\beta \vee \neg\,\gamma$$

Ex: 2.7 (a)
$$
\begin{aligned}
(p \vee q) \wedge (\neg p \wedge \neg q)) &\equiv ((p \vee q) \wedge \neg p) \wedge \neg q\\
&\equiv ((p \wedge \neg p) \vee (q \wedge \neg p)) \wedge \neg q\\
&\equiv (\text{FALSE} \vee (q \wedge \neg p)) \wedge \neg q\\
&\equiv (q \wedge \neg p) \wedge \neg q\\
&\equiv q \wedge \neg q \wedge \neg p\\
&\equiv \text{FALSE} \wedge \neg p\\
&\equiv \text{FALSE}
\end{aligned}
$$

$$
\begin{aligned}
(p \vee q) \wedge (\neg p \wedge \neg q) &\equiv (p \vee q) \wedge \neg (p \vee q)\\
&\equiv \text{FALSE}
\end{aligned}
$$

The second approach just uses DeMorgan's law and contradiction.

(b) First note that DeMorgan's law generalizes to 3 terms as shown in Exercise 2.6. To the right side of the equivalence, apply the conditional law, the 3-way DeMorgan law and finally double negation, to get the left side of the equivalence.

Ex: 2.9   Truth tables omitted.

(a) $(p \vee q)$ means that at least one of the operands is TRUE. This is surely implied by p being TRUE.

(b) $(p \to q)$ says that q is TRUE in those states where p is TRUE, but the left side makes the stronger statement that q is TRUE, period. The stronger statement implies the weaker.

(c) If the truth of p yields the truth of q and moreover p *is* TRUE, then indeed q is (also) TRUE.

(d) If $(p \rightarrow q)$ and q is FALSE, then p had better be FALSE too, since p being TRUE would lead to q being TRUE as well as FALSE, a contradiction.

Ex: 2.10 The truth tables are omitted for this problem.

(a) The left side of the principal implication operator says that the truth of p guarantees that of q which in turn guarantees that of r. If this holds, it follows that p leads (indirectly) to r. In other words, implication is a transitive operator.

(b) If at least one of p and q is TRUE and if also the truth of each alone insures the truth of r, then r must be TRUE.

Ex: 2.11 (a)

p	q	$\neg p$	$\neg p \wedge q$	$p \vee (\neg p \wedge q)$	$p \vee q$
T	T	F	F	T	T
T	F	F	F	T	T
F	T	T	T	T	T
F	F	T	F	F	F

(b)
$$
\begin{aligned}
p \vee (\neg p \wedge q) &\equiv (p \vee \neg p) \wedge (p \vee q) \\
&\equiv \text{TRUE} \wedge (p \vee q) \\
&\equiv p \vee q
\end{aligned}
$$

Ex: 2.12

$$
\begin{aligned}
((p \rightarrow q) \wedge (q \rightarrow r)) \rightarrow (p \rightarrow r) &\equiv \neg((\neg p \vee q) \wedge (\neg q \vee r)) \vee (\neg p \vee r) \\
&\equiv (\neg(\neg p \vee q) \vee \neg(\neg q \vee r)) \vee (\neg p \vee r) \\
&\equiv ((p \wedge \neg q) \vee \neg p \vee (q \wedge \neg r)) \vee r \\
&\equiv ((\neg p \vee \neg q) \vee (q \vee r)) \\
&\equiv \text{TRUE} \vee \neg p \vee r \\
&\equiv \text{TRUE}
\end{aligned}
$$

$$
\begin{aligned}
((p \vee q) \wedge (p \to r) \wedge (q \to r)) \to r \;\;\equiv&\;\; \neg\,((p \vee q) \wedge (\neg p \vee r) \wedge (\neg q \vee r)) \vee r \\
\equiv&\;\; \neg\,(p \vee q) \vee \neg\,(\neg p \vee r) \vee \neg\,(\neg q \vee r) \vee r \\
\equiv&\;\; (\neg p \wedge \neg q) \vee (p \wedge \neg r) \vee (q \wedge \neg r) \vee r \\
\equiv&\;\; (\neg p \wedge \neg q) \vee (p \wedge \neg r) \vee (q \vee r) \\
\equiv&\;\; ((\neg p \wedge \neg q) \vee q) \vee ((p \wedge \neg r) \vee r) \\
\equiv&\;\; (\neg p \vee q) \vee (p \vee r) \\
\equiv&\;\; (\neg p \vee p) \vee (q \vee r) \\
\equiv&\;\; \text{TRUE} \vee (q \vee r) \\
\equiv&\;\; \text{TRUE}
\end{aligned}
$$

Ex: 2.13

$$
\begin{aligned}
(p \vee q) \wedge (r \vee s) \;\;\equiv&\;\; ((p \vee q) \wedge r) \vee ((p \vee q) \wedge s) \\
\equiv&\;\; (p \wedge r) \vee (q \wedge r) \vee (p \wedge s) \vee (q \wedge s)
\end{aligned}
$$

Ex: 2.14   Truth table omitted. The left side of the principal implication states that there is a *one*-way implication from p to q, but not two-way. For such a situation to exist, two-way implication would have to be prevented which can only happen with falsity of the reverse implication, that is, with $\neg\,(q \to p)$.

Ex: 2.15 $(p \to q) \wedge \neg\,(p \leftrightarrow q) \to \neg\,(q \to p)$

$$
\begin{aligned}
\equiv&\;\; (p \to q) \wedge \neg\,((p \to q) \wedge (q \to p)) \to \neg\,(q \to p) \\
\equiv&\;\; (p \to q) \wedge (\neg\,(p \to q) \vee \neg\,(q \to p)) \to \neg\,(q \to p) \\
\equiv&\;\; ((p \to q) \wedge \neg\,(p \to q)) \vee ((p \to q) \wedge \neg\,(q \to p)) \\
&\;\; \to \neg\,(q \to p) \\
\equiv&\;\; \text{FALSE} \vee ((p \to q) \wedge \neg\,(q \to p)) \to \neg\,(q \to p) \\
\equiv&\;\; ((p \to q) \wedge \neg\,(q \to p)) \to \neg\,(q \to p)
\end{aligned}
$$

The last line is of the form $(\alpha \wedge \beta) \to \beta$ and in general it can be shown:

$$
\alpha \wedge \beta \to \beta \equiv \neg\,(\alpha \wedge \beta) \vee \beta \equiv \neg \alpha \vee \neg \beta \vee \beta \equiv \neg \alpha \vee \text{TRUE} \equiv \text{TRUE}
$$

Ex: 2.16 Note that distributivity from the *left* is taken as true.

$$(p \lor q) \land r \equiv r \land (p \lor q) \equiv (r \land p) \lor (r \land q) \equiv (p \land r) \lor (q \land r)$$

Ex: 2.6
$$\begin{aligned} p \lor (q \land r \land s) &\equiv (p \lor (q \land r)) \land (p \lor s) \\ &\equiv (p \lor q) \land (p \lor r) \land (p \lor s) \end{aligned}$$

Ex: 2.18 The truth tables are omitted for this problem.

(a) $p \oplus q \equiv \neg (p \leftrightarrow q)$

(b) $p \oplus q \equiv (p \lor q) \land \neg (p \land q)$

Chapter 3: Proofs by Deduction

Ex: 3.1   Letting $\alpha = (p \vee q) \wedge (p \to r) \wedge (q \to r)$,

p	q	r	$p \vee q$	$p \to r$	$q \to r$	α	$\alpha \to r$
T	T	T	T	T	T	T	T
T	T	F	T	F	F	F	T
T	F	T	T	T	T	T	T
T	F	F	T	F	T	F	T
F	T	T	T	T	T	T	T
F	T	F	T	T	F	F	T
F	F	T	F	T	T	F	T
F	F	F	F	T	T	F	T

Ex: 3.2

1	$[(p \to q) \wedge \neg q]$	Assumption
2	$p \to q$	$\wedge$ elimination: 1
3	$\neg q$	$\wedge$ elimination: 1
4	$[p]$	Assumption
5	q	Modus ponens: 4, 2
6	FALSE	Contradiction: 3, 5
7	$\neg p$	Reduction to absurdity: 4, 6
8	$((p \to q) \wedge \neg q) \to \neg p$	$\to$ introduction: 1,7

Ex: 3.4

$[(p \to q) \wedge (q \to r)]$	Assumption
$(p \to q)$	$\wedge$ elimination
$(q \to r)$	$\wedge$ elimination
$[p]$	Assumption
q	Modus Ponens
r	Modus Ponens
$p \to r$	
$((p \to q) \wedge (q \to r)) \to (p \to r)$	$\to$ introduction

Ex: 3.5

$[q]$		Assumption
	$[p]$	Assumption
	q	From line 1
	$p \rightarrow q$	$\rightarrow$ introduction
$q \rightarrow (p \rightarrow q)$		$\rightarrow$ introduction

Ex: 3.6

$[(p \wedge (p \rightarrow q) \wedge (q \rightarrow r))]$	Assumption
p	$\wedge$ elimination
$p \rightarrow q$	$\wedge$ elimination
$q \rightarrow r$	$\wedge$ elimination
q	Modus ponens
r	Modus ponens
$(p \wedge (p \rightarrow q) \wedge (q \rightarrow r)) \rightarrow r$	$\rightarrow$ introduction

Ex: 3.7

1	$[(p \rightarrow q) \wedge \neg (p \leftrightarrow q)]$	Assumption
2	$p \rightarrow q$	$\wedge$ elimination: 1
3	$\neg p \leftrightarrow q$	$\wedge$ elimination: 1
4	$[q \rightarrow p]$	Assumption
5	$p \leftrightarrow q$	Biconditional: 2, 4
6	FALSE	Contradiction: 3, 5
7	$\neg (q \rightarrow p)$	Reduction to absurdity: 4, 6
8	$(p \rightarrow q) \wedge \neg (p \leftrightarrow q) \rightarrow \neg (q \rightarrow p)$	$\rightarrow$ introduction: 1,7

Ex: 3.8 This is half of the proof.

1	$[\neg q \rightarrow \neg p]$	Assumption
2	$[p]$	Assumption
3	$[\neg q]$	Assumption
4	$\neg p$	Modus ponens: 1, 3
5	FALSE	Contradiction: 2, 4
6	q	Reduction to Absurdity: 3, 5
7	$p \rightarrow q$	$\rightarrow$ introduction: 2, 6
8	$(\neg q \rightarrow \neg p) \rightarrow (p \rightarrow q)$	$\rightarrow$ introduction: 1,7

Ex: 3.10

1	$[((p \lor q) \lor r) \land (p \to s) \land (q \to s) \land (r \to s)]$	Assumption
2	$(p \lor q) \lor r$	$\land$ elimination
3	$p \to s$	$\land$ elimination
4	$q \to s$	$\land$ elimination
5	$r \to s$	$\land$ elimination
6	$\quad\quad [p \lor q]$	Assumption
7	$\quad\quad\quad s$	Cases:3, 4, 6
8	$\quad (p \lor q) \to s$	$\to$ Introduction: 6, 7
9	$\quad s$	Cases:2, 8, 5
10	$((p \lor q \lor r) \land (p \to s) \land (q \to s) \land (r \to s)) \to s$	$\to$ introduction: 1,9

Ex: 3.11 The first six are:

1	$[p \to q]$	Assumption
2	$\quad\quad [p]$	Assumption
3	$\quad\quad q$	Modus ponens 1,2
4	$\quad\quad p \land q$	$\land$ introduction 2,3
5	$\quad p \to (p \land q)$	$\to$ introduction 2,4
6	$(p \to q) \to (p \to (p \land q))$	$\to$ introduction 1,5

1	$\quad\quad [p]$	Assumption
2	$\quad\quad p \lor (p \land q)$	$\lor$ introduction 1
3	$p \to (p \lor (p \land q))$	$\to$ introduction 1,2
4	$\quad\quad [p \lor (p \land q)]$	Assumption
5	$\quad\quad\quad\quad [p]$	Assumption
6	$\quad\quad\quad\quad p$	copy 5
7	$\quad\quad\quad p \to p$	$\to$ introduction 5,6
8	$\quad\quad\quad\quad [p \land q]$	Assumption
9	$\quad\quad\quad\quad p$	$\land$ elimination 8
10	$\quad\quad (p \land q) \to p$	$\to$ introduction 8,9
11	$\quad\quad p$	Case analysis 4,7,10
12	$(p \lor (p \land q)) \to p$	$\to$ introduction 4,11
13	$p \leftrightarrow (p \lor (p \land q))$	$\leftrightarrow$ introduction 3,12

1	$[p \to q]$		Assumption
2		$[p]$	Assumption
3		q	Modus ponens 1,2
4		$p \land q$	$\land$ introduction 2,3
5	$p \to (p \land q)$		$\to$ introduction 2,4
6	$(p \to q) \to (p \to (p \land q))$		$\to$ introduction 1,5

1	$[p]$	Assumption
2	$p \lor q$	$\lor$ introduction 1
3	$p \land (p \lor q)$	$\land$ introduction 1,2
4	$p \to p \land (p \lor q)$	$\to$ introduction 1,4
5	$[p \land (p \lor q)]$	Assumption
6	p	$\land$ elimination 5
7	$p \land (p \lor q) \to p$	$\to$ introduction 5,6
8	$p \leftrightarrow p \land (p \lor q)$	$\leftrightarrow$ introduction 4,7

1	$[(\neg p \to q) \land \neg q]$	Assumption
2	$\neg p \to q$	$\land$ elimination 1
3	$\neg q$	$\land$ elimination 1
4	$\neg\neg p$	Modus tollens 2,3
5	p	Double negation 4
6	$((\neg p \to q) \land \neg q) \to p$	$\to$ introduction 1,5

1	$[p \to q]$			Assumption
2		$[\neg q]$		Assumption
3		$\neg p$		Modus tollens 1,2
4	$\neg q \to \neg p$			$\to$ introduction 2,3
5	$(p \to q) \to (\neg q \to \neg p)$			$\to$ introduction 1,4
6	$[\neg q \to \neg p]$			Assumption
7		$[p]$		Assumption
8			$[\neg q]$	Assumption
9			$\neg p$	Modus ponens 6,8
10			FALSE	Contradiction 7,9
11		$\neg\neg q$		Reduction to absurdity 8,10
12		q		Double negation 11
13	$p \to q$			$\to$ introduction 7,12
14	$(\neg q \to \neg p) \to (p \to q)$			$\to$ introduction 6,13
15	$(p \to q) \leftrightarrow (\neg q \to \neg p)$			$\leftrightarrow$ introduction 5,14

Chapter 4: Predicate Logic

Ex: 4.1 Parts (a) and (e) are equivalent. Parts (b) and (d) are equivalent.

    (a) $\exists x : \text{IsCarOwner}(x)$

    (b) $\neg \forall x : \text{IsCarOwner}(x)$

    (c) $\neg \exists x : \text{IsCarOwner}(x)$

    (d) $\forall x : \neg \text{IsCarOwner}(x)$

    (e) $\neg \forall x : \neg \text{IsCarOwner}(x)$

Ex: 4.2 A definition of a term can be thought of as distinguishing the members of the category it refers to from other members of some larger category. The definition should state precisely the properties that are both necessary and sufficient for something to belong to the category. Using all the correct properties and some extra ones makes too narrow a definition, while using only some of the correct properties allows too many things into the category. The biconditional - as opposed to the conditional - provides a convenient way to assert that neither the term nor its definition includes things that are not in the other. The universal quantifier lets us say that everything in the larger category must obey the definition.

Ex: 4.3 (a) $\forall x : \forall y :$ PARENTINCOMMON$(x, y) \leftrightarrow$ DIFFERENT(x, y)
$\wedge \ \exists z :$ PARENT(z, x)
$\wedge \ $ PARENT(z, y)

(b) $\forall x : \forall y :$ SISTER$(x, y) \leftrightarrow$ FEMALE(x)
$\wedge \ $ PARENTINCOMMON(x, y)

(c) $\forall x : \forall y :$ FIRSTCOUSIN$(x, y) \leftrightarrow \exists w : \exists z :$ PARENT(w, x)
$\wedge \ $ PARENT(z, y)
$\wedge \ $ PARENTINCOMMON(w, z)
$\wedge \ $ DIFFERENT(x, y)

Ex: 4.4 $\neg (p(a) \wedge p(b) \wedge p(c)) \equiv \neg p(a) \vee \neg p(b) \vee \neg p(c)$

Ex: 4.5 We include some parentheses (like the first and last) for readability.

$$\exists x : ((4 < x < 6) \wedge \forall y : ((4 < y < 6) \rightarrow (y = x)))$$

Ex: 4.6 $\forall t \in \mathcal{N} :$ TRIANGULAR$(t) \leftrightarrow \exists n \in \mathcal{N} : t = n(n + 1)/2$

Ex: 4.7 (a) TRUE. Squares are nonnegative and so is any sum of two of them.

(b) FALSE. The positive squares less than 10 are $\{1, 4, 9\}$. Unequal pairs from this set add to 5, 10 and 13, none of which is above 5 and less than 10.

(c) TRUE. Every i is even or odd. When it is even there is a j that makes the first half of the $\vee$ true and when it is odd there is a j that makes the second half true.

(d) TRUE. This calls for a single value of j that always works. That value is -1.

Ex: 4.8 (a) $\forall x \in V : \forall y \in V : \exists z \in V : \text{EDGE}(x, z) \wedge \text{EDGE}(z, y)$

(b) $\forall x \in V : \forall y \in V : \text{PATH}(x, y)$
$\leftrightarrow (x = y) \vee \exists z \in V : \text{EDGE}(x, z) \wedge \text{PATH}(z, y)$

(c) $\forall x \in V : \forall y \in V : \text{PATH2}(x, y)$
$\leftrightarrow \exists z \in V : (z \neq x) \wedge (z \neq y) \wedge \text{EDGE}(z, y)$
$\wedge \; \text{P2}(x, y, z),$

where $\text{P2}(x, y, z)$ verifies that there is a path from x to z that avoids y,

$$\forall x, y, z \in V : \text{P2}(x, y, z)$$
$$\leftrightarrow \text{EDGE}(x, z) \vee (\exists w \in V : (w \neq y) \wedge \text{EDGE}(w, z)$$
$$\wedge \, \text{P2}(x, y, w))$$

Ex: 4.9 (i) FALSE for both. The assertion is that every distinct pair of vertices is an edge, in other words that the graph is complete. With 4 vertices this would require 6 edges.

(ii) TRUE for both. The assertion is that every pair of vertices (distinct or not) is connected by a path of some length (possibly length zero), in other words that the graph is connected.

(iii) FALSE for both. Here the claim is that the graph contains a cycle, since there are two vertices connected by both a single edge as well as another path.

Ex: 4.10 It asserts that the graph is bipartite.

Ex: 4.11 (a) $\exists i \in \mathcal{I}_n : \exists j \in \mathcal{I}_n : a_i = a_j \wedge j \neq i$

(b) this is just the negation of (a); generalized DeMorgan's law can be applied.

(c) $\forall i \in \mathcal{I}_n : a_i = b_i$

(d) $\forall i \in \mathcal{I}_n : \exists j \in \mathcal{I}_n : b_j = a_i$

(e) $(\forall i \in \mathcal{I}_n : \exists j \in \mathcal{I}_n : b_j = a_i) \quad \wedge \quad (\forall i \in \mathcal{I}_n : \exists j \in \mathcal{I}_n : a_j = b_i)$

(f) $\forall i \in \mathcal{I}_n : a_i \prec b_i$

Ex: 4.12

$$\exists j \in \mathcal{I}_n : a_j \prec b_j \wedge \forall i \in \mathcal{I}_n : i < j \rightarrow a_i = b_i \text{ or}$$

$$\exists j \in \mathcal{I}_n : a_j \prec b_j \wedge \forall i \in \mathcal{I}_{j-1} : a_i = b_i$$

Ex: 4.13

$result \Leftarrow \text{TRUE}$
for $i \Leftarrow 2$ **to** n **do**
  if $a_i \neq a_1$ **then** $result \Leftarrow \text{FALSE}$
return $result$

Ex: 4.14 (a) $\forall x \in \mathcal{P} : \exists! \, y \in \mathcal{Q} : \text{MOTHER}(y, x)$

(b) $\forall x \in \mathcal{I} : \exists! \, y \in \mathcal{I} : y = x^2$

Chapter 5: Proving with Predicates

Ex: 5.1 (a) Subset rule:

$$\dfrac{\forall x \in A : x \in B}{A \subseteq B}$$

(b) Set equality rule:

$$\dfrac{\begin{array}{l} A \subseteq B \\ B \subseteq A \end{array}}{A = B}$$

(c) Transitivity of conditional:

$$\dfrac{\begin{array}{l} \alpha \to \beta \\ \beta \to \gamma \end{array}}{\alpha \to \gamma}$$

(d) Pigeon-hole principle:

$$\dfrac{\begin{array}{l} [\text{given } f : A \to B] \\ |A| > |B| \end{array}}{\exists x \in A : \exists y \in A : f(x) = f(y) \land y \neq x}$$

Ex: 5.2 As in the text, let $P(n)$ be the nth proposition, that is, $\sum_{i=1}^{n}(2i - 1) = n^2$. Also **BC** is the base case, $P(0)$, **IH** the inductive hypothesis, $P(k)$ and **IC** is the inductive conclusion, $P(k+1)$. "Summation identity" refers to the fact that a sum from 1 to $n+1$ can be written as the sum of the first n terms plus last one.

Step		Rule or Comment
1	$\sum_{i=1}^{0}(2i-1) = 0 = 0^2$	Proof of BC, $P(0)$
2	$[k \geq 0]$	Assumption
3	$[\sum_{i=1}^{k}(2i-1) = k^2]$	Assumption: IH
4	$\sum_{i=1}^{k+1}(2i-1) = 2(k+1) - 1 + \sum_{i=1}^{k}(2i-1)$	Summation identity
5	$\ldots = 2k + 1 + k^2$	Substitution: 3, 4
6	$\ldots = (k+1)^2$	Algebra; IC proved
7	$P(k) \rightarrow P(k+1)$	$\rightarrow$ introduction: 3, 6
8	$\forall n \geq 0 : P(n) \rightarrow P(n+1)$	$\forall$ introduction: 2, 7
9	$\forall n \geq 0 : P(n)$	Math induction: 1, 8

Ex: 5.3 In this case we provide an *in*formal proof of the inductive step. It is helpful to introduce notation for the key summations: S_n for the first n integers and T_n for the first n cubes. That is, $S_n = \sum_{i=1}^{n} i$ and $T_n = \sum_{i=1}^{n} i^3$. The basis is $S_0^2 = 0^2 = 0 = T_0$. With the inductive hypothesis $S_n^2 = T_n$ and $n \geq 0$ the algebra establishing the inductive conclusion is:

$$
\begin{aligned}
S_{n+1}^2 &= ((n+1) + S_n)^2 \\
&= (n+1)^2 + 2(n+1)S_n + S_n^2 \\
&= (n+1)^2 + 2(n+1)\left(\frac{n(n+1)}{2}\right) + T_n \\
&= (n+1)^3 + T_n \\
&= T_{n+1}
\end{aligned}
$$

Ex: 5.4　First note that the inequality does not hold for values of n from 1 to 9. For $n = 10$, the basis, the inequality does hold, since $2^{10} = 1024$ while $10^3 = 1000$. Note that the assumption $n \geq 10$ alone implies $n^3 > 3n^2 + 3n + 1$, by elementary algebra. (In fact $n \geq 4$ is enough.) With the inductive hypothesis, $2^n > n^3$, we get this proof of the inductive conclusion:

$$
\begin{aligned}
2^{n+1} = 2 \times 2^n \; &> \; 2 \times n^3 \\
&= \; n^3 + n^3 \\
&> \; n^3 + 3n^2 + 3n + 1 \\
&> \; (n+1)^3
\end{aligned}
$$

Ex: 5.5　The basis, $n = 2$, is given. To show for $n + 1 > 2$ assume it is true for $n \geq 2$.

$$
\begin{aligned}
&p \vee (q_1 \wedge q_2 \wedge \cdots \wedge q_n \wedge q_{n+1}) \\
\equiv \; &(p \vee (q_1 \wedge q_2 \wedge \cdots \wedge q_n)) \wedge (p \vee q_{n+1}) \\
\equiv \; &((p \vee q_1) \wedge (p \vee q_2) \wedge \cdots \wedge (p \vee q_n)) \wedge (p \vee q_{n+1}) \\
\equiv \; &(p \vee q_1) \wedge (p \vee q_2) \wedge \cdots \wedge (p \vee q_n) \wedge (p \vee q_{n+1})
\end{aligned}
$$

Ex: 5.7　Basis is $F_6 = 8 > (\frac{3}{2})^5 = \frac{243}{32}$ and $F_7 = 13 > (\frac{3}{2})^6 = \frac{729}{64}$. Assume $n \geq 7$.

$$
F_{n+1} = F_n + F_{n-1} > (\frac{3}{2})^{n-1} + (\frac{3}{2})^{n-2} = \frac{10}{9}(\frac{3}{2})^n > (\frac{3}{2})^n.
$$

Ex: 5.8　The theorem, for all $n \geq 0$, is

$$
F_n = \frac{(\frac{1+\sqrt{5}}{2})^n - (\frac{1-\sqrt{5}}{2})^n}{\sqrt{5}}.
$$

Show for F_0 and F_1, assume for all $0 \leq k \leq n$ and establish it for F_{n+1}.

Ex: 5.9   The theorem is a quantified Boolean expression:

$$\exists i \in \mathcal{N} : \exists j \in \mathcal{N} : n = 3i + 7j, \quad n \geq 12.$$

Do case analysis on $j < 2$ and $j \geq 2$. Also note that $(j < 2 \wedge n \geq 12) \to i \geq 2$.

Ex: 5.10   Use induction on the number of vertices; it is a universally quantified theorem.

Chapter 6: Program Verification

Ex: 6.1   **Sequence:**

$$p \{S_1\} q_1$$
$$q_2 \{S_2\} r$$
$$q_1 \to q_2$$

$$\overline{p \{S_1; S_2\} r}$$

Ex: 6.3   The purpose of the code is to compute $\sum_{i=0}^{n} i = \binom{n+1}{2} = n(n+1)/2$ in the variable s. Therefore we will take as part of the invariant that $s = i(i+1)/2$ inside the loop. At the time of exit, we will have $i = n$, making $s = n(n+1)/2$. In light of these considerations we take the loop invariant p to be $s = i(i+1)/2 \wedge (i \le n)$. Note that for p to be true initially we must know that $n \ge 1$. To show p is a loop invariant we need to argue that:

$$\frac{i(i+1)}{2} \wedge (i \le n) \wedge (i < n) \{\texttt{i}\Leftarrow\texttt{i+1};\ \texttt{s}\Leftarrow\texttt{s+i}\} \frac{i(i+1)}{2} \wedge (i \le n).$$

While this can easily be seen to be true, we could break the argument down into two steps, and use the sequencing inference rule:

$$\frac{i(i+1)}{2} \wedge (i \le n) \wedge (i < n) \ \{\texttt{i}\Leftarrow\texttt{i+1}\} \ \frac{i(i-1)}{2} \wedge (i \le n).$$

$$\frac{i(i-1)}{2} \wedge (i \le n) \ \{\texttt{s}\Leftarrow\texttt{s+i}\} \ s = i(i+1)/2 \wedge (i \le n).$$

Once we have established p as a loop invariant, the inference rule gives:

$$\frac{i(i+1)}{2} \wedge (i \le n) \ \{\texttt{while (i < n) do S}\}$$

$$\frac{i(i+1)}{2} \wedge (i \le n) \wedge (i \ge n).$$

so that when the loop terminates $i = n$ and so $\frac{n(n+1)}{2}$.

Ex: 6.5 (a)
```
        i ⇐ 0;
        s ⇐ 0;
        while i < n do
            s ⇐ s+i
            i ⇐ i+1
            s ⇐ s+i
```

(b) The purpose of the code is to compute $\sum_{i=0}^{n-1}[i + (i + 1)] = n^2$ in the variable s. Therefore we will take as part of the invariant that $s = i^2$. At the time of exit, we will have $i = n$, making $s = n^2$. In light of these considerations we take the loop invariant p to be $(s = i^2) \wedge (i \leq n)$. To show p is a loop invariant we need to argue that:

$$s = i^2 \wedge (i \leq n) \wedge (i < n)$$

$$\{s \Leftarrow s + i;\ i \Leftarrow i + 1;\ s \Leftarrow s + i\}$$

$$s = i^2 \wedge (i \leq n).$$

This can easily be seen to be true from the identity in (a). We could break the argument down into three steps.

(c) Once we have established p as a loop invariant, the inference rule gives:

$$s = i^2 \wedge (i \leq n)\ \{\texttt{while}\ (\texttt{i} < \texttt{n})\ \texttt{do}\ \texttt{S}\}$$

$$s = i^2 \wedge (i \leq n) \wedge (i \geq n).$$

so that when the loop terminates $i = n$ and so $s = n^2$.

Ex: 6.7 To discover a loop invariant we will analyze *cases*. Taken together, we see that in those cases where m changes it changes by 2, so that its parity (being odd or not) is unchanged at each iteration. Further, the parity of the white balls at any time, $\text{ODD}(m)$, is the same as it was in the beginning, $\text{ODD}(M)$. We can therefore take the loop invariant p to be the proposition that $\text{ODD}(m) = \text{ODD}(M)$. Note that p must be true before the first iteration, since m was initialized to be equal to M. Letting

S be the body of the while loop and
p be the loop invariant, $\text{ODD}(m) = \text{ODD}(M)$ and
B be the condition for staying in the loop, $m + n > 1$,

we have the requirements in place for applying the While inference rule:

$$(\text{ODD}(m) = \text{ODD}(M)) \wedge (m + n > 1) \{S\}$$

$$(\text{ODD}(m) = \text{ODD}(M)).$$

Applying the rule gives

$$(\text{ODD}(m) = \text{ODD}(M)) \{\texttt{while } (m + n > 1) \texttt{ do } S\}$$

$$B \wedge (\text{ODD}(m) = \text{ODD}(M)).$$

This solves the puzzle: the one ball left at the end is white — so that $m = 1$ and $\text{ODD}(m) = \text{TRUE}$ — if and only if there was originally an odd number of white balls, so that $\text{ODD}(M) = \text{TRUE}$.

Strictly speaking, the above discussion leaves a minor mathematical loose end: $m+n \leq 1$ seems to allow $m+n = 0$. In order to sharpen the result we really need a stronger loop invariant: $(\text{ODD}(m) = \text{ODD}(M)) \wedge (m + n > 0)$. The sum $m + n$ stays above zero because it is required to be at least 2 until exit from the loop and it decreases by exactly 1 in each iteration. It now follows that when the loop terminates $m + n = 1$ (since $m + n$ is an integer above 0 but not above 1).

Ex: 6.8   Assuming Y and Z are positive integers

```
x ⇐ 0;
y ⇐ Y;
z ⇐ Z;
//YZ = x + yz ∧ (0 ≤ z)
while 0< z do
      //YZ = x + yz ∧ (0 < z)
      if odd(z) then x ⇐ x + y
      //YZ = x + y(2⌊z/2⌋) ∧ (0 < z)
      y ⇐ y + y
      //YZ = x + y⌊z/2⌋ ∧ (0 < z)
      z ⇐ floor(z / 2)
      //YZ = x + yz ∧ (0 ≤ z)
```

Note that the **if** statement follows from

$$\texttt{odd(z)} \to z = 2\lfloor\frac{z}{2}\rfloor + 1 \to YZ = x + y(2\lfloor\frac{z}{2}\rfloor + 1)$$

$$= (x + y) + y(2\lfloor\frac{z}{2}\rfloor);$$

the case when z is not odd is straightforward.

Upon termination of the loop $z \geq 0$ and $z \leq 0$ so that $z = 0$ and therefore $x = YZ$.

Chapter 7: Language and Models

Ex: 7.1 (a) 7, (b) 8, (c) 0

Ex: 7.2 $3^5 = 243$

Ex: 7.3 $2^{k+1} - 1 = 1 + 2 + 4 + \cdots + 2^k$

Ex: 7.4 (a) Since $L^* = \{\ldots, aaaa, aabb, abba, bbaa, bbbb, \ldots\}$ there are 5 strings.

(b) Since $L^* = \{\ldots, aaaaa, aaabb, aabba, abbaa, bbaaa, bbbba, bbabb, abbbb, \ldots\}$ there are 8 strings.

Ex: 7.5 (a) $\{aaa, aab, aba, abb, baa, bab, bba, bbb\}$

(b) $\{aaaa, aaba, abaa, abba\}$

Ex: 7.6 (a) $\{x \mid x \in \{a, b, c\}^* \wedge |x| = 2\}$

(b) $\{x \mid x \in \{a\}^* \wedge |x| \text{ is even }\}$

Ex: 7.7 (a) $\{x \mid x \in \{0, 1\}^* \wedge |x| = 5\}$.

(b) $\{x \mid |x| \leq 5 \wedge \exists y \in \{0, 1\}^* : (x = 1y)\}$.

Ex: 7.8

$\{x = x_1 x_2 \ldots x_n \mid x \in \{b, c, +\}^* \wedge |x| \text{ is odd} \wedge (x_i = +) \leftrightarrow i \text{ is even}\}$.

Ex: 7.10 It is associative since the left to right ordering of the characters remains unchanged. For example, if $x = ab$, $y = cd$, and $z = ef$ then $(xy)z = (abcd)ef = abcdef = ab(cdef) = x(yz)$.

Ex: 7.12 (a) $\{ab\}$ (b) $\{ab, abb, aab, aabb\}$

Ex: 7.14 It is true that they are same; a string is in either language iff it is the concatenation of zero or more strings from L.

Ex: 7.15 If $L = \{a\}$ then $aaa \notin (LL)^*$ but $aaa \in L^*L^*$. For this L only even length strings are in $(LL)^*$.

Chapter 8: Generative Models of Regular Languages

Ex: 8.1 (a) $\{bcc\}$

        (b) $\{acc, bcc\}$

        (c) $\{aaa, abc, bca\}$

Ex: 8.2 (a) $\{aaaab, aaacc\}$

        (b) $\{bbbbb\}$

        (c) $\{aaaaa, aaaab, aaabb, aabbb, abbbb, bbbbb\}$

Ex: 8.3 (a) $\{bcc\}$

        (b) $\{acc, bcc\}$

        (c) $\{aaa, abc, bca\}$

Ex: 8.4 (a) a^*

        (b) a^+

        (c) a^*

        (d) $(a + b + c)^*$

Ex: 8.5 $\{\Lambda, a, aa, aaaaa\}$

Ex: 8.6 Every string with 0, 1, or 2 symbols is in the language; *bba* is one (and the only) string of length 3 not in the language.

Ex: 8.7 (a) $\Lambda + a + b + (a+b)^*(aa+ab+ba) = \Lambda + b + (a+b)^*(a+ab)$

(b) $(a+ba)^*(b+\Lambda)$

(c) $(a+ba)^*bb(ab+a)^*$

Ex: 8.8 (a) $(0+1)^*010(0+1)^*$

(b) $1^*(0+111^*)^*1^*$

(c) $1^*(0+111^*)^*010(0+111^*)^*1^*$

Ex: 8.10 Let $r_0 = 0+1+2+3+4+5+6+7+8+9$ and $r_1 = 1+2+3+4+5+6+7+8+9$

(a) $r_a = (+ + - + \Lambda)(r_0^* + r_0^*.r_0^*)$

(b) $r_b = (+ + - + \Lambda)(r_1 r_0^*(\Lambda + .r_0^*) + (\Lambda + 0).r_0^*)$ where we do permit, say, .88 but do not allow a sign on the various forms of 0.

(c) $r_c = (+ + - + \Lambda)(r_1 r_0^*(\Lambda + .r_2^*) + (\Lambda + 0).r_0^* r_1 r_0^*) + 0(\Lambda + .0^*)$

(d) $r_d = r_c E(+ + - + \Lambda) r_1 r_0^*$

Ex: 8.11   (a) [See Ex. 8.21] $r_1 = a$, $r_2 = b$, $r_3 = c$, $r_4 = c^*$,
$r_5 = bc^*$ and $r_6 = r = a + bc^*$.

$P_1 = \{S_1 \to aA_1, A_1 \to \Lambda\}$

$P_2 = \{S_2 \to bA_2, A_2 \to \Lambda\}$

$P_3 = \{S_3 \to cA_3, A_3 \to \Lambda\}$

$P_4 = \{S_3 \to cA_3, A_3 \to S_4, S_4 \to \Lambda, S_4 \to S_3\}$

$P_5 = \{S_2 \to bA_2, A_2 \to S_4, S_3 \to cA_3, A_3 \to S_4, S_4 \to \Lambda,$
$\qquad S_4 \to S_3, S_5 \to S_2\}$

$P_6 = \{S_1 \to aA_1, A_1 \to \Lambda, S_2 \to bA_2, A_2 \to S_4, S_3 \to cA_3, A_3 \to S_4,$
$\qquad S_4 \to \Lambda, S_4 \to S_3, S_5 \to S_2, S_6 \to S_1, S_6 \to S_5\}$

Removing the unit productions we get (only S_6, A_1, A_2 and A_3 are reachable though):

$P_6 = \{S_1 \to aA_1, A_1 \to \Lambda, S_2 \to bA_2, S_3 \to cA_3, S_4 \to \Lambda\} \cup$
$\qquad \{A_2 \to \Lambda, A_3 \to \Lambda, S_6 \to aA_1, S_6 \to bA_2, S_5 \to bA_2,$
$\qquad A_2 \to cA_3, A_3 \to cA_3\}$

Ex: 8.16   The basis is $k = 0$: $L^0 = \{\Lambda\}$ which is always regular. For $k > 0$ assume the statement is true for $k - 1$: since L^{k-1} and L are both regular $L^k = L^{k-1}L$ is regular (by Theorem 9.7).

Ex: 8.20   First, add S', H, and missing loopbacks.

$S' \to S$	$S \to aB$	$A \to bA$	$B \to bS$	$H \to \Lambda$
$S \to aA$	$S \to S$	$A \to H$	$B \to B$	

Remove S.

$S' \to S\ /\ S \to S\ /\ S \to aA$: $S' \to aA$

$S' \to S\ /\ S \to S\ /\ S \to aB$: $S' \to aB$

$B \to bS\ /\ S \to S\ /\ S \to aA$: $B \to baA$

$B \to bS\ /; S \to S\ /\ S \to aB$: $B \to baB$

After removing S, the remaining productions are:

$$S' \to aA \qquad A \to bA \qquad B \to baA \qquad H \to \Lambda$$
$$S' \to aB \qquad A \to H \qquad B \to (\Lambda + ba)B$$

Remove A.

$$S' \to aA \, / \, A \to bA \, / \, A \to H \; : \qquad S' \to ab^*H$$
$$B \to baA \, / \, A \to bA \, / \, A \to aH \; : \qquad B \to bab^*H$$

After removing A, the remaining productions are:

$$S' \to aB \qquad\qquad B \to bab^*H \qquad\qquad H \to \Lambda$$
$$S' \to ab^*H \qquad\qquad B \to (\Lambda + ba)B$$

Remove B.

$$S' \to aB \, / \, B \to (\Lambda + ba)B \, / \, B \to bab^*H \; : \qquad S' \to a(ba)^*bab^*H$$

After removing B, the remaining productions are:

$$S' \to ab^* + a(ba)^*bab^*H \qquad\qquad H \to \Lambda$$

Regular expression: $ab^* + a(ba)^*bab^*$

Ex: 8.21

$$S \to A \qquad\qquad B \to S \qquad\qquad A \to bS$$
$$S \to bB \qquad\qquad B \to bA$$

$$B \to A$$

$$S \to bS \qquad\qquad B \to bB$$
$$\qquad\qquad\qquad\quad B \to bS$$

Chapter 9: Finite Automata and Regular Languages

Ex: 9.1   Briefly, replace $\delta(q, \sigma) = \emptyset$ with $\delta(q, \sigma) = q'_t$, and replace $\delta(q, \sigma) = \{p\}$ with $\delta(q, \sigma) = p$. Further q'_t must make a transition to itself on all symbols. These are the only changes.

Ex: 9.2   (a) $q_0, \{q_0, q_1\}$, (b) $q_0, \{q_0\}$, (c) $q_2, \{q_0, q_2\}$, (d) $q_1, \{q_0, q_1\}$, (e) $q_1, \{q_0, q_1\}$

Ex: 9.3

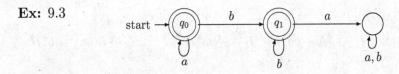

Ex: 9.4

(a)

(b)

(c)

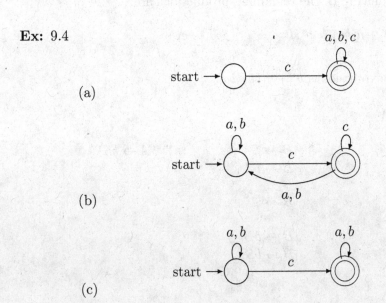

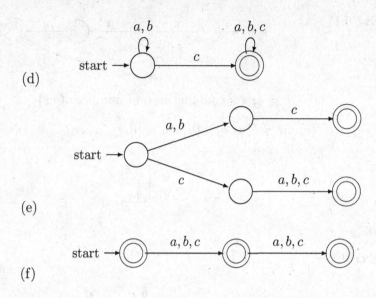

(d)

(e)

(f)

Ex: 9.5 Hint: consider (e) and (f) of the previous problem.

Ex: 9.7 $L_1 = \{a\}^*$ and $L_2 = \{b\}^*$.

Ex: 9.9 It is the same machine as in the example with d replaced by /, c replaced by * and "a, b" replaced by the elements in the set difference $\Sigma \setminus \{*, /\}$.

Ex: 9.10 $M = (\{A, B, C\}, \{a, b\}, q_0 = A, \delta, \{A\})$, where C is the trap state and

$$\delta = \quad \begin{array}{c|cc} & a & b \\ \hline A & A & B \\ B & A & C \\ C & C & C \end{array}$$

Ex: 9.11 (a)

(b) $L = \{x \mid x \text{ contains an odd number of } as\}$

(c) $M = (\{q_0, q_1\}, \{a\}, q_0, \delta, \{q_1\})$, where

$$\delta = \quad \begin{array}{c|c} & a \\ \hline q_0 & q_1 \\ q_1 & q_0 \end{array}$$

Ex: 9.12

$$\delta = \quad \begin{array}{c|cccc} & a & b & c & d \\ \hline q_0 & q_5 & q_5 & q_5 & q_1 \\ q_1 & q_5 & q_5 & q_2 & q_5 \\ q_2 & q_2 & q_2 & q_3 & q_2 \\ q_3 & q_2 & q_2 & q_3 & q_4 \\ q_4 & q_5 & q_5 & q_5 & q_5 \\ q_5 & q_5 & q_5 & q_5 & q_5 \end{array}$$

Ex: 9.13   (a) q_2, (b) q_1, (c) q_5, (d) q_2, (e) q_2, (f) q_4

Ex: 9.14

$$
\begin{array}{lll}
\delta^*(q_0, dad) & = \delta(\delta^*(q_0, da), d) & \text{Def 9.2 with } x = da \text{ and } \sigma = d, \text{ so } x\sigma = dad \\
& = \delta(\delta(\delta^*(q_0, d), a), d) & \text{Def 9.2 with } x = d \text{ and } \sigma = a, \text{ so } x\sigma = da \\
& = \delta(\delta(\delta(q_0, d), a), d) & \text{Theorem 9.1} \\
& = \delta(\delta(q_2, a), d) & \text{Evaluating the inner } \delta \\
& = \delta(q_2, d) & \text{Evaluating the inner } \delta \\
& = q_2 & \text{Evaluating } \delta
\end{array}
$$

Ex: 9.15 (a)

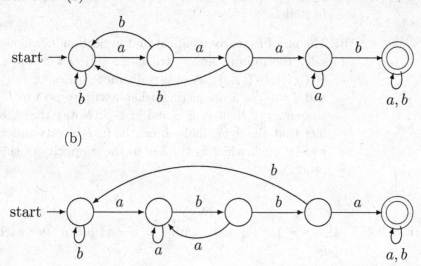

(b)

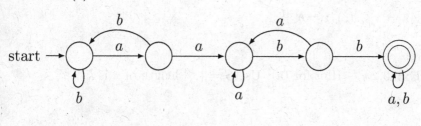

Ex: 9.17 (a)

(b) omitted

Ex: 9.19   Recall $L_1 \setminus L_2 = L_1 \cap \overline{L_2}$ and the closure of intersection and complementation.

Ex: 9.24 (a) $L_2 \subset L_3 \subset L$; ()() separates L_2 and L_3;))((separates L_3 and L.

(b) The proof is nearly identical that in Section 9.7. Consider the infinite set of strings $S = \{ (^i \mid i > 0 \} = \{ (, ((, (((, (((, ((((, \ldots \}$. Any two distinct strings, $x = (^i$ and $y = (^j$, in S are distinguishable with respect to L, since if $z =)^i$ then $xz \in S$ and $yz \notin S$. Notice that the fact that the symbols in L can be in arbitrary order was ignored, which is the key to the simplicity of the proof.

Ex: 9.25   Use $S = \{ a^n \mid n > 0 \}$, with $x = a^i$ and $y = a^j$, for each part.

(a) $z = ba^i$

(b) $z = ba^i b$

(c) $z = b^{i+1} c$

Ex: 9.26   Hint for (a): Use $S = \{ x \mid \text{length of } x \text{ is } k \}$

Ex: 9.29 (a) Each production is a generalization of a right-regular production; instead of 0 or 1 terminals followed by a nonterminal, the productions now have zero or more terminals followed by a nonterminal.

(b)

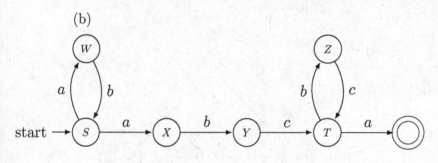

(c) $S \to aX \mid aW$
$W \to bS$
$X \to bY$
$Y \to cT$
$T \to bZ \mid a$
$Z \to cT$

$A \to a_1 a_2 \ldots a_n B$ is, in general, replaced by
$A \to a_1 A_1$
$\vdots$
$A_{n-1} \to a_n B$

Ex: 9.30 q_0 - no as, bs, or cs
q_a - as but no bs or cs
q_b - bs but no as or cs
q_{ab} - as and bs but no cs
q_c - at least one c

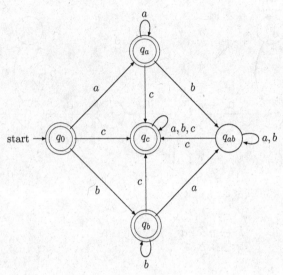

Ex: 9.31

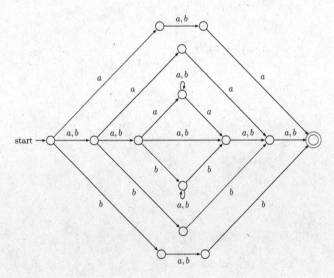

Chapter 10: Context-Free Grammars

Ex: 10.1   It is the language of odd-length strings of as. It is easy to prove by induction, on the length of the derivation, that an string derived has any odd number of symbols.

Ex: 10.2   (a) $S \Rightarrow SS \Rightarrow (S)S \Rightarrow ()S \Rightarrow ()(S) \Rightarrow ()((S))) \Rightarrow ()(())$; trees omitted

       (b) $S \Rightarrow (S) \Rightarrow ((S)) \Rightarrow ((SS)) \Rightarrow (((S)S)) \Rightarrow ((()S)) \Rightarrow (((()(S))) \Rightarrow ((()()))$

Ex: 10.3 $\{S \to \Lambda,\ S \to SS,\ S \to \{S\},\ S \to \langle S \rangle\}$

Ex: 10.4   (a) $L_r = \{(), ()(), ()()(), ()()()(), \ldots\}$ and $L_n = L_3$ the set of balanced parantheses.

       (b) $L_r = \{(^i)^j \mid i, j > 0\}$ and $L_n = L_2 = \{(^i)^i \mid i > 0\}$.

       (c) Since any finite language, including $\emptyset$, is regular, any two disjoint non-regular languages would work.

Ex: 10.5   (a) We will use induction on the length, n, of x. The basis, $n = 0$, is trivial. Assume that it is true for any $n - 1$ character string and that $x = x_1 x_2 \ldots x_n$. By the inductive hypothesis $S \overset{*}{\Rightarrow} x_1 x_2 \ldots x_{n-1} S x_{n-1} x_{n-2} \ldots x_1$. Clearly with one more derivation step we can establish $S \overset{*}{\Rightarrow} x\, S\, x^R$.

       (b) If w is an arbitrary element of the language of even-length palindromes then $w = xx^R$ for some string x. From part (a) we know $S \overset{*}{\Rightarrow} x\, S\, x^R$ and with the final production $S \to \Lambda$ we derive w.

Ex: 10.6   Add these productions $S \to a$ and $S \to b$, since any odd-length palindrome w is $w = xax^R$ or $w = xbx^R$ for some x. See previous answer.

Ex: 10.7   (a) $S \to aSbb \mid abb$

(b) $S \to S_1 S_2$
$S_1 \to aS_1 b \mid \Lambda$
$S_2 \to bS_2 c \mid \Lambda$

(c) $S \to S_1 C \mid AS_2$
$S_1 \to aS_1 b \mid \Lambda$
$S_2 \to bS_2 c \mid \Lambda$
$A \to aA \mid \Lambda$
$C \to cC \mid \Lambda$

(d) $S \to aSb \mid S_1 \mid S_2$
$S_1 \to aS_1 \mid a$
$S_2 \to bS_2 \mid b$

Ex: 10.8   Let B_1 be set as originally defined and let B_2 correspond to the new definition; we wish to show $B_1 = B_2$. First we argue that $x \in B_1 \to x \in B_2$. Assume, for the purpose of contradiction that $x \in B_1$ and $x \notin B_2$. That means for some prefix y of x there are more)s than (s; but by the definition of B_1 each) is preceded by a unique matching (, so there must be at least as many ('s as)'s. Second we argue that $x \in B_2 \to x \in B_1$. We prove this by strong induction on n the length of x. The basis, $n = 0$, is trivial. Assume it is true for strings with fewer than n symbols. Let y be the shortest non-empty prefix of x for which $m(y) = n(y)$. If $y = x$ then it follows that $x = (z)$ and $z \in B_2$. By the inductive hypothesis $z \in B_1$, and hence $x \in B_1$. Otherwise $x = yz$, and both y and z are in B_2 and hence both are in B_1. By definition $yz = x$ is in B_1.

Ex: 10.9

$$S \to \Lambda \mid aSbS \mid bSaS$$

We prove that any derivation of k steps generates a "good string," one with an equal number of as and bs and perhaps some Ss. For the basis of an induction proof, we see it is true is of 0 (and 1) step derivations. Assume, for $k > 1$ that it is true that any $k - 1$ step produces a good string then one more of our three productions will also result in a good string.

We also need to show that every string of L_e is in $\mathcal{L}(G_e)$. We show it by induction on, n, the length of the string $x \in L_e$. The basis, $n = 0$, is trivially shown $(S \Rightarrow \Lambda)$. Suppose x begins with an a (the remaining case is symmetric). We need to argue that $x = aybz$ for some strings $y \in L_e$ and $z \in L_e$. If that were true we are done; since y and z have lengths less than n the induction hypothesis means that both can be derived from the S symbol, and so x can be derived via the second production.

To show that y and z must exist for $x = x_1 x_2 \ldots x_n$, consider the function

$$d(i) = (\text{ the number of } as \text{ in } x_1 x_2 \ldots x_i) -$$

$$(\text{ the number of } bs \text{ in } x_1 x_2 \ldots x_i).$$

We define $d(0) = 0$ corresponding to the empty string. As i increases from 0 to n, $d(i)$ begins at 0 and first increases (since x begins with an a), then it decreases, perhaps going up and down repeatedly, and eventually ends up at $d(n) = 0$ (since x is a good string). Let $j > 0$ be the least index such that $d(j) = 0$. Clearly $x_1 x_2 \ldots x_j = ayb$ for some $y \in L_e$ (perhaps Λ). Further $x_{j+1} \ldots x_n = z \in L_e$.

Ex: 10.10

$$E \to E \lor T \mid T$$
$$T \to T \land F \mid F$$
$$F \to \neg G \mid G$$
$$G \to (E)$$
$$G \to \text{TRUE} \mid \text{FALSE}$$
$$G \to p \mid q \mid r \mid \cdots.$$

Ex: 10.11 Let Σ be the symbol set for the REs and the set of terminal symbols for each grammar. Recall the REs are: $\emptyset$; Λ; each symbol of Σ; and whatever can be constructed from REs by concatenation, alternation and closure. We prove by mathematical induction on the number of operators in an RE; the base case of the definition corresponding to the basis of the proof.

A grammar for the RE $\emptyset$ is $(\{S\}, \emptyset, S, \emptyset)$.

A grammar for the RE Λ is $(\{S\}, \emptyset, S, \{S \to \Lambda\})$.

For each $\sigma \in \Sigma$, a grammar is $(\{S\}, \{\sigma\}, S, \{S \to \sigma\})$.

Suppose that we already have CFGs G_1 and G_2 for the REs r_1 and r_2; that is
$$G_1 = (V_1, \Sigma, S_1, P_1) \text{ and } \mathcal{L}(G_1) = \mathcal{L}(r_1), \text{ and}$$
$$G_2 = (V_2, \Sigma, S_2, P_2) \text{ and } \mathcal{L}(G_2) = \mathcal{L}(r_2).$$
Then
$$G_3 = (V_3, \Sigma, S_3, P_3) \text{ is a CFG that generates}$$
$\mathcal{L}(r_1 + r_2)$, where $S_3 \notin V_1 \cup V_2$
$$V_3 = \{S_3\} \cup V_1 \cup V_2$$
$$P_3 = \{S_3 \to S_1, \ S_3 \to S_2\} \cup P_1 \cup P_2$$

$G_4 = (V_4, \Sigma, S_4, P_4)$ is a CFG that generates
$\mathcal{L}(r_1 r_2)$, where $S_4 \notin V_1 \cup V_2$
$$V_4 = \{S_4\} \cup V_1 \cup V_2$$
$$P_4 = \{S_4 \to S_1 S_2\} \cup P_1 \cup P_2$$

$G_5 = (V_5, \Sigma, S_5, P_5)$ is a CFG that generates
$\mathcal{L}(r_1^*)$, where $S_5 \notin V_1$
$$V_5 = \{S_5\} \cup V_1$$
$$P_5 = \{S_5 \to S_1 S_5, \ \ S_5 \to \Lambda\} \cup P_1$$

Consider G_3, for simulating alternation of REs. In addition to all the existing symbols and rules, we add – using set union – a new start symbol and include it in the new set of variables. Then we add new rules that generate S_1 and S_2, to get the component grammars (G_1 and G_2) started. Similar strategies go into the construction of grammar G_4 for simulating concatenation and G_5 for closure.

Ex: 10.12

$$S \to A\,S \mid \Lambda$$
$$A \to B\,d$$
$$B \to C \mid D$$
$$C \to a$$
$$D \to E c$$
$$E \to b E \mid \Lambda$$

Ex: 10.15 As in the proof, just as $u = vwxyz \in L \to u' = vwwxyyz \in L$ it is also true that $u \in L \to u'' = vxz \in L$; the upper subtree rooted at A is replaced by the lower subtree rooted at A. Consider $u = a^m b^{m+1} c^{m+2}$ where m is sufficiently large, as in the proof, to guarantee such an A is repeated. It follows again that w and y are both homogeneous. If w contains no cs then u' is not in L. If w is all cs (and so y is all cs too) then u'' is not in L since we are decreasing the number cs.

Chapter 11: Pushdown Automata and Parsing

Ex: 11.1 (a) $(q_0, S) \vdash_0 (q_1, X) \vdash_0 (q_1, XX) \vdash_1 (q_2, X) \vdash_1 (q_2, \Lambda)$

(b) $(q_0, S) \vdash_0 (q_1, X) \vdash_0 (q_1, XX) \vdash_1 (q_2, X)$, the input runs out without an empty stack.

(c) $(q_0, S) \vdash_0 (q_1, X) \vdash_0 (q_1, XX) \vdash_1 (q_2, X) \vdash_1 (q_2, \Lambda) \vdash_1 \emptyset$, the $\emptyset$ denotes there is no configuration since there is no transition from an empty stack.

Ex: 11.3 (a) $(q_0, S) \vdash_a (q_1, X) \vdash_b (q_1, YX) \vdash_a (q_2, XYX) \vdash_a (q_2, YX) \vdash_b (q_2, X) \vdash_a (q_2, \Lambda)$

(b) $(q_0, S) \vdash_a (q_1, X) \vdash_a (q_1, \Lambda) \vdash_b \emptyset$, since aa is the longest prefix it can accept.

Ex: 11.5 (a) $(q_0, S) \vdash_((q_0, SR) \vdash_((q_0, RSR) \vdash_) (q_0, SR) \vdash_((q_0, RR) \vdash_) (q_0, R) \vdash_) (q_0, \Lambda)$

(b) $(q_0, S) \vdash_((q_0, SR) \vdash_((q_0, RR) \vdash_) (q_0, R) \vdash_) (q_0, \Lambda) \vdash_) \emptyset$, since $(())$ is the longest prefix it can accept.

Ex: 11.7 (a) $(q_0, S) \vdash_((q_0, AB) \vdash_((q_0, AAB) \vdash_) (q_0, AB) \vdash_((q_0, AAB) \vdash_) (q_0, AB) \vdash_) (q_0, B) \vdash_\lhd (q_0, \Lambda)$

(b) $(q_0, S) \vdash_((q_0, AB) \vdash_((q_0, AAB) \vdash_) (q_0, AB) \vdash_) (q_0, B) \vdash_) \emptyset$, since there is no configuration since there is no transition on inputs B and).

Ex: 11.9 (a) The DPDA will **PUSH** a symbol (*"I"*) for each *a* it sees; *b*s will not change the stack; a stack symbol is **POP**ped for each *c*. If the stack goes back down to just the start symbol *S* while reading *c*s it goes to q_A. Only in q_A will the sentinel be properly processed. Further the machine will move through the states q_a, q_b, and q_c to force all the *a*s to come before all the *b*s, and all these before all the *c*s.

(b)

from	input	stack	change
q_0	a	S	$\{(q_a, IS)\}$
q_0	b	S	$\{(q_b, S)\}$
q_0	c	S	$\{(q_A, S)\}$
q_a	a	I	$\{(q_a, II)\}$
q_a	b	I	$\{(q_b, I)\}$
q_a	c	I	$\{(q_c, \Lambda)\}$
q_b	b	I	$\{(q_b, I)\}$
q_b	b	S	$\{(q_b, S)\}$
q_b	c	I	$\{(q_c, \Lambda)\}$
q_b	c	S	$\{(q_A, S)\}$
q_c	c	I	$\{(q_c, \Lambda)\}$
q_c	c	S	$\{(q_A, S)\}$
q_A	$\triangleleft$	S	$\{(q_A, \Lambda)\}$

Ex: 11.10 The set of productions is
$\{S \to S_1 \mid S_2, \ S_1 \to a\,S_1\,b \mid ab, \ S_2 \to a\,S_2\,bb \mid abb\}$

Ex: 11.11 Sketch: Work with PDA-A model since it is more like a FA. Use a DFA. Take the PDA and the DFA and create a "cross-product" of the two machines; i.e. do a simulation that runs both in "parallel." The resulting machine, a PDA, does not have any competition for the one stack, since the DFA it is simulating does not use it. Accept a string if both machines accept it.

Ex: 11.12   Since $L' \cap \{a^i b^j c^k \mid i, j, k \geq 0\} = \{a^n b^n c^n \mid n \geq 0\}$ and the latter language is not a CFL, it follows that L' cannot be a CFL.

Chapter 12: Turing Machines

Ex: 12.1 (a) the perfect squares

$$
\begin{array}{ccccc}
0 & 1 & 2 & 3 & 4 \quad \cdots \\
\updownarrow & \updownarrow & \updownarrow & \updownarrow & \updownarrow \\
0 & 1 & 4 & 9 & 16 \quad \cdots
\end{array}
$$

(b) the set of all integers (including the negatives)

$$
\begin{array}{ccccccc}
0 & 1 & 2 & 3 & 4 & 5 & 6 \quad \cdots \\
\updownarrow & \updownarrow & \updownarrow & \updownarrow & \updownarrow & \updownarrow & \updownarrow \\
0 & 1 & -1 & 2 & -2 & 3 & -3 \quad \cdots
\end{array}
$$

Ex: 12.3   We only explain the design; it can be built with 15 states. First we find the center of the input. We bounce back and forth changing as to As and bs to Bs starting from each end working towards the middle. (If the string is of odd length it should eventually fail to find a matching lower-case symbol and halt without accepting.) This first phase should end with the tape head positioned over the first symbol of the second half of the input, and the input shifted into upper-case symbols but otherwise unchanged.

We are now going to match symbols in the second half with the first half; matched symbols will become Xs. The second phase has a series of supbphases, each consisting of a back and forth pass. To begin a subphase we change the symbol scanned into an X while first "remembering" if it was an A or a B (by going into a set of states corresponding to A or to B) and then go back to the first unmatched symbol of the input looking for a match. It should find an A if it is remembering an A or a B if it is remembering a B; if the matching symbol is found it is replaced by and X and we continue, otherwise we halt without accepting. We continue by scanning back to the first unmatched symbol in the second half (that is, after the middle X, or Xs) and begin another subphase. We halt and accept the input when all the input has been changed into Xs.

Ex: 12.4 Note that the FA knows that the last batch of 1s, in an encoding of a single transition, will have zero or one 1 because it is encoding the μ subscript.

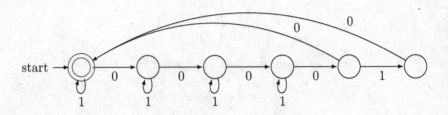

Ex: 12.5 (a) Any derivation begins with one symbol, the start symbol, so a derivation of strings of non-decreasing length cannot end up with zero symbols, that is Λ.

(b)

$$
\begin{aligned}
S &\rightarrow WDZ \\
D &\rightarrow ABCD \mid B \\
CA &\rightarrow AC \\
CB &\rightarrow BC \\
BA &\rightarrow AB \\
WA &\rightarrow aW \\
WB &\rightarrow aX \\
XB &\rightarrow bX \\
XC &\rightarrow bY \\
XZ &\rightarrow bc \\
YC &\rightarrow cY \\
YZ &\rightarrow cc
\end{aligned}
$$

This is similar to the version in the text, except that W and Z are not bracketing symbols that get erased; they are still bracketing symbols but the W turns into an a like A does and Z turns into a c like Y does.

Appendix A: Logic Programming

Ex: A.1
```
father(X,Y) :- parent(X,Y), male(X).
grandmother(X,Z) :- mother(X,Y), parent(Y,Z).
child(X,Y) :- parent(Y,X).
grandchild(X,Y) :- grandparent(Y,X).
descendant(X,Y) :- ancestor(Y,X).
```

Ex: A.2 (a) $\forall X : \forall Y : female(X) \wedge parent(X,Y) \rightarrow mother(X,Y)$

(b) $\forall X : \forall Y : mother(X,Y) \leftrightarrow female(X) \wedge parent(X,Y)$

Ex: A.3 (a) `wife(X,Y) :- husband(Y,X).`

(b) `spouse(X,Y) :- wife(X,Y); husband(X,Y).`

```
spouse(X,Y) :- wife(X,Y).
spouse(X,Y) :- husband(X,Y).
```

(c) `spouse(X,Y) :- husband(X,Y); husband(Y,X).`

Ex: A.4
```
aunt(X,Y) :- sister(X,Z), parent(Z,Y)
          ;  wife(X,Z), sibling(Z,W), parent(W,Y).
```

Ex: A.5
```
fullsibling(X,Y) :- different(X,Y), parent(W,X),
                    parent(W,Y), parent(Z,X),
                    parent(Z,Y), different(Z,W).
```

Ex: A.6
```
firstcousin(X,Y) :- sibling(X,Y), !, fail
                 ;  different (X,Y), parent(W,X),
                    parent(Z,Y), fullsibling(W,Z).
```

Ex: A.7　　higher(X,Y):- on(X,Y)
　　　　　　　　; on(X,Z), higher(Z,Y).

Ex: A.8 (a)　olderthan(X,Y):- age(X,M), age(Y,N), M > N.

　　　　　(b)　bigsib(X,Y)　:- sibling(X,Y), olderthan(X,Y).

Ex: A.9 (a)　employee(_,X,pp,_,_).

　　　　　(b)　employee(_,X,Y,_,Z), Z >= 1998.

　　　　　　　Note that Z would printed out after any successful query. In general such superfluous output can be omitted by querying with an auxiliary predicate, such as

　　　　　　　shorter(X,Y) :- employee(_,X,Y,_,Z),
　　　　　　　Z >= 1998.

　　　　　(c)　employee(_,X,_,_,Z), Z >= 1991, Z =< 1999
　　　　　　　; employee(_,X,_,Y,1990), Y >= 7
　　　　　　　; employee(_,X,_,Y,2000), Y =< 6.

Ex: A.10 (a)　works_in(X,Y) :- employee(_,X,Y,_,_).

　　　　　(b)　started(X,Y,Z) :- employee(_,X,_,Y,Z).

　　　　　(c)　payroll_employee(W,X,Y,Z) :-
　　　　　　　employee(W,X,pay,Y,Z).

　　　　　(d)　senior_hr_employee(W,X,Y,Z) :-
　　　　　　　employee(W,X,hr,Y,Z), Z < 1997.

Ex: A.11　　setof(X,employee(_,X,pp,_,_),Y).

Ex: A.12 (a) `all_info(A,B,C,D,E,F,G) :-`
`employee(A,B,C,D,E), dob(A,F,G).`

(b) `senior_employee(A) :-`
`all_info(A,_,_,_,E,_,G), E > G + 50`
`; all_info(A,_,_,D,E,F,G), E = G + 50, D >= F.`

Ex: A.13 (a) `later(W,X,Y,Z) :- X > Z ; X = Z, W > Y.`

(b) `senior_to(X,Y) :- employee(X,_,_,A,B),`
`employee(Y,_,_,C,D), later(C,D,A,B).`

(c) `senior_div_mate_of(X,Y) :- employee(X,_,Z,_,_),`
`employee(Y,_,Z,_,_),`
`senior_to(X,Y).`

Ex: A.14 Let `employs(a,b)` mean that person *a* owns a firm that employs person *b*. Note that it is possible to work in your own firm. Write eleven Prolog queries, each having an argument pattern that differs significantly from all of the others. For each of your eleven queries, write down a question in English that expresses the idea of that query.

One kind of significant difference between argument patterns is having a different kind of argument — constant versus named variable versus anonymous variable ("_") — in one of the argument positions. When two argument positions both have a constant (or both have a named variable) there is a significant difference between the case in which those two constants (or named variables) are the same and the case of them being different.

employs(a,b).	Does a employ b?
employs(a,a).	Is a self-employed?
employs(a,X).	Who does a employ?
employs(a,_).	Does a employ anyone?
employs(X,b).	Who employs b?
employs(X,Y).	Who employs whom?
employs(X,X).	Who is self-employed?
employs(X,_).	Who are the employers?
employs(_,b).	Is b employed (by anyone)?
employs(_,X).	Who is employed (by anyone)?
employs(_,_).	Is anyone employed (by anyone)?

Ex: A.15 (a) `delete_first2([_,_|Result],Result).`

(b) ```
delete_last2(L,Result) :-
    append(Result,[_,_],L).
```

(c) ```
delete22(L,Result) :-
    append([_,_|Result],[_,_],L).
```

Ex: A.16 (a) It succeeds for even length palindromes and fails for those of odd length.

(b) For X to be the reverse of Y, they must be the same length. Together they form Z, so Z is twice as long, hence of even length.

Ex: A.17
```
evenlength([ ]).
evenlength([_|X]) :- oddlength(X).

oddlength([_|X]) :- evenlength(X).
```

Index